THE PACIFIST IMPULSE IN
HISTORICAL PERSPECTIVE

Peter Brock

The Pacifist Impulse in Historical Perspective

Edited by

HARVEY L. DYCK

UNIVERSITY OF TORONTO PRESS

Toronto Buffalo London

© University of Toronto Press Incorporated 1996
Toronto Buffalo London
Printed in Canada

ISBN: 0-8020-0777-5

Printed on acid-free paper

Canadian Cataloguing in Publication Data

Main entry under title:

The pacifist impulse in historical perspective

Essays in honour of Peter Brock, all but one of
which were presented at an international conference
on The pacifist impulse in historical perspective,
in May, 1991 at the University of Toronto.
Includes bibliographical references and index.
ISBN 0-8020-0777-5

1. Pacifism – History – Congresses.   I. Brock,
Peter, 1920– .   II. Dyck, Harvey L. (Harvey Leonard).

JX1938.P33 1996   303.6'6   C95-932773-8

Frontis photo: Louisa Yick,
Arts and Science Photographic
Facility, University of Toronto

University of Toronto Press acknowledges the
financial assistance to its publishing program
of the Canada Council and the
Ontario Arts Council.

For Peter Brock
on his seventy-fifth birthday
30 January 1995

Contents

viii   Contents

Preface

This volume of twenty-three essays appears in recognition of the emergence of peace history as a relatively new and coherent field of learning. All but one of these essays were first presented at an international conference, 'The Pacifist Impulse in Historical Perspective,' which met on the downtown campus of the University of Toronto in May 1991. The conference coincided with the landmark publication of a comprehensive three-volume history of pacifism to 1914 by Peter Brock, the doyen of peace history. Opening with an essay entitled 'Peter Brock as a Historian of World-wide Pacifism: An Appreciation,' this volume honours Brock's pioneering leadership and unmatched scholarly attainments in the field.

Since their appearance early in this century, the words 'pacifist' and 'pacifism' have been used with various meanings, some of them contradictory. In the title of this book, 'pacifism' is taken to mean, in the words of Martin Ceadel, a belief that 'all participation in or support for war [is] wrong' (*Thinking about Peace and War*, Oxford, 1987). But some contributors use it in the broader sense of a 'doctrine that the abolition of war or violence is desirable and possible' (*Concise Oxford Dictionary of Current English*, seventh edition, 1982).

Together these essays explore the ideas and activities, over two millennia, of persons and groups rejecting war and often urging non-violent means of settling conflicts. They probe the limits and branches of pacifism and peace history, pacifist pioneering and the relationship of pacifism and internationalism, including its contemporary phase. The essays highlight new interpretations where various of these have emerged in recent studies. They address topics that have been previously neglected such as the role of women in peace thinking and peace movements and the idea of peace in non-Western thought and religions.

Reflecting some of the main areas of contemporary scholarship in peace history, the essays are grouped in four major thematic divisions. The three essays of Part I, 'Approaches to Peace History,' explore conceptual issues and approaches in peace history. The eight essays in Part II, 'Christian Traditions of Pacifism and Non-resistance,' range quite widely from the problem of non-violence and war in the Early Church through the non-resistant traditions of the Mennonites and Brethren from the sixteenth century onwards to aspects of the Quaker peace witness down to the present day. Part III, 'Gandhi and the Indian Tradition of Non-violence,' surveys violent and non-violent impulses in Hindu and Buddhist thought and practice as well as aspects of Gandhi's intellectual and moral formation and outlook.

From the emergence of an international peace movement in 1815, the history of pacifism often became closely intertwined with the history of the broader movement advocating world peace. This intertwining is at the centre of the seven essays of Part IV, 'Pacifism and Peace Movements in the Modern World, 1890–1955.' The volume concludes with a bibliography of Peter Brock's scholarly contributions to peace history. There is an introduction to each of the parts that profiles the subjects of the individual essays and their relationship to one another.

The idea for an international gathering of scholars working in peace history originated in a small group of University of Toronto faculty engaged in peace history within the Department of History and University College's Program in Peace and Conflict Studies. The organizing committee consisted of Harvey Dyck (co-chair), History, University of Toronto; Ingrid Epp, Library, University College, University of Toronto; William Klassen (co-chair), Principal, St Paul's United College, Waterloo, Ontario; Arthur Sherk, University College, University of Toronto; Thomas P. Socknat, History, University of Toronto; Metta Spencer, Sociology, University of Toronto; and William Westfall, History, Atkinson College, York University, Toronto.

The editor and conference organizers thank Peter Brock for his friendly counsel and assistance at every stage of the undertaking. As well, they are grateful to the following individuals and institutions for their encouragement and financial support of the conference and of this publication: Conrad Grebel College, Waterloo, Ontario; Department of History, University of Toronto; Faculty of Arts and Science, University of Toronto; Shirley Farlinger, Toronto; Theodore Friesen, Altona, Manitoba; Good Foundation, Inc., Breslau, Ontario; Frieda and Vern Heinrichs, Toronto; Rosemarie and Victor Heinrichs, Toronto; Anne J. Konrad, Toronto; The Mennonite Central Committee (Ontario), Kitchener, Ontario; President and Provost, University of Toronto; Richard and Anne Rempel, Hamilton, Ontario; School of Graduate Studies, University of Toronto; Social Sciences and Humanities Research Council of Canada, Ottawa; University College, University of Toronto; Louise Wolfenden, Toronto; Derek Wulff, Toronto. The index was prepared by Thomas P. Socknat. The efforts of Kate Baltais, Anne Forte, and Ron Schoeffel, of the University of Toronto Press, in seeing this book into print are warmly acknowledged.

The University of Toronto conference provided a stimulating international forum for significant contemporary scholarship in the field of peace history. The editor and contributors nourish the hope that these proceedings will help to define and enrich this new and active field while pointing the way for fresh scholarly work in it.

Contributors

Irwin Abrams is university professor emeritus of history at Antioch University, Yellow Springs, Ohio.

Roy C. Amore is a professor of religious studies at the University of Windsor, Windsor, Ontario.

Hugh Barbour is professor emeritus of religion at Earlham College, Richmond, Indiana.

Y. Aleksandra Bennett is an associate professor of history at Carleton University, Ottawa.

Martin Ceadel is a fellow and tutor at New College, Oxford, and a lecturer in politics at the University of Oxford.

Charles Chatfield is a professor of history at Wittenberg University, Springfield, Ohio.

Sandi E. Cooper is a professor of history at the College of Staten Island, City University of New York.

Donald F. Durnbaugh is a fellow of the Young Center for the Study of Anabaptist and Pietist Groups at Elizabethtown College, Elizabethtown, Pennsylvania.

Harvey L. Dyck is a professor of history at the University of Toronto.

Stephen Hay is emeritus professor of history at the University of California, Santa Barbara.

James D. Hunt is a professor of religion at Shaw University, Raleigh, North Carolina.

Norman Ingram is an assistant professor of history at Concordia University, Montreal, Quebec.

Thomas C. Kennedy is a professor of history at the University of Arkansas, Fayetteville.

Klaus K. Klostermaier is university distinguished professor of religion at the University of Manitoba, Winnipeg.

Michael A. Lutzker is an associate professor of history at New York University, New York, New York.

Jack D. Marietta is an associate professor of history at the University of Arizona, Tucson.

Richard A. Rempel is a professor of history at McMaster University, Hamilton, Ontario.

Luise Schottroff is a professor of theology at Kassel University, Kassel, Germany.

Thomas P. Socknat teaches history and peace and conflict studies at the University of Toronto.

James M. Stayer is a professor of history at Queen's University, Kingston, Ontario.

Peter van den Dungen is a lecturer in peace studies at the University of Bradford, Bradford, United Kingdom.

Jo Vellacott is an honorary fellow of the Simone de Beauvoir Institute of Concordia University, Montreal, Quebec.

John H. Yoder is a professor of theology at the University of Notre Dame, Notre Dame, Indiana.

THE PACIFIST IMPULSE IN
HISTORICAL PERSPECTIVE

1

Peter Brock as a Historian of World-wide Pacifism: An Appreciation

HARVEY L. DYCK[1]

It seems to me that the world is faced by three problems: war, overpopulation, and pollution. I can't write the history of overpopulation because I'm not a demographer. Pollution is something new and has a short history. But I feel I can perhaps contribute something to the history of peace. Mind you, I'm not saying that pacifists are the only people who contribute to peace, far from it.

In the living-room of his midtown Toronto duplex, Peter Brock, widely esteemed as the world's leading historian of worldwide pacifism, reflects on his recent scholarship. He does so typically with a self-deprecating aside. We are joined briefly by his wife, Carmen, a Quaker volunteer involved in the settlement of Central American refugees. The doorbell rings. A colleague deposits luggage for a mainland Chinese student who will live with the Brocks while he seeks permanent housing. An electrician repairs the range in the kitchen, a puzzling contrivance for Peter (who does not drive a car). I have caught the Brocks just before they leave for a month-long indulgence of a shared passion, cathedral hopping, this time in Portugal.

Peter Brock has written sixteen noteworthy books and at least fifty major articles, and he has edited several important collections. His scholarship roams, in detailed monographs as well as sweeping syntheses, across a vast terrain of ages and cultures. While he is equally at home among the Fathers of the Christian Church in the early centuries AD and Gandhi's India, his studies are neither episodic nor meandering. They are tightly woven around two major and distinct, though overlapping, subjects. In both he has become a scholar without peer.

Peter Brock is a pre-eminent authority on Polish and East European history. What is remarkable here is that his mastery extends to many different nationalities and that he has become highly respected for work in all of them. He is an historian of Poland but also of the Czechs, Kashubs, Hungarians, Slovaks, Sorbs, and Ukrainians.[2] In each case he has been able to ferret out important patterns of their past from the sources. To do this he has also mastered all of their often difficult languages. Brock's writing concentrates on, but is not exclusively about, populist and nationalist ideas and movements. These aimed in modern times at freeing groups from the tutelage and domination of elites and empires. He is inclined to take his stand with the 'little peoples' of the regions, with their underdogs. His writings have often helped to restore to an ethnic community or social stratum part of its memory and its fuller voice. As one of Brock's knowledgeable friends has written, 'Just as he champions the rights of downtrodden peoples to independence and the peaceful enjoyment of their fundamental human rights, so he deplores and condemns any abuse of this freedom to restrict the liberties of others.'[3] Eastern Europe, a minefield for less sure-footed scholars, has been Peter Brock's first scholarly love. It has also remained almost the exclusive area of his teaching, and over the years students have acclaimed him as a devoted guide and source of inspiration.[4]

What elevates Peter Brock from the ranks of fine historians and places him among a handful of the truly exceptional, is his second academic career, as an historian of pacifism. Some eight of his books and many of his smaller publications are about pacifism. These writings cut across the ages and circle the globe.

Peter Brock's earliest work on pacifism was about peace ideas and movements among Czechs.[5] He then turned to the English-speaking world on both sides of the Atlantic. *Pacifism in the United States* (1968), a volume of more than a thousand pages, his first major study devoted wholly to pacifism, was a critical and popular success.[6] It was described as 'the definitive account' and a 'prodigiously solid and well-based work on a theme that is in an odd way both a marginal and a fundamental aspect of American history.'[7] Against a background of the early peace witness of Quakers, Mennonites, and others, Brock traces the development of more widely based peace movements in the nineteenth century. Sensitive to the sovereignty of detail and the need for nuance, he became the first scholar to track the intricate changes that the peace movement underwent in the colonial environment and then in the perfectionist atmosphere of post-revolutionary American reformism.

To Peter Brock's surprise, his book on American pacifism appeared at a fortunate moment, just as anti-Vietnam war sentiment in America was crystallizing into what became, over the next years, a triumphant crusade. Striking a resonant chord, the book was widely read and helped give that movement a distinctively American home-grown pedigree, native roots. To make the study more easily accessible, Princeton University Press reprinted two parts as separate paperbacks.[8] Then, in the late 1960s and early 1970s, as the number of those keen about war resistance grew further, Peter Brock addressed his next book on the subject to a more general reader and university student. *Twentieth-Century Pacifism* (1970) examined peace movements globally. It was perhaps strongest on the ideas and fortunes of opponents of war during the First and Second World Wars. One reviewer wrote, 'The strength of this book is its balanced and analytical framework ... It outlines a program of peace research in modern history.'[9]

There followed quickly Brock's *Pacifism in Europe to 1914* (1972), a work of seasoned learning. It maps a vast terrain from the early Christian peace thinkers through the Anabaptists, Mennonites, and Quakers, to the ideologues and activists who futilely tried to prevent the outbreak of the first global war of this century. As he further broadened his studies, it was almost inevitable that Peter Brock would try also to fathom the ideas and worldwide influence of Gandhi as this century's chief theorist and practitioner of non-violence, and its greatest martyr. After a year of research in India, this round of scholarship appeared as *The Mahatma and Mother India: Essays on Gandhi s Non-Violence and Nationalism* (1983). Brock's passionate interest in specific forms of peace witness led also to important articles. Invariably grounded in work in original languages, as are all his writings, they examine the peace views of groups like the Quakers, Czech reformers, Hutterites, Dukhobors, Polish Anabaptists, Hungarian Nazarenes, Tolstoyans, and the early Plymouth Brethren.

More than twenty-five years ago, at Columbia University, at the start of Peter Brock's work on pacifism, my wife and I first heard about the Brocks from my doctoral supervisor, Henry Roberts. He described an unusual interview he had had with a candidate for a major appointment in East European history. 'Your usual applicants, all fine scholars,' he said, 'invariably asked about salary levels, workloads, sabbatical leaves, and pensions.' After inquiring about students, a certain Peter Brock, however, had put only one question: 'Were there places nearby on Manhattan Island where [he and Carmen] could go for long walks?'

I met Peter Brock for the first time, when, now as colleagues at Colum-

bia, we walked a picket line together at St John's University on Long
Island, protesting an odious abuse of academic freedom. It was about
then that he and I started talking about Mennonites and pacifism, and I
began reading his work. At the time, as a historian of Russia, I was pon-
dering Stalinism and was viscerally attracted to the 'Christian realism'
of Reinhold Niebuhr: the lesser evil as a moral choice. I even audited
Niebuhr's disquieting lectures and pondered his sermons across Broadway Avenue at Union Theological Seminary and Riverside Church. At
the time my own commitment to categorical non-resistance was, at best,
pretty shaky. Reading Peter Brock's masterfully told and engrossing
story of Czech Christian non-resisters braving injustices and daunting
political dilemmas was an eye-opener for me. Here was moral courage
in the face of huge ambiguities and obstacles. The reading got me thinking further about my own position.

In 1966 Peter Brock and I took up appointments in history at the
University of Toronto. Since then, over a quarter of a century, I have
followed Brock's career closely in several settings: in seminars, a team-
taught course on comparative nationalism, academic planning sessions,
lunches (usually with rich, creamy desserts for Peter's sweet tooth), and
in shared, sometimes anguished, stands on contentious issues of the
day.

The author of significant research across a breadth of eras and cultures, Peter Brock seems at first glance difficult to classify as a historian.
One asks, What are the links among the foremost strands of his scholarship – populism, nationalism, and pacifism? Several years ago, while
getting together a small talk for Peter Brock's retirement dinner, I surrounded myself with his writings. I paused to read a chapter here, to dip
into a particularly apt description there, looking for bits of analysis, conclusions, or a revealing dedicatory note among this wonderful body of
printed material. I had previously read many of his books and articles,
but not nearly all. I was sampling, looking for connections among the
main themes of his scholarship.

One clue is that Peter Brock's consuming interest is people who take
personal stands against injustice, oppression, or war. In his own scale of
values, courage, the making of personal choices about significant moral
issues, excites his curiosity. He is equally curious about the ideas behind
such hard moral stands, ideas, he states in one place, 'in the realm of
practical living.' He also focuses on trail-blazers, the pioneers of those
ideas, and on the meaning and implications of the texts that they composed. His scholarship is most riveting when it deals with beginnings.

These were heroic dawns when choices were made, lines were being drawn, and seminal ideas worked out. Despite Peter Brock's undeniable identification with the men and women he studies, he writes history with rare detachment, wholly avoiding advocacy or propaganda.

The roots of his own pacifism have many ironic and endearing twists. Peter Brock was born in 1920 on the Channel Island of Guernsey, United Kingdom. On both his mother's and his father's side he comes of distinguished military stock. One relation was conspicuously involved in the British burning of the White House in 1812 and another, Sir Isaac Brock, in the Battle of Queenston Heights in the same year. His maternal grandfather was also a British general. Yet, already as a child, he seems to have begun to buck the family tide. A favourite story of his wife, Carmen – his loving companion and support for more than three decades – tells how younger members of the family were expected to address grandpapa as 'general,' and regularly did so. Peter Brock, however, always called him simply 'grandfather.'

Brock attended Oxford as an undergraduate in the late 1930s. This was a time in his life, he recalled, when he was in 'rebellion' against the Church of England, had 'inchoate religious views,' and was quite 'disinterested in sectarianism.' Secular pacifism, however, was then much in the air. So he read into the subject a little, got involved in the peace movement, and joined a pacifist society at Oxford. It was not until the onset of the Second World War, however, that his views began to cohere. This was partly under the intellectual tutelage of a Dutch pacifist, Bart de Ligt. Peter Brock had read a French version of a book by de Ligt, *Creative Peace*, written in the 1930s on a large scale and with great enthusiasm.[10] It traced the history of peace from classical times through the sects to the socialist movements. On re-reading it later, Brock saw that, despite the author's learning, it was a little chaotic in organization and sometimes based on inadequate sources. In 1939, however, it was for him a 'book at the right time,' which had a great influence intellectually. It introduced him to sectarian pacifism, sparked his ardour and became a source of his desire one day to write his own synthetic global history of pacifism.

When war came Peter Brock persevered in his beliefs and took his stand as a conscientious objector. He was briefly imprisoned and served out the rest of the conflict on alternative service, including work in an English hospital. In the meanwhile he had been strongly drawn to Quaker ideas about war and social justice, although remaining religiously 'a little bit of an outsider.' The war over, he was accepted for work with Quaker relief, first among displaced persons in Western Germany and then in devastated Poland. This was his introduction to Eastern Europe. There followed graduate study at the universities of Cracow, Poland, and Oxford, England, from each of which he holds doctorates in history. Brock first came to the University of Toronto for the one year, 1957–8. He then taught successively at the University of Alberta, Smith College, and Columbia University. He returned to Toronto in 1966, and since then it has been his home.

Peter Brock, now well into his formal retirement from the department of history of the University of Toronto, has in recent years completed his most ambitious undertaking to date, a three-volume historical synthesis of worldwide pacifism and war resistance from the Middle Ages to the First World War. The first volume is on sectarian non-resistance;[11] the second explores the Quaker peace witness;[12] and the third, devoted to non-sectarian pacifism, touches on the ideas of various peace societies, of Gandhi, Tolstoy and the Tolstoyans, and Japanese peace groups.[13] The trilogy does no less than define for our generation the subfield of peace history to 1914. It is a significant and sympathetic personal summing up for Peter Brock, though he will, of course, write on this theme again. To celebrate this landmark, a major international conference on the history of pacifism met at the University of Toronto in May 1991.

Peter Brock's new three-volume global synthesis is naturally based on research from previous books, but it also incorporates significant new scholarship published in recent years. The synthesis is, for one thing, broader in scope, embracing the experience of groups and lands he has not dealt with very much before. These include Nazarenes, Plymouth Brethren, Seventh-Day Adventists, and Polish Anabaptists, and places like Wales, Canada, Scandinavia, South Africa, and Japan. He touches also, for the first time, on non-pacifist sections of the American peace movement during the decades before 1914, and, generally, he pays closer attention to broader peace movements.

How does Brock deal with the recent spate of revisionist writing on pacifism? Is he perhaps himself revising his former views? In detail he is, he says, where new research warrants this, but he has not changed his main conclusions. The possible linkage between social class and pacifism is one new area of current scholarship that interests him greatly. Scholars of Quakerism, he observes, seem to produce a new book every two or three years. A number of these are reinterpretations of the class foundations of Quaker Pennsylvania, and they have pinpointed how that society accepted military measures – more easily than previous historians had believed.[14] Brock accepts, on the whole, this modified view of Quaker pacifism in that colony. He is more dubious, however, about recent suggestions that the influential British Peace Society in the nineteenth century was essentially class-bound in impulse, promoting peace chiefly as a way of ameliorating class conflicts in England.[15] Ever meticulous, his review of the evidence indicates to him that while some members of the society were doubtless socially conservative, many others, keenly sensitive to issues of social justice, fought hard for reform.

Brock appears warmly appreciative of some recent reinterpretations of Anabaptist pacifism. He shares, for example, the view of someone like George Williams that the Polish Brethren belonged to the mainstream of Anabaptism, and he treats them accordingly.[16] He is not, however, in agreement with everything suggested by the main revisionists on Anabaptism, represented, for example, by James Stayer of Queen's University, Kingston, Ontario,[17] and his numerous followers. Nevertheless, Brock does find their work solidly based, measured, and well reasoned. He accepts the particular point that Harold Bender, for all his achievement in delimiting and developing the field of Anabaptist scholarship, was mistaken in defining the mainstream of Anabaptism as exclusively peaceable. A balanced understanding must deal with both the peaceable and militant Anabaptists, Brock feels. This he tries to do himself.

While Brock is encouraged by the abundance of stimulating new work on Anabaptist pacifism, he laments the serious gaps in the scholarship regarding the Mennonite peace witness across much of Europe. 'For good or bad,' Brock observes, 'Mennonites are very important in the history of pacifism.' On a general level he notes the absence of an all-embracing synthetic work on the vicissitudes of Mennonite pacifism. 'With the same idea running through it and the same problems confronting it, it seems to hang together,' he says. He makes an interesting point about sources, commenting that he feels his own writing devotes disproportionate space to the Quaker story relative to that of the Mennonite. 'But this is to some degree the Mennonites' own fault,' he explains. 'They left many fewer records. For a time they thought it was wrong to leave records. The Quakers were tremendous record keepers, and were also introspective. Literally dozens of them kept personal journals. So there is a vast quantity of Quaker material and, until recently, a meagre amount of Mennonite material.'

Over the years Peter Brock and I have often talked about the relationship, and sometime sharp tension, between the moral imperatives of peace and of justice. In fact, a recurring theme in his writings is the conflict that often emerged between these two goals. Brock is interested in how some pacifists have tried to reconcile and justify their aspirations for both and how, on occasion, they have achieved neither. For principled pacifists the classical issue is a difficult one: if one rejects the use of force under all circumstances, does one not risk becoming an absolutist in regard to means but a relativist in regard to ends? Crassly put, might not non-resistance as an unequivocal stance embolden the likes of a Hitler, Stalin, or Pol Pot? Ought one then to try to be peaceable only in regard to one's personal relations? Peter Brock, who answers this question with a firm 'no,' continues to wrestle with the implications of his personal convictions in all areas of his life (in recent years he has chosen to become a vegetarian). But he admits to worrying about this dilemma, 'sometimes feeling awkward about it and slightly embarrassed. And yet if one didn't worry one should perhaps be more worried.'

The story is told that the child Peter Brock was once asked what he wanted for a birthday present. He replied that he wished to climb the tower of St Paul's Cathedral to look out as far as it was possible for him to see. Figuratively, Peter Brock has taken his worldwide readership by the hand on many such a long climb to share with it the vistas he has uncovered. By mapping the vast terrain of pacifist history, its uplands and watersheds, as well as its wastelands, he has advanced and given the field clarity, coherence, and boundaries. He has also identified grey areas on the map in need of further scouting.

As we read his careful but luminous sketches of the heroes great and small of populist, nationalist, and pacifist thought, we recognize that Peter Brock often writes about individuals who have some of the same qualities he has found, or somehow managed to create, in himself. His pacifism, in the absence of anything in his own background pointing in this direction, is a highly personal, lifelong commitment. It has made him highly sensitive to social oppression and war. Peter Brock himself, in a kind of personal credo, puts the matter much more simply. 'I'd like my scholarship to be as impartial as I can make it,' he has said, 'but also that it be something of significance.'

Notes

1 Parts of this essay come from my, 'Peter Brock and the History of Pacifism,' *Conrad Grebel Review*, 147–57, and I thank the editors of the *Review* for permission to use them here.

2 See John Stanley, 'Bibliography of Scholarly Writings of Peter de Beauvoir Brock,' *Canadian Slavonic Papers* 31 (June 1989), 211–20.

3 Note by John H.L. Keep, 25 Nov. 1989.

4 See the June 1989 issue of *Canadian Slavonic Papers*, entitled 'Essays in Honour of Peter Brock,' and, in particular 'Peter Brock: An appreciation,' 105–6, by a former graduate student, John Stanley.

5 *The Political and Social Doctrines of the Unity of the Czech Brethren in the Fifteenth and Early Sixteenth Centuries* (The Hague, 1957).

6 *Pacifism in the United States: From the Colonial Era to the First World War* (Princeton, 1968).

7 A.A. Ekirch Jr., *American Historical Review* 74 (1969), 1707.

8 *Radical Pacifists in Antebellum America* (Princeton, 1968) and *Pioneers of the Peaceable Kingdom* (Princeton, 1970).

9 C. Chatfield, *American Historical Review* 78 (1973), 655.

10 B. de Ligt, *Vrede als daad: Beginselen, geschiedenis en strijdmethoden van de direkte aktie tegen oorlog* (Arnhem, 1931–33). An expanded translation of vol. 1 of the Dutch appeared as *La paix créatrice: Histoire des principes et des tactiques de l'action directe contre la guerre* (Paris, 1934).

11 *Freedom from Violence: Sectarian Nonresistance from the Middle Ages to the Great War* (Toronto, 1991).

12 *The Quaker Peace Testimony, 1660–1914* (York, England, 1990).

13 *Freedom from War: Nonsectarian Pacifism, 1814–1914* (Toronto, 1991).

14 For example, Jack D. Marietta, *The Reformation of American Quakerism, 1748–1783* (Philadelphia, 1984), and Herman Wellenreuther, *Glaube und Politik in Pennsylvania, 1681–1776: Die Wandlungen der Obrigkeitsdoktrin und das 'Peace Testimony' der Quaker* (Cologne and Vienna, 1972).

15 As an example, see Eric W. Sager, 'The Social Origins of Victorian Pacifism,' *Victorian Studies* 23 (1980).

16 George H. Williams, *The Radical Reformation* (London, 1962).

17 James M. Stayer, *Anabaptists and the Sword* (Lawrence, Kansas, 1976; originally published 1972). A good example of scholarship by a member of this group is Werner O. Packull, *Mysticism and the Early South German-Austrian Anabaptist Movement, 1525–1531* (Scottdale, 1976).

PART I:

APPROACHES TO PEACE HISTORY

PEACE HISTORY IS A COMPARATIVE NEWCOMER to the historical discipline. Yet a number of approaches have already emerged, as have differences in regard to such issues as, say, terminology, categories, or parameters. Martin Ceadel in the first essay of this section elaborates ten distinctions he believes will help clarify the content of peace history, giving greater precision to scholarship on its various strands and ideologies. He urges, in particular, greater clarity for such frequently used terms as 'pacifism' and 'peace movement' – and even 'pacificism.' Charles Chatfield carries the argument further in the next essay, which he entitles 'Thinking about Peace in History.' While supporting the plea for clearer distinctions among intellectual categories and historical traditions, he cautions against overly rigid typologies that might 'compartmentalize and marginalize ideas' about peace. He concludes that 'it is necessary to group peace advocates, but categories apply sometimes more and sometimes less.'

Peter van den Dungen discusses two Dutch scholars, Jacob ter Meulen and Bart de Ligt, in a case study in early peace historiography. The two men represented contrasting approaches to the subject. Ter Meulen, who held the post of chief librarian at the Peace Palace in The Hague for many years, was primarily interested in the development of internationalism. It was to this theme that he devoted his *magnum opus*, a work of profound research in three volumes. If, however, 'for ter Meulen the idea of peace was tantamount to that of international organization,' for de Ligt this idea signified something different. His *magnum opus*, likewise the fruit of deep learning, was a 'history of ... radical pacifism and antimilitarism,' of civilian resistance and direct action against war, a struggle de Ligt traces from its roots in antiquity to the interwar years of the twentieth century when he composed his major works. Himself a peace activist, de Ligt exercised considerable influence on later students of non-violence. It should be noted that the divergent approaches of these two scholars have continued to recur in the subsequent writing of peace history.

2

Ten Distinctions for Peace Historians

MARTIN CEADEL

No ideology owes more to one academic than pacifism owes to Peter Brock. That the scope and richness of its historical tradition can now be recognized is largely the result of Brock's sympathetic and dedicated scholarship, which was begun, moreover, at a time when pacifism was an unfashionable subject, particularly when compared with equivalently radical viewpoints in domestic politics. When I started research on the 1930s British peace movement in 1969, just a year after the appearance of Brock's *Pacifism in the United States: From the Colonial Era to the First World War*, I was struck not only by the lack of published work on pacifism and its related ideologies and movements but also by the lack of interest in such topics.[1] I remember reading *Twentieth-Century Pacifism*, the second volume of Brock's remarkable first trilogy, on train trips to pacifist archives in 1970 and discovering guidance that was available from no other source. And I can no less vividly recall reading the third volume, *Pacifism in Europe to 1914*, soon after its publication in 1972 at a time when I was struggling to write the first drafts of a doctoral thesis that by then had narrowed its focus to the pacifist core of the peace movement. In fact, the direction that my work has subsequently taken has owed much to the typology of six varieties of pacifism with which, albeit somewhat tentatively, he concluded that book.[2]

Brock, however, has never been particularly interested in categorization: though always clear-minded and rigorous in his definitions, he has concentrated on providing a chronological record of the pacifist tradition and an exegesis of its early texts. Brock's work has thus not principally been designed to dispel the conceptual confusion that irritated me as a postgraduate student. When, for example, I told people who were well informed about Britain in the 1930s that I was working on the paci-

fism of that decade, surprisingly few made the correct inference that I
was dealing mainly with Canon Dick Sheppard and the Peace Pledge
Union. Many more assumed that I was working on the literary reaction
against the First World War, on support for the League of Nations and
collective security, on the appeasement of Germany, or on some other
topic in the general area of attitudes to war. Moreover, in the *viva voce*
examination of my thesis, I was asked by one of my examiners why I
had not discussed E.D. Morel. I replied that it was because Morel (who
had anyway died in 1924, seven years before my starting date) was not a
pacifist, in the absolute sense in which I had defined and used the term
throughout my thesis, but what I had called a *pacificist*. It startled me to
have to make such a reply since the examiner in question was the person
from whose work I had, with full acknowledgment, borrowed the
pacifism-*pacificism* distinction in the first place, A.J.P. Taylor. While
working on Britain's tradition of 'dissent over foreign policy' Taylor had
suddenly, it seems, realized that this was not the same as pacifism. To a
sentence commenting that John Bright did not wish to leave England
defenceless even though he 'was sometimes nearer to pacifism' than
Richard Cobden, Taylor therefore tacked on the following footnote: 'By
"pacificism" I mean the advocacy of a peaceful policy; by "pacificism"
(a word invented only in the twentieth century) the doctrines of non-
resistance. The latter is the negation of policy, not an alternative to it,
and therefore irrelevant to my theme. Hence my disregard for the Peace
Societies.'[3]

This footnote was typical of Taylor. It combined brilliant analysis with
memorably expressed prejudice. It also, however, carelessly implied
that 'pacificism' was an older and different word instead of an etymologically more correct[4] variant of 'pacifism' that entered the language at
the same time. And it inappropriately presented a crucial point of definition as a belated (and apparently never internalized) aside, instead of
being included in the introductory discussion of other central concepts,
such as radicalism and dissent, both of which are treated with greater
sensitivity. I make these comments not to belittle Taylor, an historian
whose strengths enormously outweighed his idiosyncrasies and to
whom I was personally indebted for a number of kindnesses, but to
illustrate what seemed to me a reluctance on the part of even the finest
academics at that time to devote the same academic precision they were
lavishing on domestic political subjects to issues connected with the prevention of war.

In recent years peace-and-war studies have started to boom, largely in response to the 'Second Cold War' of the late 1970s and 1980s and its attendant peace activism, and perhaps also in response to the overgrazing of social and domestic fields by the academic herds of the 1960s and 1970s. As a result, scholars have become increasingly aware that what they once lumped together under the heading of 'pacifism' is an assortment of distant ideologies, and some have begun to debate how best these should be distinguished and labelled. Even so, I am convinced that students of the history and politics of peace movements – peace historians as I shall call them for short – still lag behind, say, the students of the history and politics of labour movements in the precision with which they disentangle different stands. Labour historians agree not only on key distinctions (for example, between socialist and non-socialist viewpoints), but also on a vocabulary for making refinements within each of these categories: they therefore are able to distinguish precisely among Marxist, Fabian, Christian-socialist, anarcho-syndicalist, and other types of socialism, and among liberal, social-democratic, labourist, and other types of non-socialism. They are aware, moreover, that such distinctions are important not only in their own right but also, since each strand flourishes in different political conditions, for any rigorous explanation of a labour movement's development. They are also alert to the importance of dogs that do not bark: they regard the absence of a strand from the labour movement of the country on which they are working – for example, the weakness of Marxism in Britain compared with continental Europe – as a significant fact and not an indication that the distinction between Marxist and non-Marxist socialism is invalid or unimportant.

Peace historians, in my view, are inclined to be vague. For example, an informative and otherwise sensitive book on Canadian pacifism[5] states on the opening page that 'pacifism is basically a Christian phenomenon,' but soon identifies a 'quite different' sort of opposition to war (a 'pacifism in the liberal tradition'), while nevertheless retaining the term 'pacifism' for both. The result, in my view, is a loss of clarity in the analysis of the various stands within the Canadian peace movement. Similarly, an innovative article entitled 'The Social Origins of Victorian Pacifism'[6] uses lists of early members of the London Peace Society and lists of petitioners to the House of Commons in support of an arbitration motion as if they were evidence of the same phenomenon, even though the former was a society which, though imposing no creed on its members, was known to be formally committed to pacifism, and the latter a *pacificist* motion worded as an anodyne, which virtually anyone other than a militarist could support. In my view, both these works lump together distinct phenomena – pacifism and *pacificism* – that require distinct analyses. They are, of course, often intertwined within the same movement and sometimes coexist uneasily within the thinking of cross-pressured individuals, but peace historians should recognize that separate elements tangled together and in tension with each other are in fact more common than undifferentiated syntheses or hybrids.

Peace historians are also too inclined to reject distinctions that do not apply to the countries they study – in other words, to consider only dogs that do bark – thereby inhibiting the development of a comparative approach to the subject. I hasten to admit that I have been as guilty as anyone of this failing: as will be noted later in this essay, I have failed to make use of the distinction, borrowed form the sociologist Karl Mannheim, between 'utopian' and 'ideological' pacifism, because it is of little use in analysing the British peace movement, forgetting that this fact is itself significant. But others working on countries, such as Germany, in which it is more applicable, have gone to the other extreme, and have implied that it is 'the central distinction'[7] that peace historians need to make, forgetting the different needs of those studying other countries. Even when undertaking single-country studies, peace historians should remember the longer-term goal of constructing a set of categories robust enough to permit cross-national comparison.

In this essay I offer a list of ten distinctions on which such a set of categories can be founded. I adopt this format for reasons of clarity, despite the impression it may give of un-Brock-like dogmatism. I must make clear that it is not my intention to assert or imply the ethical superiority of any of the viewpoints identified. The aim of the distinctions is analytical utility alone. They are necessary to define what peace historians write about: what exactly do they mean when they use 'pacifism' and 'peace movement' in the titles of their books? And they are necessary to distinguish what must be explained separately: for example, during the nineteenth century support for arbitration was generally a by-product of political liberalism, whereas support for pacifism depended heavily on certain Christian traditions. I must also point out that my interest is in the period since approximately the late eighteenth century, when a political debate about peace and war, and with it a peace movement, first developed. What Brock calls 'sectarian pacifism' originated in a pre-modern context that my distinctions are not designed to elucidate, although, since it survived to play a role peas the modern peace movement, I shall attempt to apply my distinctions to it so far as is possible.

Distinction 1

Distinction 1 is between absolutist and what for want of a better word I shall call reformist positions. Absolutist positions are those defined by their rejection of a particular activity – for example, force, killing, war, the use of nuclear weapons – as impermissible. (As we shall see, pacifism is an absolutist position, or rather a cluster of absolutist positions, but not the only one to be found in the peace-and-war debate.) It is, however, wrong to regard absolutist positions as necessarily negative: they can form part of more positive ideologies such as the spiritual conception of socialism or anarchism. It is not, however, unfair to describe them as apolitical in the normal sense of that word.

Reformist positions are those which seek the abolition of war through a restructuring of the political order – for example, by transferring sovereignty to supranational bodies, by ending capitalism, by introducing greater democratic accountability within states, or by curbing patriarchy – rather than by rejecting a particular activity. (As we shall see, *pacificism* is a reformist position, but not the only one.) Reformist positions are thus essentially political: it is through the creation of new political structures, domestic or international, that war will be abolished.

Much of the history of peace movements – and indeed of other philanthropic movements – can be explained in terms of the struggle by organizations and individuals to combine absolutist and reformist approaches: a good example is provided by Britain's First World War peace society, the No-Conscription Fellowship, which attempted to reconcile the pacifist and *pacificist* versions of socialism.[8] But it should be recognized that they are fundamentally different.

I must here anticipate an objection to the hard-and-fast distinction I have drawn between absolutist and non-absolutist positions. What, it might be asked, about contingent positions? Not all pacifists make the unqualified assertion that all war is wrong; some admit the theoretical possibility of a justifiable war. For example, as my recent research on the origins of the British peace movement has taught me, a number of early nineteenth-century peace activists conceded the theoretical possibility of a truly defensive (and therefore justifiable) war, though they were convinced that they had never met it in practice. And, more recently, moral philosophers have defined a contingent form of pacifism. How are these to be classified? I believe that they can be treated either as absolutist or non-absolutist, depending on the rule of thumb adopted by peace activists faced with a remote contingency. Those who decide to behave as if

there is no chance of a foreseeable war being a justifiable one are absolutists. In other words, the contingent belief 'that while there is in principle
the possibility of a war being justified, this is in practice a possibility so
remote that we can disregard it'[9] results in a pacifism indistinguishable
in practice from that arising from an unqualified belief that war could in
no circumstances be justified. Peace activists who behave as if there is a
significant chance of a foreseeable war being justifiable, and who therefore decide to keep an open mind until it actually breaks out, are not
absolutists. They may be *pacificists* of an extreme kind, but not pacifists.

The most difficult case to classify is provided by a pre-modern survival, 'eschatological pacifism,' the belief that true believers should
reject all wars for the present but should expect the millennium, in the
course of which they may be called upon to fight holy wars. This is number three on Brock's list of six types of pacifism, and he describes it as a
'kind of nonviolent interim-ethic' lying 'in the border zone between a
principled and conditional pacifism.' Nevertheless, as Brock implies, a
distinction can be made according to the intensity of the apocalyptic
expectation. Those who believe the millennium – and consequently the
possibility of a holy war – to be imminent are not pacifists in the full
sense. But, as Brock notes, 'What begins as an interim-ethic may eventually be transformed into a settled moral code if the expected "final
things" do not take place.' In other words, those who do not seriously
expect the millennium to occur for the foreseeable future, and who
therefore take for granted that the next war will be one in which they
cannot participate, are indistinguishable from pacifists. In practice,
therefore, it is generally possible to distinguish between eschatological
sects that have retained their apocalyptic hopes, and with them a barely
repressed crusading zeal, and those which have become indistinguishable from religious pacifists.

Distinction 2

Distinction 2 is between both absolutist and reformist positions, on the
one hand, and the just war tradition, on the other. Just war thinking is
an increasingly important source of ethical objections to the practice of
modern warfare, as responses to the 1991 Persian Gulf War have
reminded us. It is, however, neither a moral theory nor an ideology of
peace and war, being instead a set of additional rules to which those
whose moral theories or ideologies permit the use of force must also
adhere before they can in practice employ that force. It is thus possible

to be a 'realist' supporter of orthodox defence preparedness – in other words, a 'defencist,' to use the term I have had to coin because of the extraordinary lack of an established word to describe this commonest of viewpoints – and still to feel that certain uses of force are impermissible. The just war tradition is thus, I feel, best distinguished from the peace-movement tradition, as is done, for example, by James Turner Johnson.[10]

Distinction 3

Distinction 3 is between those types of reformism that allow aggressive force and those that do not. Just as in domestic politics some advocates of fundamental change have been revolutionaries prepared to use violence, so in international politics some reformists have been crusaders willing to use aggressive war to impose their ideology and thus hasten the abolition of war. We must distinguish these crusaders from *pacificists*, who, like the gradualists and constitutionalists among domestic reformers, wish to implement their war-abolishing reforms by peaceful persuasion. Admittedly, this line is sometimes hard to draw. Many nineteenth-century liberals accepted Mazzini's idea that European peace could be established only on the basis of democratic nation states, and they were thus tempted to view revolutions and wars of national liberation against autocratic dynastic states as steps towards peace. Thus, some European groups that are conventionally classified as peace societies – such as Charles Lemmonier's Ligue Internationale de la Paix et de la Liberté, established at Geneva in 1867 at a meeting chaired by Garibaldi – exhibited a barely repressed crusading streak that unsettled their peace-movement colleagues.[11]

Distinction 4

Distinction 4 is between intellectual distinctions and labels. The former matter much more than the latter. As long as peaceful reformism is recognized as a category, I do not mind if people cannot bring themselves to label it *pacificism*.[12] Undoubtedly *pacificism* is etymologically artificial, difficult to pronounce, and visually easy to confuse with pacifism (which is why I sometimes have italicized it, as here, and at other times have written it as pacific-ism). The argument in its favour is simply the absence of any obvious alternative. 'Irenicism' is a possibility that quite appeals to me, though it is a little pretentious. 'Peace advocacy' fails to convey the fact that peaceful reformism is as much an ideology – an 'ism' – as pacifism and is best kept as an umbrella term covering both *pacificism* and pacifism.

Because they dislike *pacificism*, some writers use the word pacifist to cover the peaceful-reformist position and describe the absolutist view as 'absolute pacifism' or, in the case of writers in France, where this practice is almost universal, 'integral pacifism.' Others have used a qualifying adjective for the broad position too. For example, my understanding of Yvonne Bennett's usage in her dissertation on Vera Brittain and the Peace Pledge Union during the Second World War is that the reformist position is 'low' pacifism and the absolutist position 'high' pacifism (although the latter can be 'broad' pacifism in a particular political orientation).[13] One reason for disliking adjectives such as 'low' and 'high' is that they bring value judgments with them. My main reason for disliking the use of pacifism as a label for the reformists position, however, is that it seems odd to describe as in any sense 'pacifist' the League of Nations Union, Britain's largest peace society, when after 1936 it advocated collective resistance to Nazi aggression and opposed the Conservative government's policy of appeasement. It was the body founded as a reaction against this policy, the Peace Pledge Union, which preached pacifism in the sense then understood by most Britons. But this brings me back to a point I have already touched on, namely, that most of us when introducing supposedly universal schemes of labelling and classification are in fact conditioned by parochial concerns. As I have implied, it is because I began my research on 1930s Britain, where the absolutist tradition was strong and the most influential elements within the *pacificist* tradition came strongly to support collective security, that I have used pacifism in the strict way I do. Conversely, those working on France and Germany have tended to adopt the broader usage of pacifism because of the distinctive characteristics of their countries of study: absolute pacifism has been so much weaker in both countries than in Britain that there seems no point in reserving the more convenient label, pacifism, exclusively for it; and the political culture has been so much less favourable to *pacificism* in both countries as to make this a more subversive-seeming position than in Britain and therefore deserving of as bold a term as pacifism. Labels are thus a matter of contextual convenience as well as individual taste, and it may be impossible to all agree on a common system. Let us nevertheless agree on substantive intellectual distinctions, such as those among pacifism, *pacicism*, and the just war tradition.

Distinction 5

Distinction 5 is among the varieties of *pacificism*, as I shall continue to label it. There are as many of these as there are ideologies. Since ideology is a contentious word that I have already used a number of times here without clarification, I must before going any further explain that I do not use it with the pejorative implication that it is a false perspective that can be contrasted with an objective one. I use it in the neutral sense of a world-view or structured set of beliefs that all of us rely on, consciously or otherwise, to help us to filter out of the enormous amount of information about the world with which we are constantly confronted what is important and desirable. We have been strangely reluctant to recognize the ideological structure of the peace-and-war debate. In domestic politics, by contrast, most of us accept that ideology plays a considerable role; we take for granted that, say, conservatives and socialists take different views not merely of the values that human beings should be promoting but also of the way the world works, and that it makes sense therefore to interpret debates about such issues as the educational system and the economy as being to some extent structured by an underlying ideological dispute. But we have tended to see the peace-and-war debate taking place at the level of policy options – for example, on the merits of détente, disarmament, or international organizations – rather than among underlying positions that carry over from one policy to another. Insofar as we have acknowledged an ideological structure to the debate between the different elements of the peace movement and their various opponents, we have done so in terms of crude dichotomies between hawks and doves, realists and idealists, pacifists and militarists. I have tried in a previous book[14] to set out an ideological structure for the peace-and-war debate, dividing the opponents of the peace movement into militarists (advocates of aggression on the grounds that war alone promotes human development), defencists, and crusaders, and the supporters of the peace movement into *pacificists* and pacifists.

More relevant for present purposes is that I have also tried to identify the various ideologies underpinning the variants of *pacificism* that I have come across in my work on the British peace movement. The most important of these has been liberalism: it has argued that there is no inherent conflict of interests among nations and that only an obsession with state sovereignty has caused people to overlook this fact; and it has a proposed remedies ranging from free trade via international organizations to supranationalism. Liberalism's most conspicuous challenger has been socialism: this has insisted that it is not nationalism but capitalism that causes war and that only the spreading of socialism can guarantee peace. The third major ideology, less influential than liberalism and less intellectually coherent than socialism, has been radicalism, a left-wing variety of populism: it assumes that left to themselves the people would abolish war and that it has been the machinations of elites (such as diplomats) and vested interests (such as arms manufacturers) that have ensured that this has not been achieved. The first British peace society to be set up during the First World War was called the Union of Democratic Control because it believed that popular control of foreign policy was the way to achieve peace. And, although you will have to turn to my book for illustrations of this point, I believe that radical thinking has also been strongly influential within the nuclear-disarmament movement in Britain. Liberalism, socialism, and radicalism have been the dominant strands of *pacificism* for much of the history of the British and indeed most other peace movements. In the 1980s, however, these were strongly challenged by two other strands. The first was feminism, which often strongly implies, even if it hardly ever explicitly asserts, that patriarchy is the cause of war and that its overthrow can alone bring peace. The second was ecologism, the green ideology, which sees the upsetting of the balance of nature by industrialization as the cause of war.

These five, then, are the principal types of *pacificism* that I have identified, but of course it would be possible to draw ideological lines in different ways. For example, whereas my classification assumes that Christian *pacificists* have borrowed their thinking about war prevention from the various ideologies just discussed, others might wish to treat Christianity as a *pacificism* in its own right.

Distinction 6

Distinction 6 is between the intellectual content of an anti-war ideology and its sociopolitical context. This distinction is acknowledged, though its implications are not fully recognized, in Roger Chickering's sophisticated and path-breaking study of the pre-1914 German peace movement. Attempting 'to isolate the central distinction among varieties of pacifism' (this last word being employed to cover both *pacificism* and pacifism), Chickering offers 'a distinction based upon their socio-political context as well as their integrated intellectual content.' To this end he adopts Karl Mannheim's dichotomy between 'utopian' and 'ideological' views. Chickering explains this as follows:

Using the orientation of a pacifist doctrine towards politics and society as the basic criterion of differentiation, it is useful to distinguish between pacifism as utopia and pacifism as ideology. Utopian pacifism conceives of war as an inseparable aspect of a social and political order that is utterly corrupt and beyond rehabilitation. Ideological pacifism rejects war because of the threat it poses to a social and political order that is basically sound and praiseworthy. Differences in nuance and emphasis among varieties of pacifism are subordinate to this central distinction.[15]

This distinction is also favoured by Norman Ingram in his valuable recent study of interwar pacifism in France, though not to the exclusion of other distinctions.[16] The adoption of this terminology in the contexts of Wilhelmine Germany and interwar France suggests that 'utopian pacifism' is a phenomenon found particularly in what I have elsewhere analysed as 'illiberal' or 'non-liberal' political cultures,[17] in which the peace movement has been viewed as treacherous and subversive rather than idealistic and legitimate. In more liberal cultures, such as Britain, almost the entire *pacificist* movement, except perhaps its Marxist fringe, would have to be classified as 'ideological pacifists,' since they have regarded the social order not as 'utterly corrupt and beyond rehabilitation' but as 'basically sound and praiseworthy,' in the sense that they believe it capable by normal constitutional processes of delivering the reforms that would abolish war. That was why I ignored the distinction between 'utopian' and 'ideological' pacifism when first writing about Britain.

As already indicated, however, I now believe I was wrong to do so. The fact that 'utopian' pacifism is a dog that does not bark in Britain is a significant one to which attention should be drawn. By the same token, I feel Chickering is wrong to use it as the central distinction that needs to be made. In particular, there is no justification for believing that it removes the need for the pacifism–*pacificism* distinction, since there is a significant difference between a pacifist utopian (such as a Garrisonian non-resister) and a *pacificist* one (such as a Marxist war-resister). The best practice is to use both distinctions, as Ingram does.

It is also helpful to take Chickering's distinction between 'socio-political context' and 'integrated intellectual content' even further than he does.[18] Whereas Chickering believes that the two can be combined, I believe them to be conceptually separate. Intellectual content alone should be the criterion for identifying the various anti-war ideologies. But in addition, sociopolitical context may be used to explain why the latter differ so considerably in their political implications, and consequently in their popularity, from country to country. Let me give an illustration. In trying to analyse the major trends of opinion within the nineteenth-century international peace movement, we should begin by considering intellectual content: for example, we should identify a 'Cobdenite' version of radical *pacificism* by its set of assumptions about aristocratic power, free trade, the reduction in arms spending as part of a general reduction in government spending, and so on. Having done so, however, we may note that such a position was relatively uncontroversial in certain countries, such as Britain and the United States, yet seemed unpatriotic and almost subversive in much of continental Europe. In Mannheim's terminology Cobdenism was relatively 'ideological' in some countries, but almost 'utopian' in others. This shows that Mannheim's distinction has less to say about anti-war ideologies as such than about the political environment in which they operate. The latter is an important subject; elsewhere I have offered a general explanation of the cross-national variations in the acceptability of different anti-war theories with reference to the strength of liberalism within a country's political culture and the measure of security afforded by its strategic situation.[19] But before we can study the sociopolitical implications of an ideology, we must first establish its intellectual content. Though complementary, the study of ideologies and of their sociopolitical context must be recognized as distinct tasks.

Distinction 7

My remaining distinctions all have to do with absolutism. Distinction 7 is between pacifism and other, superficially similar, forms of absolutism that, however, fall short of being rejections of all modern war. The latter can for convenience be divided into modern and historic absolutism.

Modern absolutisms reject only the use of certain kinds of modern weapons, most notably nuclear weapons, but also chemical or biological weapons. In recent years it has become common to call the first of these positions 'nuclear' pacifism'; but insofar as it does not object to conventional warfare it cannot be recognized as a truly pacifist position. It would be better described as anti-nuclear-weapons absolutism, and the other positions as anti-chemical-weapons absolutism or anti-biological-weapons absolutism. We should note, however, that the view that the use of such weapons in any war is so probable that all future war must be rejected is indeed pacifism. (Because it deals with probabilities rather than certainties, it is a contingent rather than an unqualified position; but, as it leads to the rejection of all future warfare, it is an absolutist one nevertheless.) It should ideally be described as nuclear-era pacifism, or chemical- or biological-era pacifism, so as to make clear that the absolutist objection is not to the use of particular weapons but to all warfare in an era in which such weapons are available. These modern absolutism present few difficulties. Few scholars would think it helpful to regard nuclear pacifism and the like as a true form of pacifism, and many nuclear pacifists go out of their way to make clear they are not pacifists in the full sense.

The historic absolutisms present greater difficulties, however. Though sometimes treated by scholars as legitimate forms of pacifism, I shall argue that they are either forms of 'exemptionism' or secondary characteristics of a pacifism whose primary inspiration must be sought on other grounds.

I have defined 'exemptionism' as the view that war is all right for others, but not for members of the elite or the elect. It is best illustrated in pure form by the alleged retort of one young member of Britain's Bloomsbury Group in the First World War to the question why he was not fighting for civilization like most other men of his age: 'Madam, *I* am the civilization they are fighting for.'[20] The secular basis of such a claim has usually been the higher calling of the artist with special creative gifts, while its religious basis has been the higher calling of members of a monastic order or sect who submit to special spiritual disciplines. Brock regards these positions as instances of 'vocational pacifism,' the first of his six types of pacifism, which he defines in the following terms: 'Although for the vocationalists nonviolence is absolute in respect to an individual who has accepted it for his own way of life, they make no claim for its integral acceptance by others who have not chosen the same calling. For the rules of one calling are not incumbent on those who have adopted another, even if a less elevated one.'

Brock, however, admits that it 'scarcely fits within the definition of pacifism' he has been using. In my view, the key issue is whether vocational pacifists *want* those others who 'have not chosen the same calling' to espouse pacifism too. If not, they are preaching exemptionism. After all, when churches support a war and wish their ordinary members to fight in it, their simultaneous wish that their monastic orders be especially excused from military service has nothing to do with pacifism. Only if vocational pacifists wish others to take the same position are they true pacifists. And in this case, of course, they must explain why they and others are justified in being pacifists. Vocational pacifism is therefore either exemptionism or a behavioural characteristic – an unpriggish reluctance to point out to others what they themselves regard as correct behaviour – of those who are pacifists on other grounds. It is not itself a form of pacifism.

Similar points can be made about 'soteriological pacifism,' another pre-modern position, which is number two on Brock's list and that he defines as 'an objection to shedding human blood (and sometimes animals' as well) because it leads to ritual impurity and thus to the loss of personal salvation, at least until some form of purification is undergone.' As Brock admits, it 'is not easily comprehended within the normative pacifism' he has outlined. Unlike the objection to idolatrous military oaths, which played some part in the early Christian objection to service in the Roman army, it is an objection that goes directly to the heart of war, since the latter cannot be carried on without killing. But it might be exemptionist, if the aversion to shedding blood is regarded as a sign of the heightened fastidiousness of the elect. That this has indeed often been the case is borne out by Brock's observation: 'Vocationally this has been the standpoint of the priesthood in various primitive religions.' I would argue therefore that, as in the case of vocational pacifism, the test is whether soteriological pacifists want others to take the same stand. If not, they are exemptionists, but if so, they are indeed pacifists. In the latter case, however, they still must explain why ritual impurity arises from killing, and in doing so they will presumably show soteriological pacifism to be less a type of pacifism in its own right than one of the many forms that religious pacifism can take.

Similar observations apply to Brock's third type of pacifism, 'eschatological pacifism,' to which some attention has already been paid. As we have seen, when apocalyptic hopes are high this is, in Brock's words, too 'conditional' a rejection of war to count as 'principled' pacifism: in the terms used here, it is a temporary exemptionism, valid only until the millennium. But, after such hopes have faded, it may develop into a 'settled moral code' indistinguishable from pacifism. Even if it does so, however, it needs to explain why it rejects war in a world whose spiritual transformation looks increasingly far off, and the answer it gives is usually a religious imperative. Like 'vocational' and 'soteriological' pacifism, therefore, 'eschatological pacifism' can be either exemptionism or a particular form of religious pacifism.

Distinction 8

My final three distinctions are among those types of absolutism that are unambiguously pacifist. In *Nevertheless: Varieties of Religious Pacifism*, John H. Yoder argued that pacifism should be viewed as 'not just one specific position .. but rather a wide gamut of varying, sometimes even contradictory positions.'[21] Warning against the forcing of such positions into 'the ready-made slots of the ethicists,' he gives a long, unstructured list. I believe it is useful to structure these different pacifisms according to three criteria: what it is they object to; what their ethical inspiration is; and what their orientation towards politics is.

Distinction 8 is thus among the various things to which pacifism can object. The most extreme is to physical force of any kind: the best known theorist of this view was Tolstoy. Less extreme is the objection to killing, which entails an objection to capital punishment as well as war. Next comes the objection to war as such, which permits forms of killing that do not count as war. At the moderate end are the objections only to modern war or war in the nuclear era, which accept that in past ages wars were sometimes justified. Because different pacifisms thus object to different things, it follows that an argument against one is not an argument against all. Though a 'killing pacifist' could not consistently support a violent revolution, for example, the same would not be true of a 'war pacifist.'[22]

Distinction 9

Distinction 9 is among the three or four main ethical inspirations for pacifism. The latter must, in other words, be grounded either in a religious faith (usually Christianity), or in a political creed (notably anarchism or the spiritual conception of socialism), or in a philosophical position (such as humanitarianism or utilitarianism). Except that I now would place more emphasis upon the difference within the philosophical strand between the humanitarians, whose ethical position is deontological and unqualified, and the utilitarians, whose approach is consequentialist and contingent, I see little need to change what I wrote about pacifist inspirations in my first book. Indeed my subsequent research has increased my conviction that such distinctions are useful. After all, pacifism as an idea is inexorably linked to the development of three or four ethical traditions, and pacifists spend much of their time trying to persuade those in the same tradition that it entails pacifism. Religious pacifists have sought to so persuade their fellow Christians, political pacifists their fellow socialists, and philosophical pacifists their fellow humanists or consequentialists. To some extent, moreover, the dynamics of the pacifist movement are explained by tensions among religious, political, and philosophical approaches. For example, as a British Christian pacifist observed some years ago of his relations with the rest of the peace movement: 'A question that continually arises but is usually brushed under the carpet is what kind of relationship there can be between Christian pacifists and secular pacifists or those who simply claim to be "religious" ... To ignore these differences is to pretend that they don't matter but the Christian cannot honestly behave as if Christianity did not matter without some strain, and the equivalent beliefs of other groups are perhaps comparably important to them.'[23]

Distinction 10

Distinction 10 is among the three main orientations towards politics that pacifists can adopt. This brings me to my original debt to Brock, since it was his fourth, fifth, and sixth pacifist categories that first alerted me to the need to classify pacifism according to its view of politics as well as its ethical inspiration. Brock's separational pacifism was what I now call the pessimistic orientation: in peacetime it adopts a sectarian approach to politics; in wartime it seeks to maintain a quietist witness, often in pacifist communities. Brock's integrational pacifism was what I now call the mainstream orientation: in peacetime it collaborates with *pacificist* proposals for war prevention; in wartime it mainly attempts to serve society through humanitarian and relief work. Brock's goal-directed pacifism was what I now call the optimistic inspiration: in peacetime it believes that to develop a capacity for Gandhi-style non-violent resistance will be an effective way of deterring invasion; in wartime it attempts to stop the war effort.

I am convinced that these distinctions have been useful to the historical analysis of pacifism, and I have been generally unpersuaded by attempts to vary them.[24] But I should make clear that there is no implication that these three orientations will be found in every pacifist movement. That the non-violent orientation was not found in interwar France does not, as Ingram implies,[25] reveal a weakness of this typology: it is another example of a non-barking dog.

I have now set out ten distinctions: between absolutism as a whole and reformism as a whole, between each of these and the just war tradition, between the crusading and *pacificist* versions of reformism, between substantive intellectual distinctions and descriptive labels, between the intellectual content of an anti-war ideology and its sociopolitical context, among the varieties of *pacificism*, between pacifist and non-pacifist absolutism, among the things to which different varieties of pacifism object, among the ethical inspirations for pacifism, and among pacifism's orientations towards politics. If these distinctions are conceived as the different axes of a multidimensional grid, then there are sufficient slots to embrace all the many types of anti-war position without straitjacketing. Perhaps I am exhibiting a *déformation professionelle* in questing for that holy grail of political science, the comprehensive taxonomy. But I am convinced that such a quest is needed if the study of the history and politics of peace movements is to catch up with comparable branches of study, such as that of labour movements, in making rigorous distinctions among, for example, intellectual traditions, ideological structures, political tactics, and contextual factors.

Notes

1 This was reflected in the fact that neither of the doctoral theses on aspects of modern British pacifism which I read early in my work had been published: K.G. Robbins wrote books on two other subjects before publishing a revised version of 'The Abolition of War: A Study in the Organisation and Ideology of the Peace Movement, 1914–19,' DPhil thesis, Oxford University (1964) in 1976; and, so far as I am aware, Joyce A. Berkman, 'Pacifism in England, 1914–39,' PhD dissertation, Yale University (1967) remains unpublished.

2 Peter Brock, *Pacifism in Europe to 1914* (Princeton, 1972), 472–6. The quotations from Brock's typology later in this essay are all from these pages. I must admit with considerable shame that I did not read John H. Yoder's stimulating book *Nevertheless: Varieties of Religious Pacifism* (Scottdale, 1971) until the Bodleian Library acquired a copy (of the 1976 edition) in 1989.

3 A.J.P. Taylor, *The Trouble Makers: Dissent over Foreign Policy, 1792–1939* (London, 1957), 51n.

4 The once revered English linguistic authority H.W. Fowler was in 'no doubt that the longer form is the better' but in no doubt either that the 'barbarous' shorter form would oust it: *A Dictionary of Modern English Usage* (Oxford, 1926), 300–1, 418. For the first use of pacifism, see the entry by Sandi E. Cooper on Emile Arnaud, in Harold Josephson (ed.), *Biographical Dictionary of Modern Peace Leaders* (Westport, 1985), 36–7.

5 Thomas Socknat, *Witness against War: Pacifism in Canada, 1900–1945* (Toronto, 1987) 3, 7, 8.

6 By Eric W. Sager, in *Victorian Studies* 23 (1979–80), esp. 214.

7 Roger Chickering, *Imperial Germany and a World without War: The Peace Movement and German Society, 1892–1914* (Princeton, 1975), 18.

8 See Jo Vellacott, *Bertrand Russell and the Pacifists in the First World War* (Brighton, 1980), and Thomas C. Kennedy, *The Hound of Conscience* (Fayetteville, 1981).

9 Jonathan Glover, *Causing Death and Saving Lives* (Harmondsworth, 1977), 258, summarizing John Rawls, *A Theory of Justice* (Cambridge, Mass., 1971), section 58, where the term 'contingent pacifism' can be found.

10 James Turner Johnson, *The Quest for Peace: Three Moral Traditions in Western Cultural History* (Princeton, 1987), xii.

11 F.H. Hinsley, *Power and the Pursuit of Peace: Theory and Practice in the History of Relations between States* (Cambridge, 1963), 120–1.

12 Peter Brock has used it on one occasion: see his *The Roots of War Resistance: Pacifism from the Early Church to Tolstoy* (Nyack, 1981), 76. A.J.P. Taylor came to dislike his own terminology; see his review of my *Pacifism in Britain, 1914–1945* (Oxford, 1980), in *London Review of Books* (2 Oct. 1980), 4. A significant if passing early use of the pacifism–*pacificism* distinction can be found in David A. Martin, *Pacificism: An Historical and Sociological Study* (London, 1965), 205.

13 Yvonne Aleksandra Bennett, 'Testament of a Minority in Wartime: The Peace Pledge Union and Vera Brittain 1939–1945,' PhD dissertation, McMaster University (1984), 11.

14 Martin Ceadel, *Thinking about Peace and War* (Oxford, 1987; paperback ed., 1989).

15 Chickering, *Imperial Germany*, 18–19.

16 Norman Ingram, *The Politics of Dissent: Pacifism in France, 1919–1939* (Oxford, 1991), 13.

17 Ceadel, *Thinking about Peace and War*, 168–76.

18 Chickering, *Imperial Germany*, 18.

19 Ceadel, *Thinking about Peace and War*, ch. 8.

20 Michael Holroyd, *Lytton Strachey: A Critical Biography* (London, 1967), vol. 1, 416. See also Ceadel, *Pacifism in Britain*, 43–6.

21 Yoder, *Nevertheless*, 10–11.

22 I have sometimes implied otherwise in my own work, but I came to realize my error thanks to a helpful discussion with Norman Ingram.

23 Richard Thomas, 'Communications with the Peace Movement,' *Reconciliation Quarterly* (Sept. 1974), 22.

24 For example, Yvonne Bennett's category of 'broad pacifism' (Bennett, 'Testament of a Minority,' 10) seems to me to offer no advance on Brock's 'integrational' or my 'collaborative' category, and I am unclear whether her 'high' pacifism is a general position of which 'broad' pacifism is a subset or whether

it is a different orientation altogether. Similarly, I do not agree with Norman Ingram (*Politics of Dissent*, 11) that the non-violent orientation is 'no more than a case of extreme collaboration': the essence of collaboration is that pacifists support non-pacifist measures as a second best but a step in the right direction, whereas non-violence is not a second best and involves pacifists in no compromise with physical force.

25 Ingram, *Politics of Dissent*, 11.

3

Thinking about Peace in History

CHARLES CHATFIELD

This essay has an intentionally ambiguous title, for it addresses both how we think about peace in historical terms (thinking about peace-in-history) and how peace has been considered historically (thinking-about-peace in history). My own thought has been stimulated in each respect by Martin Ceadel's critical analysis of the positions taken in what he has called the war-and-peace debate, notably by the typology he advanced in *Thinking about Peace and War* and by his subsequent essay, 'Ten Distinctions for Peace Historians.'

In each case Ceadel develops categories for the purpose of offering interpretive distinctions with which to clarify our discourse and enable us to get beyond description. In the first instance he frames his typology in the theoretical context of international relations – how we think about peace and war. In the second he applies his typological distinctions to the history of peace movements – how peace has historically been considered – and he does so in an historically sensitive, nuanced manner. This is not surprising, because Ceadel's earlier *Pacifism in Britain, 1914–1945* was a sophisticated excursion into the consequences of thinking about peace in particular ways.[1]

The difference between thinking about war and peace, on the one hand, and reflecting on the historical consequences of war and peace thought, on the other, is itself a critical distinction. It is not an absolute one, of course; it is a matter of relative emphasis which, however, establishes parameters of judgment. I would like to reflect a bit on those parameters and then to explore them in terms of some aspects of historic peace thought and organization.

Categories and Characterization

In his 'Ten Distinctions' Ceadel distinguishes between the 'intellectual distinctions,' required for understanding, and those 'labels' that constitute a kind of shorthand for schemes of classification. He identifies the threshold of our problem with language when he observes that 'most of us when introducing supposedly universal schemes of labelling and classification are in fact conditioned by parochial concerns ... Labels are thus a matter of contextual convenience as well as individual taste.' They are also a matter of historical context, as I will note below.

Labels are a kind of signs that point to generalized classifications. To be sure, there is a difference between descriptive labels and the intellectual distinctions on which typologies are based. Still, words that originate in attempts to free thought from imprecision or stereotyping can be turned into labels that, in turn, compartmentalize and marginalize ideas.

The history of the word *pacifism* illustrates this process. It was created in 1901 in a deliberate effort to distinguish peace advocacy from anti-patriotic defeatism and shirking of social responsibility.[2] It meant the belief that international disputes should be resolved by peaceful means instead of war. Subsequently, the word was narrowed in common Anglo-American usage to connote the principled refusal to sanction any war or participate in military service.[3] Thus, labels do matter because the more they are used, the more they constitute a new language – whether technical or political – and the further removed they become from their historic usage. Perhaps it is for this reason, more than difficulties in pronunciation and etymology, that I prefer the phrase *peace advocate* to the word *pacific-ism* (although in his own historical writing Ceadel imbues the more technical term with content and context, thus making it more than a typological category).

Adding difficulty, labels with contradictory meanings are fixed in the secondary literature. Thus, Roger Chickering and James Turner Johnson use the word *utopian* to ascribe opposite characteristics to peace advocacy.[4] Each use makes sense within the author's context, but the word cannot be generalized without losing the very distinctions to which each author points. And the substitution of another word does not resolve this problem. The word *pacifism* itself is a classic example of multiple usage. Peter Brock's historical canon is based on the use of *pacifism* in the strict sense of the principled refusal to sanction or participate in war, but the word is still used in its original and more general sense of substituting peaceful processes for warfare, especially in European writing (and in Sandi Cooper's definitive history of the nineteenth-century European peace movement[5]). Introducing a new word (such as pacific-ism) does not relieve us of the task of interpreting the existing secondary and primary literature.

There is also a subtle difference between definitions and distinctions. By definition we identify a subject of discourse in terms of precise outlines or boundaries, giving it a decisive and exclusive identity. By making a distinction, we use particular qualities to differentiate related subjects of discourse that can be understood only in relation to one another. Thus, having defined 'pacifism' as an exclusive position that rejects warfare altogether, Ceadel makes telling distinctions in relation to the focus, ethical inspiration, and political orientation of that rejection. Specific labels are not essential to the distinctions he makes, but context is crucial to relationships.

Clearly defined categories are essential for political and historical distinctions, but analysis necessarily becomes modified in historical interpretation. Otherwise, the intellectual clarity implicit in typological categories would contravene the very ambiguity that is part of real life – and therefore of real-life history. Perhaps this is why Peter Brock and John Howard Yoder, among others, willingly acknowledge variations in pacifism but resist rigid, definitive typologies of it.[6] Ideas and ideologies interact only through persons and groups. People and organizations may be categorized, and that exercise contributes to our analytical description of their interactions. But this is not to be confused with understanding what they were about or thought they were about, or even what they thought about peace and war.

Moreover, since distinctions beget distinctions, types beget types: absolutism, contingent absolutism, exemptionism. This may contribute to clarity of comparative analysis. But thus refined, intellectual distinctions can be misleading *insofar as* they articulate variations of thought as though they were discrete rather than relative positions, as abstract instead of contextual.

In sum, linguistic fine-tuning is most appropriate to thinking about thought. In thinking about peace advocates and movements, though, it must not obscure the ambiguity of purpose that is often a fact of the life we seek to understand.

These preliminary reflections on the value and limitations of categorical analysis can be extended in terms of some conventional categories of historic peace thinking.

Just War, Peace Advocacy, and Pacifism

There is indeed a sense in which just war thought differs from both strict pacifism and peace advocacy in general.[7] The just war tradition, although it limits war, accepts warfare as a given fact of social organization. By contrast, peace advocates have held that the abolition of war is possible and desirable, and strict pacifists have repudiated war altogether (although there is within the non-resistance tradition an important line of thought that regards violence as a given for unredeemed society). This distinction holds, however, only insofar as just war thought is understood as an *intellectual* and *political* paradigm (a model, for instance, of international relations).

Understood as an *ethical* paradigm, the distinction breaks down.[8] The just war tradition is, of course, misnamed, because it has not interpreted war as 'just' *per se*. It has held, rather, that warfare may be justifiable – may constitute an ethical choice – if and only if it meets certain criteria for the authority and conduct of war (*jus ad bellum* and *jus in bello*). Insofar as the tradition delineates choices rather than wars, it offers an ethical paradigm.

It was as moral philosophy that it was given systematic development by sixteenth- and seventeenth-century scholars – notably Franciscus de Victoria and Francisco Suares, William Ames and John Locke, and especially Hugo Grotius. Although they grounded their thought in natural law rather than formal theology, they were concerned with moral theory. Grotius sought an alternative to those who, as he wrote, 'believe that in war nothing is lawful' and those 'for whom all things are lawful in war.'[9] That was the objective of St Augustine well before Grotius and of Reinhold Niebuhr long after: to bring warfare within the purview of moral law.

Although the moral theory of justifiable war has been interpreted quite differently in various eras, it has consistently been assumed that a choice for or against warfare is relative to and contingent upon political circumstances. As an ethical model, therefore, it could be (and has often been) consonant with peace advocacy in general, insofar as both are moral theories of relative goodness. Limiting the scope of war is consonant with increasing the sphere of peace. In Ceadel's terms, both are reformist. In this respect, the just war tradition has differed from strict, or absolute pacifism, for which war is intrinsically unethical (at least for the pacifist community), but even here one must be careful. In some of its early versions, as again recently, the tradition incorporated the obligation of conscientious objection to specific wars in the light of just war criteria.[10] Moreover, Immanuel Kant framed his views on *Perpetual Peace* (1795) on the explicit assumption that there is no fundamental dichotomy between practical politics and intrinsic values. Whatever the merits of that position, its meaning derives from an ethical paradigm.

Understood as a *historical* paradigm, too, just war thought has been consonant with general peace advocacy. It is becoming clear, for example, that the medieval formulation of just war codes such as the Peace and Truce of God was part of a vast process of social transformation.[11] A similar process seems to have taken place during the Renaissance, when aggressive war was defined and proscribed in recognition of national sovereignty.[12] Or, to return to Grotius, his historical context dictated that his exposition of just war thought presaged peace advocacy: why else was he and not his predecessors remembered as 'the father of international law'? It was, as one of his translators remarked, 'that Europe, with feudalism in its death-throes and Church and Empire riven asunder, had urgent need of a general theory of the State, of the nation, and its organization. The contractual theory of government was now rising out of the dissolving feudal system, and here was Grotius frankly developing that theory by a bold assimilation of public powers to private rights. So it was the general course of events, the very atmosphere of a rapidly changing and developing Europe, that determined the reputation and influence that the *De Jure Belli* was to enjoy and command.'[13] As a historical phenomenon, then, the just war tradition has been consonant with the program of peace advocates.

Indeed, the internationalism of the nineteenth and early twentieth centuries heralded a social transformation on a global scale. One part of this has been the development of the law of war as an encompassing and 'homogeneous body of rules applicable to the modern state of war.' These rules are fully consolidated and codified, and they are now widely acknowledged even when they are violated. The law of war epitomizes the just war tradition. Whether or not it has limited warfare, it has expanded the concept of international community to include protection for individuals, and it has also imposed obligations upon state and non-state groups (both intergovernmental agencies and such non-governmental groups as liberation movements and guerillas), all of which are bound together 'by the reason of equality of belligerence.'[14] In this historical context the just war tradition has been not only consonant with peace advocacy but an instrument of it.

In any case, the relationship of the just war tradition, peace advocacy, and strict pacifism hinges on a distinction between intellectual or political constructs and ethical or historical paradigms. As an intellectual construct or political program, warfare itself is not a justifiable institution for peace advocates or pacifists. In a specific historical situation or in a relative and contingent ethic, however, a war can command the reluctant endorsement of peace advocates as being justifiable, although not the endorsement of strict pacifists (at least not for themselves). Existential circumstances determine to what extent peace advocates respond to political possibilities or a sense of ethical obligation. Moreover, the interplay between these three traditions over time suggests that periods and processes of historical transformation offer categories of peace history as important as specific ideologies of war and peace.

Varieties of Peace Advocacy

Perhaps it would be useful to redefine the relationship of the three conventional traditions in historical terms. To begin with, we might identify all intellectual positions, organization, and activity designed to limit, eliminate, or reject warfare as forms of peace advocacy. Quite simply, our universe of discourse is that which denies the inherent, positive value of war and seeks alternatives to it.[15] It is the alternative to militarism. This definition is not quite arbitrary, since it encompasses all those who historically have claimed to favour and advance peace over war, even if they believed that warfare is in some sense inescapable. It does not include those who have argued that war is inherently good, even if they claimed that it results in some kind of peace.

Until at least the later medieval phase of Western civilization, war was indeed regarded as an inevitable characteristic of social organization. That assumption qualified two broad categories of peace advocacy: efforts to limit and control warfare, and refusals to participate in it. The first was developed in the diplomacy of the Greek city states and the rules of warfare assumed by the Roman empire. It was articulated by St Augustine and others in terms of moral criteria, which in conjunction with codes of chivalry, custom, and canon law, evolved into the just war tradition. The second was institutionalized in the early Christian church. It was periodically revived within monastic orders and religious reform groups, evolving into a tradition of individual or group non-resistance to violent force. Each of these approaches to peace was articulated in relation to a variety of ideologies.[16]

Throughout this period there were also recurrent assertions that peace (in the sense of social order) could be imposed by a moral authority that was secured by force of arms. The empires of Cyrus and Alexander, Augustus, and Charlemagne were rationalized under the aegis of this notion. Under it popes and Holy Roman emperors claimed leadership of a Christian empire and justified their armed crusades. Notions of an imposed peace and a 'final war' for a peaceful order survived into the modern era. They were articulated in the French and Bolshevik revolutions by Anacharsis Cloots and V.I. Lenin, but they surfaced also in Allied propaganda of the First and Second World Wars and on both sides of the Cold War. So prevalent and powerful a view must be taken seriously as peace-related thought; but it need not be included with peace advocacy except insofar as its proponents explicitly sought to replace the force of arms as the basis of social order. To the extent that they did so, they can be related to the just war tradition, albeit uncomfortably.[17]

There seems to be consensus that from the sixteenth through the nineteenth centuries peace advocacy acquired a new thrust. The belief grew that war was not a morally justifiable institution and should be replaced by non-violent processes of conflict resolution: warfare could and should be brought within the purview of law or even eliminated. To a large extent, this represented a conscious extension of the nation state centralized under the rule of law and of the contract theory of sovereign authority.

The new orientation did not begin as a systematic ideology, and it was not necessarily viewed as an alternative to the older traditions. Probably its influence helped to reshape the non-resistance tradition for Quakers, for example (varieties of pacifism in the strict sense will be explored below), and certainly it was incorporated into just war treatises from Grotius to Kant. Its growing influence is suggested by comparisons of, say, Sully's 'Grand Design' (ca. 1620–38) with William Penn's peace proposal (1693), or of Saint-Pierre's 'Project for Perpetual Peace' (1711–38) with Rousseau's version of it (1760).

In the nineteenth century the new orientation was combined with the growth of representative government and voluntary associations to form the modern peace movement. It is in that sense that Sandi Cooper observed in 1976, 'Pacifism – in its definition as an organized propaganda movement opposing wars among nation states – has a fairly short history in the modern world, confined to the last 150 years.'[18]

Thus organized, peace advocacy took several forms. These can be dis-

tinguished by their constituencies, by their various theories about the
origins of war (as Ceadel tends to do),[19] or by their strategies for containing or eliminating it. On the one hand, for example, there were efforts to
limit the scope and destructiveness of warfare through negotiated laws
of war, and there were attempts to limit the occasions for war through
arbitration and diplomacy. Together, these approaches constituted an
emphasis on international law. A second broad emphasis was on international organization, both that of non-governmental peace (and socialist)
societies and – especially in the early twentieth century – of states.

Broadly speaking, then, the orientation of modern peace advocacy has
been internationalist, although a distinction is required between forms
of internationalism designed to work within the existing order of sovereign states (as in international law or Cobden models of free trade) and
efforts to restructure the state system in ways that would modify sovereignty. Collective security arrangements are one outgrowth of the latter
approach, and collective problem-solving agencies (such as the International Monetary Fund) are another. Although they are quite different as
regards war *per se*, they are both forms of interstate cooperation
designed to limit the scope and occasion for warfare.

It must be added that twentieth-century peace advocacy has been profoundly influenced by a pervasive and growing transnationalism. That
was manifested early in the rhetoric of peace advocates (notably pacifists in the strict sense, socialists, and feminists). Subsequently it has
been institutionalized in international problem-solving agencies and has
become the accepted frame of reference for conflicts on a global scale
(such as the Cold War, socio-economic disparities, and ecological
threats). In this sense, the view of the planet Earth from the moon, the
first universal image in history, is recognizably a peace symbol.

What is the point of this cursory survey? It is to suggest that categories
of peace advocacy can be interpreted as responses to changing realities
as well as to changing perceptions of reality. I take it to be Ceadel's central point that varieties of peace thought can be distinguished by their
intellectual content (their attitudes towards war and peace, order and
change, or self and society), and that the distribution and consequences
of those variations can be interpreted by historical (socio-political) contexts. That is a very helpful suggestion. It offers points of comparison
across time and across political cultures.

It is still possible, within that framework, to interpret categories of
peace advocacy as variations on a central theme, rather than as discrete
ideologies, and to explain their variety in terms of the real-world issues

to which individuals and groups have responded. The difference is perhaps one of nuance; but it may imply that we understand categorical ideologies as the result, and not necessarily the determinants, of historic struggles to come to terms with war. The difference is perhaps one of subject matter: whether we compare different ways of thinking about war and peace or interpret the meaning and consequences of the different ways in which war and peace have been approached.

Varieties of Pacifism

Of the classic approaches to the problem of war, pacifism in the strict sense has perhaps been the most problematic for historians – as also for politicians and the general public. This difficulty is largely a twentieth-century phenomenon. Accordingly, Peter Brock accepts 1914 as the terminus for his treatment of pacifism as an integral tradition noting that it was then poised 'on the threshold of a new era just when humankind itself was entering on a new – and infinitely dangerous stage in its development.'[20]

The rejection of war could be understood to be 'absolute' as long as it was total and sectarian, a form of non-resistance to both violence and civil authority. 'Sectarian' pacifism is a meaningful term insofar as violence is prohibited altogether for members of the sect, for whatever reason, even if it assumed it to be requisite for the larger, unredeemed society.[21] Those who accept that proscription for themselves may be called pacifists. The same principle may be applied to vocational and soteriological pacifists.[22]

The cases where war is rejected for all practical purposes, even though theoretically it might be justified, are simply incidences of practical or even eschatological but not necessarily absolute pacifism. Here descriptive adjectives are sufficient to distinguish that which is contingent: *nuclear pacifism*, for example, refers precisely to the rejection of war that might involve nuclear warfare although not necessarily all forms of military force.

What is involved here is a distinction between the absolute (unremitting) refusal to participate in war, on the one hand, and the contingent grounds for that refusal, between the principles that make absolute claims and the claims they make.[23] It is between the varied bases of refusing to participate in warfare, which divide pacifists, and the practice of refusal, which they have in common. What is contingent is the grounds for pacifism, not the fact of commitment that defines it.

The difficulty in characterizing strict pacifism is not merely verbal, it is substantive. About the same time that the word *pacifism* was narrowed from its original broad connotation of peace advocacy to the refusal to sanction or participate in war, the principle of rejecting war was coupled with an activist orientation. Many strict pacifists have participated in movements that challenged foreign public policy without challenging the ultimate recourse to war. This is largely a twentieth-century phenomenon, and one which probably reflects a pervasive ethical relativism. Two broad considerations are involved. One is the multiplicity of roles open to individuals and groups. The other is the dynamics of advocacy.

The participation of pacifists in political action is a paradox only if pacifists are relegated to the single role of espousing their own principles. In fact, numerous individuals and groups have played dual roles as strict pacifists and as citizens. As pacifists they rejected war altogether, on whatever grounds of principle. They even fostered the rejection of war as an instrument of national policy. As citizens they tried to prevent or limit warfare on realistic, empirical grounds. They acknowledged the relative claims of justice and security. From at least the First World War to the present, there were individuals and groups that promoted absolute pacifism while at the same time they participated in the relative politics of peace advocacy.[24] Without question, they often felt torn between or confused by these roles. Sometimes they were marginalized by adversaries who confused intellectual consistency with personal authenticity.[25]

Finally, then, this brings us to what Martin Ceadel calls the 'dynamics' of pacifist movements. Here we can benefit from the careful language and considerable literature of social movement theory, especially that on resource mobilization.[26] The dynamics of movements (here the interaction of peace groups with one another and with the public) is conditioned by specific social and historical circumstances. Very practical considerations contribute different orientations to politics, at least as much as ideologies do. The relevant concerns include identifying salient issues and mobilizing resources – funds, expertise, leadership, and constituencies – so as to generate public pressure and political influence. These considerations come into play when peace organizations attempt to form coalitions and to generate public campaigns. The resulting organizational and strategic tensions, inherent in activism, offer a basis on which to distinguish and compare various peace campaigns.

The history of successive peace coalitions also reinforces the merit of a distinction advanced by German sociologist Ferdinand Tönnies and applied by Sondra R. Herman to the American peace movement of the Progressive Era.[27] Tönnies and Herman contrast those who stress institutional reform, what Herman called 'polity,' with those who emphasize personal, community-based values.

Polity-oriented peace advocates prefer alternatives to war, but most of them endorse force when necessary to maintain peace in the sense of order. They are attracted to formal internationalism. They trust institutions and seek access to decision-making elites. They tend to organize around single issues and for short-term goals. By contrast, community-oriented peace advocates tend to think of peace as harmony, to emphasize a spirit of fellowship embracing the peoples of the world. They are attracted to transnationalism. They respond to values and popular movements. They tend to organize for multiple issues and the long-term goals of social transformation.[28] In the succession of peace coalitions, strictly pacifist groups are important precisely because their community and value orientation endures beyond specific policy crises. They become storehouses of values, leadership, constituencies, experiences, and other resources on which more ephemeral, issue-directed peace coalitions are built.[29]

Coalition politics in periodic peace campaigns is complicated by the interaction of people and groups with these alternative orientations, as well as by the changing issues and political contexts that produce varied movement strategies. Since the forms of interaction evolve over time, the changing relationships of peace advocates to one another and the public itself offers important categories of interpretation.

Categories and Characterization

I do not know how to interpret history without telling stories. That medium is my message. Accordingly, I conclude these reflections by recalling two 1969 conversations.

The first one was with Friederich Siegmund-Schultze. His adult life spanned both world wars, and it was a three-fold amen: he was at once a leader in the continental movements for ecumenism, the social gospel, and pacifism. Prior to the Second World War he went into exile from Germany to Geneva. There during the war he worked for the International Fellowship of Reconciliation, but he also passed on sensitive information from the German and Dutch resistance movements to the Allied governments. 'Didn't that contradict [his] pacifist principles?' I asked.

He answered, 'One must always know one's principles and be true to them. Sometimes conditions make it possible to pursue them more and sometimes less. One must consider the circumstances, but one must always know and be true to one's principles.'

The second conversation was with Premysl Pitter, a Czechoslovakian pacifist, pastor, and founder of a youth home where he saved many Czech and Jewish children from the Nazis. Threatened by Soviet repression in 1948, he escaped to Zurich. It was there that we talked of the Second World War. Pitter admitted that he had been pleased with each Allied victory that brought the Nazi regime closer to ruin, even though he understood the cost in human life and the likelihood that military victories would only displace and not end warfare. 'Wasn't that a dilemma for a pacifist?' I asked. He looked at me as though I were one of the naive children from his youth home, and said simply, 'Life is dilemma.'

Historians must approach peace ideas and movements with Siegmund-Schultse's sense of contingency and Pitter's appreciation for dilemma. Analytical distinctions are very important for clarity, of course, but they must be tempered with an appreciation for the contingent dilemma of living out ideas. The limit of peace history is not only a function of historical discipline. That constraint is real enough, but even the most effective scholarship only exposes the boundaries of the peace impulse in the lives of its advocates.

Beyond the variety of peace ideas and the distinctions we apply to them for analytical purposes, there is a quest of which they are a part. It is what James Turner Johnson called 'a moral tradition.' It is, as he wrote, 'something that develops through human reflection and action, and it is the continuity that links such reflection and action which defines the tradition.' The tradition embraces not only the peace advocates and organizations of whom we write, but also our characterization of them. At best, historians of peace are engaged, in Johnson's words, in 'the conscious act of forging connections with the past and utilizing connections already forged' to give their own era 'moral identity.'[30]

Beyond the generic limitations of historical scholarship, peace research in history is constrained by the limitations of peace advocates and pacifists to know their own principles and to apply them in an ambiguous, dilemma-filled world. The limits of their understanding are the limits of ours. As for divisions in peace history, the most useful classifications are those which most help us to convey how people and groups thought and acted for peace, how they dealt with the tensions of ethical consistency and political possibility, of vision and obligation, of intellectual clarity and real-life ambiguity. It is necessary to group peace advocates, but categories apply sometimes more and sometimes less. History is dilemma. We consider the circumstances, but we try to be true to the people whose principles we characterize.

Notes

1 Martin Ceadel, *Pacifism in Britain, 1914–1945: The Defining of a Faith* (Oxford, 1980), and *Thinking about Peace and War* (Oxford, 1989).
2 Irwin Abrams established in 1957 that *pacifisme* was coined in 1901 by Emile Arnaud, French lawyer and president of the *Ligue Internationale de la Paix et de la Liberté*, and was introduced by him in a report of the International Peace Bureau meeting in September 1901. There had been a widespread search for a term that could disarm charges of anti-patriotism and negativism, but one more distinctive than the commonly used 'friends of peace.' Research notes courtesy of Irwin Abrams.
3 The original, broad meaning of *pacifism* still is favoured by the Webster's and Oxford dictionaries.
4 As quoted by Ceadel, Chickering refers to utopian peace advocacy as conceiving of war 'as an inseparable aspect of a social and political order that is utterly corrupt and beyond rehabilitation.' Quoted from Chickering, *Imperial Germany and a World without War: The Peace Movement in German Society, 1882–1914* (Princeton, 1975), 19. James Turner Johnson means by utopian pacifism the view that war is transitory and society perfectible. *The Quest for Peace: Three Moral Traditions in Western Cultural History* (Princeton, 1987), xi–xii, passim.
5 Sandi E. Cooper, *Patriotic Pacifism: Waging War on War in Europe, 1815–1914* New York, 1991).
6 Noted in Ceadel's essay: Peter Brock, *Pacifism in Europe to 1914* (Princeton, 1972), 472–6, and John H. Yoder, *Nevertheless: Varieties of Religious Pacifism* (Scottdale, 1971).
7 This distinction is developed in Ceadel's Ten Distinctions,' and it formed the basis of Johnson's *Quest for Peace*. It is my intent to use 'peace advocacy' at this point in the sense that Ceadel uses 'pacific-ism.'
8 Although J.T. Johnson describes the just war as a moral tradition in his enormously erudite and valuable studies, it seems to me that he obscures the implications of this paradigm for the relationship to peace advocacy in general. See his *Quest for Peace* and also his *Ideology, Reason, and the Limitation of War: Religious and Secular Concepts, 1200–1740* (Princeton, 1975) and *Just War Tradition and the Restraint of War: A Moral and Historical Inquiry* (Princeton, 1981).

9 Hugo Grotius, *The Law of War and Peace*, 'Prolegomena,' section 29.

10 This line of thought was especially well developed by canonists and theologians in the thirteenth century. Ronald G. Musto, *The Catholic Peace Tradition* (Maryknoll, NY, 1986), 104–9.

11 See Harold J. Berman, *Law and Revolution: The Formation of the Western Legal Tradition* (Cambridge, Mass. 1983), 90 passim, and Udo Heyn, '*Pax et Iustitia*: Arms Control, Disarmament, and the Legal System in the Medieval Reich,' *Peace and Change* 8 (Spring 1982), 23–36. In fact, Berman does not separate or even index just war thought, so integral was it to the evolution of law and institutions.

12 See Joycelyne G. Russell, *Peacemaking in the Renaissance* (Philadelphia, 1986) and esp. the case study by Gerald Mattingly, 'An Early Non-aggression Pact.' *Journal of Modern History* 10 (1938).

13 W.S.M. Knight, 'Introduction to *Selections from De Jure Belli ac Pacis by Hugo Grotius* (London, 1922 [a Grotius Society publication 1), 19.

14 Ingrid Detter de Lupis, *The Law of War* (Cambridge, England, 1987), xx, 364.

15 For the purposes of this discussion, I accept the definition of war advanced by Ingrid Detter De Lupis in *The Law of War*, 24: 'War is thus a sustained struggle by armed force of a certain intensity between groups, of a certain size, consisting of individuals who are armed, who wear distinctive insignia and who are subjected to military discipline under responsible command.' In this section of my essay, I am of course suggesting that 'peace advocacy' encompasses what Ceadel calls 'pacific-ism.'

16 I use the word 'ideology' in the sense that Ceadel employs it in his 'Ten Distinctions': 'a world-view or structured set of beliefs that all of us rely on, consciously or otherwise, to help us to filter out of the enormous amount of information about the world what is important and desirable.'

17 The classic crusades of the late medieval period are so treated by Musto, *The Catholic Peace Tradition.* See also the fine study by Frances A. Yates, *Astraea: The Imperial Theme in the Sixteenth Century* (London, 1975).

18 Sandi E. Cooper, ed., *Internationalism in Nineteenth-Century Europe: The Crisis of Ideas and Purpose* (New York, 1976), 21.

19 This is the basis for distinctions in terms of related ideologies. The terminology itself is problematic because 'liberalism,' 'socialism, ' 'radicalism,' and 'feminism' convey multiple structures of thought. Liberalism is especially difficult, since English usage (classical or free trade liberalism) differs so sharply from American.

20 Peter Brock, *The Quaker Peace Testimony, 1660 to 1914* (York, England, 1990), 298, Brock here referred explicitly to Quaker pacifism. The extraordinary canon of his work has culminated in a trilogy including also *Free-*

dom from War: Nonsectarian Pacifism, 1814–1914 and *Freedom from Violence: Sectarian Nonresistance from the Middle Ages to the Great War* (both Toronto, 1991). It should be noted, though, that Brock's *Twentieth-Century Pacifism* (New York, 1970) is still the only comprehensive treatment of the subject.

21 The sectarian principle of exempting members of the sect from the prevailing mores of society is what I take Ceadel to mean by 'exemptionism.' The converse is that society is not expected to meet the standards of the sect: it is in fact society that is exempted from the law of Christ, as it were. Members of the sect who accept a non-resistance tenet are no less pacifists for the fact that they do not impose the principle on others, since they accept the tenet as absolutely binding on themselves.

22 In another sense the pacifism that derives from these positions is 'contingent' upon ideologies which themselves are absolutely binding. This does not make the pacifist commitment less absolute, although it mitigates the extent to which pacifism is an 'absolutism.' The linguistic difficulty disappears when descriptive adjectives are used to identify varieties of pacifism in lieu of subcategories of nouns.

23 I suppose that this is close to Ceadel's distinction between 'inspirations' and 'orientations' in *Pacifism in Britain*, ch. 2, 9–17.

24 Certainly this has been the American experience, and it accords with what I know of the British, Australian, continental, and Indian experiences.

25 A classic example of this was the diatribe of Reinhold Niebuhr in the late 1930s. A contemporary instance is Guenter Levy, *Peace and Revolution: The Moral Crisis of American Pacifism* (Grand Rapids, 1988). For a critique of the latter see Charles Chatfield, 'Misplaced Crisis,' in *Peace Betrayed?* (Washington, 1989), 41–65.

26 To date this methodology has been applied systematically to peace movements in David S. Meyer, *A Winter of Discontent: The Nuclear Freeze and American Politics* (New York, 1990), less effectively in Frances B. McCrea and Gerald E. Markle, *Minutes to Midnight: Nuclear Weapons Protest in America* (Newberry Park, Calif., 1989), and comparatively in Robert Kleidman, *Organizing for Peace: Neutrality, the Test Ban, and the Freeze* (Syracuse, 1993). The latter is a study of the 1930s Emergency Peace Campaign, the 1950s test-ban campaign, and the 1980s freeze. Resource mobilization theory is formally applied to the whole American peace movement in the concluding chapter of Charles Chatfield, *The American Peace Movement: Ideals and Activism* (Boston, 1991).

27 See Herman, *Eleven against War: Studies in American Internationalist Thought, 1898–1921* (Stanford, 1969). Reflections on this sociological theme can be

found in F. Tönnies, *On Sociology*, eds. Werner J. Cahnman and Rudolf Haberle (Chicago, 1971).

28 In some measure the orientations of polity and community-oriented peace advocates correspond to Johann Galtung's distinction between negative and positive peace, between peace as the absence of war, and peace as a more just and humane world.

29 See Chatfield, *The American Peace Movement*, concluding chapter. This notion was referred to as the 'halfway house' function of movement organizations by Aldon D. Morris in *The Origins of the Civil Rights Movement* (New York, 1984).

30 Johnson, *Quest for Peace*, 284.

4

Jacob ter Meulen and Bart de Ligt as Pioneers of Peace History

PETER VAN DEN DUNGEN

[Our descendants] will naturally value the history of earlier times ... only from the point of view of what interests them, i.e., in answer to the question of what the various nations and governments have contributed to the goal of world citizenship, and what they have done to damage it. (Kant, *Idea for a Universal History from a Cosmopolitan Point of View*)

Even though in recent years the reputation of Sir Basil Liddell Hart as a serious historian of warfare has been somewhat tarnished, this need not detract from the value of much of his writing. *Why Don't We Learn from History?*, first published in 1944, is regarded as a classic in the philosophy of history. Two of the lessons that this 'Captain who teaches Generals' (J.F. Kennedy) learned from history may be recalled here because of their bearing on our general theme: 'We learn from history that the critics of authority have always been rebuked in self-righteous tones – if no worse fate has befallen them – yet have repeatedly been justified by history. To be "agin the Government" may be a more philosophic attitude than it appears. For the tendency of all "Governments" is to infringe the standards of decency and truth.' Liddell Hart also found that 'it is unrealistic ... to underrate the force of idealism.'[1]

Shortly before his death in 1970, Liddell Hart revised this slim volume, and concluded his new Foreword thus: 'I would add that the only hope for humanity, now, is that my particular field of study, warfare, will become purely a subject of antiquarian interest.'[2] The advent of atomic weapons signified either the end of major war, or of history (of course, in this case the 'end of history' meant something far less benign than the way in which the phrase has recently been interpreted). The hope that we can live without war is premature and likely to remain long unfulfilled, as will be Liddell Hart's wish to see his subject lose its contemporary relevance. However, it is possible to derive some satisfaction and encouragement when a more limited perspective is adopted. Wars have been not only fought, but also fought against – in order to conquer war itself.

The documentation and interpretation of this aspect of history and of war, is no less interesting than the traditional study of war. Thus, we can now add to the ranks of the historians of war and militarism, in small but increasing numbers, historians of peace, pacifism, anti-militarism, and internationalism. It is no coincidence that peace history has emerged at a time when historians of contemporary war wish to become a redundant species, and when at the same time one can witness a slow but increasingly perceptive process in which the emancipation of the idea of peace is accompanied by the delegitimization of the idea of war. Is it wholly presumptuous to believe that the pursuit of peace history constitutes not only a contribution to history (as a scholarly pursuit), but even to peace? Unless this is a misreading of Kant, he did not believe so: in the eighth thesis of his *Idea for a Universal History from a Cosmopolitan Point of View*, he precisely affirmed that 'the Idea can help, though only from afar, to bring the millennium to pass.'[3] Although Kant's 'Idea' is far from synonymous with the idea of peace history, it seems that the latter enterprise may legitimately be subsumed under it. But the value of peace history, like that of history in general, does not in the first instance depend on its perceived utility: 'to show what actually happened' (von Ranke) is a sufficient rationale. Much of peace history is inherently interesting and captivating: it is a story with its own heroes and battles (moral, social, intellectual, political – rather than physical), victories, and defeats. It confirms what Bertha von Suttner (drawing on Gabriel Tarde and Arthur Schopenhauer) observed about the evolution in the acceptance of the peace idea, namely, that 'in the history of thought, every new movement has to go through three phases: in the first one, it is being ridiculed; in the second, it is being fought; and in the third, it is being accused of kicking in open doors.'[4]

Peace history, like peace thought and peace action, seems to have been stimulated by war, and it is not surprising that the first peace historians emerged in the twentieth century's interwar period. One of them, A.C.F. Beales, wrote in his (perhaps immodestly but certainly ambitiously titled) *The History of Peace*: 'The history of peace has at present [1931] only four prominent historians at work on it,' and he mentioned Lange,

Curti, ter Meulen, and Koht.[5] For the United States he might have added to Curti's name those of Allen, Galpin, and Phelps, and in Holland ter Meulen's work was being complemented by that of de Ligt. It is worthwhile to note, however, that some initiatives had been taken before the First World War – of which one of the most interesting was Gilbert Murray's proposal (in a letter to Andrew Carnegie) to establish chairs of 'Peace History' in universities that supported chairs of military history.[6] Had Murray's proposal been accepted, a small but distinguished group of possible incumbents was available. It included not only academics such as Curti and Koht, but also activists such as de Ligt and Allen, and administrator-scholars like Lange and ter Meulen. In the following pages the contributions of two somewhat forgotten figures from the early days of peace history will be highlighted.

The Hague was the city where Jacob ter Meulen (1884–1962) was born and died and where he lived most of his life. It also shaped his life in a very real sense. For what was once known as 'The Work of the Hague' (next to 'The Spirit of Geneva') also became, in a way, *his* work. We do not know what influence the First Hague Peace Conference had on the youngster, but it seems certain that this momentous diplomatic event, which dominated also the social life of his small city for several months during the summer of 1899, cannot have escaped his attention. When the Second Hague Peace Conference met in 1907, ter Meulen was studying international law (and also municipal law and economics) at Amsterdam University. He was greatly impressed, he wrote a few years later, by 'the scientific reputation and practical activities during the deliberations of the Second Hague Peace Conference'[7] of Max Huber, a member of the Swiss delegation, and became his student at the University of Zurich. Huber encouraged ter Meulen to undertake 'cultural-historical researches in the field of pacifism'; these were crowned with the award of a doctorate in public law in January 1914. Three years later, when his dissertation was about to be published, ter Meulen noted that his research 'had been a comforting occupation at this wild time when the entire building of international law is threatening to fall apart.'[8] In 1924 ter Meulen was appointed director of the library of the Peace Palace, the institution which was created thanks to the munificence of Andrew Carnegie (and as a result of the 1899 conference).[9] It was to remain ter Meulen's home until his formal retirement in 1952 (and even in the decade afterwards he was a frequent visitor, continuing his research).

Ter Meulen's first publication, leaving aside a couple of newspaper articles, was titled 'On the Significance of Alfred H. Fried for the Peace Movement' (1912) and appeared in the leading Dutch peace movement journal, *Vrede door Recht* ('Peace through Justice').[10] His last publication, half a century later, was a bibliography of seventeenth-century writings on Grotius (1961), a work that complemented his authoritative and definitive bibliography of Grotius, undertaken together with P.J.J. Diermanse (1950). Between them, these two peace figures – Fried and Grotius – not only span ter Meulen's productive writing career, but also serve as symbolical representatives of two distinct but complementary peace approaches and traditions. Fried was concerned to enlighten the masses and thus to build up a well-informed and powerful but non-official peace movement. Grotius, on the other hand, who is often regarded as the founder of modern international law, addressed in the first instance the governments and rulers of states. Whereas Fried confidently predicted the total abolition of war (in the years preceding the Great War), Grotius, writing during the Thirty Years War, aimed to reduce the frequency of war and to limit its destructiveness.

Although Fried constantly talked of 'pacifism,' and claimed to be promoting strictly 'scientific pacifism,' he was anxious to distance himself and his cause from what he called 'dilettantish' or 'romantic' pacifism. As one student of his writings has noted, 'Deliberately, and certainly against his better instincts, [he] eschewed all moral opposition to war, and denounced all Christian or Tolstoyan criticism of war as "utopian."'[11] It seems that ter Meulen, at least in his youthful article, shared Fried's goal of 'turning pacifism from a utopia into a science,' for he wrote, 'Preachers against war there have always been, for as long as war has existed, but Fried does not *preach* peace, he ... "merely" announces its arrival; he is addressing not so much the emotions as common sense or, better: he simply wants to open one's eyes.' Ter Meulen regarded Fried's main achievement (which had resulted in the award of a Nobel Peace Prize, the event that had led ter Meulen to write his article) to have been the demonstration that the modern peace movement saw war merely as one of the many consequences of international anarchy and that the latter was gradually being replaced by international organization. Fried regarded this as an organic and natural process that was occurring even without people being aware of it. The modern peace movement aimed to understand this process, to make it better known, and to hasten it.

When ter Meulen wrote his article, he had already decided to concentrate his studies on the history of the idea of international organization, having been encouraged to do so by Huber in 1910.[12] Perhaps ter

Meulen conceived this project in order to document the growth of the idea of international organization – published as *Der Gedanke der Internationalen Organisation in seiner Entwicklung* in three volumes in 1917, 1929, and 1940 – as a complementary study to Fried's *Handbook of the Peace Movement* (first published in 1905, and expanded into a two-volume edition which appeared in 1911–13). If so, the project was far from providing an historical underpinning of Fried's thesis, since it emphasized rather than derided the value of all those historical 'utopian' projects for peace and international organization. In the Foreword to his second volume (1929) ter Meulen felt compelled to justify explicitly the value of considering such projets when, for the first time in history, a number of international political organizations had been created in the closing decade of the nineteenth century, culminating in the Hague peace conferences, and the creation of the League of Nations and the Permanent Court of International Justice in the aftermath of the Great War. He believed that students of peace and internationalism had recently been stressing one-sidedly the value of 'acts of peace' at the expense of that of 'words of peace': 'Today, scholarship pays scant value to the influence of peace utopias of earlier times.' Ter Meulen argued that in the course of centuries a number of interrelated factors had affected the development of legal thought and organization, both within and between states. The international structures that were emerging in The Hague and Geneva were, in part, also the result of the international peace projects of the thinkers and dreamers of previous centuries. They formed a vital link in the chain of development that leads from anarchy to organization. For this volume ter Meulen had chosen the motto: 'But be patient! Let a few centuries go by; Utopia will have taken shape in society' (F. Laurent). Ter Meulen was suggesting that the eventual realization of utopia was not unconnected with its bare and earlier formulation.[13]

More than ten years earlier a different perspective, more akin to Fried's, can be found in the reflections with which ter Meulen concluded the first volume of his trilogy. Then he had written that one can view the development of 'pacifism' in the same way in which Schiller had once painted his own intellectual-spiritual (*geistig*) development in his poem 'The Ideal' (1795): poetic rapture at the beginning, followed by great disappointment at the discovery that the beautiful utopias are but castles in the air, and ending with restless activity to bring the ideal nearer. Ter Meulen wrote, 'In the period up to the French Revolution pacifism was nothing more than a great series of phantasies, expressions of the pantheistic ideals of the young human race ... But now, for a more mature humanity, the era has commenced in which it can no longer lose itself in poetic dreams, but must summon all its energies so that through restless labour it can fulfill its noble task, the achievement of the highest perfection.'[14] Seemingly oblivious to the war raging around him, ter Meulen quoted the following words on his title-page: 'That which perceives itself as unity, also wants to strengthen and nurture this unity' (Jellinek). This was very much a Friedian sentiment, at least as long as the material rather than the moral aspects of that experience and perception were envisaged.

The rather different views that ter Meulen expressed in his second volume (already referred to), he reiterated in more general terms in the concluding volume, where he addressed the question of the significance of his entire enterprise, which had stretched out over three decades, punctuated by two world wars. To the question, 'What is the value of studying the myriad peace plans of the past?' he replied, 'The value of such an overview finally is to be found in the plans themselves, not in the value of each one separately but all of them together. Together they form a power whose influence so far has been small, a power which temporarily can be forced back, possibly can appear in new forms, but can never completely disappear. For it is a fact that the human consciousness contains not only a sense of the real but also of the ideal. Both elements are necessary for the organization of human society. They are also vital for the future shaping of the relations between peoples.'[15] Ter Meulen was thus able to challenge the claims of those who denied the value of the plans he had studied. For instance, in the *Times Literary Supplement*, the reviewer of the first volume of his trilogy wrote, 'We cannot see that all these plans and projects have ever had the slightest influence upon that which actually happened.' The reviewer saw the reason for this failure in their authorship: these plans were written by onlookers and outsiders, rather than by protagonists.[16] Also the individuals whose ideas and activities Bart de Ligt documented – the radical anti-militarists – might be regarded as outsiders, but they were no onlookers; their frequent persecution clearly confirms that they – questioning as they did, for example, the right of the state to conscript and enforce a duty to take life on its citizens – were held to be anything but irrelevant or ineffective by those in authority.

Incidentally, ter Meulen's view of assessing the peace projects of the past seems to have been shared by Carl Becker when he successfully convinced a young and uncertain Merle Curti of the value of peace history. Becker urged him not to attempt a narrow cost-benefit evaluation of the historic peace movement but to correlate it 'with the general intellectual history of the century' – 'The more ruthless the world the more it needs idealistic compensation.'[17]

It seems that in his early studies ter Meulen was not only influenced by the writings of Fried and the teaching of Huber, but also by Walther Schücking's *Die Organisation der Welt* ('The Organization of the World'). This was originally the text of a lecture held in Vienna in the immediate aftermath of the Second Hague Peace Conference, and it was subsequently extended and published as a book in 1909.[18] Schücking sketched in it the ideas of a world state or a union of states, in classical times, the Middle Ages, and the modern period, and he also highlighted the threads of the peace movement that were woven into the history of humanity. Instead of the world state of the ancients (*Weltstaat*), history was now witnessing the emergence of a world league of states (*Weltstaatenbund*), and Schücking believed that this could develop even into a federal world state (*Weltbundesstaat*). Increasingly, war was losing its legitimacy.[19] It is significant that ter Meulen focused on this book in his obituary article on Schücking, published in a special issue (devoted to Schücking's memory) of *Die Friedens-Warte* (1935).[20] He wrote that it 'had an inspiring effect in a twofold manner: The ideas about the evolution of the world community developed in it were a revelation for many. [And:] The study of the history of peace approaches received a strong impetus.' It is tempting to infer that ter Meulen was referring to his own experience and that his large work is likely to have been inspired, or at least encouraged, by Schücking's sketch.[21]

It is interesting to read in the same article on Schücking which writers ter Meulen regarded as having documented the fact that 'the peace movement has its history' before the appearance of Schücking's book. Ter Meulen mentions H. Hetzel (1891), de Bloch, W. Evans Derby, H. La Fontaine, and A.H. Fried (and, as regards the question of an international court of arbitration, Kamarowsky, Revon, and Dreyfus).[22] He was very much involved at this period in attempts to make the subject of peace history a more professional one, and the title under which he commemorated Schücking is indicative of this interest and concern. We do not know whether there was much contact between ter Meulen and Schücking in the years 1930–5, when the latter joined the former in the Peace Palace following Schücking's appointment as a judge to the Permanent Court of International Justice.

For ter Meulen, the idea of peace was tantamount to that of international organization, specifically the creation by national states of a league of nations. This has become, he wrote in 1947, 'the present ideal of the organization of peace.' Hence, the importance that he attached to the growth of international law and international arbitral and juridical organs and, hence also, ter Meulen's lifelong interest in Grotius. Ter Meulen reminded his readers that, in an age of incessant warfare, Grotius was fully preoccupied with regulating its practice, rather than with suggesting schemes for its total elimination, and that Grotius devoted only a few lines to the idea of a league of nations.[23] It would be wrong, however, to regard ter Meulen as an internationalist 'pure and simple,' for he was – or became – also a pacifist.[24] On more than one occasion he expressed the view that the Peace Palace had two spiritual fathers: Grotius and Erasmus,[25] and it seems that ter Meulen's loyalties encompassed both of these European countrymen of his. It was thanks to ter Meulen that the library of the Peace Palace developed both a unique collection of Grotiana and a very large collection of early literature on pacifism and the peace movement. His own scholarly and bibliographical studies comprised both areas. Ter Meulen's main bibliographical works concerning Grotius appeared in the years 1925, 1950, and 1961. His studies of the history of peace and internationalism stretched out over a similarly lengthy period, from before the First World War until the Second World War. They consisted of two separate but clearly related projects, the second being a natural outcome of the first.

Before he had completed his first project, the 'History of the Development of the Idea of International Organization,' ter Meulen started what was meant to be an exhaustive bibliography of the historic peace literature. The need for it had occurred to him during the preparation of *Gedanke*: in the Foreword of the first volume (1917) he indicated that he did not claim for it any completeness since many of the precursors of the idea of international organization, whose names were known to the author, could not be discussed because he had been unable to find their writings, whether published or unpublished.[26] When the second volume of *Gedanke* appeared (1929), he suggested to C.L. Lange, his fellow peace historian (who was also a peace librarian, being the first director of the Norwegian Nobel Institute and creator of its library), the formation of an association of 'all those who are interested in the study of the history of pacifism.' During 1929–30 ter Meulen persuaded the *Revue de Droit International* to publish in its pages on three occasions a 'Special Bulletin Devoted to the History of Pacifism,' which he wrote and which was meant to be an information exchange for research on the subject .

By 1932 ter Meulen had established a 'Committee for the Bibliography of the Peace Movement in History' under the auspices of the International Committee of Historical Sciences. Besides ter Meulen, who was its secretary, the committee's members were Lange, Curti, Hans Wehberg, and Rafael Altamira. Ter Meulen was the driving force of this rather nominal committee and the provisional *Bibliography of the Peace Movement before 1899*, which was published in 1934 (for the period 1776–1898) and 1936 (for the period 1480–1776), was largely his work and that of his collaborators at the Peace Palace (supported financially by the Norwegian Nobel Institute as well as by ter Meulen himself). He requested and received much new and additional information from fellow peace historians and librarians to whom copies of the provisional lists were sent. Although in subsequent years ter Meulen continued sporadically to work on the compilation of a comprehensive and fully annotated bibliography of the early peace literature, it was not brought to a successful completion and did not result in the publication of the projected definitive bibliography. This would have consisted of some 10,000 references; as it is, the provisional lists, comprising less than half that number, are still today by far the largest available compilation of the historic peace literature and continue to be an important and unrivalled source for peace historians.[27]

Ter Meulen was not only hampered by the absence of such an instrument in the course of writing his *Gedanke*, but had also become alert to the rarity and precarious existence of much of the early peace literature. He knew that even the most important collections in the field, at the Nobel Institute and at the Peace Palace, revealed many gaps. When he first suggested the idea for a comprehensive bibliography (together with a committee to undertake it) to Lange (1932), ter Meulen wrote, 'In a common effort we have ... to preserve what exists, to rescue that which is in danger of being lost, and to publicise that which is available.'[28] A few years later, the growth of Nazism and Fascism in Europe had made this task all the more urgent. In his third report on the work of the committee (1936), ter Meulen noted, 'We hope not only to produce a useful instrument of study, but also to assist with the preservation of material which for a large part has been neglected for too long. We are aware of more than one important collection in the world which is in danger of being lost forever if the necessary measures are not undertaken soon.'[29] In the United States, early peace historians such as Merle Curti and Devere Allen, as well as Ellen Starr Brinton, the first curator of the Swarthmore College Peace Collection, were voicing similar concerns. Both Curti and Brinton were valuable collaborators on ter Meulen's project.

How and where did ter Meulen draw the boundary lines for his peace bibliography? They were roughly the same as those applied to his *Gedanke* as regards the historical period to be covered. He had concluded his large study with the year 1889, the *annus mirabilis* of the peace movement, stating: 'We stopped precisely there, where the developing peace idea began to interest more effectively and persistently the political organs [of states] for the great cause of the organization of peace (Inter-Parliamentary Union, Pan-American Congresses) and when a governmental initiative was to some extent being prepared. The Hague Peace Conference and its immediate pre-history belong to a new period.'[30] He concluded the provisional bibliography of the peace movement with the year 1898, when Tsar Nicholas II issued his call for what would be the First Hague Peace Conference. It not only resulted in a flood of peace literature but also heralded the emergence of an official peace movement. On both scores it made sense to let the bibliography finish at this point.

Ter Meulen started *Gedanke*, his survey of individual plans for peace, with Pierre Dubois, King George of Bohemia, and Erasmus. (This was preceded by a discussion of the nature of peace and world-unification ideas of the medieval world that set it apart from the later period, when Christian unity under pope and emperor had been shattered.) The bibliography started with the end of the Middle Ages and Erasmus. To Lange who apparently wanted to see it start with the Middle Ages, ter Meulen wrote, 'I believe that the name of Erasmus is an excellent beginning for a bibliography of pacifism. The teachings of this author have, for a large part, a modern flavour. The pacifism of Erasmus is not too much linked to political goals such as the war against the Turks. As soon as one deals with the Middle Ages it will be difficult to establish a starting point.'[31]

For the bibliography covering the early period ter Meulen applied the following considerations for deciding on the appropriateness of including certain authors and titles: 'In the first place we have retained works which, either in their entirety or predominantly, have a pacifist content or tendency, followed by those which deal with projects for a federation of states or with general plans for peace ... We have excluded works which deal with religious, personal or familial peace, or with a particular peace treaty. Difficulties frequently arose with writers who preached peace among Christian princes and at the same time counselled them to combine in combat against the Turks ... a large category of works by religious sects which profess non-resistance [proved problematical].'[32]

One of ter Meulen's most valued correspondents, Ellen Starr Brinton, queried in one of her letters (1938) why 'the name of Hugo Grotius is

nowhere mentioned in your bibliographies.' He replied, 'We consider
Hugo Grotius more a jurist than a pacifist in the strict sense of the word,
although he was deeply interested in the subject and had made great
efforts towards the unity of the churches.'[33] It is perhaps prudent to
point out that many authors included in the bibliographies were not
pacifists 'in the strict sense of the word,' starting with Erasmus. As ter
Meulen had correctly noted in his *Gedanke*, 'On occasion Erasmus sanctioned defensive war, and war against the Turks.'[34]

This is an appropriate moment to inquire about ter Meulen's own
viewpoint, and to consider him as a peace activist (rather than peace historian). His father's family, which came from the northern part of Holland, had a firm Mennonite tradition. Ter Meulen's membership in the
Mennonite brotherhood probably influenced his peace activism and
peace scholarship. However, there are several indications that (like other
Dutch Mennonites) he only gradually rediscovered the pacifist basis of
his faith. At the time of the outbreak of the First World War, when there
was a general mobilization in Holland, he fulfilled his military service.
This is unlikely to have caused him any problems of conscience, because
of his country's neutrality. In a biographical reference work, published
in 1938, we read, 'Character, work environment and world situation
brought him more and more into contact with the peace movement, particularly that based on Christian anti-militarism. He is especially
attracted by the old Mennonite position.'[35] 'Old' in this context seemed
to mean not so much venerable or traditional as forgotten, lost. The
refusal of military service had become a 'curiosity' among Dutch Mennonites by the time of the French revolution, and although there were
instances of individual Mennonites emigrating to 'free' America in order
to avoid military service, 'the principle had died.'[36]

Ter Meulen's rediscovery of it led him in the late 1920s and throughout the 1930s to an 'active Christian pacifism'[37]; it seems an exaggeration to say that he became 'a fierce champion of Christian anti-
militarism.'[38] He was certainly not as 'fierce' a campaigner, nor as pro-
lific or effective a pamphleteer in this cause as, for instance, Bart de
Ligt (see below); however, ter Meulen increasingly started to address
this issue, in writing and speaking, as he had not done before. Several
of his anti-militarist articles appeared in the periodical 'Letters issued
by the ... Mennonite Brotherhood,' starting with 'The Rebirth of Militarism' (1930). In 1932 he was instrumental in setting up a Dutch 'Mennonites Working-Group against Military Service,' of which he was the
secretary. At about the same time he wrote two pamphlets, 'We Want

to Be Good Citizens, But We Shall Not Bear Arms,' and 'Do Not Judge,' both published by the 'International Mennonite Peace Committee' in The Hague, whose secretary-treasurer was ter Meulen. It seems that he was largely responsible for setting up both organizations, which were meant to encourage a renewed witness of the brotherhood's pacifist belief. In 'We want ...' he wrote, 'If Christians do not realize that modern war is fully contrary to the Gospels, their faith no longer has any value. And if Mennonites no longer know that they have a special task to fulfill in this matter, our Brotherhood has lost its historic calling. For us this task can only be peaceful action [Vredesdaad].'[39] The Statement of Principles of the Working-Group declared, 'We see it as a neglect of our Christian fellowship that this truth is too little recognised and acted upon.'[40]

Ter Meulen's initiatives in establishing contacts with members of the brotherhood abroad in 1934, together with Harold Bender's visit to Holland in the following year, resulted in the plan to form an international committee that would try to promote the peace idea in a Mennonite spirit. In 1936 an international (mainly Dutch-American) Mennonite congress took place in Holland, and ter Meulen used the opportunity to promote the plan. At a specially convened 'peace meeting' in Fredeshiem (Friesland), an International Mennonite Peace Committee was formed with ter Meulen as secretary-treasurer and Bender as chairman. It issued a Mennonite Peace Testimony that had been drawn up following consultations with Mennonites worldwide. The committee aimed to strengthen and publicize the Mennonite peace witness both among the brotherhood and beyond, as well as to provide moral and material assistance to those who refused military service or who suffered because of their pacifist beliefs.[41] Like Bender, ter Meulen took a special interest in the provision of alternative service for conscientious objectors to military service; several of his last publications, in the 1940s and 1950s, were on this subject.

Ter Meulen's interests comprised international law and organization, and pacifism and the peace movement. His studious temperament and profession (librarianship) meant that he was more involved with the historical rather than contemporary aspects of these subjects; he was above all a scholar rather than an activist. The personal peace witness emerged only in his mature years. Very different are the development and contributions of Bart de Ligt: he was in the forefront of the radical peace movement during the interwar period. His speeches and writings were highly revolutionary and inflammatory; his deep knowledge (in the first place

of the history of peace thought and action) served to inspire and invigo-
rate the radical peace movement of his day.

It is instructive to sketch the life and work of Bart de Ligt (1883–1938)
in comparison with that of Jacob ter Meulen. While the latter's religious
orientation became increasingly manifest and specific as he grew older,
de Ligt developed in an opposite direction. His father was a clergyman
who belonged to the orthodox, Calvinist wing of the Netherlands
Reformed Church. The son also studied theology and from 1910 to 1915
was pastor in Nuenen (in the same small vicarage where Vincent van
Gogh had lived). However, during his student days, he slowly and painfully extricated himself from his Calvinist milieu. By 1919 de Ligt considered himself no longer a Christian, and he adhered instead to a more
universal, cosmic religious outlook, declaring that he had outgrown
Christianity. In the same year he left the 'Union of Christian Socialists,'
which he had joined in 1910 and in which he had played a prominent
role.[42] Upon the outbreak of war, when still a pastor, de Ligt drafted a
manifesto entitled, 'The Guilt of the Churches,' which was condemned
by the synod of his church. In June 1915 the military authorities banned
him from the country's southern provinces because of a fiercely anti-
militarist sermon he had preached. Later that year, he was one of the
first to sign the 'Manifesto against Military Service,' and this led to his
imprisonment in 1916. De Ligt served another prison sentence in 1921
for attempted sedition, following his vocal support for the conscientious
objector Herman Groenendaal, who was in prison and on a hunger
strike. The campaign which de Ligt organized in his support resulted in
the passage in 1923 of the first Dutch law providing for (limited) conscientious objector status. In 1921 de Ligt also co-founded and became
president of the International Anti-Militarist Bureau. This was an
attempt to breathe new life into the organization that carried a similar
name and had been founded in 1904 by the grand old man of Dutch
socialism (and anarchism), F. Domela Nieuwenhuis. Throughout his life
de Ligt was the driving force behind the creation of several radical anti-
militarist organizations whose purpose was to unite all those who were
fighting against war and militarism and thus to strengthen their efforts
(for example, War Resisters International).

In 1925 he moved to Geneva, for health reasons, and continued to live
there until his death.

Whereas 'the work of the Hague' and that of ter Meulen were largely
identical, the same cannot be said of de Ligt and the approach to peace

that has become associated with the name of his adoptive city. 'The spirit of Geneva' (involving respect for the League of Nations, the promotion of disarmament, and a conciliatory and compromising approach) for de Ligt could only result in a phoney peace. While ter Meulen was an enthusiastic supporter of the league (regarding it as the first, embryonic, realization of the proposals contained in many of the classical peace plans he had written about), de Ligt treated it as an irrelevancy or, more accurately, as an attempt to consolidate an unjust and unpeaceful world order in which the forces of nationalism, colonialism, imperialism, and militarism persisted. De Ligt noted that, just as in the days of Erasmus it was said, 'the nearer to Rome, the further from God,' now it could be said, 'the nearer to Geneva, the further from world peace.'[43] He regarded instead the 1927 Brussels Congress against Colonial Oppression and Imperialism as the beginning of a real world forum: it included colonial peoples and the gathering represented a much wider geographical area than the league was able to claim. De Ligt was also highly sceptical that the league would effect any real disarmament. Moreover, disarmament pure and simple was for him not enough, since it implied a conservative outlook.

For de Ligt, true peace also meant freedom and justice for the oppressed, in the colonies as well as at home, and this could only be obtained by struggle. He was therefore concerned to arm – but only with non-violent means – all those involved in this work. Lastly, nothing was further from de Ligt's approach than compromise: he was always a principled opponent of the use of violence, and this accounts for his criticism of Gandhi (in a celebrated correspondence in 1928–9 and during their meetings in Switzerland in 1931) and of George Lansbury (whose personal crusade in 1937 to preserve peace involved appeasement of the dictators). In both cases de Ligt was one of the very few dissenting voices from within the peace movement.

Whereas ter Meulen frequently wrote on Grotius, Erasmus was the subject of de Ligt's last work (which has autobiographical overtones). De Ligt often made a clear distinction between 'official, state-supporting pacifism' and the anti-militarism of direct action. The former approach he associated with a tradition going back at least to Grotius: it aimed to tame war, but did not condemn defensive war. But de Ligt distinguished between those who condemned war and those who strove for a comprehensive peace (and for the creation of a society from which it could emerge). In today's terminology, he adhered to a positive concept of peace in which the latter is equated with the establishment of a just social order, rather than merely with the absence of interstate war, and thus leaving much violence untouched. He recognized in Erasmus a kindred spirit who, four centuries before, had fought, even though in a feudal-Catholic form, not only against war and violence, but also for the idea of free thought and for the liberation of humanity. Erasmus, like de Ligt, wanted to sweep away a stale, bigoted, degenerate, and militaristic Christianity.

While ter Meulen was a peace historian who became moderately active in the peace movement, de Ligt was a theorist, as well as an historian, of peace (which he understood in a deeper sense than ter Meulen did), the productivity and originality of whose intellectual work was always matched by an equally intensive personal involvement in the social and political developments of his time, foremost those concerning war and peace. De Ligt's first article, published in a student newspaper, was in defence of a conscientious objector (1904). It is not surprising that *La Paix Créatrice*, his *magnum opus*, is a history of the idea of peace as witnessed in the concrete acts of individuals and small groups. He discussed not so much the theoretical peace plans of past thinkers as the actual peace deeds of past and contemporary war resisters. De Ligt chronicled the history of radical pacifism and anti-militarism rather than internationalism. In this two-volume work (the French translation was meant to comprise four volumes, but the author did not live to complete them), subtitled 'Principles, History, and Method of Struggle of Direct Action against War,' de Ligt documented the origin and development of the personal witness against war in the tradition and culture of China, India, Sumeria, Egypt, Persia, Israel, Greece, Rome, and of Europe up to his day.[44] He was able to demonstrate that non-violent struggle was a widespread phenomenon not confined to any historical period, group, race, or moral or religious belief. His examples were drawn from all periods of history and from all parts of the world. Aldous Huxley, a friend and admirer of de Ligt's work, called it 'a work of wide and profound learning, indispensable to those who would study the history of peace and of "the things that make for peace."' In his *An Encyclopaedia of Pacifism* (a misnomer for this popular pamphlet, but a title which would have been apt for de Ligt's study), Huxley called it 'the most complete history of pacifist ideas and practice.'[45]

Today's leading historians of non-violent struggle, direct action against war, and pacifism, such as Gene Sharp, Gernot Jochheim, and Peter Brock, have confirmed the unique nature of *La Paix Créatrice*. Brock has paid tribute to it not only as representing 'a truly pioneering venture,' but also as one which inspired him to study the subject further.[46] De Ligt's power to inspire, through the written and the spoken word (he was an effective orator and pamphleteer, in addition to being a scholar), made him a charismatic leader of the radical peace movement in Holland and abroad. His life and writings continue to inspire both scholars and activists today.[47] Among the factors that account for his enduring appeal are: the prophetic nature of his message, the passion of its delivery, his belief in the power of the utopian vision to move the world forward and his attempts to make each person realize his or her responsibility and power for bringing about a better world – one characterized by the liberation and emancipation of all humanity (and living in harmony with the rest of creation). It was de Ligt's fate, one of his friends wrote after his death, that he was born in a small country while, as no other, he promoted the coming together of religious-anarchist, libertarian-socialists, and revolutionary–anti-militarist movements.[48] De Ligt was much more than a fighter against war – he wanted to lay the foundations of a new culture that would be based on 'a free order.' He regarded war merely as the most characteristic feature of the prevailing social system and the struggle against it as part of a wider struggle for a new society.

De Ligt was both a peace historian and activist and a theoretician of war and peace, violence, and revolution. His rejection of revolutionary violence was based on both moral and pragmatic grounds, and he argued instead for the need to develop non-violent methods of struggle (which had become all the more necessary given the developments affecting the instruments of violence and the way modern warfare had become total). He stressed the need for a two-fold revolution: not only of the social structures, but also within each person (who had to become more truly human), and for 'a revolution of the revolution' (by the elaboration and application of non-violent means of struggle). He asserted, 'The more violence, the less revolution,' and 'Violence will always be the weakest, and never the strongest side of the revolution.'[49] Born in the same year that Marx died (1883), de Ligt held anarchism to be superior to Marxism, since it stressed the principles of self-activity, self-development, self-education, and self-government. He valued Marxism for the insights it offered of the workings of capitalist society (and from which anarchists could learn), but criticized its neglect of the individual as well as its acceptance of violence in the revolutionary struggle. These ideas he developed in *The Conquest of Violence*, his only book published in English.[50] Charles Chatfield has called it 'the most influential exposition of war resistance in the interwar period,' next to Richard Gregg's *The Power of Nonviolence*, and regards it as 'the great departure for systematic analysis and plans of civilian nonviolent resistance.'[51] Some students of this book called de Ligt 'a Gandhi of the West,' but he disliked any cult of personality and, as regards Gandhi, condemned his social goals for being frequently reactionary (while regarding him as a revolutionary for the *means* of struggle that Gandhi advocated).

Ter Meulen's creation in 1932 of a committee to foster the study of the history of peace was in some ways parallelled by de Ligt's establishment of a Peace Academy in 1938, which aimed to lay the foundations for a multidisciplinary *Science of Peace*, the title of de Ligt's inaugural lecture.[52] Although both initiatives were short-lived, they were not without results. Moreover, they can now be seen as noteworthy predecessors of more recent initiatives taken at a time when the study and pursuit of peace have become so imperative.

Notes

1 B.H. Liddell Hart, *Why Don t We Learn from History?* (London, 1944), 17, 31.
2 (New York, 1971), 12.
3 Immanuel Kant, *On History*, ed. Lewis White Beck (Indianapolis, 1963), 22. The quotation at the start of this chapter is the penultimate sentence of Kant's essay.
4 Quoted by A.H. Fried in his *Handbuch der Friedensbewegung* (Vienna and Leipzig, 1905), vi.
5 A.C.F. Beales, *The History of Peace* (London, 1931), iv.
6 Duncan Wilson, *Gilbert Murray OM, 1866–1957* (Oxford, 1987), 245. Full details in my 'On the Historiography of Peace, '*Peace and Change* 20, no. 1 (Jan. 1995), 68–9.
7 Jacob ter Meulen, *Beitrag zur Geschichte der Internationalen Organisation, 1300–1700. Inauguraldissertation* (The Hague, 1916), Vorwort.
8 Ibid.
9 Ter Meulen thus followed again the path of Huber, who in 1921 had been appointed a member of the new Permanent Court of International Justice and remained a member of it until 1930. The court had its seat in the Peace Palace.
10 Jacob ter Meulen, 'Iets over de beteekenis van Alfred H. Fried voor de Vredesbeweging,' *Vrede door Recht* 13 (1912), 23–4.
11 Daniel Gasman in his Introduction to A.H. Fried, *Handbuch der Friedensbewegung* (New York, 1972 reprint), vol. 1, 9.

12 Jacob ter Meulen, *Der Gedanke der Internationalen Organisation in seiner Entwicklung* (The Hague, 1929), vol. 2, ix.

13 Ibid, x–xi. It was his aim, he wrote modestly, to 'cast a glance' at the profusion of old, often forgotten, plans and ideas concerning the organization of peace and a league of nations. In this way he hoped 'to have facilitated, in no mean way, the work of later historians of pacifism' (xii). When ter Meulen's final volume appeared (1940), Hans Wehberg found that he had brilliantly succeeded in this and that 'no better author could have been wished for.' Cf. Hans Wehberg, 'Die Entwicklung des Gedankens der internationalen Organisation: Zur Vollendung des grossen Werkes von Jacob ter Meulen,' *Die Friedens-Warte* 41, no. 5/6 (1941), 221.

14 (The Hague, 1917), vol. 1, 362.

15 (The Hague, 1940), vol. 3, 353.

16 'The Avoidance of War,' *Times Literary Supplement* (8 March 1917), 111.

17 Merle Curti, 'Reflections on the Genesis and Growth of Peace History,' *Peace and Change* 11, no. 1 (Spring 1985), 1–18 (at 8). Curti's *The American Peace Crusade, 1815–1860* had just been published (1929).

18 Walther Schücking, *Die Organisation der Welt* (Leipzig, 1909).

19 Ibid., 82–3.

20 Jacob ter Meulen, 'Walther Schücking als Historiker der Friedensbewegung,' *Die Friedens-Warte* 35 (1935), 217–18.

21 A further indication of the importance which ter Meulen ascribed to Schücking's 1909 study is the fact that it appears, together with Fried's *Handbuch*, in the very selective bibliography which he appended to his article 'The Idea of Peace through the Centuries,' published in a Dutch encyclopedia in 1947. Cf. Jacob ter Meulen, 'De Vredesgedachte in de Loop der Eeuwen,' in *Eerste Nederlandse Systematisch Ingerichte Encyclopedie* (Amsterdam, 1947), vol. 3, 185–9.

22 'Walther Schücking,' 217–18.

23 'De Vredesgedachte,' 185–6.

24 He is, appropriately, represented in both the *Biographical Dictionary of Internationalists*, ed. W.F. Kuehl (Westport, 1983) and the *Biographical Dictionary of Modern Peace Leaders*, ed. H. Josephson (Westport, 1985). The fact that he is one of only seven individuals included in both is fortuitous and should not be regarded as indicating the existence of a sharp dividing line between internationalists and, for example, pacifists. Many have, in the course of their lives, shifted their position and the question of whether someone is an internationalist or a pacifist is frequently one of balance and judgment. (The overlapping noted is largely, no doubt, the result of editorial oversight.)

25 Jacob ter Meulen, *Report on the Library during the World War, 1939–1945* (The Hague, 1945), 5. That ter Meulen was not alone in this view is, in a symbolic

way, suggested perhaps by the following story. When in 1938 the Dutch government presented Hildo Krop's statue of Erasmus to the Carnegie Foundation for display in the palace's gardens, it proved much less impressive in height than had been anticipated. This invited so many protests that finally the statue was put on a plinth, making it thereby much more prominent. Cf. Arthur Eyffinger, *The Peace Palace* (The Hague, 1988), 119, 127.

26 *Gedanke*, vol. 1, vii.

27 They have recently been reprinted; cf. my (ed.) *From Erasmus to Tolstoy: The Peace Literature of Four Centuries; Jacob ter Meulen's Bibliographies of the Peace Movement before 1899* (Westport, 1990). The Introduction provides full details on the history of this project.

28 *From Erasmus*, 6.

29 Ibid., 12.

30 *Gedanke*, vol. 3, 352. Cf. also Beales: 'After 1878 [Berlin Congress] the history of Peace becomes an integral part of the history of international relations; and arbitration and disarmament, once the nostrums of a few cranks, become the commonplaces of diplomacy,' *The History of Peace*, v. This had become even more so ten years on.

31 *From Erasmus*, 10.

32 Ibid., 11–12.

33 Ibid., 40, n57.

34 *Gedanke*, vol. 1, 125 n1. Strictly speaking, it is thus not true to say that 'Erasmus did not concede ... that there could be any circumstances under which war would be justified,' or that he, 'unlike More and Grotius ... did not consider that there could ever be a just cause for war.' Cf. Michael Howard in his *War and the Liberal Conscience* (London, 1978), 16, 19. For an authoritative and accurate account of 'Erasmus and the Theory of the Just War,' see Robert Regout, 'Erasmus en de Theorie van den Rechtvaardigen Oorlog,' in *Voordrachten gehouden ter Herdenking van den Sterfdag van Erasmus op 10 en 11 Juli 1936 te Rotterdam* (Lectures held to commemorate the day of Erasmus's death; The Hague, 1936), 155–71.

35 'Jacob ter Meulen,' in *Persoonlijkheden in het Koninkrijk der Nederlanden* (Amsterdam, 1938), 1005.

36 Bart de Ligt, whom we are following here, argues that its incipient revival during the First World War can be attributed to the 'Anti-Conscription Movement' (in which de Ligt himself played a leading role). Cf. Bart de Ligt, *Vrede als Daad* (Arnhem, 1931), vol. 1, 227–31; Bart de Ligt, 'Kriegsbekämpfer in den Niederlanden,' in Franz Kobler (ed.), *Gewalt und Gewaltlosigkeit* (Zurich, 1928), 198–214. De Ligt's view is confirmed by H. Bremer, who sees the revival of the Mennonite peace principle following the First and Second

World Wars as the result of the ideas of Tolstoy and de Ligt, and later also of G.J. Heering and the Quakers. In addition, contacts with Mennonites abroad led their Dutch adherents to an awareness of their own tradition. Cf. H. Bremer, 'Doperse Weerloosheid' (Mennonite Non-resistance) in J. de Graaf et al. (eds.), *Handboek voor de Vredesbeweging: De Radicaal-Pacifistische Stromingen* (The Hague, 1954), esp. 26–7.

37 The expression is used by P.J.J. Diermanse and B. Landheer in their obituary article on their colleague in the *American Journal of International Law* 57 (1963), 391–3.

38 A. Eyffinger in *From Erasmus*, ix. See also Merle Curti's comments on ter Meulen's moderate views on Mennonite war resistance in his 'Reflections,' 12. Curti met ter Meulen during his research in 1929–30 in the Peace Palace.

39 Jacob ter Meulen, *Wij Willen Goede Burgers Zijn, Maar de Wapenen Zullen Wij Niet Dragen* (The Hague, 1932?), 3–4.

40 Ibid.

41 *Samenkomst van Doopsgezinden ... Een Vredesgetuigenis en de Vorming van een Internationaal Doopsgezind Vredescomité* (Meeting of Mennonites ... A Peace Testimony and the Creation of an International Mennonite Peace Committee; The Hague, 1937), 1–4. In the absence of further information, it is assumed that the committee formed in 1936 was a fuller embodiment of its namesake which ter Meulen had established some years before. See also the reports of the 1936 meeting in joint articles by ter Meulen and Bender in *Brieven* (etc.), 20 (1937), 19–22, and in *Kerk en Vrede* 12 (1936–7), 144–5.

42 For biographical information on de Ligt in English see, Peter van den Dungen, Herman Noordegraaf, and Wim Robben, *Bart de Ligt: Peace Activist and Peace Researcher* (Boxtel, 1990); Peter van den Dungen, 'Introduction to the 1989 Edition,' in Bart de Ligt, *The Conquest of Violence* (London, 1989), ix–xxvii; Herman Noordegraaf, *Niet met de Wapenen der Barbaren: Het Christen-Socialisme van Bart de Ligt* (Baarn, 1994), 389–95 (English summary).

43 Bart de Ligt, *Erasmus* (Arnhem, 1936), 68.

44 Bart de Ligt, *Vrede als Daad* (Arnhem, 1931–3); French translation: *La Paix Créatrice* (Paris, 1934).

45 Aldous Huxley, Introduction, in Bart de Ligt, *Conquest*, xxviii; Aldous Huxley, *An Encyclopaedia of Pacifism* (London, 1937), 18.

46 Peter Brock, *Pacifism in Europe to 1914* (Princeton, 1972), 505; Gene Sharp in *Bart de Ligt*, 4–9; Gernot Jochheim, *Antimilitaristische Aktionstheorie, Soziale Revolution und Soziale Verteidigung* (Assen/Amsterdam/Frankfurt a.M., 1977); Nikola Bock, *Pazifismus zwischen Anpassung und 'Freier Ordnung': Friedensdiskussionen in der Weimarer Republik und die Gewaltfreiheitstheorie des Holländischen Pazifisten Bart de Ligt (1883–1938)* (Hamburg, 1991).

47 Cf. the contribution by Wim Robben in *Bart de Ligt*.

48 Bram Storm in *Bart de Ligt, 1883–1938* (Arnhem, 1939), 163, 167.

49 Bart de Ligt, *Conquest*, 162; Rudolf de Jong,'Antimilitarisme en Geweldloos-heid bij Bart de Ligt,' *de As*, 11, no. 62 (April–June 1983), 23.

50 First published in 1937 (London); reprinted in 1972 (New York) and 1989 (cf. n42).

51 Charles Chatfield (ed.), *International War Resistance through World War II* (New York, 1975), 33, 44 (n39), 558.

52 Bart de Ligt, *Introduction to the Science of Peace* (London, 1939). Nearly half a century later, Jochheim notes that de Ligt's reflections read as if they had been written today. See his excellent contribution, 'Bart de Ligt: Gewalt-losigkeit und Antimilitaristische Aktion,' in Christiane Rajewsky and Dieter Riesenberger (eds.), *Wider den Krieg: Grosse Pazifisten von Immanuel Kant bis Heinrich Böll* (Munich, 1987), 103–10.

PART II:

CHRISTIAN TRADITIONS
OF PACIFISM AND
NON-RESISTANCE

TWO MAJOR TRADITIONS HAVE BEEN PRESENT in the history of Christian pacifism, the 'separational' and the 'integrational' (to adopt the typology formulated some years ago by Peter Brock). Both traditions have drawn their inspiration from the record of the New Testament and from the example of the early Church.

In her essay, 'Non-violence and Women's Resistance in Early Christianity,' Luise Schottroff, on the basis of a feminist analysis, examines several documents of early Christianity, including the Sermon on the Mount and the little known Acts of Thekla, and then briefly discusses the implications of the non-violent resistance on the part of women revealed there for present-day Christian pacifism. She argues that 'women's resistance is resistance in daily life that can make it clear to men that their resistance also belongs in everyday living.'

In the following essay John H. Yoder surveys 'War as a Moral Problem in the Early Church' and reviews the 'hermeneutical assumptions' of recent historians who have dealt with this subject. The problem for him lies not so much in any further examination of the few surviving texts from this period of church history bearing on war, but in scrutinizing such things as historians' vocabulary, terms of reference and perimeters of the debate, and the Jewish background of early Christianity. In his view, such an approach would also cast new light on the survival of the pacifist impulse within the 'just war tradition.'

After Christianity became the state religion of the Roman Empire, war became for the Church an acceptable practice under certain conditions, even though it continued to pursue various forms of peacemaking throughout the Middle Ages. The idea of non-resistance reappeared again in the high and later Middle Ages with such sects as the Waldenses and the Czech Brethren in Bohemia, but had largely disappeared by the beginning of the sixteenth century. Then, around 1525, the idea of non-resistance re-emerged with the Swiss Brethren. In that year they broke with the mainstream Reformation when they rejected infant baptism and replaced it by the baptism of adult believers. Out of the sixteenth-century Anabaptist movement the Mennonites and Church of the Brethren emerged, and they became the main protagonists of separational pacifism in the modern world.

By no means all early Anabaptists were non-violent, however. The extent of, and relationship between non-resistant and 'revolutionary' Anabaptism has been debated among historians of the Radical Reformation, particularly during the past generation. The view expressed by the Mennonite historian, Harold S. Bender, that non-resistance formed one of the core beliefs of the Anabaptist mainstream, whereas violence existed only briefly and on the peripheries of the movement, has come under increasing criticism. The leader of the revisionist school, James M. Stayer, contributes an essay entitled, 'Anabaptists and the Sword Revisited: The Trend from Radicalism to Apoliticism.' The essay, as he explains, offers a commentary on, and amendment of, his original views on the subject developed in his *Anabaptists and the Sword* (1972). Stayer concludes that Anabaptism in the sixteenth century witnessed a dynamic trend from an at first dominant social radicalism towards an apolitical quietism that eventually gave the tone to Mennonite sectarian non-resistance.

The Mennonites were not the only religious group to champion non-resistance. Early in the eighteenth century, non-resistance was adopted by the closely related Brethren (also known as Dunkers), who had gathered in the Palatinate. Soon, as a tiny group, they emigrated to North America, leaving none of their co-religionists behind in Europe (unlike the Mennonites, many of whom remained in Central Europe and the Netherlands, or moved to Russia, after a large emigration to the New World). In his essay on 'The Brethren and Non-resistance,' Donald F. Durnbaugh surveys the attitude of this group to war and military service from their genesis under the impact of Radical Pietism through the American Revolution and the American Civil War to the post–Cold War period. By then the Church of the Brethren had become the largest of the United States's three 'historic peace churches.' The situation today, he writes, is one in which 'non-resistance ... is certainly alive among the Brethren but it would be too much to say that it is a predominant position.'

The pacifism of the Quakers (also known as Society of Friends) became more closely integrated with the surrounding world than did the non-resistance of the Anabaptist-Mennonites and Brethren. The following four essays are devoted to aspects of Quaker pacifism from its hesitant beginnings in Cromwell's England. The first essay – by Hugh Barbour – is entitled, 'The "Lamb's War" and the Origins of the Quaker Peace Testimony.' It deals with the controversial issues of when and why Quakers first declared themselves to be pacifists. There were a number of Quakers in Cromwell's armies in the 1650s, while some of the sayings during this period of George Fox, the founder of Quakerism, were quite bellicose. On the basis of the printed works of prominent early Quakers, Barbour argues that the peace testimony of early Friends did not spring from the inspiration of an individual or a few Bible verses, but evolved out of their perception of the Christian way to overcome evil in what they came to call the Lamb's War. This was a non-violent struggle and not a merely negative abstention from killing that left the control of evil to the unregenerate.

The more favourable attitude to the state on the part of Quakers emerged most fully in the so-called Holy Experiment of Quaker Pennsylvania between 1682 and 1756. A large body of literature exists on this subject, produced by both non-Quaker and Quaker historians. Among those who have given scholarly depth to this well-known episode in American history is Jack D. Marietta, who focuses on its social and political context. Here Marietta discusses the problems arising during the aftermath of the Holy Experiment and the implication of this period – that ended with the outbreak of revolution in 1775 – for the Quaker peace testimony.

Since its beginnings women have played a prominent role in the Society of Friends. Margaret Fell, Elizabeth Fry, Lucretia Mott – to name just three outstanding women Quakers – shaped their religious community in ways rarely found among other denominations. Thomas C. Kennedy has chosen a comparatively recent period of Quaker history for his study in this area, 'Quaker Women and the Pacifist Impulse in Britain, 1900–20.' His essay covers the latter part of the so-called Quaker Renaissance as well as the First World War. In that period Quaker women were prominent in efforts to renew the Society's peace testimony. Some of them supported a radical peace witness in the First World War and backed the stand of the absolutist conscientious objectors as the only legitimate Quaker response to conscription. This stance, in turn, endowed the British Quaker doctrine immediately after the First World War with a somewhat radical pacifist cast.

If this kind of orientation hardly made Quakers generally popular, the relief work for the victims of war that the Society of Friends carried on during and after the First and Second World Wars brought out the positive aspects of its rejection of war. It also made the Society widely known throughout many parts of the world as an agent of international reconciliation. In 1947 the Friends Service Council in Britain and the American Friends Service Committee were jointly awarded the Nobel Peace Prize for their peacemaking activities. In an essay entitled, 'The Quaker Peace Testimony and the Nobel Peace Prize,' Irwin Abrams surveys the background leading up to this award and assesses the relative weights assigned to the pacifist and humanitarian aspects of Quaker work by those involved in making the award. Irwin shows that in the minds of the Norwegian Nobel Committee, 'there was full recognition that the relief work was a translation in deeds of the inner life of the Society [of Friends] and that the peace testimony was an integral part of the Quaker way of life.'

5

Non-violence and Women's Resistance in Early Christianity[1]

LUISE SCHOTTROFF

In this essay I pursue the question of non-violent resistance on the part of women in early Christianity. To begin with I focus on the particular history of women's resistance during this period in comparison with men's resistance and go on to examine how women's resistance and their gender role in a patriarchal society relate. In conclusion I present, to my thinking, basic consequences for pacifism and non-violent resistance of both women and men. My approach is based on a critical feminist analysis of Christian theological discussion on non-violence and the andro-centrism of particular text passages in the Sermon on the Mount. My aim is not limited to an historical clarification. Rather, I want to contribute to the practice of present-day women's resistance – of which I consider myself a part – and thereby contribute a change also in men's resistance.

The Persistent Widow (Luke 18:1–8)

The parable of the persistent widow tells a story of women's resistance against injustice and holds the resisting widow up as an example for all faithful in their relations with God and humanity.

The injustice inflicted on the widow occurs on two levels. She is the victim of a man, who threatens her livelihood, and against whom she seeks to defend herself with the help of the judge. In the parable this man is described as the 'opponent.' In addition to that she falls victim to an unjust jurisdiction, which is regardless of her rights. According to the parable, the judge dismisses her several times. Both Old Testament material and the parable indicate that they see this double injustice against widows as a *structural* injustice. The Old Testament texts already indicate through the continual repetition of the indictment that the injustice is structural. The New Testament parable does this by describing this predicament as a typical case. This text shows an awareness, in both early Christianity and in the Judaic tradition, that a patriarchal society can commit a structural injustice, against which God intervenes.[2]

The resistance of the widow against the double injustice to which many widows are subjected is her accusation in court and her refusal to be dismissed by the judge. She returns too often and conducts herself in so burdensome a fashion that the judge calls her a nuisance. He administers justice to avoid her obstinacy.

The parallels to this case found in antique texts allow a more detailed examination of the widow's behaviour. In many of these examples, the emphasis is both on the persistence of the accuser and his or her vocal opposition to the unjust judge. These cases of resistance behaviour allow for a different perspective of the widow's behaviour in Luke 18:1–8. She continually returns to court to *demand justice*, while also *reproaching* the judge and *reminding* him of his duties. She knows that he is an unjust judge, who does not want to be anything else; nevertheless, she induces him to pronounce *justice* through her persistent accusations and speaking. How many experiences of unjust jurisdiction, especially against widows, emerge out of this text and the parallels? The widow is within a recognizable tradition of resistance.

The tenacity with which people fight for injustice in these texts is linked in several examples with an infringement of social roles. This violation of social norms is quite clear in Luke 18:1–8: no widow – presumably no woman – is allowed to act this way. This exceeding of social roles has often led to the interpretation of the judge as 'sarcastic.'[3] The judge realizes that he will see her righted, 'so that she will not finally hit him in the face.' Since some editors find the assertion that the widow would hit someone 'peculiar,' they usually render the word weaker, that is, 'so that she will not wear me out with her persistence.'[4] This mitigation is improper. The judge's 'sarcasm' is the sexist sarcasm about a woman who does not behave like a woman: now they believe anything, including violence, can be ascribed to her.

The sarcasm is an expression of sexism and a cynical reversal of reality, in which the accusers are more likely to be hit by court clerks than the judge by a claimant. The transgression of the women's role by the widow can also be recognized by the mitigation of her behaviour in the interpretation tradition, for instance, when the parable is entitled 'The

Pleading Widow,' as in the Luther Bible. This is how we can imagine a widow in court: she begs, rather than asks, or 'is a nuisance.'

The Androcentrism of the Sermon on the Mount

The Sermon on the Mount is – and this applies to the entire New Testament – a male-centred text, whose language and perception is strictly male biased. Women are mentioned exclusively in the context of male behaviour, for example, as the object of the male's desiring gaze or in divorce or marriage (Matt. 5:28–32). The situations presented as examples are taken from the daily life of men. I name two: the quarrel between brothers (Matt. 5:22) and the building of a house (Matt. 7:24–26).[5] Presumably, the 5th and 6th 'Antitheses' on the renunciation of violence and love for the enemy are also based on male experience. Accordingly, one must ask: (1) Are these assumptions correct? (2) Is the socially prescribed gender role for men pivotal in the described behaviour? (3) If the behaviour is applicable for women, what would this imply for women?

In interpreting Matt. 5:38–48 I will proceed from an understanding that the passage is a set of directions for peace practice and not for an accepting passivity nor for private life, such as in dealing with an unfriendly neighbour.

I have chosen as an example for this interpretation of the Sermon on the Mount the work of Walter Wink. He pictures the following situations for Matt. 5:38–41: Evil should not be met with the same means. The subordinate is hit in an insulting manner with the back of the hand. By turning the other cheek, he prevents the subjugator from humiliating him. The creditor, who wins the undergarment in court, is embarrassed when the debtor, in addition, gives his coat voluntarily. The debtor leaves court naked, and friends and neighbours gather around him in solidarity. Love of the enemy 'can free the oppressed from subservience as well as liberate the oppressor from sin.'[6]

If a woman is hit by her husband – or by any man for that matter – and she turns the other cheek, then it is most likely that he thinks she has learned her lesson, that her female subordination dictates this behaviour. The turning of the cheek as an active strategy is only effective if the offender expects a return blow. Walter Wink is aware of this problem: 'How many abused and oppressed women were advised on the strength of a *literal* interpretation, to turn the other cheek.'[7] Wink accordingly demands the adjustment of the concrete behaviourial recommendations of Jesus to the given situation. They are not to become literal laws.

The male-centredness of non-violent situations is even more evident in the case of the creditor and the soldier, who exacts compulsory service. Had a woman undressed publicly in court in antique society, she would have been inviting rape. Women sentenced to animal fights were often raped before being driven into view of the spectators in the arena.

Also, a soldier who had forced a woman into compulsory service – for example, that she carry his load – would have interpreted the willingness of the woman to accompany him as a sexual provocation. What this means is that the three model situations in Matt. 5:39–41 presuppose, that the victim hits back, that a debtor would defend himself in court, and that the compulsory service would be rendered grudgingly. The three situations presuppose the male role in society, which stipulates that one wrong rights another and that violent self-defence is the socially 'proper' behaviour for men.[8] The effectiveness of these situations is based upon the fact that men renounce their *right to violence* and self-defence.

It is worth contemplating at this point, whether women, whose role obliges them to non-violence, would attain the goal which Jesus preaches by not turning the other cheek but rather by hitting back. The question is, therefore, what peace practices according to Matt. 5:38–48 should look like for women. One reference to women's resistance is the story of the persistent widow (Luke 18:1–8), who fights for her rights and in doing so becomes a role model for the faithful. However, she does exactly the opposite of what is expected of Christians as put forth in Matt. 5:40. She argues tenaciously for justice in court. The simile of the persistent widow, in which her behaviour is lauded, illustrates once more that in Matt. 5:40 male behaviour is intended and, that at the same time, the Jesus tradition shows an awareness, that women's resistance has a *form* of its own. So we must examine sources that reveal more about women's resistance along the lines of Matt. 5:38–48.

Before an examination of women's resistance can be attempted, however, a further examination of the androcentric interpretation of the male-centred Sermon on the Mount is necessary. Both the male-centred sermon and its interpretation must be subjected to a critique of patriarchy. Otherwise, they will continue to oppress or repress women in the realm of peace practices. In this construction of the sermon, the alternative to the armed revolutionary is the non-violent resistance fighter, who is not critically questioned on his patriarchal and renewed legitimized role. The historical experience of women who are treated equally when needed in the revolutionary phase of resistance, and then referred to their 'women's role' at the end of this process, also corresponds to the androcentric reality and patriarchal practice of non-violent resistance. Until sexual oppression is not included in non-violent resistance, androcentric perception and patriarchal practice of pacifism will maintain sexual injustice.

The Acts of Thekla

The Acts of Thekla[9] are an outstanding document on women's resistance during early Christianity. Although they must be regarded as a novel-like story (similar to the other Apocryphal Acts of the Apostles) and not as historical reports, they are nevertheless not to be underestimated in their relevance to the reconstruction of historical reality. Women's resistance is a continuous theme of the Acts of Thekla. Thekla herself, (the queen) Tryphäna, the women in Antioch, the women of Iconium, and even a lioness fight against injustice and submission.

Thekla is – so the story goes – a beautiful virgin from an upper-class family in Iconium. She is engaged to Thamyris. From a neighbouring house, she hears Paul's sermon on abstinence and resurrection, which addresses women in particular.[10] She refuses to marry Thamyris and is punished. Her punishment of death through burning is harsher than that of Paul, whose message brought about her change of mind. She is sentenced to death because her refusal to marry is seen as a threat to public order and as a political misdemeanour. The central issue here is the rights of men over women.[11]

Thekla's 'no' to marriage, like all refusals of Christian women in the ancient church, is seen by non-Christian society as a danger to the stability of public order. On the other hand, women experience virginity as liberation and empowerment. Although the Christian message on abstinence is directed at both sexes, more women than men are attracted to it, and therefore more women are persecuted than men. Thekla continues her fight for her virginity in court in Antioch. Her course is constantly threatened by the possibility of rape by those who feel threatened by her message.[12]

The refusal to marry on the part of women is seen here as an attack on the social order of patriarchy. The basic unit of the state is marriage, said Cicero.[13] Male supremacy is a decisive part of the social ruling order. Virginity presents a possibility for women to withdraw from direct male subjugation and to develop the power of their own counter-culture.

Even during the animal fight in the arena of Antioch, to which she is condemned for her defence against an attempted rape, Thekla manages to avoid being seen as a victim. She prays with her hands spread apart. Earlier, during the attempt to burn her in Iconium – I am summarizing Thekla's martyrdom here – she made 'the shape of the cross' with her body. She makes it very clear that she has been condemned to death *as a Christian*. Her self-baptism in the arena in Antioch also transforms her role as the victim of wild beasts into that of a believing and courageous woman, who in the hour of her death uses the pond full of crocodiles as a christening font.[14]

So, as we can see, Thekla defends her virginity against all attempts to force her into a woman's role in a patriarchal society and thus brings about not only her *religious* identity, but also a new *female* identity. This explains why she has been a role model for many Christian women. She must defend her self-determined female identity also against Paul. He refuses to baptize her with the remark that she is beautiful and thus seducible. In addition, Paul lets her down when Alexander tries to rape her publicly on the street. This means that Paul has tried to force Thekla into her role in a patriarchal society twice, despite the fact that virginity became an instrument of Thekla's emancipation through *his* sermon.

A description of the resistance of a group of women is found in the context of Thekla's animal fight in Antioch. The women are already present in court when Thekla's verdict is pronounced, and they criticize the verdict. The text verbatim: 'But the women caused a disturbance [exeplagesan] and cried out before the throne of the judge: 'An evil judgement! A Godless judgement!'[15] The text depicts in detail the women's public protest against the verdict and in the arena. It is interesting that the women only become Christians through their expression of solidarity as women of the town with Thekla.

Despite the novel-like character of this passage, it becomes clear that the text presupposes similar occurrences and invites women to emulate the behaviour of Thekla and the women in Antioch. Furthermore, the behaviour of the women in Antioch suggests that women in this city are not acting as a group for the first time when they appear in court to pro-test the misogynist trial. Because we know a similar capability for orga-nizing and solidarity of women in Damascus from Josephus – in this case for the Jewish minority in the city – and repeatedly hear about inde-pendently acting women's groups, we can assume that in actuality politically active women's groups existed in some places in which women developed an awareness of the inferior status of women.[16]

In some respects the Galilean women's group that, according to the gospels, accompanied Jesus and the male disciples from Galilee to Jerusalem can be compared to the women from Antioch. Although according to Mark they stood at a distance from the cross, they accompanied the crucifixion and the burial together, whereas the male disciples fled.[17]

The Acts of Thekla are a unique document of the history of women's resistance.[18] According to this text, women's resistance evolved by women refusing their role, which again and again is forced on them by agents of the patriarchal order. These agents are both female and male. Thekla's mother, for example, is the harshest judge of her daughter. The women's group, which criticizes the court publicly, has also broken with the role of women. Public speaking on the part of women was considered in the Roman Empire and in arenas of early Christianity as unsuitable and politically inappropriate. The pressure on the loudly protesting women in Antioch was without a doubt considerable.

It would be inaccurate to see this resistance as the universal resistance of all women against all men. It is rather the resistance of women against the patriarchal system, which shackles them in their role. The subordination of women by means of their role is experienced by women as a continuum in life, beginning with their daily 'private' life and relationships and extending into the area of their public possibilities. The description of the sentencing of Thekla in the Acts of Thekla shows that women's subordination is understood here in its political dimensions, that this is a beginning analysis of patriarchy in the direction of feminist liberation theology. The term 'patriarchy' is used here to denote a complete socially organized power structure, in which dominance over women – but also over men who do not comply with their allotted roles – is secured by means of subtle and outright force. Militarism as part of this patriarchal system is also recognizable in the Acts: soldiers patrol the animal fights as a public presentation of a (forced) consensus of the population with the violent structure of patriarchy. If the people did not attend the animal fights voluntarily, they were forced to do so by the military. The resistance of women in Antioch in the arena takes place exactly at the spot of the victories of violence of the Roman patriarchy and exposes the connection between animal fights, the military, the administration, and the subordination of women.

The Non-violent Church as Co-perpetrator – A Woman's Role

Women's role in society includes the co-perpetration of patriarchy. For example, women support the male trait of force by admiring strong men and by tending to the wounded. The feminist analysis of female co-perpetration is vital for modern peace research, but it is not my intention at this point to explain female co-perpetration. Let me point out, however, that my description of women's resistance sketches an alternative to co-perpetration. And in the following, I will subject *Christian pacifism* to feminist scrutiny, because I think it is necessary to differentiate between a conforming pacifism and a pacifism based on resistance.

The word 'pacifism' was defamed by its opponents in the German debate during and after the Persian Gulf War as a conforming pacifism. Only these two possibilities were mentioned in the public discussion during the Gulf War: a pacifism that did not want to dirty its hands and its so-called alternative, the just war. The peace movement was rebuked for practising the pacifism that 'leaves everything to dictators and mass murderers.' This, however, does not apply to the majority of the German peace movement. The peace movement tries to find democratic ways and means to prevent military production and export and to publicize and introduce into the political process alternatives to defending human rights with military might.

A pacifism which 'leaves everything to dictators and mass murderers' is, however, a form of non-violence, which particularly in the context of churches – as far as they are integrated into the power structure of their countries – plays a role. I would like to illustrate this kind of pacifism by analysing an example, the book on Jesus by Gerd Theissen. I chose this book not to criticize the author, but because it has been published in fifteen languages and has an enormous following in present-day Christian circles.[19] I will criticize this book from a feminist perspective. The purpose of this book is to advocate Jesus' non-violence and his love for the enemy as the alternative to resistance with force, as the Christian mode of behaviour. The concept of resistance coupled with force is taken in Theissen's book from the history of German terrorism, specifically that of the Red Army Faction (RAF). Repeatedly, Theissen confronts the non-violent forms of resistance with violent forms.

Jesus' course – to follow Theissen – is not one of resisting action, because this is immediately categorized as terrorist: 'But we [the Zealots] are convinced, that God only helps those, who help themselves. He only helps those, who are prepared to revolt against and show force to the enemy.' Active participation or 'helping themselves' is disqualified as wrong by associating it with the terrorist use of violence.[20]

A church that follows the concept of Jesus' non-violence as depicted in Theissen's book, would be – seen from a feminist vantage point – in the female role of nurturing and supporting the perpetrator and not offering resistance to his offences. The non-violent church policy would, in this sense, be supporting male supremacy, the despots of the *pax Romana*, which Theissen describes as a beast. That generations of Christian women and men after Jesus worked against war and violence and for justice and will continue to do so, finds no mention in this book.

The non-violent Church as co-perpetrator is therefore to be distinguished fundamentally from a pacifism that works actively and publicly for the goal of a peace without violence. The alternative – violence or pacifism – regardless of the form it may assume – ignores the 'third path,' the active pacifism of non-violent resistance.

Concluding Remarks on Women's Resistance and Men's Resistance

'Every women, who refuses "to stay put in a woman's place" contributes to the resistance against sexism.'[21] Every man who refuses to stay put in his place, contributes to the resistance against sexism. Resistance against sexism should be considered as part of resistance against force in all its forms. Pacifism without resistance against sexism leaves the roots of violence and co-perpetration untouched. Pacifism without resistance against sexism leaves the gut of class exploitation untouched: the poverty of women and children in the Two-thirds World. I suggest making the feminist analysis of patriarchy part of peace research. Only then will it become clear that non-violent resistance and pacifism cannot be singular actions in unspecific political situations, but have to be a part of daily life. Only this will make it possible to live in times of military posturing and ecological catastrophes. A real life is, to my mind, one that carries the vision of a healed creation which directs all its energies to protecting and passing life on.

Women's resistance is resistance in daily life, and it can make clear to men that their resistance also belongs in everyday living. 'We want to break the spell of powerlessness and subjugation and practise a responsible dealing with ourselves and others by assuming comprehensive responsibility and control in areas accessible to us.'[22] For the present that means breaking up the gender roles that work together to cement the structures of force and coercion in this world. Resistance in daily life means, in addition, taking all those small seemingly insignificant steps to liberation: to recognize violence in language and to learn to speak and teach differently, to avoid waste and superfluous consumption, to boycott companies and products that are linked to military production. In the Christian tradition the lifelong resistance in daily life is called *Umkehr* or 'conversion.'

Notes

1 The editor would like to thank Gaby Donicht for her help with the translation and editing of this essay.
2 For non-biblical examples of the treatment of widows, see Luise Schottroff, 'Frauen und Geld im Neuen Testament,' in *Reader der 4. Kasseler Feministisch-befreiungstheologischen Sommeruniversität* (Gesamthochschule Kassel, 1991). See also Mark 12:40.
3 Hans Weder, *Die Gleichnisse Jesu als Metaphern* (Gottingen, 1978), 270 n139, and Wolfgang Harnisch, 'Die Ironie als Stilmittel in Gleichnissen Jesu,' *Evangelische Theologie* 32 (1972), 421–2, 433.
4 Walter Bauer, *Griechisch-deutsches Wörterbuch zu den Schriften des Neuen Testaments und der frühchristlichen Literatur*. See also J. Duncan M. Derrett, 'Law in the New Testament: The Parable of the Unjust Judge,' *New Testament Studies* 18 (1972), 178, 189–91.
5 Luise Schottroff, 'Wanderprophetinnen: Eine feministische Analyse der Logienquelle,' *Evangelische Theologie* 51 (1991), 76–87.
6 Walter Wink, *Angesichts des Feindes: Der dritte Weg Jesu in Südafrika und anderswo* (Munich, 1988), 43.
7 Ibid., 49.
8 See a similar interpretation by Paul Hoffmann, 'Eschatologie und Friedenshandeln in der Jesusüberlieferung,' in *Eschatologie und Friedenshandeln*, ed. Ulrich Luz et al. (Stuttgart, 1981), 133.
9 The Acts of Thekla, in R.A. Lipsius and M. Bonnet, *Acta Apostolorum Apocrypha* (1891; reprint ed. Darmstadt, 1959), vol. 1, 235–6. The text was created between 185 and 195 AD in Asia Minor.
10 Acts of Thekla, verses 7, 9, 12, 15.
11 Ibid., verses 15–21.
12 Lipsius-Bonnet, 271–2.
13 Cicero, *de republica I*, 38, and *de officiis I*, 54.
14 Acts of Thekla, verses 22, 34.
15 Ibid., verse 27.

16 Josephus, *Bell. jud. II*, 560–1, and Luise Schottroff, *Befreiungserfahrungen: Studien zu einer Sozialgeschichte des Neuen Testaments* (Munich, 1990), 291–2.

17 Schottroff, *Befreiungserfahrungen*, 134–5.

18 For the history of women's resistance the Acts of the Xanthippe and Polyxene are also important. See L. Davies, *The Revolt of the Widows: The Social World of the Apocryphal Acts* (Carbondale, Ill., 1980), 64–9.

19 Gerd Theissen, *Der Schatten des Galiläers* (1986). Between 1986 and 1990 this book had a print run of 50,000 copies.

20 Theissen, 126. See also Acts of Thekla, verse 15.

21 Beverly W. Harrison, 'Die Kraft des Zorns in der Arbeit der Liebe,' in *Die neue Ethik der Frauen*, ed. B.W. Harrison (Stuttgart, 1991), 169.

22 Christine Schaumberger, 'Radikal in kleinen Schritten? Die Ökumenische Initiative EINE WELT und ihr Versuch eines alternativen Lebens,' in *Theologisch-politische Protokolle*, ed. Tiemo Rainer Peters (Munich/Mainz, 1981), 87.

6

War as a Moral Problem in the Early Church: The Historian's Hermeneutical Assumptions

JOHN H. YODER

There has been no significant new information on the topic of war as a moral problem in the early Church for a long time. When Peter Brock began his 1972 history with twenty-two pages on early Christianity, the sources he summarized, written from 1905 to the 1960s, added little to what had already been treated by Harnack[1] and Cadoux[2] generations before. Some new authors came to the same old material with new perspectives, but there was even very little of that. Most new authors brought the same old perspectives, although the tone changed as Roman Catholic historians joined the discussion. There have been no new patristic texts adduced,[3] and the progress of archaeology has not changed much. The number of people continuing to run over the same ground still grows, as recorded in Peter Brock's own recent *Selected Bibliography*,[4] but with little change in the shape of the data.

The survey by Jacques Fontaine[5] restates the above summary, adding the complaint that the literature is marked by an 'emotional' tone reflecting the respective authors' own leanings on the issue of pacifism. That is another thing that has not changed.[6]

What is needed today is not one more effort towards a still more careful, or still more partisan, fine reading of those same few dozen pages from the first three centuries. As an ethicist, my work in history has not centred on the early centuries, but rather on the later epoch we call 'Renaissance' and 'Reformation.' This was the time when the process of looking back to the early centuries began in a new key, introducing two new ideas: the application of critical historical methods to interpreting the distant past and the critical use of the past as a guide in renewal. It is the tension between these two kinds of criticism that creates the 'emotion' noted by Fontaine.

The need is thus for a review not of the slender literary base but of the hermeneutical assumptions that tend to determine how the texts are read. These assumptions need to be made more conscious and to be subjected to methodological scrutiny on grounds other than whether or not the texts can be called on to support one's own ethical predilections.

Vocabulary

The tilt begins already with the word 'pacifism,' whose definition is not as univocal as some may assume. I used to think that with good manners people on both sides of the ethical debate could agree to define their terms 'objectively' enough that the argument could be about substance rather than about words. Accordingly, I used to accept the term 'pacifism' as a description of my own view, though with the carefully stated awareness that for others it has many meanings.[7]

That hope, however, has not been sustained. A great disappointment is the slanderous characterization in the neoconservative journal *First Things* of pacifism as 'a doctrine that holds that it is morally preferable to allow Dr Mengele to continue to perform medical experiments on men, women, and children than it is to kill him.'[8]

Ronald Musto, author of *The Catholic Peace Tradition*[9] and editor of a bibliography in the same area,[10] proposes that we should abandon the defence of the term. Musto notes[11] that according to a *New York Times* story of 21 February 1991, Pope John Paul II wants to avoid 'pacifism' because he does not want 'peace at any cost.' Musto points, too, to James T. Johnson's characterization of pacifism as 'withdrawal from the world and all its ills.' He could have added the neoconservatives George Weigel[12] and Guenter Lewy,[13] who have written patronizingly of what 'pacifists' would have to do to earn their respect.

In the early 1950s I saw the term 'pacifism' used by secular journalists in France to describe the fact that the then Secretary of State John Foster Dulles, the father of brinkmanship, was inclined not to go to war against continental China over the Pescadores, despite the signals he had been giving in that direction. Others used the term to label Neville Chamberlain's postponing war against Hitler. As Musto indicates, 'pacifism' for the first generations of its usage meant the stance of politicians who considered war not immoral or illegal but inopportune. The same was true of the use of the phrase 'peace at any price' by France's foreign minister Georges Bonnet. In the late 1940s in France 'pacifism' was the label given both to Vichy and to the communist fronts.

James T. Johnson has further complicated that conversation by suggesting yet another set of meanings.[14] He calls people like Erasmus, Dante, and Marsilius of Padua 'pacifist' because of their 'utopian' vision of peace as a possible political program under a new world order. Yet these visionaries approved of war under three circumstances: (a) for self-defence until the new world order comes; (b) in the hands of the dominant government in order to impose the new world order in the first place; and after that (c) to police the peace. Most ethicists would call this a subset of just war thinking. It would complicate our assignment to study the first three centuries if we were to add that definition.

Unfortunately, Ronald Musto does not have a new word to propose which would not be subject to the same kinds of abuse. All of the other words in the conversation – 'peace,' 'violence,' 'non-violence' – are equally polyvalent in current usage. I shall thus continue here to use the old term, although under protest. For the rest of this essay 'pacifist' shall denote the moral rejection of war as incompatible with fidelity to Jesus Christ as Lord.[15]

Who Speaks for Christians?

Who are the early Christians whose attitudes or behaviour we are asking about? Today the bureaucratic leaders of the 'mainstream' Protestant denominations in the United States and of the National Council of Churches routinely make statements about public matters, including war and peace, without there being any formal way to know how many of their constituencies support it. The National Conference of Catholic Bishops in the United States does the same. Similar things happen in Canada as well.

Americans who have been baptized and who tell the census-takers that they are 'Catholic' seem to commit the canonically prohibited actions of contraception, of entering a new sexual union after divorce, or even of abortion, in proportions not very different from the rest of the American population. The people who have carried out torture on behalf of the several fascist regimes of Latin America were mostly baptized at birth and mostly felt free to continue to frequent parish worship, so that whether they could and should be excommunicated has been a serious theme of episcopal deliberation in some Latin American countries. Do Roman Catholics support dictators? Does that mean that on all these matters the position of Catholic Christianity is to be determined by a descriptive statistical reading on how many people do what, rather than ascribing to the bishops and the theologians any magisterial status?

Few would challenge the label of 'pacifist' for the Society of Friends, even though only a minority of draft-age men from that constituency took conscientious objector status during the Second World War. Even those young Friends who accepted military service made no attempt to change either the documents or the public image of Quakerism that their individual action undermined.

As these examples demonstrate, the meaning of normativity is multiple in any setting. In any community some interpreters are more 'authorized' than others. Shepherds and sheep do not weigh the same.[16] There is no point in citing over against each other the comportment of young men before the draft, on the one hand, and the statements of morally articulate authors, on the other. The way normativity 'works' depends on quite diverse understandings of the status of clergy, of the role of canon, of the status under God ascribed to (non-Christian) civil rulers, and a handful of other variables.

Those who say 'the early Christians were pacifist' base the generalization mostly on a few writings from literate laymen. Those who most strongly deny the thesis base their claim on circumstantially attested actions of men under arms from whom we have no literary communication.[17] The statements on both 'sides' may both be true, since they are not talking about the same people. The literate laymen made moral claims that we can read; the men under arms did not. Some of the writers (notably Origen and Tertullian) were later accused of heresy, by other literate men, on grounds unrelated to the issue of military service. Does any of that make any difference? Bishops, who according to most accounts were supposed by the end of the second century to be quite important, are not generally available for personal comment, although we do have some disciplinary texts likely written by them.

Appreciating and Deprecating the Appeal to Origins

Since the age of the Renaissance and Reformation all of the parties within divided Christendom have appealed to the early centuries for validation. It is a serious misrepresentation of the ecumenical debate to suggest or to assume, as both some 'pacifists' and some of their detractors tend to do, that only the 'radicals' appealed to the 'myth of Christian origins.' The mainstream Protestant appeal to 'Scripture' was one form of appeal to the early centuries, but the alternative 'Catholic' claim was that the development of tradition, leading all the way to the Council of Trent, was also mandated in the first century, and in fact derived from the Apostles the unwritten wisdom which had been handed down 'as if from hand to hand' ever since. The Roman Catholic pietists of Port Royal and the Anglican Pietists like Wesley appealed to original Christianity in practically identical terms.[18] The Tractarians of the nineteenth century were no less 'primitivist' about the availability and the authority of models from the earliest centuries than were their contemporaries the Campbellites.

A fascinatingly flexible verbal key to this hopeless debate is the use of the adjective 'pristine.' For some it means original as opposed to developed; for others simple as opposed to complicated, or pure as opposed to mixed, or uniform as opposed to diverse. Yet *none* of these value-laden connotations belongs to the word. 'Pristine' means simply 'earliest.' All of the other evaluative overtones are derived from the bias about change through history. Those for whom 'pristine' is pejorative are those for whom history moves necessarily (and/or has in fact properly moved) in a welcome direction. Those for whom 'pristine' is good are the critics of later development, but they seldom use the word, since it has taken on a pejorative secondary penumbra like 'unrealistic' or 'imaginary.'

Jonathan Z. Smith has reviewed with his customary thoroughness and verve a number of the most current ways in which the contrast between 'original' and 'degenerate' has served to hide some historians' value biases under the cover of what pretends to be simple historical description. The historian reports how Jesus was replaced by Paul, Hebraic thought patterns were replaced by Greek, historic modes of perception were overruled by 'cyclical' timelessness, biblical religion was replaced by 'paganism,' and so the story goes on, usually downhill. The invidious comparisons can be shown generally to be petitionary, usually anti-catholic in the modern Protestant world, and usually anti-Jewish.[19] This description is well demonstrated for the cases Smith has pursued; he watched closely one chosen concept, that of 'mystery,' and one narrative, that of the dying and rising god.

What Smith does not do is to round out the picture by identifying an alternative. Would it be possible to get along without facing the question of normative identity in historical communities? Could one avoid it by recourse to a monolinear historical evolution validating itself by the power of its univocality? Would the wholesome alternative be a mode of appeal to prior history or present community that would be less naive than the specimens Smith shows to be too simple? Would it be a 'map' not subject to being invalidated by its not fitting the world?

I need not pursue further the theme of the deceptiveness of describing our problem as 'primitivism.' This is not the place for a careful evalua- tion or restatement of the case for canonical accountability, or for any other forms of appeal to the 'fathers.'

For the present let it suffice to note that were there no notion at all of an early model, since lost or betrayed, to serve as a criterion for reform, then there would be no reason for the non-pacifists to contest the bias of which they accuse the pacifist account, or vice versa. For my purposes, the question of the moral attitude of early Christians to war should therefore be considered as an historical issue, independently of whether we look to them a priori as models to be emulated or as primitives to be left behind. Most of the reformers who claimed to be returning to 'the New Testament pattern' did not do so in the mood of ahistorical naivete that is often ascribed to them by critics,[20] but to make that apology is not my present concern.

The Moral World of Jewish Christians

Thus far I have been noting the complexities that beset our reading the history. Now I turn to more important matters, namely, to those parts of the setting that the 'pacifism' debate usually ignores. The debate usually begins in the middle of the second century in the form of a petty legal- ism concerned only for a 'yes' or 'no' answer to the minimal punctual question: 'Was military service forbidden or not?' Thereby most of what mattered and matters for morals is lost, namely, the thickness of the nar- rative of the Gospel as a new social style.

To begin with, the earliest Christians were Jews. Even Gentile believ- ers claimed Abraham as their father and were taught to pray *maranatha* and *abba*. The Jewish world-view does not need to be referred to explic- itly by second-century writers precisely because they take it for granted. Twentieth-century readers, on the other hand, do not. Moderns can read Tertullian or Lactantius as if they were our contemporaries, sifting them through modernity's assumptions about how moral reasoning works. It takes a careful exercise of retrieval to name those elements of the Jewish world-view of the time that make a difference for how Caesar looked at Christians. Some are pertinent to how one looks at war, or at Caesar.

Sovereignty and Suffering

God, the all-wise and all-powerful, is in charge of the world. We are not in charge of the course of events, responsible (as in most settings we are not able) to prevent atrocities or vindicate justice. We need not defend ourselves; God has always protected his own, and will protect us in the future if that is his will. If it is not his will, our mobilizing for our own defence may be against his providential purposes. He may want to chastise us for our sins. Or He may want to use our suffering to 'sanctify his name,' that is, through martyrdom, the opposite of chastisement. If evil has its way, it is under God's permission and will not last. When he does triumph it will not be of our doing and will not depend on our providing His troops. This is the explicit instruction of Rom. 12:19, leaving vengeance to God. This vision undercuts without needing to say so the consequentialism that is indispensable to the case for war in the name of social 'responsibility.'

Diaspora as Mission

Since Jeremiah the calling of the believing people was to 'seek the peace of the city where I have sent you.' After having yielded grudgingly to the Israelites' wanting a king like the Gentiles (Judges 9, 1 Samuel 8), after having let both the northern and the southern kingdoms give it a chance, Jeremiah said that God had given up on kingship. Ezra and Nehemiah rebuilt a worshipping community under the control of the Gentile emperors whose sovereignty they acknowledged. Despite the periodic rise and fall of Jewish settlements in Palestine from then on, the cultural centre of Judaism stayed in Babylon for a millennium and a half.

By the time when Paul and his unnamed contemporaries propagated the messianic movement among the synagogues around the known world, Judaism had six centuries of experience surviving healthily as a tolerated minority, with an unprecedented cosmopolitan viability, whether under the Persian or the Roman Empire, amid Greek or Galatian, Coptic or Cypriot cultures, accustomed to a healthy relativism about local power pretensions. This undercut the provincialism that characterizes any nationalism, even one as large as the Roman Empire. The Hellenistic Christians who gradually began arguing that they were pro-Roman[21] were still non-violent.

The Failure of Military Zeal

Three times the military restoration vision of zealous Jews was given a fair chance: by the Maccabees, by Menachem in 66–70, and by Bar Kochba in 132–5. Some of the faithful were already then critical of the

Maccabees. More of the rabbis were critical of the zealots,[22] even when for the first few years they seemed to be succeeding. All of the rabbis were anti-zealot from then on; they rejected the zealots for presuming upon divine sovereignty, trying to achieve by human arms what only the Messiah can do. God had chosen not to aid them, thereby manifesting His disapproval.

Inclusive Monotheism

If the one true God is creator, world sovereign, then all nations and peoples have a place in His scheme (Acts 14:17); no one ruler, no one empire can be His favourite. This dimension of the Jewish vision was most easily extrapolated into the kind of universal vision of the human race as a unity that was held by Lactantius: 'If we all derive our origin from one man, whom God created, we are plainly of one blood; and therefore, it must be considered the greater wickedness to hate a man, even though guilty. On which account God has enjoined that enmities are never to be contracted by us, but that they are always to be removed, so that we soothe those who are our enemies, by reminding them of their relationship.'[23]

Exclusive Monotheism

That the early Christians were heirs to the Jewish rejection of polytheism and of the cult of idols is more broadly understood than the other distinctives noted above. Yet even here the Christian rejection of idolatry is less adequately understood if its Jewish roots are forgotten. Later understandings of the wrongness of idolatry may be founded Neoplatonically in a deprecation of the external, or merely legalistically or even superstitiously, in a simple unexplained prohibition. How deeply the rejection of idolatry is rooted makes a difference for assessing its place in the rejection of military service.[24] Idolatry is more heinous when contrasted to the holiness of Jehovah of hosts than if we contrast it to the invisible immutable God of the Greeks. Willingness to die rather than honour a graven image is more Hebraic than Hellenistic. It takes the idol as spiritual reality more seriously than did most of the soldiers who went through the cultic motions.

The People of God and the Meaning of History

Ever since Abraham, it has been believed by his heirs that the purpose of

God is to bless all the nations through his seed. The divine purpose is pertinent to all peoples, ultimately, but mediately. God will bless the world *by means of* those who know His Name. Whether it be the Meso- potamian Empire which Abraham left behind, or the Roman one under whose claims to be the whole world Jesus was born, the people of God deny to any earthly empire, even the biggest and best, the claim to be the elect vehicle of divine historical purpose. All kings, the 'good' and the 'bad' ones alike, are willy nilly pawns of the Divine providence, so that their battles can be interpreted by believers within a providential frame; yet that does not make of any of them an independent revelator of God's purpose for His confessing people.

Sometimes the earliest Christians expressed their conviction of the priority of God's purposes over those of Caesar in the genre we call 'apocalyptic.' This has made it easy for modern interpreters, in the wake of Albert Schweitzer, to conclude that their attitude to the empire was *derived from* or *dependent upon* the certainty of an early end to the world.[25] That is a modernization. Since *we* reason consequentially that the justification for war, in favour of the regimes we prefer, is that prag- matically it prevents the triumph of worse regimes, within a perspicu- ous cause-and-effect matrix, we conclude that the only grounds for renouncing war would be an apocalyptic suspension of the cause-and- effect matrix.

Nothing like that fits the early sources. The church versus world dual- ism of the second-century writers – all of them, not merely the ones who happen to have written against war – is not derived from apocalypti- cism, but from their exclusive monotheism and their faith in the histori- cal calling of the people of God.[26]

Synthesis of the Pertinence of the Jewishness of Christianity

All of the above brought into the Roman world of the centuries we are interested in the cosmological and sociological wherewithal for ethical nonconformity. This world-view undercut the very notion that the Roman Empire was the bearer of the meaning of world history. This the- istic vision of the dignity of all mankind and therefore of the modesty incumbent on all rulers is several stories closer to the ground, if we would understand the deep forces that move a community's moral dis- course, than are the arguments one might construct for helping Caesar with his wars. Their total impact is to reinforce with an alternative world-view the lifestyle that eschews Caesar's wars.

As a matter if fact, of course, it is we who have to construct an argument for serving Caesar. There are no written testimonies, no signs of accountable advocacy, to explain what the people thought they were doing who were at the same time Christians and soldiers. They might have agreed with Tertullian that they were bad Christians, maybe even committing sins for which they would need absolution, but believed that they needed the perks. They might have held to some other more affirmative view of their calling, but there is no evience that any of them said so. Even the strongest critics of the Cadoux/Hornus thesis do not bring to the surface a single text indicating that killing in war was being interpreted positively as an act of fidelity to Jesus Christ, as praise to God the Creator of all, as an expression of the unity of the human race, or even as an imperative of natural law.

The Edges of the Debate

I have already said that this is not the setting for a detailed review of the old debate, not only because the question is usually clumsily phrased or because of the large and messy bulk of textual and logistic detail it would demand. The argumentative texts on both 'sides' are not commensurate. Those who find 'pacifism' in the early church write books. Cadouxs' work was much longer than that of Harnack to which he was responding, in a way that Harnack said convinced him.[27] Hornus has two hundred pages of text on the time before Constantine, with another hundred of thorough documentation. The strongest recent synthetic statements 'on the other side' are fewer than a hundred pages in Helgeland[28] and fewer than eighty in Swift,[29] with no chapter-and-verse response to the vast historical or linguistic argument. Johnson[30] has just over forty. To be fair to the sketchy arguments in these brief treatments would take more care, and no less space, than to summarize a full one, if there were one. It will, however, be possible to lift out of the larger discussion a few specimen subquestions that may perhaps be moved forward a little.[31]

Militare but Not Bellare

Roland Bainton at first characterized as 'baffling' the provision of Canon III of the Synod of Arles (314) excluding from communion 'those who throw down their arms in peacetime'; yet it is not too difficult after all for him to explain. 'Bearing arms' in peacetime does not mean killing but civil service.[32] Henri Secretan is credited with first pointing out that the army had long since taken over the bureaucratic management of the *pax Romana*. What counted to hold the empire together was not the threat of death but the relatively reliable centralized rule of law. The army filled that vacuum. If the presence of idolatrous practices had been what made military service unacceptable to Jews and Christians, it would have been no different in wartime or in peacetime.[33] If, on the other hand, there were ways in which Christians, whose services were appreciated by their superiors, could serve the state while avoiding involvement in the cult, but it was killing that made difference, then it would follow that they could very well have seen peacetime service in social management as a duty, without any change in the prohibition of killing. The story of Martin of Tours, ready to serve in peacetime but not in battle, supports the same pattern.

Much of the discussion which goes on under the heading 'early Christians and war' is really mislabelled. It is about 'Christians and service in the Roman army.' During the epoch which understood itself as *pax Romana*, even battle-ready units seldom saw battle. Most of the time, what most of the people under military authority did was what we would call peacetime civil bureaucracy. Without seeking to review adequately the historians of the empire, I note that according to Ramsey MacMullen soldiers were seldom warriors.[34] They built roads as well as forts, surveyed and distributed land, supervised commerce, collected customs, administered crown lands, carried the mails, and kept records of taxes and of citizenship. Many soldiers spent most of their time farming and never needed to drill. Although marriage was technically forbidden until 197, many lived a settled family life with wife and children. The advantage of the army which drew to it such non-belligerent social functions was its firm hierarchical structure more than its right to recourse to arms. Thus, the distinction between the permissible *militare* and forbidden *bellare* was no mere verbal distinction.

The Thunderstorm of 172

Eusebius recounts the legend of a rain- and thunderstorm that saved the Twelfth Roman Legion, while on campaign in Bohemia, both from dying of thirst and from their enemy, in response to the prayers of Christian soldiers. A commemorative column erected in 176 in honour of Marcus Aurelius portrays the same event, with Marcus praying and Jupiter sending down the lightning bolt and pouring out the rain. The pagan historian Cassius Dio wrote the same story a century before Eusebius, crediting an Egyptian magician with the miracle. Later imagination connected the storm with the fact that the Twelfth Legion was named *fulminata*, literally 'thunderstruck' or 'thrown like a thunderbolt.' In fact, the name had been given to the unit before the time of Christ and can have nothing to do with the storm in Bohemia. The legion was wiped out in the Jewish war of 66, but reconstituted during the next century, stationed in Cappadocia to guard the Parthian frontier. Oddly enough, our earliest witness to the event is Tertullian, who cites a letter from the emperor Marcus Aurelius himself about the event, as evidence that Christians are good citizens.

What does this account demonstrate? That Christians' prayers are answered does not prove that they are good Christians. That a miraculous storm caused the enemy to flee without a fight does not prove that Christians were shedding blood.[35] The legend sounds more like the holy war accounts of Exodus 14 or 2 Chronicles, where the miracle dispenses the faithful from battle. The letter purporting to be from Marcus Aurelius, presumably forged by Christians for apologetic purposes, says that the Christians were not armed. Maybe they were quartermasters. Eusebius does not say how many of the soldiers who prayed were Christians. Most Christians did not believe that only Christians could pray to their God.

Hippolytus and the Conditions for Baptism

Despite my renouncing in principle a general analysis of the hopeless state of the debate about detail, I should illustrate it with one example. Hippolytus of Rome is credited with gathering, in the early third century, a collection of 'Apostolic Traditions' which can be reconstituted only through a trail of translations through the Coptic, Arabic, and Ethiopic. Amidst a list of forbidden occupations, provided in connection with instructions about the conditions for baptism, we read: 'The soldier who is of inferior rank [or 'who is in authority'] shall not kill anyone. If ordered to, he shall not carry out the order.' Helgeland et al. translate 'must be told not to execute men,' as if the forbidden killing could be held to have nothing to do with battle.[36] They offer no argument for the special rendering of *occidere*. Swift[37] and Easton, on the other hand, translate 'kill no one,' and Swift comments that 'the prohibition ... is so absolute that it could even require disobedience to a direct command.'

Hornus[38] adds near parallels, the *Testament of Our Lord*, a little younger, and the *Canons of Hippolytus*, yet a little younger, further witnesses to the same tradition, which state the same kind of rule: 'let them not kill in any case, even if they received the order to kill.' Helgeland et al. and Swift make no reference to these further witnesses. The later they are, the more striking it is that such witnesses preserve, in the setting of a document concerned mostly for regulating the form of worship,[39] a rigour reflecting an earlier age. Again the status of soldier is permissible, but killing is not, and becoming a soldier, if one is not already in the service, is not.[40]

Trial Balance

Were Christians before Constantine pacifist? Certainly not, if we give the term an ahistorically modern definition. They did not advocate arms reduction negotiations nor an alternate world order that would do away with the occasion for war. The *pax Romana* in fact claimed already to be that. They were not consulted by Caesar about how to run the empire, since neither he nor they knew about 'the consent of the governed.' Thus, they neither asked Caesar to implement the non-violent Christian ethic from his throne nor measured the Christian ethic consequentially by whether it could be used to run an empire. They did not refuse to serve when subject to universal conscription, since there was none. They accepted non-lethal work in the service of the peacetime military bureaucracy. Their clash with the military establishment was not rooted *only* in their abhorrence of killing. Nor was it limited *only* to their abhorrence of idolatry.[41] It was rooted in a fundamentally anti-tyrannical and anti-provincial vision of who God is and of God's saving purposes in the world.

Yet none of these ways in which they were not *modern* pacifists allows us to say they were non-pacifist or anti-pacifist. The presence of a pacifist 'impulse' is not denied by those who claim that Cadoux and Hornus exaggerate its normativity. There is no record of a militaristic, a machiavellian, or a crusading 'impulse.' There is not even an Augustinian statement.[42]

There is good evidence, on the other hand, of an 'impulse' towards loyalty to the empire, which in peacetime (and in apologetics) was not incompatible with the rejection of bloodshed. There is likewise evidence that with the passing of the generations, and with numerical growth, especially during the decades of respite between waves of persecution, the Church's disciplinary patterns relaxed, and martyrdom became a rhetorical ideal type rather than the real cost of discipleship. This certainly began before the end of the second century. Thus, the notion that 'Constantine' brought about an instantaneous flipflop, whereby the Church changed direction, is incorrect. The critical readers of history, beginning with the Joachimites and the radical Franciscans, then the Waldenses, then the Czech Brethren, did not invent the myth of the Constantinian turnaround. It had been introduced into the standard account of Christian imperial history by Eusebius, who considered it a good thing, in fact, an apocalyptically good thing, the beginning of the millennium. All that the 'radicals' did was to stand the already dominant myth on its head.[43] The shift that Constantine symbolizes had begun well before him, in the growth of loyalty to the empire and pastoral laxity,[44] and it was not concluded until a century after him, when imperial sanctions against pagans and against Donatists were normal. Even when the shift was complete, the 'pacifist impulse' did not disappear; it survived in the eremitic and monastic life, in the lifestyle enjoined upon Christian women, paupers, and slaves, in minorities called heretical, and among Jews.[45] It survived indirectly in the occasional efforts of bishops to mitigate the excesses of war by meditation, the Truce of God, and the Peace of God.[46]

Some say that in the middle of the third century Christians were 10 per cent of the population of the empire, and most of them (even according to the account of Helgeland et al.) were not soldiers. In the sixth century, thanks to the changed definition of the noun, 'Christians' may have comprised 95 per cent of the population, but still most of them were women, religious, paupers, and serfs, to whom killing was still forbidden. Then the total number of people called to the non-violent life must have been considerably larger than three centuries before. What the fourth-century shift changed was not the 'pacifist impulse' but the definition of 'Christian.'[47]

The 'pacifist impulse' survived as well in the strict version of the just war tradition that the pastoral concerns of the bishops beginning with Ambrose set out to develop. If war cannot be eschewed, perhaps it can be disciplined.[48] The just war tradition is the synthesis, which would have not arisen had the pacifist impulse not provided the antithesis.

Even when the story has advanced well into the next epoch, with Augustine as the unchallenged landmark, it is noteworthy that no wholehearted case is made for war as a good work, a moral imperative. Augustine's argument is negative legalism, not a clear imperative. War cannot be forbidden, he argues, because John the Baptist did not forbid it, Jesus did not scold the centurion, Peter did not tell Cornelius to resign, God may have providentially subjected you to an ungodly king, Christian emperors have conquered pagan nations, and the world is miserable anyway. There is in Augustine never a joyful Gospel confidence that bloodshed pleases or praises God; never a clear command (as there is later in Bernard). As Bainton summarizes about forty brief allusions[49] – never an entire treatise or even a dozen pages on the subject – Augustine's mood was a 'mournful' pastoral adjustment to a world of which we cannot in any case ask that God's will be done.[50] What has changed is not one ruling on *what* God's will is, but the entire setting in which doing God's will can be thought about. The Neoplatonic grid, according to which God's will cannot really be done,[51] and the sociology of the imperial Church, according to which 'Christian' means everybody, have defined a whole different world. There had been a profound change, but the issue of military service was not the centre of what it was about. That was just what the second-century writers would have said if they could have been there.

Notes

1 Adolf von Harnack, *Militia Christi: Die christliche Religion und der Soldaten-stand in den ersten drei Jahrhunderten* (Tübingen, 1905; Philadelphia, 1981).

2 C.J. Cadoux, *The Early Christian Attitude to War: A Contribution to the History of Christian Ethics* (London, 1919).

3 By no means do I assume that there are no texts that still await discovery. Yet the additional contributions to the debate since Cadoux have not been based on broader reading of the sources.

4 Peter Brock, *The Military Question in the Early Church: A Selected Bibliography of a Century's Scholarship* (Toronto, 1988).

5 Jacques Fontaine, 'Christians and Military Services in the Early Church,' in *Concilium* VII, Paulist (1965), 107–19.

6 James T. Johnson, *The Quest for Peace* (Princeton, 1987) says of Cadoux, and Helgeland says of Cadoux, Bainton, and Hornus that their readings are predisposed by their pacifism (John Helgeland, 'Christians and the Roman Army from Marcus Aurelius to Constantine,' in *Aufstieg und Niedergang der römischen Welt*, vol. 2, 23/1, 729–32). That is correct; but the opposite view is not exempt from the same critique. Part of the 'hermeneutical' self-awareness to which my title refers has to do with the need for a higher level of sophistication about method, which issues like this call for.

7 See my spectrum of 'pacifisms' in *Nevertheless: The Varieties of Religious Pacifism* (Scottdale, 1972; rev. ed. 1992). The essay by Martin Ceadel in this collection testifies to the degree of confusion that prevails in the use of the term.

8 Dennis Praeger, identified only as 'a radio speaker in Los Angeles,' in 'Judaism and Public Life: A Symposium,' in *First Things* no. 11 (March 1991), 29. Most of the people who did not kill Dr Mengele were in fact not pacifists. None of the people who say Mengele merited death prevented his atrocities. No pacifist I know of opposes preventing atrocities.

9 Maryknoll, 1986.

10 *The Peace Tradition in the Catholic Church* (New York, 1987).

11 'The Pope Shouldn't Buy "Peace at Any Price" Fallacy,' in *National Catholic Reporter* (15 March 1991), 7.

12 *Tranquillitas Ordinis* (New York, 1987), 344ff; *Catholicm and the Renewal of American Democracy* (New York, 1989), 163ff.

13 *Peace and Revolution* (Grand Rapids, 1988) 231ff, also 228ff in Michael Chromartie (ed.), *Peace Betrayed?* (Washington, 1990).

14 Johnson, *Quest for Peace*; see index under 'utopian.'

15 'Pacifism' thus defined is compatible with more than one view regarding the persistence of war in non-Christian societies, and regarding the Church's way of dealing pastorally with people who commit morally unacceptable behaviour. Some 'pacifists' think they can stop non-Christians from waging war, and others do not. The Ceadel essay in this volume suggests a taxonomy for clarifying the most proper meanings of the term. I doubt that such greater consistency in respecting the internal rules of a scholar's taxonomy will help to straighten out the problems posed by popular usage.

16 That shepherds weigh more than sheep tends to be more markedly the case in the more inclusive churches. It is not refuted but rather intensified by the fact that the shepherds often differ among themselves. Yet in more egalitarian churches it remains the case that some spokespersons are esteemed more representative than others.

17 That there were such men serving is clear. Were they the exception or the rule? Even those who make the most of their existence do not try to estimate how numerous they were. 'The historians all know and agree that the army on both sides [i.e., both under Constantine and under Licinius] had never drawn more than a handful of recruits from Christians.' Ramsey MacMullen, *Christianizing the Roman Empire, (AD 100–400)* (New Haven, 1984), 44. Yet for it to prove Helgeland's point there would have needed to be many of them.

18 'The few that truly call Thee Lord / And wait Thy sanctifying word / And Thee their utmost Savior own / Unite and perfect them in one / *In them let all mankind behold / How Christians lived in days of old* / Mighty their envious foes

to move / A proverb of reproach and love' (my emphasis). Charles Wesley, 'Jesus, from Whom All Blessings Flow.' Modern hymnal editors chose these from among twenty verses in two original poems both entitled, 'Primitive Christianity.'

19 Jonathan Z. Smith, *Drudgery Divine* (Chicago, 1990). Modern Jewish historians reviewing the same history in the same way still could claim the same right to be anti-Gentile, and Catholic historians anti-Protestant (and anti-modern).

20 See my *Priestly Kingdom* (Notre Dame, 1985), 127ff. The most naive avoidance of historical consciousness is to assume that one's own position is at the pinnacle of past progress. Numerous 'restitutionists' have been naive; but so is most progressivism. Helgeland et al. note (at 2) quite rightly that a theological case can be made against considering the New Testament (to say nothing of the belief and practice of the post-apostolic Christians) to be theologically normative; yet they do not argue that case, nor suggest what kind of arguments would count theologically if all historically rooted theological claims were to be set aside.

21 Origen, while refusing bloodshed, prayed for the emperor's prospering against his enemies. The Gospel love of enemy, the Jewish relativizing of Gentile nationhood, and the cosmopolitan monotheist relativizing of loyalty to the empire have by Origen's time all been diluted, *and yet* the rejection of killing remains.

22 The *term* 'Zealot' may first have been applied to the generation of Menahem in the war of 66ff. The phenomenon was, however, present in the time of Jesus' public ministry and helped to define his public choices, as is demonstrated by the fact that Luke (even if anachronistically) uses the term (6:15, Acts 1:13). Another case of the same kind is alluded to in Acts 21:38. Cf. my *Politics of Jesus* (Grand Rapids, 2nd ed., 1994), 97ff.

23 Lactantius, *Institutes* 6, cited in Arthur Holmes, *War and Christian Ethics* (Grand Rapids, 1975), 51ff.

24 Helgeland has studied 'Roman Army Religion' in depth. (*Aufstieg und Niedergang,* vol. 2, 16/2, 1470–1505). His characterization of 'religion' merges two dimensions: 'idolatry' as an offence against the honour of a jealous God and 'religion in the army' as a tyrannically all-encompassing community. Both are important in understanding the Christians' refusal; the former is most representative of the Jewish monotheist focus. The latter might be of no less theological importance.

25 'A desire to separate themselves from the world so as to live the morally pure life of the "new age" that they expected soon to dawn.' Johnson, *Quest for Peace*, 13. Likewise Robert L. Phillips: 'serene waiting in faith for the end of

the world,' *War and Justice* (Norman, 1984), 23. Such simple caricatures fly in the face of recent scholarship's concern to understand 'apocalyptic' as a world-view and a literary genre with its own dignity.

26 See the description of the critical stance of Christians within the Roman culture in Klaus Wengst, *Pax Romana* (Munich 1986), 73–166.

27 Harnack wrote in the *Theologische Literaturzeitung* (1921), 126, that Cadoux had taken account of all previous sources, including Harnack's own work, so that his work 'als Abschluss der Bemühungen über diese Frage gelten darf. Der Widerspruch des alten Christentums gegen den Krieg tritt noch schärfer hervor, und ich finde keinen Grund, dies für die altchristliche Theorie zu beanstanden.' David McInnes Gracie, who prefaced his Fortress Press translation of Harnack with a review of some other literature, treating Cadoux critically, omitted this positive statement about Cadoux from Harnack himself. So does Johnson, although he seems to say (*Quest for Peace*, 11 n24) that Harnack claimed to have set Cadoux aside.

28 See above note 6. The more accessible overview of the same argument, in John Helgeland, Robert J. Daly, and J. Patout Burns, *Christians and the Military: The Early Experience* (Philadelphia, 1985), is still briefer. In neither text are details of debatable translation or historical interpretation pursued. Nor are they acknowledged by Johnson, who simply repeats Helgeland.

29 Louis J. Swift, *The Early Fathers on War and Military Service* (Wilmington, 1983).

30 Johnson, *Quest for Peace*, 17–50.

31 I make no effort here to return thoroughly to the original sources; it must suffice to look more carefully at the accounts of Hornus and Helgeland.

32 Bainton's discussion of this point is in his *Christian Attitudes to War and Peace* (Nashville, 1961), 80ff. Helgeland (*Aufstieg*, 793) overdoes Bainton's use of the term 'police,' as if Bainton had meant to claim that there were two separate kinds of armed forces. The point is rather that the one army discharged many kinds of functions, most of them non-lethal and many of them unarmed.

33 Helgeland fails to note that the presence of Christians in army service raises the same problems of consistency in the light of his 'religious' explanation of the reason for not serving, centring on pagan cult, as would the 'moral' explanation centering on prohibited bloodshed. In either case most soldiers must have been unfaithful to the normative Christian vision. The difference is that according to the 'pacifist' thesis they were unfaithful only in wartime; according to the 'idolatry' thesis they were unfaithful regularly, unless dispensed ad hoc from normal cultic requirements.

34 Gracie (in the Introduction to Harnack, *Militia Christi*, at 15 quotes Mac-

Mullen: 'Many a recruit need never have struck a blow in anger, outside a tavern.' Johnson (*Quest for Peace*, 38–43) describes well the changing shape of the army.

35 Helgeland, whose general account I here have followed (*Aufstieg* version, 766ff., Fortress Press version, 31ff.) says that the legionnaires 'mopped up.' The sources do not say that. Jean M. Hornus, *It Is Not Lawful for Me to Fight: Early Christian Attitudes toward War, Violence, and the State* (Scottdale, Pa., 1980), at 129 considers the legend apocryphal.

36 Dom Gregory Dix, *The Treatise on the Apostolic Tradition of St Hippolytus* (London, 1968), vol. 16, no. 17, also translates 'execute,' also without explaining why he rejects the ordinary meaning 'kill,' or what the moral difference between 'killing' and 'executing' would be. The verbs in the oriental versions allow no such distinction. There is no reason that the difference of rendering would make the prohibition less 'pacifist.'

37 Swift, *Early Fathers*, 47.

38 Ibid., 161ff.

39 Helgeland et al. (at 37) write, 'It is the only place in all of Hippolytus' extant work where he mentions the topic of military service, an obvious indication of the apparently small importance he gave to it.' By the ordinary criteria of literary criticism the opposite would have to be the case. For a tradition listing forbidden professions to have been preserved within a corpus concerned mostly with worship patterns is a stronger index of authenticity and antiquity than if evaluating those professions ethically had been the compiler's current concern. The matter is clearly important for 'Hippolytus,' that is, for the clergy who made rules. There might be more grounds for arguing that despite the bishops' concerns for making rules, the rule was not obeyed, but that is not the point Helgeland is making.

40 The latest text is the most rigorous. It adds that one who has shed blood shall be excluded from the sacraments. Now it might be the case that Helgeland et al. could make an argument for their different translation of *occidere* or for ignoring the later, stronger witnesses to the Hippolytus tradition. They might make an argument to support the flat assertion that although killing even under direct order in peacetime is forbidden, killing in war to defend or expand the empire is still licit *e silentio*. What makes further scholarly (and ecumenical) dialogue cumbersome in this setting is that the questionable translations and assertions are not even argued.

41 Helgeland is certainly right that idolatry was a major reason for soldiers' disobedience, sometimes the only one mentioned. But he is not convincing when he presupposes without arguing it a thoroughgoing dichotomy

between 'religious' and 'moral' considerations, and thereby between idolatry and bloodshed as reasons for rejecting Caesar's service. This is one further way to underestimate the Jewishness of the first Christians.

42 What is meant by Augustine's reshaping of moral thought, so as to move the doable good from centre stage, is suggested more fully below.

43 The nature of the Constantinian shift is misunderstood when the ethics of war is made central. It was only a small part of a much larger transformation, including such matters as the validity of pagan religiosity, the value of missionary propagation of the faith, the special authority of clergy, the status of women, the shape and meaning of formal worship, the substance of individual religious experience, the meaning of conversion, the theological meaning of history, and the morality of wealth 135–47 in my *Priestly Kingdom*). Johnson (*Quest for Peace*, 95), misinterprets the issue by saying that it centres on 'all forms of Church involvement in the secular government of the world.'

44 See note 21 above on the beginnings of loyalty to empire.

45 It also continues in outspoken pacifist individuals like Paulinus of Nola and Victricius of Rouen, both bishops around 400 (Swift, *Early Fathers*, 152–6).

46 See Bainton, *Christian Attitudes*, 110ff., 116ff. Cf. the themes 'peace' and 'truce' in the index to Johnson, *Quest for Peace*.

47 Helgeland (*Aufstieg*, 818ff.) borrows from historians of religion the concepts of adherence versus conversion, or of native versus diaspora religion, as ways to describe how the meaning of being a Christian, and the meaning of monotheism, had changed. Just how the several patterns of classification work, to handle either causation or evaluation, would call for complex debate, but the point Helgeland makes is the same as mine. For one kind of Christian, Jesus' Lordship is radically normative; for the other, Jesus fits within a larger cosmos.

48 If so, there would need to be defined criteria to distinguish between the licit and the illicit, condemning the latter. This is the meaning of the just war tradition properly so-called, as it slowly evolved. There is also a non-strict version of the just war tradition, which while providing a vocabulary for political discourse does not name or sanction the illicit. The debate between the two versions was renewed in the 1950s in response to Hiroshima and again in response to the Persian Gulf War.

49 *Christian Attitudes to War and Peace* (Nashville, 1960), 98.

50 If it be argued that Augustine's views were not new, 'it becomes impossible to account for the time and space which Augustine (and others) devote to defending just war theory. That is, Augustine is very much on the *defensive* in these writings, suggesting that he is arguing against the settled view to the

contrary.' Phillips, *War and Justice*, 147. Phillips holds personally to a conservative version of the just war view.

51 Robert A. Markus, 'St Augustine's Views of the "Just War,"' in W.J. Shiels (ed.), *The Church and War* (Oxford, 1983), 1–12, accentuates that what is decisive for Augustine is a shift not in his ethics but in his general view of the world.

7

Anabaptists and the Sword Revisited: The Trend from Radicalism to Apoliticism[1]

JAMES M. STAYER

Michel Foucault's 'What Is an Author?'[2] expresses the standpoint of a new theory of criticism that insists that texts should stand on their own merits, without being tied to their authors. At the same time the trend in intellectual history has been to move away from forcing the writings of people in the past into systematic consistency. Instead of assuming that any thinker worth studying is consistent, the assumption now is that most interesting thinkers change their minds (which is not to say or imply that someone qualifies as an interesting thinker by changing his or her mind).

Anabaptists and the Sword[3] is loose in the world. I have moved away from its particular intellectual history methodology and from its implied neoconservative outlook, but I know that there are people around who prefer where I was in the years from 1972 to 1976 to where I am now,[4] and, to the extent that they are sound in their judgments, the text will hold its ground against the later vagaries of its author. In at least one respect it is superior to the present essay – it is more thoroughly researched.

'Anabaptists and the Sword Revisited' was not a book but an article by John Howard Yoder, that appeared in *Zeitschrift für Kirchengeschichte* in 1974, in a special issue devoted to the anniversary of the Peasants' War that was edited by Heiko Oberman.[5] The article was one of the last of Yoder's writings in Anabaptist studies before he moved on to other fields. It was, I have reason to believe, originally written as a response to Hans Hillerbrand's published Erlangen dissertation, *Gewaltlosigkeit in Taüfertum*,[6] and then revised into a response to my book of 1972. The result was that neither Hillerbrand's work nor mine was focused on very satisfactorily. Where Yoder was on very weak ground, I think, was in trying to synthesize a position on Anabaptist non-resistance that represented all 'mainstream Anabaptists' (by whom he meant the groups affiliated with Conrad Grebel, Michael Sattler, Pilgram Marpeck, Jacob Hutter, and Menno Simons), as though it had a historical existence, and the mainstream Anabaptists were one historical group. The works of Gottfried Seebass, Christoph Bornhäuser, Claus-Peter Clasen, Werner Packull, and Klaus Deppermann in various ways stressed the plurality of the Anabaptist phenomenon and the implausibility of excluding figures like Hans Hut and Melchior Hoffman, who did not exactly fit the non-resistant mould, from the story of Anabaptist origins.[7] However, Yoder was right, in a way that I have only grasped with greater distance, to complain about my approach in Anabaptists and the Sword, which was to treat the 'teaching on the Sword' as a theological standpoint to be detected not only in writings of leaders but to be inferred from the interrogation records of rank-and-file Anabaptists and from the behaviour of the various groups. He said, correctly I now think, that one could not (as I did) compare the views of schooled theologians like Luther, Zwingli, and Müntzer with the behaviour and occasional expressions of nonconformist laymen.[8]

Another major criticism might have been added, although Yoder was not of the right mind-set to do it – I refer to the objection of Rodney Sawatsky to my taking over and using 'apoliticism' in relation to Anabaptist non-resistance.[9] 'Apoliticism' implied quietism, detachment from the world and its business, which Fritz Blanke and Clarence Bauman assumed to be the quality of sixteenth-century Anabaptism,[10] while Walter Klaassen[11] and Sawatsky saw the early Anabaptist non-resistants to be involved in a radical rejection of the world, which was 'political' in any reasonable use of that term. Here I ran into the difference between the perspectives of two generations of North American Mennonites, an older generation that tried to relate to the surrounding society with conservative withdrawal and a younger one that opted for radical critique.[12] Each found justification in the sixteenth-century Anabaptist heritage for its particular approach. Anabaptists and the Sword fudged the difference between these two perspectives (without knowing that that was what it was doing) when it declared both apoliticism and radicalism to be typical of sixteenth-century Anabaptism and their point of intersection to be the most typical expression of sixteenth-century Anabaptism.[13] The problem was that I was here taking a static view of Anabaptism from the 1520s to the 1560s. Later interpreters of the subject like Hans-Jürgen Goertz have shown me that instead of seeking a static resolution of the tension between radicalism and apoliticism, I ought to have recognized that there was a dynamic tendency from radicalism to apoliticism.[14] But my research was by no means totally independent of the Bender school that had preceded it. Hence, I concurred with Bender and Yoder and Heinold Fast[15] that an original Grebel-Sattler line crystallized early in Anabaptism (specifically in 1527 with the Seven Articles of Schleitheim) and that this normative non-resistance outlasted and survived all its competitors, because it was best fitted for survival as the most appropriate expression of the sectarian experience in a world of hostile governments and social majorities. It is precisely that conclusion that, I think, stands in need of re-examination and qualification.

The big problem with accepting the well-known Article Six of the Schleitheim Articles as an Anabaptist norm is that there was a relative lack of interest in the subject among early Anabaptists in comparison with believers' baptism, anticlerical ecclesiology, separation from the world, administration of the ban, or personal holiness. In the writings of Conrad Grebel there are virtually no relevant expressions, except for his aside about true Christian believers being sheep for slaughter and his admonishing postscript about not using the fist, in the letter of September 1524 to Müntzer.[16] This comment can be taken as a caution against becoming involved in the violence of the early Reformation and Peasants' War, but it was co-signed by Heini Aberli, who was, at least to some degree, implicated in a prime example of what was warned against, the defence of Waldshut against the Habsburgs.[17] Pilgram Marpeck has no writings on non-resistance, only passing remarks fending off Schwenckfeld's or Bucer's attempts to push him into a corner on the subject[18] – unless, indeed, he is, as Walter Klaassen argues, the author of the anonymous *Uncovering of the Babylonian Whore*,[19] a strident attack on the Protestant estates' willingness to resist the emperor through the Schmalkaldic League, after Luther's innumerable admonitions not to resist higher authorities. Balthasar Hubmaier, who wrote many books on baptism, has one book, *On the Sword*,[20] opposing a standpoint recognizable as that of the Schleitheim Articles. Hans Hut does not mention the topic of non-resistance in his few writings; he explicitly rejects the Schleitheim Articles under interrogation in Augsburg, following his arrest in late 1527, but, since he was a disingenuous witness in those hearings, it is hard to know in which of his statements he was merely throwing sand in the eyes of his interrogators.[21] In the numerous extant writings of Melchior Hoffman, non-resistance is simply not a topic. He does appear to have made a vocational distinction between his immediate sectarian followers, who were to set an example of obedience to constituted authority, and godly rulers or magistrates, who wielded the sword as a matter of course.[22] Bernhard Rothmann, the Münster ideologist, wrote a tract on the apocalyptic vengeance of the people of God.[23] With Menno Simons the subject virtually disappears, with no writings devoted to it.[24] Numerous asides show that Menno Simons opposed war and rebellion, whether that of dynasts or militant Anabaptists,[25] but in early writings Menno Simons approved 'the ordinary sword of government' and even intervention in church affairs by godly rulers.[26] Only in the last decade of his life does Menno Simons draw the line against capital punishment on the part of Christian rulers.[27] The existence of Christian rulers he took for granted throughout his life.

If we do not, heeding Yoder's criticism, apply methods of analysis only appropriate to school theology to these statements but look at them as early Anabaptist responses to the wars of the Reformation era, we should consider Anabaptist attitudes towards the Peasants' War, the Schmalkaldic League and eventual Schmalkaldic War, the siege of Münster and related events in the Netherlands, and the Dutch war of independence against Spain. Anabaptists and many persons who later became Anabaptists had a bad experience in the Peasants' War.[28] Anabaptists were involved in the Peasants' War in Waldshut, as well as in the rural territories of Schaffhausen and St Gallen, most notably in Hallau, a village subject to Schaffhausen.[29] The bitter aftermath of the Peasants' War helped Grebel and Blaurock to recruit Anabaptists in the Grüningen territory of Zurich, Hans Hut to win adherents to Anabaptism in Franconia, and his various lieutenants to do the same in Hesse and Thuringia.[30] The uprising of Michael Gaismair, the Anabaptist mission of Georg Blaurock, and the emergence of Jakob Hutter as an Anabaptist leader all took place in the same small area of the south Tyrol and were intertwined in various ways, only some of which can be established from the surviving evidence.[31] In general, although not unanimously, the Anabaptists who had participated in the Peasants' War repudiated it and regarded its outcome as a judgment of God on the mixture of religious and worldly motives among the commoners who had attempted in that way to create a new order based on the Gospel.[32] But in 1534 and 1535 in Münster and the Netherlands, in areas of the Germanic world untouched by the Peasants' War, Anabaptists inspired by apocalyptic hopes became much more violently involved in a militant struggle against established authority than had been the case in

1525–6.[33] This terrible experience led David Joris to seek a way to renounce militancy without exactly renouncing the militants, and Menno Simons to denounce both the Münster experience and the leaders of the 'corrupt sects' engaged in it, while offering refuge and consolation to the deluded rank and file.[34] The background of the Peasants' War led the anonymous author of the *Uncovering of the Babylonian Whore* to predict that rebellion of the Protestant princes against the emperor would lead to even more bloodshed than in 1525[35] – a point on which he was wrong, at least so far as the sixteenth century was concerned. The brutal Habsburg persecution of Anabaptists of all sects in the Netherlands – which still awaits precise quantitative study[36] – precluded a similar response of peaceful Anabaptists to the Dutch war of independence. Waterlander congregations assisted Prince William of Orange financially with a free gift 'for the advancement of the common cause.'[37] In the period from the *Uncovering* (ca. 1530) to the later century the Anabaptist stance on Protestant wars had shifted from radical rejection to the non-violent assistance allowed by the forms of apoliticism (and it hardly needs to be added that those in authority were usually quite agreeable to having the heirs of the Münsterites remain apolitical).

In this framework Article Six of Schleitheim becomes a problem calling for historical explanation, rather than the force that generated the norm of Anabaptist non-resistance and that somehow accounts for it. Arnold Snyder has outlined the process by which Mennonite interpreters of the late nineteenth and twentieth centuries gradually developed the unproven contention that the Schleitheim Articles were the progenitor spirit behind sixteenth-century Anabaptism, articulating 'characteristic Anabaptist emphases.' But his textual study of the distribution of the Schleitheim Articles leads him to the conclusion that in the sixteenth century 'the Schleitheim Articles were considered important only by a minority of Anabaptists.'[38] Despite a fair amount of periodical literature on the subject, there is no generally accepted account of the motives that led the leaders to agree as they did at Schleitheim. It remains in dispute whether their purpose was to distinguish Anabaptists from other Protestants, one Anabaptist group from others, 'pure' Anabaptism from impure elements to be excluded, or some combination of these.[39] It is tempting to regard Article Six as a chastened response to the militancy of 1525, when so many Anabaptists or future Anabaptists were involved on the side of the commoners, but this is a speculation. It is also worth considering that Article Six, by its teaching on the non-Christian character of the ruler, may have had as one of its objects the pre-

vention of rulers becoming 'principal members' of Anabaptist congregations as they were in Protestant churches.[40] The early Swiss Anabaptists seem to have directed a similar exclusion at *rentiers*, persons
living on income from invested wealth without working.[41] Against the
background of the Peasants' War this principled exclusion of rulers
from Christian congregations must be regarded as radically provocative, and it was so regarded at the time by rulers and theologians of
established Protestant churches.[42]

In the regions north of the Main River the Schleitheim Articles, specifically Article Six, do not appear to have been a topic of discussion among
Anabaptists. This was the case with Melchior Rinck and his followers
and with the followers of Melchior Hoffman and all the Melchiorite successor groups. The Melchiorite groups concerned themselves, up to the
death of Menno Simons, with the doctrine of Christ's heavenly flesh,
with whether or not to practise believers' baptism, with whether or not to
practise polygamy, with the identity of the promised David, with the
application of the ban among married couples – but not with the Schleitheim Articles.[43] The Schleitheim Articles only came north in 1560,
accompanying descriptions of the martyrdom of Michael Sattler, and
they appear to have gained authority in connection with Sattler's martyr
testimony.[44]

The Schleitheim Articles gained hostile attention from Hubmaier and
from Hut (if his interrogation record is to be trusted). They were cited by
Marpeck's associate Leupold Scharnschlager;[45] and allusions to the substance of Article Six appear as an Appendix to Hans Denck's *On the True
Love*.[46] In relation to Denck's expressions, it has been questioned
whether they softened the legalism of the Seven Articles (they probably
did) and whether or not they might be apocryphal addenda (they are
probably authentic).[47]

When Zwingli polemicized against the Schleitheim Articles in his
Elenchus in the year of their appearance, he assumed that they were
widely circulated. Evidence of the influence of Article Six in the territories of Bern is that its substance was made an issue for debate between
the Reformed pastors and the Anabaptists in Zofingen (1532) and Bern
(1538). In these disputations the Anabaptist participants adhered strictly
to the arguments and proof texts of Schleitheim, Article Six, elaborating
it chiefly by their contrast between the ethical requirements of the Old
Testament and New Testament.[48]

The early traditions of Swiss Anabaptism accompanied the flight into
Moravia to escape persecution that was undertaken by many Swiss and

South German Anabaptists in the late 1520s. Thus, we find the only independent tradition of the Zurich baptisms of January 1525 in the *Hutterite Chronicle*.[49] The Schleitheim Articles were reproduced in Hutterite codices,[50] and in the sectarian disputes that marked the beginning of the Anabaptist century in Moravia, non-resistance as outlined in Article Six was a prominent factor. An issue that may have helped to push Schleitheim, Article Six, into the spotlight was resistance against the Turks and the war tax levied to finance it. Lord Leonhard von Liechtenstein, the 'principal member' of Hubmaier's Anabaptist congregation in Moravia, had a duty to help his ruler wage war against the Turks; Sattler in his last trial told his Habsburg tormentors that they were Turks 'after the spirit,' while the Ottomans were merely Turks 'after the flesh,' and many of Hut's followers looked on the Turks as instruments of God's vengeance in the apocalyptic *finale*.[51] Resistance against a 'war tax,' unique to Moravian Anabaptism,[52] implies resistance to the ongoing Turkish war for which that tax was intended. So Hubmaier opposed Schleitheim, Article Six, in his *On the Sword*; and the Austerlitz *Stäbler*, Clemens Adler, wrote a tract in 1529 against Hubmaier's *Schwertler*, elaborating upon and extending the positions of Schleitheim, Article Six. It is significant that this first treatise on non-resistance was written in Moravia, not Switzerland.[53] The Schleitheim formulae of non-resistance went into Hutterite writings, were upheld in Peter Riedemann's *Account of Our Religion, Doctrine, and Faith*,[54] and were engulfed in a more extensive, less discriminating mustering of proof texts in the *Five Articles* of 1547[55] and in Peter Walpot's *Great Articlebook* (ca. 1577).[56] Here for the first time we have writings on Anabaptist non-resistance comparable in extent to those devoted to other characteristic themes of the movement.

This is only the faintest beginning of an explanation of the striking of the theme of Anabaptist non-resistance in Schleitheim, Article Six, and of the assessment of its influence in sixteenth-century Anabaptism. My impression, that I will not try to document here, is that at first the topic of Anabaptist rejection of the sword, in both its implications, rejection of killing and rejection of rulers, bulked larger in anti-Anabaptist polemics than among the Anabaptists themselves. It was the sort of thing Zwingli, Bucer, Calvin, and Schwenckfeld were glad to hold against the Anabaptists. It was certainly present, but not really prominent, among early Swiss Anabaptists, and it became an embroidered and elaborated theme at first only among the Hutterites. As Anabaptist non-resistance turned out, it went well with the later Anabaptist-Mennonite experience of a tolerated sectarian life encapsulated in a host community to which the nonconformists owed a certain qualified gratitude. To the extent that the Hutterites anticipated this encapsulated sectarian life, it was appropriate that they should have pioneered in transmuting the undoubted radicalism of Sattler's purpose at Schleitheim into something that can sensibly be labelled 'apoliticism.'

The notion that a teaching of non-resistance essentially based upon Schleitheim, Article Six, was the expression of a sixteenth-century 'Anabaptist minority' and that it gained genuine confessional status only through twentieth-century Anabaptist research (abetted and confirmed by my *Anabaptists and the Sword*) has been advanced in published statements by Hans-Jürgen Goertz and Howard Loewen.[57] It is a noteworthy but insufficiently subtle conclusion. The issue of whether a majority or a minority of Anabaptists were non-resistants in the sixteenth century is a badly posed research question – dictated by Mennonite or Brethren concerns in the twentieth century about whether their historic peace testimonies had majority or minority support in their denominational constituencies. Among Swiss Anabaptists non-resistance seems at first to have been a lesser teaching, imperfectly understood despite the Schleitheim Articles and, hence, not unanimously held. It was not in the beginning a 'sectarian distinctive' for Anabaptists in Switzerland. In the disparate Anabaptist sects in south and central Germany it was apparently no more than a peripheral issue. In Moravia, however, which became the major Anabaptist centre in the southern German-speaking territories, non-resistance established itself as a 'sectarian distinctive,' a principal article of faith, early in the Anabaptist settlement there. Here the radical, non-resistant *Stäbler* clearly outweighed the more conservative *Schwertler*. In the first three decades of Melchiorite Anabaptism in the north, during part of which Anabaptism became a militant mass movement, the question of whether Anabaptism was to be warlike or peaceful was an urgent, essential one, but the distinctive ideas of Anabaptist non-resistance in its specific sense were unknown. Afterward, however, in the tolerated sectarian life of second-generation Mennonites such ideas became very widely disseminated. The question of whether a majority of Anabaptists were 'non-resistant,' or even the better posed question of whether a majority were peaceful, cuts across the grain of the sixteenth-century reality. The real issue was whether the sixteenth-century Anabaptists were socially radical (whether non-resistant or militant) or socially quietistic (whether they sought exemption from military service or not), and the real story of sixteenth-century Anabaptism is of the trend away from radicalism towards quietism.

Notes

1 First published in translation as, 'Noch einmal besichtigt: Anabaptists and the Sword. Von der Radikalität zum Quietismus,' *Mennonistische Geschichtsblätter* 47 (1990/91), 24–37.

2 Michel Foucault, 'What Is an Author?' in Josué V. Harari (ed.), *Textual Strategies: Perspectives in Post-Structuralist Criticism* (Ithaca, 1979), 141–60.

3 James M. Stayer, *Anabaptists and the Sword* (Lawrence, 1972). A 2nd printing in 1973 corrected typographical errors; a 2nd ed. (1976) added introductory 'Reflections and Retractions,' xi–xxxiii.

4 Vernard Eller, *Christian Anarchy: Jesus' Primacy over the Powers* (Grand Rapids, 1987), 32–40.

5 John H. Yoder, '"Anabaptists and the Sword" Revisited: Systematic Historiography and Undogmatic Nonresistants,' *Zeitschrift für Kirchengeschichte* 85 (1974), 270–83. The discussion between Yoder and me was continued at the Institute of Mennonite Studies, 28–9 June 1977, Goshen, Indiana. Two unpublished papers of mine, 'Anabaptist Nonresistance and the Rewriting of History: On the Changing Historical Reputation of the Schleitheim Articles and the Four Hundred Fiftieth Anniversary of Hans Denck's *Concerning Genuine Love*' and 'Anabaptist Nonresistance and the Rewriting of History: Or, Is John Yoder's Conception of Anabaptist Nonresistance Historically Sound?' are held by the Mennonite Historical Library, Goshen College, Goshen, Indiana.

6 Hans J. Hillerbrand, *Die Politische Ethik des Oberdeutschen Täufertums* (Leyden and Cologne, 1962).

7 Gottfried Seebass, 'Müntzers Erbe. Werk, Leben und Theologie des Hans Hut (gest. 1527),' unpublished Habilitationsschrift, University of Erlangen (1972); Christoph Bornhäuser, *Leben und Lehre Menno Simons'* (Neukirchen-Vluyn 1973); Claus-Peter Clasen, *Anabaptism: A Social History, 1525–1618 – Switzerland, Austria, Moravia, and South and Central Germany* (Ithaca and London; 1972); Werner O. Packull, *Mysticism and the Early South German-Austrian Anabaptist Movement, 1525–1531* (Scottdale, 1977); Klaus Deppermann, *Melchior Hoffman: Soziale Unruhen und apokalyptische Visionen im Zeitalter der Reformation* (Gottingen, 1979). Additional facets of the Anabaptist phenomenon were illuminated by later works like Heinrich Beulshausen, *Die Geschichte der osthessischen Täufergemeinden* (Giessen, 1981); S. Zijlstra, *Nicolaas Meyndertsz van Blesdijk: Een bijdrage tot de geschiedenis van het Davidjorisme* (Assen, 1983); Gary K. Waite, *David Joris and Dutch Anabaptism, 1524–1543* (Waterloo, 1990).

8 Yoder, '"Anabaptists and the Sword" Revisited,' 129–30; 'Thus by definition the temptation is to compare what cannot be fairly compared: On the one hand, careful, measured thought from the pens of professional intellectuals,

and on the other statements wrung under torture from fugitive preachers and recently converted peasants. Ideals on the one hand ... and immediate practical situational decisions on the other.'

9 Rodney Sawatsky, review of *Anabaptists and the Sword* in the *Mennonite* (29 Oct. 1974).

10 Fritz Blanke, 'Anabaptism and the Reformation,' in Guy E. Hershberger (ed.), *The Recovery of the Anabaptist Vision* (H.S. Bender *Festschrift*) (Scottdale 1957), 68, where he uses the term 'apolitism'; Clarence Bauman, *Gewaltlosigkeit im Täufertum* (Leyden 1968), 274–90, devotes a chapter to 'Täuferische Apolitie.'

11 Walter Klaassen, 'The Nature of the Anabaptist Protest,' *Mennonite Quarterly Review* 45 (1971), 291–311.

12 See James M. Stayer, 'The Easy Demise of a Normative Vision of Anabaptism,' in Calvin Wall Redekop and Samuel J. Steiner (eds.), *Mennonite Identity: Historical and Contemporary Perspectives* (Lanham, New York, and London 1988), 109–16.

13 Stayer, *Anabaptists*, 337: '*The essential qualities of the early Anabaptist teaching on the Sword were apoliticism and radicalism.* The most typical Anabaptist stance was one like that of Sattler and Ridemann which was both radical and apolitical.'

14 Hans-Jürgen Goertz, 'The Confessional Heritage in Its New Mold: What Is Mennonite Self-Understanding Today?' in Redekop and Steiner, *Mennonite Identity*, 3–6, describes a 'crisis of the Mennonites' in which the sectarian distinction of refusing to bear arms changed from being a 'great refusal' directed against the Christian-feudal order into a special privilege bestowed by subsequent bourgeois society. Thus, in his view, Anabaptist non-resistance became apolitical by virtue of its loss of 'any basis in social experience.' (Goertz does not use the term 'apolitical,' but I think it corresponds with his intention to apply it to the period when Anabaptist non-resistance had lost the immediate social relevance that originally called it into being.)

15 See John H. Yoder, 'Der Kristallisationspunkt des Täufertums,' *Mennonitische Geschichtsblätter* 24 (1972), 35–47; Heinold Fast, '"Die Wahrheit wird euch freimachen": Die Anfänge der Täuferbewegung in Zürich,' *Mennonitische Geschichtsblätter* 27 (1975), 7–33. Behind Yoder, Fast, and my *Anabaptists and the Sword* is the common assumption, voiced in Harold Bender's review of Beatrice Jenny's book on the Schleitheim Articles that they stated 'characteristic Anabaptist emphases,' *Archiv für Reformationsgeschichte* 47 (1956), 136.

16 Leonhard von Muralt and Walter Schmid (eds.), *Quellen zur Geschichte der Täufer in der Schweiz*, vol. 1, Zürich (Zurich, 1952), 17, 20.

17 Johann Loserth, 'Die Stadt Waldshut und die vorderösterreichische

Regierung in den Jahren 1523–2526,' *Archiv für österreichische Geschichte* 77 (1891), 102–3; von Muralt and Schmid, *Quellen ... Zürich*, 196.

18 Johann Loserth (ed.), *Quellen und Forschungen zur Geschichte der oberdeutschen Taufgesinnten im 16. Jahrhundert: Pilgram Marpeck's Antwort auf Kaspar Schwenckfelds Beurteilung des Buches der Bundesbezeugung von 1542* (Vienna and Leipzig, 1929), 303–4; Manfred Krebs and Hans Georg Rott (eds.), *Quellen zur Geschichte der Täufer*, vol. 7, *Elsass 1 (Stadt Strassburg, 1522–1532)* (Gütersloh, 1959), 505–6.

19 Text in Hans J. Hillerbrand, 'An Early Treatise on the Christian and the State,' *Mennonite Quarterly Review* 32 (1958), 34–47; Walter Klaassen, 'Eine Untersuchung der Verfasserschaft und des historischen Hintergrundes der Täuferschrift "Aufdeckung der Babylonischen Hurn ...,"' in Alfred Raddatz and Kurt Lüthi (eds.), *Evangelischer Glaube und Geschichte: Grete Mecenseffy zum 85, Geburtstag* (Vienna, 1984), 113–29; James M. Stayer, *The German Peasants' War and Anabaptist Community of Goods* (Montreal and Kingston, 1991), 118–20, 207–8.

20 Gunar Westin and Torsten Bergsten (eds.), *Quellen zur Geschichte der Täufer*, vol. 9, *Balthasar Hubmaier Schriften* (Gütersloh 1962), 432–57. H. Wayne Pipkin and John H. Yoder (trans. and eds.), *Balthasar Hubmaier: Theologian of Anabaptism* (Scottdale 1989), 492–523.

21 Christian Meyer, 'Zur Geschichte der Wiedertäufer in Oberschwaben, 1: Die Anfänge des Wiedertäuferthums in Augsburg,' *Zeitschrift des Histori-schen Vereins für Schwaben und Neuburg* 1 (1874), 227–8; Packull, *Mysticism*, 119–21.

22 Melchior Hoffman, *Die eedele hoghe ende troostlike sendebrief, den die heylige Apostel Paulus to den Romeren gescreuen heeft, verclaert ...* (n.p., 1533), T8vo–Vro. There is a lost tract, *von dem swert*, in which Hoffman 'clarified for everyone to what extent it is proper to be obedient to the sword,' presumably in terms that correspond with early Wittenberg influences on his preaching. See James M. Stayer, 'Melchior Hoffman and the Sword,' *Mennonite Quarterly Review* 45 (1971), 265–77.

23 'Bericht van der Wrake,' in Robert Stupperich (ed.), *Die Schriften Bernhard Rothmanns* (Münster 1970), 284–97.

24 *Against the Blasphemy of Jan of Leyden* is devoted to the characteristically Melchiorite topic of King Jan's claim to be the 'promised David.' Besides, there are difficult problems concerning its authenticity. See James M. Stayer, 'Oldeklooster and Menno,' *Sixteenth Century Journal* 9/1 (1978), 65–6.

25 Menno Simons, *Opera Omnia Theologica* (Amsterdam, 1681), 55, 148–9, and *Dat fundament der christelycker leere* (Amsterdam, 1616), ff. 96vo–97ro

26 Menno Simons, *Fundament*, sig. A, ff. 99vo–100ro, 112vo–113vo; Menno, *Opera*, 520. This finding is confirmed by Bornhäuser, *Menno Simons*, 121–32.

27 Menno Simons, *Opera*, 603.

28 James M. Stayer, 'Anabaptists and Future Anabaptists in the Peasants' War,' *Mennonite Quarterly Review* 62 (1988), 99–139; updated and expanded in Stayer, *German Peasants' War*, 61–92, 186–200.

29 James M. Stayer, 'Reublin and Brötli, the Revolutionary Beginnings of Swiss Anabaptism,' in Marc Lienhard (ed.), *The Origins and Characteristics of Anabaptism* (The Hague, 1977), 83–102.

30 Matthias Hui, 'Vom Bauernaufstand zur Täuferbewegung: Entwicklungen in der ländlichen Reformation am Beispiel des zürcherischen Grüninger Amtes,' *Mennonitische Geschichtsblätter* 46 (1989), 113–44; Gottfried Seebass, 'Bauernkrieg und Täufertum in Franken,' *Zeitschrift für Kirchengeschichte* 85 (1974), 284–300.

31 Werner Packull, 'Die Anfänge des Täufertums im Tirol,' in Günter Vogler (ed.), *Wegscheiden der Reformation: Alternatives Denken vom 16. bis zum 18. Jahrhundert* (Weimar, 1994), 179–209.

32 Meyer, 'Anfänge,' 241–2 (Hans Hut); Georg Berbig, 'Die Wiedertäufer im Amt Königsberg in Franken 1527/1528,' *Deutsche Zeitschrift für Kirchenrecht* 35 (1903), 312 (Georg Volk); Günther Franz (ed.), *Urkundliche Quellen zur hessischen Reformationsgeschichte*, vol. 4, *Wiedertäuferakten, 1527–1626* (Marburg, 1951), 64–71 (Sorga congregation).

33 For an overview of the literature, see James M. Stayer, 'Was Dr Kuehler's Conception of Early Dutch Anabaptism Historically Sound? The Historical Discussion of Münster 450 Years Later,' *Mennonite Quarterly Review* 60 (1986), 261–88. The most recent significant treatment is by R. Po-chia Hsia, 'Münster and the Anabaptists,' in R. Po-chia Hsia (ed.), *The German People and the Reformation* (Ithaca and London, 1988), 51–69.

34 James M. Stayer, 'Davidite vs. Mennonite,' *Mennonite Quarterly Review* 58 (1984), 459–76; Stayer, 'Oldeklooster and Menno,' 51–67.

35 Hillerbrand, 'Treatise,' 37: 'Werden noch mit grösserm vnn erschröcklicherm blutuergiessen / als im Bauernkrieg beschehen.'

36 Clasen, *Anabaptism*, 358–422, esp. 372–3, shows the prominence of the Habsburgs in Anabaptist persecution in the southern part of German-speaking Europe.

37 W.J. Kühler, *Geschiedenis der Nederlandsche doopsgezinden in de zestiende eeuw* (Haarlem, 1961), 339–42. Peter Brock, *Freedom from Violence: Sectarian Nonresistance from the Middle Ages to the Great War* (Toronto, 1991), 101–3.

38 Arnold Snyder, 'The Influence of the Schleitheim Articles on the Anabaptist Movement: An Historical Evaluation,' *Mennonite Quarterly Review* 63 (1989), 323–44.

39 Fritz Blanke, 'Beobachtungen zum älteste Täuferbekenntnis,' *Archiv für Refor-*

mationsgeschichte 37 (1940), 242–9; Beatrice Jenny, *Das Schleitheimer Täuferbe-kenntnis* (Thayngen, 1951); H.W. Meihuizen, 'Who Were the "False Brethren" Mentioned in the Schleitheim Articles?' *Mennonite Quarterly Review* 41 (1967), 200–20; Yoder, 'Kristallisationspunkt,' 35–47; Klaus Deppermann, 'Die Strass-burger Reformatoren und die Krise des oberdeutschen Täufertums im Jahr 1527.' *Mennonitische Geschichtsblätter* 30 (1973), 24–41; John H. Yoder and Klaus Deppermann, 'Ein Briefwechsel über die Bedeutung des Schleitheimer Bekenntnisses,' *Mennonitische Geschichtsblätter* 30 (1973), 42–52.

40 This is implied in the concern that all members of an Anabaptist congrega-tion be like-minded with Christ, 'darmit kein spaltung in dem lip sige, dar mit er zerstöret werde.' Heinold Fast (ed.), *Quellen zur Geschichte der Täufer in der Schweiz*, vol. 2, *Ostschweiz* (Zurich, 1973), 32–3.

41 Stayer, *German Peasants' War*, 95–106, 200–3, esp. 98–9.

42 Clasen, *Anabaptism*, 180: 'Yes, if the peasants were told that their lords, ser-vants, and priests were not Christians and would not be saved, they would soon seize us, tear our hair, and strike us to the ground.'

43 William E. Keeney, *The Development of Dutch Anabaptist Thought and Practice from 1539–1564* (Nieuwkoop, 1968) is a North American Mennonite attempt to correct Dutch historiography by applying a Schleitheim model to early Dutch Anabaptism. See the polemical assessment of Keeney's book in Stayer, *Anabaptists*, 319–20 n40.

44 Samuel Cramer (ed.), *Bibliotheca Reformatoria Neerlandica – Geschriften uit den tijd der Hervorming in de Nederlanden* (The Hague: 1909), vol. 5, 585–6. The let-ter written in 1557 to Menno Simons by the Rhineland ministers, Zyllis and Lemke, is the unique contemporary source that establishes Michael Sattler's authorship of the Schleitheim Articles. Abraham Hulshof, *Geschiedenis van de Doopsgezinden te Straatsburg van 1525 tot 1557*, published ThD dissertation, Amsterdam University (1905), 229.

45 'Ein Frag – Ihr wollet nicht dass ein Christ möge ein Oberer werden,' in *Kunstbuch*, ms. copy by Samuel Geiser, Mennonite Historical Library, Gos-hen, Indiana, 285–6.

46 Georg Baring and Walter Fellmann (eds.), *Quellen zur Geschichte der Täufer*, vol. 6, *Denck Schriften* (Gütersloh, 1955–60), part 2, 83–6; trans. in Edward Furcha (ed.), *Selected Writings of Hans Denck* (Philadelphia 1976), 114–19.

47 In my view the scattered challenges to the authenticity of the material cited in note 45 are very weak. There is continuity of style and content; for instance, the discussion on non-resistance appears in both the disputed and the undis-puted part of the tract. See the critical discussion in *Denck Schriften*, part 1, 34–6; Robert Friedmann, 'Eine dogmatische Hauptschrift der hutterischen

Täufergemeinschaften in Mähren,' *Archiv für Reformationsgeschichte* 29 (1932), 9–17.

48 Fritz Blanke (ed.), Huldreich Zwingli, 'In catabaptistarum strophas elenchus,' in Emil Egli, etc. (eds.), *Huldreich Zwinglis s mtliche Werke*, vol. 6, part 1 (Zurich 1982), 1–196. Blanke's editorial comment is that 'die Schleitheimer Konfession schon fünf Monate nach ihrer Entstehung stark verbreitet war.' Martin Haas (ed.), *Quellen zur Geschichte der Täufer in der Schweiz*, vol. 4, *Drei Täufergespräche* (Zurich 1974), 189–97, 419–39. For other evidence of the influence of Schleitheim, Article Six, on early Swiss Anabaptist spokesmen, see Stayer, *Anabaptists*, 125–7.

49 A.J.F. Zieglschmid (ed.), *Die älteste Chronik der Hutterischen Brüder* (Ithaca 1943), 47; trans. *The Chronicle of the Hutterian Brethren* (Rifton 1987), vol. 1, 45. See H.W. Meihuizen, 'De Bronnen voor een Geschiedenis van de eerste doperse Doopstoediening,' *Doopsgezinde Bijdragen*, no. 1 (1975), 54–61; Heinold Fast, 'Wie doopte Konrad Grebel?,' *Doopgezinde Bijdragen*, no. 4 (1978), 22–31; James M. Stayer, 'Was There a Klettgau Letter of 1530?,' *Mennonite Quarterly Review* 61 (1987), 75–6.

50 Snyder, 'Influence of Schleitheim,' 336, n41.

51 Arnold Snyder, 'The Schleitheim Articles in Light of the Revolution of the Common Man: Continuation or Departure?' *Sixteenth Century Journal* 16 (1985), 430, n33; Packull, *Mysticism*, 88–9, 135–6.

52 Hillerbrand, *Politische Ethik*, 70–3.

53 See the short description in Stayer, *Anabaptists*, 169–70. The text, entitled, 'Das Urteil von dem Schwert mit unterschidlichem gewalt dreier furstenthum der Welt, Juden vnd Christen,' is unpublished. I used a ms. copy by Samuel Geiser in the Mennonite Historical Library, Goshen, Indiana.

54 Peter Riedemann, *Account of Our Religion, Doctrine, and Faith ...* (Bungay, 1950), 105–7, 113, 217, 220.

55 Zieglschmid, *Älteste Chronik*, 296–308; *Chronicle*, I, 276–86.

56 Robert Friedmann (ed.), *Quellen zur Geschichte der Täufer*, 12: *Glaubenszeugnisse oberdeutscher Taufgesinnter* (Gütersloh 1967), vol. 2, 230–98.

57 Hans-Jürgen Goertz, 'Zwischen Zwietracht und Eintracht: Zur Zweideutigkeit täuferischer und mennonitischer Bekenntnisse,' *Mennonitische Geschichtsblätter* 43–4 (1986–7), 23; Howard J. Loewen, *One Lord, One Church, One Hope, and One God: Mennonite Confessions of Faith* (Elkhart 1985), 27–8.

8

The Brethren and Non-resistance

DONALD F. DURNBAUGH

On 16 June 1705 the Swiss Reformed pastor and the mayor of the village of Frenkendorf, near Basel, complained to the Basel city council that a certain Andreas Boni (1673–1741) was causing trouble. A native of Frenkendorf and a weaver by trade, Boni had as a journeyman lived in Heidelberg, where he came into contact with Radical Pietist views. After his wife's death, Boni returned to his home, where he communicated his new convictions to others, first of all to his family. The local officials expressed fear that a dissenting movement would spread rapidly unless it were immediately checked.[1]

According to the pastor and mayor, Boni was guilty of three 'Anabaptist' errors: (1) he refused to bear arms or drill with the militia, (2) he categorically rejected the taking of oaths, and (3) he renounced the sacrament of Holy Communion. More than a year later, during which Boni was again in the Palatinate, the pastor complained again. He reported that Boni had shown up at a service of infant baptism and publicly challenged the pastor with the New Testament ('which he always carries with him') to prove where pedobaptism and godparents were commanded. At the time he was not wearing the customary sidearm bayonet. Boni and his brother were haled before the Basel magistrates. Their interrogation revealed that Boni had often visited local Mennonites.

An assessment by the Basel clergy reported that an early examination had revealed that Boni rejected the use of the sword. Now, after another sojourn in Heidelberg, 'he has absorbed all the other errors of the Anabaptists, enthusiasts, and fanatics.' 'He holds so obstinately and stubbornly to these doctrines that, although he is defeated and done in with God's Word, he still remains firm in his opinion ... He is completely assured of it through Scriptures as well as through the inner instruction of the Spirit.'

Although these incidents took place several years before the inception of the Brethren in 1708, they reveal the basic orientation of its founders, of whom Andreas Boni was one. They were separatists of Radical Pietist persuasion who adopted an Anabaptist view of the church. Largely stemming from the Reformed faith, the separatists were profoundly influenced by Anabaptism and Pietism.

Anabaptist Non-resistance

Much attention has been given, and rightly so, to the topic of Anabaptist non-resistance. An older generation of largely Mennonite scholarship found the tenet to be close to the core of Anabaptist essence, with Harold S. Bender's 'Anabaptist Vision' a useful symbol. It will be recalled that the third element in his delineation of the Anabaptist Vision was 'the ethic of love and nonresistance as applied to all human relationships.' More recent scholarship has questioned that interpretation. Scholars such as James M. Stayer in North America and Hans-Jürgen Goertz in Europe, to take leading examples, have demonstrated a variety of Anabaptist reactions to the problem of violence, ranging from absolutist rejection to apocalyptic crusade. Intriguing and important as the discussion is, it can be bypassed for the present topic. There is consensus that by the end of the sixteenth century the Anabaptist-Mennonite position was almost entirely non-resistant. Thus, Stayer can conclude his narrative analysis: 'By the late sixteenth century virtually all Anabaptists had adopted the idea Sattler derived from Grebel and Mantz, that "the Sword is ordained by God outside the perfection of Christ."' The position of the Brotherly Union of Schleitheim (or Schleitheim Confession) of 1527 had become normative for the movement.[2]

The point is that by the early eighteenth century the form of Anabaptism that Brethren encountered was thoroughly non-resistant. This was graphically recognized by Alexander Mack, Sr (1679–1735) in some early writing. In responding to an interlocutor who asked if he felt that his movement would turn out better than had the former Anabaptists, Mack replied:

We cannot testify for our descendants – as their faith is, so shall be their outcome. Nevertheless, we can say this, that the outcome of the former Anabaptists has turned out far better than that of all other religions. The Anabaptist seed is far better than the seed of L[uther], C[alvin], and also that of the C[atholics]. These have had a completely wild, yes, bestial outcome, which is self-evident. The Jews and the Turks are scandalized by the horrible wickedness of these three religions. Not even with gallows and torture can they keep them, who are of one faith, from murdering one another in their homes ... What is still more horrible, they go publicly to war, and slaughter one another by the thousands.

Mack considered that the Mennonites he knew had lost much of their original fervour, had indeed been sadly diminished. Yet, he averred: 'No Anabaptist will be found in war ... The majority of them are inclined to peacefulness ... It would indeed be desirable that the whole world were full of these "deteriorated" Anabaptists.'[3]

Peter Brock's studies have described the attenuation of the non-resistant position among the rapidly acculturating Dutch and north German Mennonites in modern times. However, the Palatine Anabaptists with whom the early Brethren had contact in the first decades of the eighteenth century were from Switzerland and south Germany and still faithfully maintained the peace testimony.[4]

A bridge from the Anabaptist stance on peace to the Brethren is offered by the *Dompelaars* (also *Dompelaers*), a little-studied immersionist movement among seventeenth-century Mennonites with congregations in Hamburg-Altona and in Krefeld. The mystic Christian Hohburg (1606–75), a Lutheran pastor who became Reformed, often preached at the Dompelaar congregation in Altona. He called for Christians to follow the path of suffering because their weapons are 'not muskets, but Bible and prayer to God.' When the Brethren movement became active in the early eighteenth century, members established links with these congregations, and were themselves called *Dompelaars*.[5]

Pietist Non-resistance

One man played a predominant role in winning whose who became Brethren to Radical Pietism. This was the itinerant evangelist Ernst Christoph Hochmann von Hochenau (1670–1721). Hochmann was a thoroughgoing non-resistant. This became clear in several interrogations he underwent in the course of his wandering ministry. They revealed that he had read the works of Quaker theologian Robert Barclay (1648–90). Hochmann was also directly influenced by Gottfried Arnold (1666–1714), noted Radical Pietist historian. Arnold's books on the early Christians and on heretical movements included sections on non-resistance. He is sometimes credited with being the first historian to treat the Anabaptists sympathetically.[6]

Hochmann preached directly against Christian participation in war; although wars would continue, sincere Christians would reject military service because of its incompatibility with Christ's commandment of love. If all who claimed to be Christians were Christians in reality, actually following Christ's message of brotherly love, then wars would cease. In any case, it was totally offensive to Hochmann that Christians would fight against fellow Christians. A symbol of Hochmann's non-resistance was his name for a retreat in the village of Schwarzenau – he called it *Friedenstadt*.[7]

Separatists influenced by Hochmann shared this attitude. Under interrogation, members of a conventicle of Radical Pietists meeting at the home of buttonmaker Martin Lucas in Heidelberg testified that love of enemy was central for them. Christian practice for them required, besides meeting for worship and Bible study in small groups, that 'they love foremost God and their neighbor as themselves, even their enemies.' Many of this group later joined the Brethren.[8]

Early Brethren Non-resistance

To the surprise and disappointment of modern Brethren, little discussion on peace issues has been recorded among the early Brethren. Why would something so central to their faith pilgrimage be scarcely mentioned in the early records? Besides the evident fact that only scraps of documentation can be gleaned from the early records, there are two other reasons for the silence. Early Brethren arose in conscious rejection of the Reformed and Lutheran state churches and what they considered their hyper-creedalism. They specifically refrained from compiling a creed, or even a confession of faith, that would give systematic expression to their views; they wished to stay open to new light. As Alexander Mack, Jr (1712–1803) expressed it in colonial America, in dealing with differences of church practice: 'I want to say this, that if a brother or some other person can in love and humility demonstrate by the word of the Lord something other than what is now done, we are willing to accept it ... Indeed, we do not intend to rest upon old practice but the word of the Lord alone is to be our rule and guideline ... Therefore, dear brethren, let us watch and be careful, and above all preserve love, for thus one preserves light.'[9]

Because they were not writing complete statements of faith, the few writings they did publish dealt with controversial points. With the Radical Pietists they debated the necessity of church discipline; with the Mennonites, they debated the method of baptism. Because both of these informing movements held to a staunch non-resistant position, the Brethren had no occasion to dispute this shared tenet in published form. This explains the relative absence of expression on it. Similarly, they engaged in some published controversy with a contemporary group, the charismatic New Prophets or Community of True Inspiration, who have become well known in North America as the Amana Society. These Inspirationists also held a consistent peace stance, so that this did not become a point of argument.[10]

Colonial Period

Space does not permit an extended historical review of the peace witness of the Brethren in the centuries since the foundation in 1708, even though their story, unlike that of the Mennonites and the Quakers, is principally an American one. (By the early 1740s the Brethren had been transplanted in North America, primarily in Pennsylvania; those remaining in Europe either reverted to an individualist Radical Pietism or merged with the Mennonites.) The story of Brethren non-resistance has been told well in the magisterial studies by Peter Brock, *Pacifism in the United States* (1968) and *Freedom from Violence* (1991), as well as in the earlier monograph by Rufus D. Bowman, *The Church of the Brethren and War* (1944). A few highlights will illustrate initial Brethren grounding in non-resistance and recent changes in position.[11]

In the familiar irony of history, most documentation on peace churches arises when governments make military demands on their citizenry, including those of pacifist persuasion, so that we know most about the Brethren attitude towards peace during times of war. The rise of American independence efforts as they came to focus in the Revolutionary War brought sharp demands upon the Brethren and other peace groups. During this time Brethren held staunchly to the non-resistant principle as attested by all contemporary accounts. Proud's *History of Pennsylvania* records of them: 'Those people in Pennsylvania, called Dunkards, Tunkers, or Dumplers ... hold it not becoming a follower of Jesus Christ to bear arms or fight; because, say they, their true Master has forbid His disciplines to resist evil.' Proud borrowed his language from the Quaker historian Samuel Smith.[12]

Basically, the Germanic peace sects wished to stay neutral in the struggle. Their tragedy was that it was in the American interest not to permit this. By a variety of means, such as test or loyalty acts, the revolutionary camp forced all colonists to take sides. Most often these peace groups – Mennonites, Brethren, Moravians, and others – came down on the Loyalist (Tory) side, and the same is true of the Quakers. This is not surprising. They were truly grateful that the British crown had allowed them religious freedom in the New World. They accepted Romans 13 and God's support for the powers that were; it was not at all clear to them that the rebel cause had supplanted the British in that status. Largely agriculturalists, they did not have the economic grievances that merchants and lawyers had with the newly restrictive English laws, such as the Stamp and Townshend Acts. Those Americans taking the most belligerent revolutionary positions came from the Puritan, Scotch-Irish, and Anglican parties who had been the most active political opponents of their interests.[13]

A classic statement of the Brethren position is contained in a joint petition of Mennonite and Brethren elders to the Pennsylvania Assembly in 1775: 'The Advice to those who do not find Freedom of Conscience to take up arms, that they ought to be helpful to those who are in Need and distressed Circumstances, we receive with Cheerfulness towards all men of what Station they may be – it being our Principle to feed the Hungry and give the Thirsty Drink; – we have dedicated ourselves to serve all Men in every Thing that can be helpful to the Preservation of Men's Lives, but we find no Freedom in giving, or doing, or assisting in any Thing by Which Men's Lives are destroyed or hurt.'[14]

A few of the Brethren and Mennonites were so opposed to the Revolutionary cause that they became active Tories. Brethren member Christopher Sauer III (1754–99), of the famous Germantown printing family, was incensed by the rough rebel actions. He became an operative for British intelligence; as such he passed on a communication from peace people in Lancaster County to British headquarters in New York; it read in part, 'Mennonites and German Baptists (the latter in derision called Dunkers) have long wished to know from Authority how to conduct themselves during the present Rebellion, that they might not give offense to His Majesty or to His Representatives in America.' Sauer was rewarded for his efforts by appointment after the war as postmaster and king's printer in Saint John, New Brunswick. Some Mennonites and Brethren were caught up in Loyalist plots in Pennsylvania and Maryland; they did insist, however, that their support would be limited to non-combatant activities such as driving wagons. In both cases, the plots never came to fruition but some participants, including sectarians, were executed anyway.[15]

This pro-British support is one reason for the migration after war's end to Ontario. Among those who left the newly established American state were Mennonites, Amish, Brethren, and the newly founded River Brethren. Because the latter two groups were both called Tunkers in Canada, there is much confusion in the literature.[16]

Nineteenth Century

Brethren practice in the Civil War followed that of the late eighteenth century. Membership in the church was still conditioned on a baptismal pledge by members that they would be faithful to the non-resistant position. Brethren held true to this during the war. They were following the direction of the Annual Meeting which pointedly answered this question that came to it in 1865: 'Can a brother be held as a member of the church who will, when put in the army, take up arms and aim to shed the blood of his fellowman?' The answer was: 'He cannot.'[17]

This abstention caused considerable sacrifice, particularly in the Confederacy. The South had greater need of all of its men of fighting age; moreover, as it was understood that Brethren hated slavery, their non-resistant principles could easily be interpreted as pro-Union sentiments. Several killings of Brethren are known, clearly caused by their non-resistance. The most noted was the assassination in 1864 by Confederate irregulars of Elder John Kline (1797–1864) of Broadway, Virginia. Kline had repeatedly crossed the battle lines to preside over church meetings held in the North. This travel, compounded by his clearly stated anti-secession and anti-slavery views, led to his murder.[18]

Yet, Kline had carefully articulated the Brethren view that non-resistance included acceptance of proper authority. In a letter to the governor of Virginia in 1861, Kline wrote:

We teach and are taught obedience to the 'powers that be,' believing as we do that 'the powers that be are ordained of God,' and under his divine sanction so far as such powers keep within God's bounds. By God's bounds we understand such laws and their administrations ... as do not conflict with, oppose, or violate any precept or command contained in the Divine Word which he has given for the moral and spiritual government of his people. By government ... we understand rightful human authority. And by this, again, we understand, as the Apostle Paul puts it, 'the power that protects and blesses the good, and punishes the evildoer.'[19]

Brethren had not developed much literature on peace, but they presented a small book emerging at this time as their statement to the Confederate government. It was *Non-Resistance, or the Spirit of Christianity Restored* (1862); its author was William C. Thurman (ca. 1830–1906), a Virginia Baptist, who had become non-resistant through his own biblical study. He joined the Brethren during the war and soon was given leadership positions. This did not last long, because Thurman came to question certain traditional practices, such as the form of feetwashing. Somewhat later he caused a schism with his adventist views of Christ's second coming. Thurman died in 1906 in a poorhouse in Richmond, Virginia, predicting that the world would end in 1917.[20]

Twentieth Century

By 1917, when the United States entered the Great War, the attitude of the Brethren towards war had changed. This was because the Brethren had changed. No longer German-speaking farmers living in isolated enclaves, Brethren had moved with the times. Beginning in 1876 they had established 'normal' (teacher-training) schools, which eventually became well-respected colleges. Many Brethren had moved from the farms to take up managerial and professional positions – particularly as teachers – in towns and cities. A well-endowed General Mission Board was sending scores of missionaries to several continents. In 1911, after painful years of controversy, the Annual Conference ruled that the plain dress or garb could be waived by congregational action.[21]

If one event were to be singled out to illustrate this transformation, it would be the election in 1914 of Martin Grove Brumbaugh (1862–1930) as governor of the Commonwealth of Pennsylvania. Brumbaugh, a minister among the Brethren and the first member of the church to earn a doctor of philosophy degree, had been a president of the oldest Brethren college (Juniata College in 1876), professor of pedagogy at the University of Pennsylvania, and commissioner of education in Cuba after the American victory in the Spanish-American War. His achievements as a reforming superintendent of the Philadelphia school system gave him the credentials for the gubernatorial race, which he won handily.

At Brumbaugh's inauguration in January 1915 he did not take an oath of office; rather, he affirmed his dedication to perform his duties. When the United States entered the war, one of these duties was to command the Pennsylvania militia, which was soon incorporated into the regular United States military. Although this involvement, in the eyes of traditional Dunkers, cast doubt about his bona fides as a member of the church, many in the denomination were proud of his standing.

The Annual Conference for 1918 was asked to define the church's position 'as regards the propriety of our members holding any office under our Civil Government which would necessitate their using, or causing to be used, physical force, carrying carnal weapons, or administering oaths.' The answer was equivocal:

1) Annual Meeting reaffirms her position on nonresistance and does not permit the holding of office by her members when such office compels them to violate these nonresistant principles and the taking or administering of oaths. 2) However, we recognize that, in a democracy, it is not wrong for Brethren to serve their communities and municipalities to promote efficiency and honesty in social and civic life when the nonresistant principles and the New Testament doctrines are not violated. 3) Anyone who violates this decision subjects himself to the discipline of the church.

Brumbaugh was never called to task for his war involvement and continued to be respected. He was, however, also never called to the highest positions in the church.[22]

The change in tone of the resolutions of the Brethren Annual Conferences also documents the shift from consistent non-resistant to a more activist pacifism. Through the nineteenth-century conferences dealt with issues involving the church and its members in regard to war. There was no hint that the church felt itself responsible for social or governmental problems. The Annual Meetings of 1875 and 1885 turned down requests for Brethren to cooperate officially with peace associations and conferences.[23] Resolutions in the twentieth century urged such cooperation. More strikingly, by 1915 the church thought it appropriate to praise the course of President Woodrow Wilson in 'his efforts to discourage war and maintain peaceable relations with all the world,' commending his 'spirit of conservativism, his words encouraging restraint and self-control, his calm temper and manly character.' The resolution also applauded Wilson's 'humanitarian course in securing advocacy of Christian ideals in all walks of public and private life.'

The same conference resolved that 'the church renews its allegiance to its time-honored stand for peace and the brotherhood of man, and urged the judicial arbitration of all international differences.' It pledged greater zeal in spreading the 'peace gospel,' more relevant discussions among members, and frequent sermons by ministers 'to the end that it may be an increasingly effective power in the hands of the master for the maintenance of peace and goodwill among men and among the nations of the world'[24]

The shift from apolitical non-resistance to a Social Gospel-type of pacifism had been initiated by the conference action of 1910 to appoint a Peace Committee. The language of the second part of the assignment is noteworthy for the sweeping quality of its parameters:

First: to propagate and aid in the distribution of such literature as may be helpful to the better understanding as to the sinfulness and folly of resorting to arms in the settlement of differences;
Second: to use every lawful gospel means in bringing about peaceful settlements of difficulties when such may arise between governments or societies;
Third: to keep the Brotherhood informed, from time to time, through our publications, as to the true status of the peace movement.[25]

The fact that the conference did not provide any funds to aid the Peace Committee in this undertaking does not decrease the significance of the sea change in orientation. No longer were the Brethren thinking in terms of two realms or kingdoms, that of the church and that of the world. They began to think of the church as co-responsible with the government for the solution of the world's problems. Bowman quite rightly, if understatedly, regarded the action as marking a change in the church's thought: 'The Brethren were beginning to sense the need of a peace educational program within the church and the necessity for the church to become an active force for peace among the nations.'[26]

The change in attitude was tested when the entry of the United States into the First World War in April 1917 brought after it draft legislation in May. Conscientious objectors (COs), such as the Brethren, were excused from combatant duty but required to perform non-combatant service; the exact nature of such service was to be defined by executive order. Such clarification did not come for almost a year, much complicating the plight of the COs. At this time the leadership of the Church of the Brethren was divided in its advice to young members who began to be drafted. Many, such as the important church leader Henry C. Early (1855–1941), believed that as loyal citizens, young Brethren men should accept non-combatant service. Others, arguing that this made them part of the military machine, urged them to avoid such activity and, indeed, to refuse to wear uniforms or participate in any way.[27]

Charles D. Bonsack (1870–1953), another key churchman, summarized the situation:

The First World War brought new issues that confused our church people ... The church had strong decisions about peace and war; but its members were also careful citizens of the state, paying taxes, conforming to its laws and upholding its institutions. Between these two conflicting attitudes in the time of war, the church became ... somewhat uncertain about the direction it should take. To train for war and engage therein seemed impossible to our people. On the other hand, to lie in a detention camp and do nothing seemed contrary to our loyal citizen idea through the years ... Meanwhile mistakes were made by all parties involved. But the result of it was that some accepted service in the regular armed forces; most of the young men found service in the noncombatant service of the army and some remained in the detention camps.[28]

The confusion led to the calling in January 1918 of a special Annual Conference, one of the very few times this has happened; it convened in Goshen, Indiana. The most significant conference action was an incisive restatement of the Brethren position on war:

Therefore this Conference of the Church of the Brethren hereby declares her continued adherence to the principles of nonresistance, held by the Church since its organization in 1708.
I. We believe that war or any participation in war is wrong and entirely incompatible with the spirit, example, and teachings of Jesus Christ.
II. That we can not conscientiously engage in any activity or perform any function, contributing to the destruction of human life.[29]

These conclusions were buttressed by extensive biblical citations, a statement on church-state relations, and the creation of a Central Service Committee to liaise with the government. Officials of the latter were informed by a high-level delegation of the conference action. President Woodrow Wilson sent a courteous letter to Elder H.C. Early acknowledging its receipt, suggesting that the list of non-combatant services would probably to broadened enough to satisfy the conscience of the Brethren. The Goshen Statement, as it came to be called, was printed in pamphlet form for distribution to the denomination, for particular use by those men being drafted.

Among the recommendations of the Goshen Statement was one directing Brethren men, when drafted, to refrain from wearing military uniforms and from drilling. This proved to be fateful. When the statement, with these recommendations, came to the attention of the War Department in the summer of 1918, the office of Advocates General threatened prosecution of the officers of the conference. It grounded its threat on the provisions of the Espionage Law, which called for severe penalties for those discouraging military service. Religious leaders (particularly Jehovah's Witnesses), political radicals, and union leaders were in fact given stiff sentences on this basis.

Brethren leaders managed to avoid prosecution by pledging to cease distribution of the Goshen Statement. J. Maurice Henry (1880–1966), a Brethren participant in the negotiations with the government, wrote, 'The Central Service Peace Committee – guided by wisdom from a gracious heavenly Father – had saved the church from a tragic situation: the church which the peaceful saint, Alexander Mack, had founded, for which Christopher Sower had been persecuted, and for which John J. Bowman and John Kline had suffered martyrdom in times of war.' Later commentators found this statement fraught with irony; their judgment was that the retraction seriously weakened the church's non-resistant position.[30]

Second World War

Young Brethren who had been caught in the draft machinery of the First World War disliked the mixed signals from the church's leadership. Several among them decided to avoid this kind of problem in the future by devoting their lives to strengthening the Brethren peace witness. They included such figures as M.R. Zigler (1891–1985) and Dan West (1893–1971), who became known both nationally and internationally as peace advocates. Other peace proponents who moved into leadership positions included Paul H. Bowman, Sr (1887–1964), Rufus D. Bowman (1899–1952), and Kermit Eby (1903–62). These men were largely influenced by the liberal pacifism of the time. While always referring to the non-resistant tradition as their foundation, in practice their orientation was liberal and activist rather than conservative and withdrawn. They sought to combine what the church called 'creative citizenship' with active peacemaking strategies, hoping to eliminate the causes of war by social strategems, political intervention, and church activity.[31]

Moreover, they were keenly ecumenical in attitude. They hoped to extend the Brethren peace witness to the broader Christian world. Quite naturally, they reached out first to sister churches with peace traditions. These were principally the several varieties of Mennonites and Friends, as well as the Schwenkfelders and others. A little-known series of ten conferences held between 1922 and 1931, in which Brethren played active roles, sought to deepen a sense of unity initiated by shared experience as COs during the First World War. The first conference was held at Bluffton College, Ohio, in 1922; its title gave the orientation — Conference of Religious Bodies Who Hold that Peace between Nations Can Be Maintained by Following the Teachings of Jesus. Such interaction doubtless influenced one of the most cited Annual Conference papers of the Brethren in 1935, including these words:

We believe that all war is sin; that it is wrong for Christians to support or to engage in it; and that war is incompatible with the spirit, example, and teachings of Jesus ... Those beliefs are not based upon a popular peace doctrine of our own; they arise from our application of Christian standards to all human relations, whether individual, group, class, or national. To settle conflicts in any of these relationships by war is not efficient, nor constructive, not permanent, and certainly not Christian.[32]

The same year, 1935, saw a landmark conference at North Newton, Kansas, which coined and popularized the term 'Historic Peace Churches.' Because the storm clouds of the next war were already forming on the horizon, the unresolved theological differences in peace positions of those attending (which were many) were not allowed to deter the cooperative peace effort which ensued. Along with active peace education, seminars, publications, and pronouncements, the Historic Peace Churches sent weighty delegations to the United States government. These delegations, which met twice with President Franklin D. Roosevelt and often with other high officials, wanted to accomplish at least two things: first, to place their peace position on record, with particular attention to the vigorous programs they were carrying on through their service agencies in several countries; and second to lay the groundwork for a plan for dealing with conscientious objectors in wartime. They did not want a repetition of the unhappy experiences of the First World War.[33]

As it happened, their foresight was rewarded in September 1940 when the Burke-Wadsworth Bill became law as the Selective Training and Service Act, mandating the first peacetime conscription in United States history. The Historic Peace Churches had lobbied for improvements in the bill with partial success. While not achieving all they had asked for, they did secure more generous provisions for COs than originally planned by legislators. The upshot was the creation in 1940–1 of the Civilian Public Service (CPS) program, which was intensely studied during its fiftieth anniversary. It was administered by a cooperative body, chaired by M.R. Zigler, called the National Service Board for Religious Objectors.[34]

The Church of the Brethren, as well as several other smaller Brethren bodies, supported this program of alternative service in a sacrificial way, contributing $1,300,000 as well as much material aid. A church survey in 1945 estimated that 10 per cent of draft-age Brethren men entered CPS, and that another 10 per cent accepted non-combatant military service. A majority followed full military participation, without falling under the censure of their home congregations.[35]

Of the 12,000 men in the entire CPS program, the Mennonites had by far the largest contingent, and the Brethren the second largest with over 1,500. Many Brethren COs accepted the CPS alternative as being the best option; it satisfied the military obligation in a sacrificial way and held true to Brethren tradition. Some men, however, opposed the arrangement, concluding that the Brethren were cooperating too closely with the military. These absolutists, who refused CPS or walked away from the CPS assignments, were tried and received prison sentences.[36]

CPS men had volunteered for overseas duty in relief work during the Second World War, but this was blocked by the United States Congress. At war's end many secured places with the expanded operations of the Historic Peace Church service organizations – the American Friends Service Committee (AFSC), the Mennonite Central Committee, and the Brethren Service Committee. They assisted these voluntary agencies in worldwide programs of material aid, resettlement, and other assistance to refugees, displaced persons, and other war victims. This activity received much favourable attention, symbolized by the awarding of the Nobel peace prize to the Friends Service Council and the AFSC in late 1947.[37]

Later Twentieth Century

The end of the twentieth century finds the Church of the Brethren in a divided position in relation to its peace tradition. Repeated Annual Conference statements have rearticulated the position and at the same time have attempted to deal with diversity. On one end of the continuum are those who still hold tightly to traditional non-resistance. They are two-kingdom people who pray for the government, criticize those Brethren attempting to be politically relevant, and at the same time are totally opposed personally to military service. On the other end are accultur-ated Brethren, who are unhappy with the traditional peace emphasis of the Brethren, write bitter letters to the denominational journal question-ing the lack of patriotism of the church's leaders, and still consider them-selves good members. In between are a small, articulate, and rather influential group who could be called Neo-Anabaptist. They follow a line that seeks to speak to political issues while keeping at the same time a clear distinction between an agape ethic of love within the church and an ethic of justice and fairness, seen as appropriate for the state. Also present are classical liberal pacifists who seek to extend the way of love through all sectors of society by education, social action, and govern-ment programs. A small number follow a just war ethic, especially as currently expressed in liberation theology. Most members are content to support and maintain the denominational peace tradition, without nec-essarily feeling personally obliged to follow it in their own lives. Several Annual Conference study papers have sought to bring clarity by identi-fying these positions, but have not succeeded in bringing unity.[38]

Brethren have given leadership since 1948 in bringing the Historic Peace Church witness to the National Council of Churches and the World Council of Churches. A number of publications, of which *Peace Is the Will of God* (1953) is the most important, were presented to World Council assemblies. A significant series of formal theological discussions took place after 1955 at the so-called *Puidoux* conferences, named after the Swiss retreat house where the first meeting was held. The formal title was 'Conference on Lordship of Christ over Church and State.' Its impact on the *Volkskirchen* of the Federal Republic of Germany was par-ticularly strong. Later initiatives have kept the peace issue before the World Council of Churches. The latest effort, *A Declaration on Peace* (1991), was prepared by a team of Brethren, Mennonite, Quaker, and Fel-lowship of Reconciliation writers; it seeks to speak to the entire Christian community.[39]

Thus, the Brethren and non-resistance has become a topic with great variety in understandings and responses. Non-resistance in the historic sense is certainly alive among the Brethren but it would be too much to say that it is a predominant position. Pacifism in a broader sense that includes such meanings as active peacemaking and non-violent resistance is definitely present among many Brethren. Other members clearly distance themselves from the historic peace position. Yet, a substantial number of Brethren are concerned to keep the peace testimony alive and well, rather than resting content with it as part of a discarded heritage.

Notes

1 The incidents are discussed in Donald F. Durnbaugh, *Brethren Beginnings: The Origins of the Church of the Brethren in Early Eighteenth-Century Europe* (Philadelphia, 1992), 15–18; many of the documents are given in translation in Donald F. Durnbaugh (ed.), *European Origins of the Brethren* (Elgin, 1958), 87–105.

2 Harold S. Bender, 'The Anabaptist Vision,' in *The Recovery of the Anabaptist Vision*, ed. Guy F. Hershberger (Scottdale, 1957), 51; the essay was originally published in *Church History* 13 (1933), 3–24. See the literature cited in John S. Oyer, 'Anabaptist Vision, The,' in the *Mennonite Encyclopedia* (Scottdale and Waterloo, 1990), vol. 5, 26. James M. Stayer, *Anabaptists and the Sword* (Lawrence, 1972), 328; rev. version (1975). Hans-Jürgen Goertz, *Die Täufer: Geschichte und Deutung*, 2nd, rev. ed. (Munich, 1988).

3 Durnbaugh, *Origins*, 342–3; the original title was *Eberhard Ludwig Grubers Grundforschende Fragen, welche denen Neuen Täuffern, im Witgensteinischen, insonderheit zu beantworten, vorgelegt waren* ([Berleburg?], 1713), no original copy extant.

4 Peter Brock, *Pacifism in Europe to 1914* (Princeton, 1972), 174–254.

5 Brock, *Pacifism in Europe*, 247–48; Durnbaugh, *Beginnings*, 34, 42, 52, 54, 57; Friedrich Nieper, *Die ersten deutschen Auswanderer von Krefeld nach Pennsylvanien* (Neukirchen/Moers, 1940), passim (simply equating the Dompelaars in Krefeld with the Dunkers); Albrecht Ritschl, *Geschichte des Pietismus ...* (Bonn, 1884), vol. 2, 61–3; F. Ernest Stoeffler, *The Rise of Evangelical Pietism* (Leiden, 1965), 230–1.

6 Heinz Renkewitz, *Hochmann von Hochenau (1670–1721): Quellenstudien zur Geschichte des Pietismus*, 2nd rev. ed. (Witten, 1969), passim. A new study of Gottfried Arnold is Peter C. Erb, *Pietists, Protestants, and Mysticism: The Use of Late Medieval Spiritual Texts in the Work of Gottfried Arnold (1666–1714)* (Metuchen, 1989). Comments on Arnold's treatment of the Anabaptists are found in Guy F. Hershberger, Introduction, in Hershberger (ed.), *Recovery* (1957), 2, and Franklin H. Littell, *The Anabaptist View of the Church*, 2nd rev. ed. (Boston, 1958), 152.

7 Renkewitz, *Hochmann*, 335–6; a critical theologian in Wesel also pointed out Hochmann's dependence on Barclay, 308. Ruth Rouse and Stephen C. Neill

(eds.), *A History of the Ecumenical Movement, 1517–1948* (Philadelphia, 1954), 83, 103–4, 228–9.

8 Renkewitz, *Hochmann*, 235; Durnbaugh, *Origins*, 76.

9 Donald F. Durnbaugh (ed.), *The Brethren in Colonial America* (Elgin, 1967), 464, 468.

10 There is a voluminous literature on the Inspired or Inspirationists; a recent study is Diane L. Barthel, *Amana: From Pietist Sect to American Community* (Lincoln, 1984). See also Peter Brock, *Pacifism in the United States* (Princeton, 1968), 438–9, 825–7; Brock, *Pacifism in Europe*, 249–50.

11 See Brock, *Pacifism in the United States* and *Freedom from Violence: Sectarian Nonresistance from the Middle Ages to the Great War* (Toronto, 1991); and Rufus D. Bowman, *The Church of the Brethren and War, 1708–1941* (Elgin, 1944), republished with a biographical sketch of Bowman (New York, 1971). See also Rufus D. Bowman, *Seventy Times Seven* (Elgin, 1945), a study guide with additional material on the Second World War, and Dale W. Brown, *Brethren and Pacifism* (Elgin, 1970), a revised and expanded version of which was issued as *Biblical Pacifism: A Peace Church Perspective* (Elgin, 1986).

12 Robert Proud, *History of Pennsylvania* (Philadelphia, 1798), 345–7, quoted from Bowman, *Brethren and War*, 71–2. The original source remained unpublished until the twentieth century: William M. Mervine (ed.), *History of the Province of Pennsylvania by Samuel Smith* (Philadelphia, 1913), 181–3, 188–90, discussed and quoted in Durnbaugh, *Colonial America*, 14–21. See also Roger E. Sappington, 'Eighteenth-Century Non-Brethren Sources of Brethren History, IV,' *Brethren Life and Thought* 2 (Autumn 1957), 65–75. These statements are well corroborated by recent studies. See, for example, Richard K. Mac-Master and others (eds.), *Conscience in Crisis: Mennonites and Other Peace Churches in America, 1739–1789 – Interpretation and Documents* (Scottdale and Kitchener, 1979); Richard K. MacMaster, *Land, Piety, Peoplehood: The Establishment of Mennonite Communities in America, 1683–1790* (Scottdale, 1985), *The Mennonite Experience in America*, vol. 1. These findings are also supported by my own research.

13 For more detail, consult Donald F. Durnbaugh, 'Religion and Revolution: Options in 1776,' *Pennsylvania Mennonite Heritage* 1 (July 1978), 2–9. For another version of the Frederick treason trial, see Emmert F. Bittinger, *Allegheny Passage: Churches and Families, West Marva District, Church of the Brethren (1762–1990)* (Camden, 1990), 220–6.

14 The original petition was published in English and German. For modern publication, see (among others) MacMaster, *Conscience in Crisis*, 266–7; Durnbaugh, *Colonial America*, 362–5.

15 See Durnbaugh, 'Religion and Revolution'; J. Russell Harper, 'Christopher Sower [III], King's Printer and Loyalist,' *New Brunswick Historical Society Collections* 14 (1955), 67–109; Carl Van Doren, *Secret History of the American Revolution* (New York, 1941).

16 See Dennis D. Martin and R. Truman Northup, 'Ontario,' in the *Brethren Encyclopedia* (Philadelphia and Oak Brook, 1983–4), 975; E. Morris Sider, *The Brethren in Christ in Canada: Two Hundred Years of Tradition and Change* (Nappanee, 1988).

17 This and other relevant minutes are found in L.W. Shultz, comp., *Minutes of the Annual Conference of the Church of the Brethren on War and Peace* (Elgin, 1935), 7. For this period, see Brock, *Pacifism in the United States*, 797–821, and Bowman, *Brethren and War*, 114–68.

18 See Roger E. Sappington, *Courageous Prophet: Chapters from the Life of John Kline* (Elgin, 1964).

19 Found in Benjamin Funk, *Life and Labors of Elder John Kline, the Martyr Missionary* (Elgin, 1900), 439, also quoted in Bowman, *Brethren and War*, 121.

20 William C. Thurman, *Non-Resistance, or the Spirit of Christianity Restored* (Charlottesville, 1862); Donald F. Durnbaugh, 'Thurman, William C.,' in the *Brethren Encyclopedia* (1983–4), 1264. See also Brock, *Pacifism in the United States*, 814–15; Bowman, *Brethren and War*, 141; Roger E. Sappington, *The Brethren in Virginia* (Harrisonburg, 1973), 190–1.

21 A thorough interpretation of this change is Carl F. Bowman, *Brethren Society: The Cultural Transformation of a 'Peculiar People'* (Baltimore, 1995), a revised version of his thesis, 'Beyond Plainness: Cultural Transformation in the Church of the Brethren from 1850 to the Present,' PhD dissertation, University of Virginia (1989).

22 Shultz, *Minutes*, 26; Bowman, *Brethren and War*, 193–4 (slightly varied); Bowman, *Brethren Society*, 245–51. Earl C. Kaylor, Jr, of Juniata College, is preparing a full biography of Brumbaugh; see relevant sections of his two books, *Truth Sets Free: Juniata, Independent College in Pennsylvania* (South Brunswick, 1977) and *Out of the Wilderness: The Brethren and Two Centuries of Life in Central Pennsylvania* (New York and London, 1980). See also Dennis L. Slabaugh, 'Brumbaugh, Martin Grove,' in the *Brethren Encyclopedia* (1983–4), 222–3, and Salvatore M. Messina, 'Martin Grove Brumbaugh: Educator,' PhD dissertation, University of Pennsylvania (1965).

23 Shultz, *Minutes*, 9, 10.

24 Ibid., 13.

25 Quoted in Bowman, *Brethren and War*, 161.

26 Ibid.

27 The best discussion is found in Bowman, *Brethren and War*, 169–233, based in

part on interviews with church leaders. See also Kenneth G. Long, 'Attitudes of the Brethren in Training Camps during the World War,' BD thesis, Bethany Biblical Seminary (1939), published in part in *Schwarzenau* 1 (July 1939), 57–77.

28 Bowman, *Brethren and War*, 173–4.

29 Shultz, *Minutes*, 17–25.

30 J. Maurice Henry, a member of the committee appointed to negotiate with the United States government, left a full description in a district history: *History of the Church of the Brethren in Maryland* (Elgin, 1936), 525–32. See also Roger E. Sappington, *Brethren Social Policy, 1908–1958* (Elgin, 1961), 38–45; Bowman, *Brethren and War*, 180–9; and Bowman, *Brethren Society*, 329–34. The latest full assessment is Robert G. Clouse, 'The Church of the Brethren and World War I: The Goshen Statement,' *Mennonite Life* 45 (Dec. 1990), 29–34.

31 Brief biographical sketches of these men are found in the *Brethren Encyclopedia*. There are biographies of West and Zigler: Glee Yoder, *Passing on the Gift: The Story of Dan West* (Elgin, 1978); Donald F. Durnbaugh, *Pragmatic Prophet: The Life of Michael Robert Zigler* (Elgin, 1989). Much of Eby's writing was autobiographical; see esp. *Protests of an Ex-Organization Man* (Boston, 1961). All are discussed in Sappington, *Social Policy*. See also D.F. Durnbaugh, 'Bowman, Rufus David,' in *Biographical Dictionary of Modern Peace Leaders*, ed. Harold Josephson (Westport, 1985), 104–5.

32 Quoted in Bowman, *Brethren and War*, 241.

33 The best recent study of these developments is Albert N. Keim and Grant M. Stoltzfus, *The Politics of Conscience: The Historic Peace Churches and America at War, 1917–1955* (Scottdale, 1988).

34 See Keim and Stoltzfus, *Politics*, 78–102, and Albert N. Keim, *The CPS Story: An Illustrated History of Civilian Public Service* (Intercourse, 1990). A non-peace-church assessment is Lawrence S. Wittner, *Rebels against War: The American Peace Movement, 1941–1960* (New York and London, 1969), 70–84.

35 The Brethren CPS program was studied in Leslie Eisan, *Pathways of Peace* (Elgin, 1948); a recent interpretation of CPS is Cynthia Eller, 'Moral and Religious Arguments in Support of Pacifism: Conscientious Objectors and the Second World War,' PhD dissertation, University of Southern California (1988), based on interviews. See also articles in a special issue of the denominational journal, *Messenger* (Oct. 1990), 10–21.

36 Mulford Q. Sibley and Philip E. Jacob, *Conscription of Conscience: The American State and the Conscientious Objector, 1940–1947* (Ithaca, 1952).

37 Brethren efforts are described in Donald F. Durnbaugh (ed.), *To Serve the Present Age: The Brethren Service Story* (Elgin, 1975). See also Durnbaugh, *Pragmatic Prophet* and Sappington, *Social Policy*.

38 Fairly recent reviews are Robert W. McFadden, 'Perspective in Pacifism,' *Brethren Life and Thought* 6 (Spring 1961), 36–52; Richard B. Gardner, 'Brethren and Pacifism: An Analysis of Contemporary Brethren Approaches to Peace and War,' *Brethren Life and Thought* 8 (Autumn 1963), 17–37. See also Harry K. Zeller, Jr, *Peace Is Our Business* (Elgin, 1947); Arthur G. Gish, *The New Left and Christian Radicalism* (Grand Rapids, 1970); Vernard Eller, *King Jesus' Manual of Arms for the 'Armless* (Nashville and New York, 1973), republished as *War and Peace from Genesis to Revelation* (Scottdale, 1981); Dale Aukerman, *Darkening Valley: A Biblical Perspective on Nuclear War* (New York, 1981); Brown, *Biblical Pacifism* (1986); Varnard Eller, *Christian Anarchy: Jesus' Primacy Over the Powers* (Grand Rapids, 1987); Bowman, 'Beyond Plainness,' esp. 349–56. Among the relevant Annual Conference pronouncements are the following: 'Statement of the Church of the Brethren on War' (1968, adapted from an earlier 1948 statement, rev. 1957, to recognize selective objection to war); 'Obedience to God and Civil Disobedience' (1969); 'Statement on Church/State Relationships' (1988).

39 The cooperative work of the Historic Peace Churches is traced, with documents, in Donald F. Durnbaugh (ed.), *On Earth Peace: Discussions on War/Peace Issues between Friends, Mennonites, Brethren, and European Churches, 1935–1975* (Elgin, 1978). The recent publication is Douglas Gwyn, George Hunsinger, Eugene F. Roop, and John Howard Yoder, *A Declaration on Peace: In God's People the World's Renewal Has Begun* (Scottdale, and Waterloo, 1991); see esp. the chronology, John Howard Yoder, comp., '40 Years of Theological Dialogue Efforts on Justice and Peace Issues by the Fellowship of Reconciliation and the "Historic Peace Churches,"' 93–105.

9

The 'Lamb's War' and the Origins of the Quaker Peace Testimony

HUGH BARBOUR

The title of this essay suggests the need to see the roots of the Quaker peace testimony in the early Friends' central message about the nature of evil and how evil is overcome, not simply in conscientious objection and international peacemaking. What is clear is that the story of the Quaker peace testimony has been studied in much detail and remains complex.

Forty years ago, James Maclear and Alan Cole explored the responses of the Quakers to the traumatic years after Nayler's ride into Bristol in 1656, amid the Puritans' backlash against toleration in Cromwell's Commonwealth.[1] They maintained that, except for individual conscientious objectors to army or navy service like William Dewsbury, Thomas Lurting, Peter Hardcastle, and George Fox himself,[2] Quakers had no collective 'peace testimony' in the 1650s. Cole and Reay cited Quakers in arms. A modern Friend wading through the complete works of Edward Burrough, Francis Howgill, and James Nayler for those years[3] must admit that negative evidence seems strong: many early Quaker tracts were written, often specifically addressed to rulers or soldiers, to warn in detail against inner and outward sins, without naming among them military force. When Friends condemned violence they referred specifically to persecution.

The death of Cromwell in September 1658 led to a crisis in England. For fifteen months his son Richard as Protector, the recalled Rump Parliament (elected in 1641, purged in 1648), and the council of Puritan army officers competed for power. Popular support for all of these waned so that within a year a royalist uprising was only narrowly put down. In the first half of 1659, the successive governments were besieged by Quakers bringing petitions with up to 15,000 signatures

regarding prisoners and tithes, and suggested 'platforms' for constitutional reform by George Fox, George Bishop, Thomas Lawson, and
Edward Billing.[4] In the summer of 1659, as the gains of three generations
of Puritan hopes and ten years of civil war were threatened, Sir Harry
Vane and the radicals in the Rump and the army appealed to the Quakers and Baptists for support. Barry Reay has compiled evidence that
twenty-five to twenty-seven Friends were listed as commissioners of the
militia; about the same number were actually enrolled under arms or
were ready to be.[5] Fifty out of 40,000 Quakers is a small total, in proportion to those among Baptists and others, and no Friends actually shed
blood; but many consciences were torn. Fox himself spent an agonized
summer and autumn before warning Friends against involvement. The
moral ambiguity of both alternatives for Friends in 1659 may have
driven Fox to minimize thereafter Friends' claims to perfection.

When General George Monck in December 1659 brought his carefully
purged garrison regiments south from Scotland, Lambert's more radical
units refused to shed the blood of former comrades-in-arms. The Restoration in 1660 of Charles II as king, of the royalist squires, and the epis-
copacy was inevitable. Barry Reay and Peter Brock view the statements
of non-violence that Margaret Fell made then, and Fox and others a year
later, as 'the transformation of Quakerism' or 'the crystallisation of
Quaker Pacifism.' For Hill, Reay, and other Marxists, Friends were
deserting the 'good old cause' of the great Puritan social revolution. Yet
a deeper look at the roots of the Quaker peace testimony is necessary in
order to see the inherent but secondary place of political involvement
within the dynamics of early Quaker experience as a whole.

Our test case, constantly quoted by Reay's group, is Edward Burrough, since James Nayler and Francis Howgill, to whom I will return,
said less on politics.[6] Burrough was one of the circle of Separatists in
Westmorland won by Fox in 1652, centred on Firbank Fell and Swarthmore Hall. Burrough was too young to have fought in the Puritan crusade against Charles I. He became nevertheless one of the five famous
Quaker preachers in London and Bristol. His 'convincement' from Sepa-
ratism into Quakerism, described in his 'Epistle to the Reader' of Fox's
Great Mistery, parallels other Friends' accounts of their harrowing experience of dark months, 'sitting still under the Light' to which Fox had
called them, as they had each searched and purged every habit and
motive: 'After long seeking, the Lord appeared to us, and ... gave us of
his Spirit, and gave us of his Wisdom to guide us, whereby we saw all
the World ... and the true condition of the Church, and ... that ... God had

given to every one of us in particular, a Light from himself shining in our hearts and consciences ... which Light we found sufficient to reprove us, and convince us of every evil deed, word and thought.'[7]

In 1654 Burrough had described his struggle in 1652 more grimly to his home village: 'It pleased the Lord to speak to me by ... G. Fox, ... that I was in the prodigal state, and above the Cross of Christ ... for I saw my self to be in bondage to my own Will ... and was full of Airy Notions; and then I saw my self to be a Child of Wrath ... and ... separated from ... all my Acquaintance and kindred, and betook my self to the company of a poor despised and contemned people called Quakers.'[8] He described in his Epistle the religious basis of the new Quaker community:

And so we ceased from the teachings of all men, and their words, and their Worships ... and we ceased from our own Words, and Professions, and Practices in Religion in times before zealously performed by us ... and we became Fools for Christ's sake ... and felt his Word in our hearts to burn up and beat down all that was contrary to God, and we obeyed the Light of Christ in us, and followed the Motions of the Lords [sic] pure Spirit, and took up the Cross to all Earthly Glories, Crowns and Ways ... And our hearts were made glad and our Tongues loosed ... and things unutterable were Known; and then begun we to sing Praises to God Almighty who ... put an end to Sin and Death.

Their mission to bring the world under judgment was a part of this new life:

We became Followers of the Lamb whithersoever he goes, and he hath called us to make war in righteousness for his Name sake against ... all the Powers of Darkness ... and gave us power ... to bind Kings in Chains, and Nobles in Fetters of Iron, and the Word of the Lord we sounded, and did not spare ... Priests and Teachers ... This we did with no small Opposition ... oftentimes we were in danger of our lives ... And the Witness of God in many stirred for us, for ... in all Consciences in our words and sufferings and wayes we did commend ourselves.

In the beginning we were but few ... that had received the Power from on high in such a measure ... Then in the Year 1654, as moved of the Lord, we spread our selves South-ward ... and came first to this City of London.[9]

Quakers travelled in pairs like Apostles; Burrough and his companion Francis Howgill, after months preaching to crowds in rented halls in London and Bristol, felt led simultaneously to work together in Ireland in 1655. Like almost all Quaker preachers they felt directly moved by

God to write as well as to preach, so *A Visitation of the Rebellious Nation of Ireland* includes warnings to judges and Catholic priests and 'an Invitation to all the poor desolate Souldiers to repent from lying, Swearing, Drunkenness and Oppression, – but not from bearing arms.' Burrough told the Puritan garrisons that 'the Light in your Consciences ... will teach you to lay your Swords in justice upon every one that doeth evil: And it will teach you not to make War but to preserve peace in the Earth.'[10]

For Burrough the heart of his message, as for Fox, Howgill, and Nayler, was that worship can be totally dependent on God. Thus, the embodiment of evil that they most often confronted was the clergy of the parish churches; earlier and later these had been Anglican in ritual and sacrament, but at this time the best were Puritans. Friends' key issue was the Puritans' compromises with sin in their own conduct and in their too gentle 'pleading for sin' of their parishioners. Quakers attacked every evil they saw, but the root of sin is pride or self-will: for early Friends this included pride of rank, wealth, and titles (the chief points at which Reay and Hill approve early Quaker ethics). By 1659, when legal reforms seemed possible, Friends stressed increasingly their opposition to the support of the parish clergy by a church tax or 'tithe,' but they ignored the portion of such tithes which had been 'impropriated' into the hands of rich laymen.[11]

Burrough's tracts of 1659 to rulers, like many earlier ones by Nayler and Howgill, thus drum repeatedly on two needs: to abolish state support for the clergy, and to end persecution, 'in the Name and Power of the Lord, though he requires nothing of you to exalt his Kingdom ... he requires, That you should do nothing against him nor against his People by limiting the Spirit of the Lord.'[12] Burrough claimed toleration in the name of God, not of humans. In editing his works in 1672, George Whitehead, Ellis Hookes, and Fox proudly included nineteen fiery political tracts Burrough wrote in 1659, and, as well, his equally stirring 1659 preface to Fox's *Great Mistery*.

Burrough, like George Bishop, was constantly in the lobbies of England's rulers; both men later knew how to present to Charles II news from Massachusetts about the hangings of Mary Dyer, Robinson, and Stephenson that prevented any more deaths there.[13] In 1657 Burrough talked with Oliver Cromwell at length about tithes and toleration; in July 1659 he gathered and reprinted for Richard Cromwell seven letters Burrough had written and delivered by hand to Oliver, five to Richard, and one to his Parliament from February 1658/59 to April 1659. Probably in May or June and early August, Burrough wrote two more appeals

to the Rump Parliament, which were never published.[14] The most striking feature of these letters, like those by George Fox 'the Younger' and
other Quakers in 1659, was Burrough's faith in God's role in the events
of daily history.[15] He unhesitatingly told Richard Cromwell that his
father 'was smitten of the Lord' because of his failure to abolish tithes, so
'that ye may learn the Lord's just Judgments in these things.' He published a warning to the Rump Parliament in September, and another in
October: 'In so much as the Lord God our deliverer hath begun to
appear for the freedom of the Nations ... these things we are waiting for
... and the hand of the Lord will accomplish it, if not by you, then even
contrary to you.'[16] In November's anarchy Burrough wrote to 'the
Present Rulers of England, Whether Comitty of Safety (so called) Council of
Officers, or Others whatsoever.' Now Burrough's scope widened: he traced
the 'sacred history' of the English Reformation from the martyrs under
'bloody Mary' to the present 'overturnings.' Finally, in the chaos of
December 1659 he wrote To the Present Distracted and Broken Nation of
England and to all her Inhabitants urging a more fundamental repentance:
'Everyone must love the Light of Christ in his own conscience, and
become a follower of it ... and he must war against the Enemies of his
own Soul ... even his own Lusts ... and deny the false Teachers and
Deceivers, and must come to be taught of the Lord ... O Nation, If it were
thus with thee, then shouldst thou be a happy People ... then shall thy
Breaches be healed, and thy Sorrows be turned into Joy ... Whatsoever
men profess to do ... Till ... men be ruled of the Lord, they can never rightly
rule for him.'[17] Early Friends' basically theocratic message contrasts with
the 'two Kingdom ethic' of the Mennonites and Lutherans.

Even in sorrow for England Burrough was unafraid and gave the
same message to the City of London and to the Convention Parliament –
even though 'I dare not say that God expects much more from you than
... to be the Executioners of Justice upon men as sinful as your selves ... and not
to persecute the people of the Lord.'[18] As a 'minimum royalist' (though
not a 'minimum pacifist')[19] he could assure King Charles II at his acces-
sion that 'God ... doth give the Kingdoms of this World to whomsoever he
will ... Charles Stuart must either be converted to God, and be ruled by him, or
else he can never rightly rule for God in this nation ... If he have a deliverance,
let him turn it into the praise of the Lord in holiness, & not into shedding blood
in ... revenge.'[20]

Since many Friends had served in Cromwell's armies before being
'convinced,' and some afterward, Burrough tried to insist that 'If any that
are now amongst us, were any way engaged in the Parliament Service in

the Wars, it was not in Rebellion against him and his father [but] upon
Sober and Reasonable Principles.' Yet he announced a Quaker peace testimony in May 1660, a month before Margaret Fell's, and eight months
before Friends' 1661 collective 'Declaration to King Charles,' saying that
'though we more than ever ... seek after Reformation, yet we do it not in
that way of outward Warring and Fighting with Carnal Weapons and
Swords.'[21] After two more years of preaching and tract writing, Burrough returned from Bristol to London expecting to die in prison, and
did so. Meanwhile he told suffering Friends 'to be patient and faithful in
this day of our tryal ... We are the Lord's, and in his cause we are tryed,
and he will judge and avenge our Persecutors in his season.'[22]

The constancy of Burrough's cosmic viewpoint rebuts ideas that
'Friends sought solace in apocalyptic ranting' only after 1659.[23] Quaker
apocalyptic hope united the inner experience of a crisis of truth with the
Puritan faith in God's purpose in history, just as Friends' faith in daily
'leadings' paralleled Puritans' trust in providences. Quakers believed as
ardently as Oliver Cromwell that they were God's agents responding to
a divine 'Day of Visitation' to each person and nation. Quakers in the
1650s had been radically convinced through a shattering personal experience of judgment and purging, followed by submission to 'the Light'
or Spirit. They were thus confident that the rapidly spreading movement witnessed to a conquest by the Spirit whereby all kingdoms of the
world would be transformed as each Quaker had been, and as the militant Puritan revolution had failed to do. The Quakers' turning inwards,
which for Marxists has seemed a turning back from revolution, was
actually its intensification. They did not simply believe in 'Primitive
Christianity revived' but that God had brought the clock back to Pente-
cost after 1600 years of apostasy. The work of the Spirit through Paul
was being continued. For it the Quakers borrowed from the Book of
Revelation the phrase 'the Lamb's War.' In that era of holy war and commonwealth, even Puritan biblicism was expressed as apocalyptic history
by images of 'the Fifth Monarchy' and the rule of 'King Jesus.' The
dynamic Quaker 'awakening' of the English Northwest evoked similar
symbols.

Religious awakenings that swept a whole region were often linked
with millennial hopes, not simply by radicals on their fringes like the
'Spiritual Franciscans' or the New York State Millerites of 1844, but by
men as sober as Martin Luther and Jonathan Edwards. Such awakenings,
as I have written elsewhere,[24] experience moral transformation and often,
but not always, expect ethical perfection, as did the Anabaptists until

1527, the Waldensians three hundred years earlier, and the Wesleyans two hundred years later. The sense of the Spirit's power may lead men or women to claims of unique inspiration, a common aspect of millennialism. Fox trusted that the prophecy of Joel was fulfilled in the pouring out of the Spirit upon all flesh. The apocalyptic message that 'Jesus Christ has come to teach his people himself' by his inward word becomes in Douglas Gwyn's and Lewis Benson's interpretation,[25] a timeless 'eternal covenant,' just as did Jesus' similar message after his own death; but such a 'realized eschatology' does not respond to the intensity of the historical moment, 'the Day of the Lord Dawning,'[26] for Nayler, Fox, and the Friends in 1652–60. Gwyn in March at Lancaster called early Quaker nonviolence and openness to a future without human plan or structure far more subversive than a military revolution.[27]

Burrough and Howgill each wrote tracts reflecting the actual spread of Quakerism from the English Northwest in 1654 by 'the Camp of the Lord in England.'[28] But their constant use of ultimate symbols ('Antichrist,' 'Babylon,' 'the Beast,' 'the Whore,') for the evil forces Quakers opposed, shows both the intensity of their inner moral struggle and the Puritan tradition of linking all moral evil and Church corruption to cosmic Catholicism. In the crisis year 1659, Burrough felt led to make in person *A Visitation and Warning ... and an Alarum to the Pope's Borders* at Dunkirk, 'in the Name and Authority of the Lord Almighty and the Lamb.'[29] He had sent a fiery epistle to the Pope in 1658. At English-held Dunkirk, taking with him Samuel Fisher of Dover who spoke Latin, he could challenge a Catholic population and their Capuchin friars, whom he asked valid and honest if naive theological questions. Dunkirk also housed a Puritan garrison, whom Burrough recalled to the Light, but also to Cromwell's Puritan Crusade: 'The Lord hath owned and honoured our English Army and done good things for them and by them in these Nations in our Age ... and the Lord once armed them with the spirit of courage ... and gave them Victory ... Return to the old Spirit of Righteousness, which will reach after the liberty of the people and the freedom of the Nations ... and avenge the Blood of the Guiltless through all the Dominions of the Pope, the Blood of the Just, it cryes through Italy and Spain ... and it would be your honour to be made use of by the Lord in ... [this matter].'[30] This sounds bloodthirsty, but it echoes the images of 'binding Kings in Chains and Nobles with Fetters of Iron' with which the preaching of 'the Lamb's War' began. Despite inconsistencies in Burrough and others we should therefore take literally the constantly quoted Quaker text from 2 Corinthians 10:4 that their weapons were spiritual, not carnal.

Early writings of Howgill and Nayler are strikingly like Burrough's; I have reprinted Howgill's narrative of his agonies under the purging Light,[31] and other modern Friends have quoted his description of their joy afterward: 'The Heavenly Presence ... did gather us in ... to our Astonishment, Amazement, and great Admiration, insomuch that we often said one unto another, with great joy of Heart, *What, is the Kingdom of God come to be with men?, and will he take up his Tabernacle among the Sons of Men, as he did of old?'*[32] Nayler is less often quoted: 'This is the Day of your Deliverance, own it with the loss of all fading pleasures ... this is the Day of your Joy, but of the World's Sorrow ... Rejoyce ye Meek of the Earth.'[33]

Symbols of conquest are endless in the early tracts both of Howgill and Nayler:

To all you who have Eyes, and yet are blind ... the Lord is proclaiming himself to be King ... and all who rule as Kings and Conquerors shall bow. [The Quakers will] spare none; bathe your Sword in the Blood of Amalek.

[And to Cromwell]: thus saith the Lord, wilt thou limit me, and set Bounds to me when, and where, and how, and by whom I shall declare myself? ... then will I break thy Cord ... and exalt myself in thy overthrow.

Let the Potsheards strive with the Potsheards of the earth. Shall the Clay question the Work of the Potter? ... God is now exalting his own Son to be King.[34]

Howgill and Nayler spoke of God as 'the Higher Power' to which all, even rulers must be subject and in general had a more positive idea than a Mennonite would have had of 'the principal End of Magistrates, to judge the Cause of the Strangers, Poor and Helpless'; 'is not the Spirit of Meekness, Justice and Mercy, without respect of Persons, the Spirit of the living God, which being in a Magistrate, he is most like God ... Honourable here and hereafter.' Nayler and Howgill also warned rulers endlessly against telling God 'that he may not speak under Pain of Imprisonment or Killing the Body in which he speaks.'[35] Like Margaret Fell and Isaac Penington, they saw that the same evil which within themselves had cost such pain to face under the Light caused the anger and violence they faced from their persecutors. They expected violence from others.[36]

Thus, the root of Friends' peace testimony was the realization that violence was the fruit of anger or 'lust,' as Fox had said when he was first asked to enlist. It was the Devil's distraction, the trick of the wounded ego to 'destroy the creature,' the physical body of an enemy rather than the source of the evil.

Nayler's tract, *The Lamb's War*, written in prison and published anonymously in 1657 and 1658,[37] best shows the early Quaker vision of the peace testimony:

God Almighty, to whom belongs all the Kingdoms in Heaven and Earth, doth nothing therein but by his Son, the Lamb: by him he Creates and Governs; by him he Saves and Condemns ... makes Peace and makes War ... with the God of this World, and to plead with his Subjects concerning their revolt from him their Creator ... *The manner of his War is* ... that he may be just who is to judge all Men and Spirits, he gives his Light into their Hearts ... whereby he lets all see ... what he owns and what he disowns, that so all may know what is for destruction ... to come out of it, lest they be destroyed with it, that so he may save and receive all ... who are willing to be undeceived ... *They are to war against* ... whatever the Eye lusts after; whatever the Flesh takes Delight in, and whatever stands in Respect of Persons ... they wrestle not with Flesh and Blood which God hath made, but with spiritual Wickedness exalted in the hearts of Men and Women.[38]

Like most early Friends, Nayler said more about self-judgment than about love:

The Lamb's War YOU must know before you can witness his Kingdom ... But say you, *God is love and we are commanded to love all and seek peace with all*. I say, is *God's love* in you otherwise than it has ever been in Christ and all the Saints whom the world ever hated ... *For we War not with Flesh and Blood* nor against the Creation of God; that we Love; but we Fight against Wickedness, which Wars against God in the Creation ... that the Creation may be delivered ... without which there can be no true Love, nor lasting peace.[39]

The conquering Lamb was no casual symbol. Nayler had more insight than any other early Quaker into the sufferings and death of Christ, as he himself had suffered:

Come try whether Christ is in you. See if your Christ be the same that was from Everlasting ... or is he changed according to the times: in Life, in Death, in Peace and Wars, in Reigning, in Suffering? ... Does he beget in your Hearts a New Nature contrary to ... the Old Nature that inclines to the World and can be at peace therein?[40]

For Mennonites, as for the medieval Jewish tradition, faithfulness under suffering is trust in God's future action. But for Nayler, non-violence was itself the way God works, part of the present victory of God's Spirit:

For with the Spirit of Judgment and with the Spirit of Burning will he plead with his Enemies; and having kindled the Fire, and awakened the Creature, and broken their Peace and Rest in Sin, he waits in Patience to prevail to recover the Creature and slay the Enmity, by suffering all the Rage and Envy and evil Entreatings that the Evil Spirit that rules in the Creature can cast upon him, and he receives it all with Meekness ... that so the Creature might see what ... Fruits he himself brings forth.[41]

Nayler could thus speak of the Kingdom of God in the present tense, without losing the Friends' dynamic sense of crisis and victory:

His Dominion he hath amongst the Heathen, and his Hands are in the Counsels of the Kings ... and there is no Place where he is not ... But his Kingdom in this World in which he chiefly delights ... is in the Hearts of such as have ... owned his Call out of the World, whose Hearts he hath purified ... and is Righteousness and Peace, in Love, in Power and Purity.[42]

Claiming to be guided as a group by the Spirit of Truth, Friends did not apologize for growing clarity in a moral testimony, just as Roman Catholics can claim that the evolution of their doctrine shows the Spirit's work. It was thus also important that early Friends did not take the peace testimony as a negative commandment like the bans on oaths or pagan month-names they shared with many Baptists, and which the conscience of any radical Puritan would have affirmed. Such testimonies often betray their origin by their dependence on single Bible texts. Quakers naturally cited, especially against violent enemies, Jesus' warning to Peter (Matt. 26:52), and the Sermon on the Mount (Matt. 5:9, 21, and 38–48), which cuts deeper (but they ignored Matt. 5:21–2 and 7:1–5). They might have learned these texts from the few Baptist or sectarian pacifists they knew.[43] Within a generation Friends had begun to oppose capital punishment. Yet most early Friends (like most of their non-pacifist Baptist contemporaries) accepted police restraint as a marginal duty for 'saints.' They attacked spiritual evil, not physical, yet they never challenged restraint of children, thieves, or drunks, nor asked sharply enough how evil men with 'seared consciences' may be restrained. We must thus mark off the Friends both from monks and absolute ('non-resisting') pacifists and from the Anabaptist tradition that saints withdraw from violence and the state and leave police duty to the unregenerate.

Friends' peace testimony, like the later Quakers' attitudes to slavery, prison reform, and care of the insane, did not arise from one man's inspiration or even from a few Bible passages. The peace testimony was the result of a consensus of Friends as a whole about the meaning of their movement as a whole[44] and about the life and spirit as well as the words of Jesus.

Notes

1 James F. Maclear, 'Quakerism and the End of the Interregnum,' *Church History* 19/4 (Dec. 1950): Alan Cole, 'The Quakers and Politics, 1652–60,' PhD dissertation, Cambridge University (1955); cf. Peter Brock, *Pacifism in Europe to 1914* (Princeton, 1972), 264–6; *Quaker Peace Testimony*, ch. 2.

2 Thomas Lurting, *The Fighting Sailor Turn'd Peaceable Christian* (1710); P[eter] H[ardcastle], *The Quakers Plea*, 1661; George Fox, *Journal*, ed. John Nickalls (London, 1985), 65, and for all these cases and others, Margaret Hirst, *Quakers in Peace and War* (New York, 1972). I ignore in this essay the evidence that some men convinced of Quakerism while on garrison duty in Parliamentary armies in Ireland or Scotland did not resign or (when called insubordinate) did so only under protest. Early Friends, for reasons discussed later, never rejected police restraint.

3 Edward Burrough, *The Memorable Works of a Son of Thunder and Consolation* (1672); Francis Howgill, *The Dawnings of the Gospel-Day* (1676); James Nayler, *A Collection of Sundry Books, Epistles, and Papers* (1716). Cf. also William G. Bittle, *James Nayler, 1618 1660* (York, England, 1986). Will Hayes, *Gray Ridge: The Book of Francis Howgill* (1942) is slight. No adequate biography of Burrough exists; good summaries are: William C. Braithwaite, *The Beginnings of Quakerism* (London, 1923), 87–91, 157–62, 182–5, 285–8; Ernest E. Taylor, *The Valiant Sixty* (London, 1947), ch. 4. The other two pioneer Quaker preachers in London and Bristol, John Camm and John Audland, wrote much less; Camm died of tuberculosis in 1657/8.

4 Edward Billing, *SA Mite of Affection ... in 31 Proposals*; George Bishop, *Honest, Upright, Faithful, and Plain Dealing*; George Fox, *To the Parliament ... 59 Particulars*; Thomas Lawson, *Appeal to the Parliament Concerning the Poor*. These tracts owed much to Leveller ideas on improving the legal and electoral systems (cf. Hugh Barbour, 'From the Lamb's War to the Quaker Magistrate,' in *Quaker History* 4/1 (1966).

5 Reay, *The Quakers*, 88–91. He also (91–107) assembles quotations from conservative Puritans trying to show the Restoration was the result of their 'Quaker fear' of Quakers' attacks on tithes, rather than interrupting worship.

6 Fox was ill at the Curtises at Reading (*Journal*, 353–6). Meanwhile, he rebutted over fifty anti-Quaker tracts by his massive *Great Mistery* (1659).

7 *Memorable Works*, b-2-verso.

8 *A Warning from the Lord to the Inhabitants of Underbarrow: Works*, 16.

9 *Memorable Works*, c-verso and c-2-verso.

10 Ibid., 93–4.

11 Reay may overstress the economic, as against the religious element in Quakers' threat to tithes and the parish church system. A notebook of handwritten statements and pledges against pastors' tithes by over 250 Westmorland Quaker women was in the Kendal Meeting House in 1959.

12 *Memorable Works*, 503; cf. 519, 585, 594.

13 George Bishop, *New England Judged* (1661); Edward Burrough, *Some Considerations Presented unto the King of England* (1660); both mainly drawing on Humphrey Norton, *New England's Ensign* (1659): see *Early Quaker Writings*, ed. Hugh Barbour and Arthur O. Roberts (Grand Rapids, Mich., 1973), 116–48. Burrough went personally to see the King.

14 Cf. Barry Reay, 'The Quakers and 1659: Two Newly Discovered Broadsides by Edward Burrough,' *Quaker History* 54/2 (1977), 101–11.

15 On lay Puritans' belief in portents and providences, see David D. Hall, *Worlds of Wonder: Days of Judgment* (Harvard, 1990), and biographies of Oliver Cromwell.

16 *Memorable Works*, 582; *To the Parliament of the Commonwealth of England* (1659), 3, which as Reay notes was omitted from the *Works* but adds little.

17 Ibid., 601, 604 (his italics).

18 Ibid., 613.

19 Hill, *World Turned*, 351, quoted in Brock, *Quaker Peace Testimony*, 26.

20 *A Visitation of Love to the King* (1660) in *Memorable Works*, 668, 671. Burrough cited for the King his letters to the Protector saying the same.

21 *Memorable Works*, 671. Reay, *Quakers*, 107, may be wrong in thinking that Burrough thought Friends only 'better informed' about violence after 1659.

22 *Memorable Works*, 767, from Epistle 'To all My Dear Companions' (1660).

23 Reay, 107.

24 'The Ethics of Movements of Awakening,' for Biblical Theologians 11 Oct. 1979. See also the writings of Timothy L. Smith and William G. McLaughlin, Jr on the American 'Holiness Movement' and 'the Third Awakening.'

25 Douglas Gwyn, 'The Early Quaker Covenant of Light, in *The Covenant Crucified* (Pendle Hill, 1995).

26 Part of the titles of Howgill's *Works* and *Nayler's The Power and Glory of the Lord Shining out of the North* (1653). Fox often 'sounded the Day of the Lord,' e.g., on top of Pendle Hill.

27 Douglas Gwyn, 'The Early Quaker Covenant of Light' anticipated a book in press. Early Friends' refusal until 1661 to promise what the Spirit might lead them to do (e.g., in Massachusetts) can be linked to their refusal until 1659 to advance concrete proposals for political reform or to enter into ordinary radical political action like the Levellers.

28 Both were written from Ireland in 1655, Howgill's is *Dawnings*, 28–33; Burrough's is *Memorable Works*, 64–7. See my *Quakers in Puritan England* ch. 3 on the mystique of the 'Quaker Galilee' and ch. 4 on 'the Lamb's War.' Nayler's corresponding tract was *The Power and Glory of the Lord, Shining out of the North* (1653), before the nationwide expansion began.

29 *Memorable Works*, 525–41. The tract to the Pope is 426–73.

30 Ibid., 537. Cited also by Reay and others.

31 *Quakers in Puritan England*, 98, 107, and *Early Quaker Writings*, 167–79; from *Inheritance of Jacob* (1655); also in Howgill, *Dawnings*, 37–71. Nayler's greater depth of prior religious experience may have minimized his self-searching phase, but his sudden call to be a Quaker prophet was equally a surprise to him: see Fox and Nayler, *Saul's Errand* in *Early Quaker Writings*, 67–8.

32 'Francis Howgil's Testimony Concerning Edward Burrough,' from *Memorable Works* reprinted also in the 'London Discipline,' *Christian Faith and Practice in the Experience of the Society of Friends* (London, 1988) as no. 184, etc.

33 'Epistle to several Friends about Wakefield' (1653), in *Collection*, 27..

34 *Dawnings* 3, 32, 5, 11; *Collection*, 85.

35 *Dawnings*, 21; *Collection*, 297, 252, 251; *Collection*, 79, cf. 40. The same dual message about the role of rulers was typical of Burrough, who asked the Rump to see 'that *Justice* sits in the *Throne*: And not men for greatness sake in Titles or Birth, chosen in *Tradition* and not by Appointment of God,' but made clear these were 'righteous judges ... over the outward man ... though to the Lord God alone we give Authority and Power to Rule us and Judge us ... over our inward man ... that the Civil Magistrate may be secluded from Judgment over us in all things concerning the worship of our God' (*To the Parliament of the Commonwealth*, 4–7).

36 Like a modern psychiatrist, feminist, or black militant, early Friends welcomed anger as a sign they had reached an opponent's conscience; they were only grieved when Oliver Cromwell treated them graciously in refusing.

37 The two quite different editions were printed in London by Thomas Simmons, one of two regular printers of Quaker books and husband of Martha Simmons, who in 1656 played a key role in Nayler's disastrous 'sign,' when

he rode into Bristol like Jesus' Palm Sunday entry into Jerusalem. Unless Nayler's companions carried the manuscript from their previous imprisonment at Exeter, it must have been written in the first months after Nayler's trial by Parliament, brutal flogging, and branding, during his long imprisonment in Newgate, where also he added for the second edition eleven additional pages to the original ten, echoing the same themes. Nayler's name was not printed on either, as he was in disgrace with Friends as well as Puritans.

38 *Collection*, 375–8.

39 Ibid., 393; this passage was among those Nayler added in 1658.

40 Ibid., 382–3. Nayler fully united the historical Christ and the inner Spirit of Christ in his approach to suffering and victory.

41 Ibid., 379–80. Nayler's famous 'dying words' are similar.

42 Ibid., 381.

43 Cf. Brock, *Peace Testimony*, 6.

44 Conventicle Act persecutions no doubt made this clearer to Friends. But the vigour of Friends' open challenge to persecution in the 1660s, often still using Lamb's War language, and the pacifism already assumed by their enemies in the same years to be typical of Friends, seem to me to need more study.

10

'The Things That Make for Peace' The Context of Pacifism in Quaker Pennsylvania

JACK D. MARIETTA

Would that even today you knew the things that make for peace!
Luke 19:42

The bumper sticker said, 'If you want peace, work for justice.'[1] It was intended as political advice, but it suggested an appropriate way to write the history of pacifism. While historians have never ignored the context of pacifism and pacifists, we have more often than not written histories of pacifist thought and ethics or pacifist sects or minorities, and neglected their historical circumstances. Social critics might allege that while writing the history of peace we insufficiently appreciate that we may be writing the history of repression, especially Westerners pacifying Third World peoples. Without conceding their case, I propose in this essay to review the political and social context of the Quaker pacifists of Pennsylvania and not confine myself to the history of the Society of Friends. While employing my own research, more often I will examine recent writings on Pennsylvania history relevant to that context and the conditions that made for peace or that inhibited it. I have organized my argument according to the following topics: Friends' practice of pacifism, government and politics, economic life, the administration of justice, and relations with Native Americans.

Friends and the Practice of Pacifism

Because Pennsylvania was one of the rare places where pacifists administered much of public life, we should inspect conditions in the colony as well as the faith and practices of its unusual leaders. Until the American Revolution, the typical Pennsylvania pacifist had very few public obligations that troubled his conscience. Freedom from concern resulted especially from the Quaker-dominated legislature that relieved all Pennsylvanians from militia service. That relief was as much as non-Quaker pacifists asked. Quaker legislators clearly facilitated the practice of peace by all men and women of conscience, and not just by their own Quaker brethren. Quaker legislators and magistrates, however, had to confront the questions of pacifist intimacy with the colony's use of force, first, through its dependence on England and its foreign relations and, second, through its justice system. The record of the Quaker legislators proved to be an uneven one, and that record finally served as a motive for some Quaker legislators' famous departure from office after 1755.

The overarching tension between the legislators' pacifism and their contrary values arose from their Whig politics – that is, their pursuit of local political power at the expense of imperial and proprietary (the Penns') power and interest. Pennsylvanians, who were mostly Quakers, accrued more constitutional power at British expense than probably any other Americans.[2] The pursuit of local power was innocent enough in peacetime, but in wartime it jeopardized Friends' pacifism. In general, to push for public power in time of war brought responsibility for waging war; even to continue in wartime to exercise powers customary in peacetime brought such responsibility. Quaker pacifism was then put 'in harm's way.'

The Quaker legislators' problem was the raising and expenditure of money for war. That their intimacy with war extended only this far was the result of the limited character of eighteenth-century imperial wars, the typical remoteness of the wars from Pennsylvania, and the usual harmony between Pennsylvania and its Native American population. The British government was normally content when Pennsylvania contributed to the expense of the wars after 1689, although it occasionally asked for more than funds. Pennsylvania assemblymen, however, often were not content to supply the funds without a consideration. At this point their Whig propensities came into play, for they either used Britain's importunity to bargain for more power for the Pennsylvania assembly or they defended the power they had already accrued.

In the first of the colonial wars, 1689–96, the sins of the legislators against pacifism may be called venial. To bargain for power the legislators had to misrepresent the Quaker pacifist ethic and posture before provincial executives as though they had some pacifist stock in trade that the governors had to deal with. It was the Quaker orthodox pacifist understanding that these Quaker legislators must supply funds – 'render to Caesar' – as long as they did not *apply* the funds to war.[3] What the executive did with the money was his, Caesar's, business. They could not honourably refuse the royal request for funds if the executive knew their ethics would not suffer when they granted the king their money. Their practice was to be silent about their ethic while the governors of the colony, Benjamin Fletcher and William Markham, mistakenly presumed that the Quakers could not give money to bellicose *uses*. Fletcher, for example, once promised them their money 'would not be dipt in blood,' as though that made a difference for their ability to grant money.[4] In that era, the assembly did not control the expenditure or application of any monies it granted and so never violated Quaker pacifism in the war. (Later, it gained a customary power over expenditure.) On all occasions when it either proffered funds or actually granted them, it did so only in exchange for power or privilege. When it twice supplied money it did so after the governors committed themselves to using the money for peaceful purposes, in deference to a presumably inhibited, pacifist assembly. But it was not for the reason of the peaceful use that the house twice granted money. Though it did not finally do so, in 1695 the assembly negotiated to grant money for clearly bellicose uses, but again, only in return for power.[5]

During the war, a pacifist issue emerged from an incipient division among Pennsylvania Friends. In 1692, a premier Friend and minister, George Keith, precipitated a schism in the Society in Pennsylvania. Keith ultimately left Quakerism and came back to irritate the Society as an Anglican missionary. But before the schism that took his name he criticized Friends for inconsistently practising pacifism; they approved of force in domestic government while they prohibited using it in foreign relations or war. The proper course for Friends, wrote Keith, was to leave public office.[6] The criticism had the attractiveness of being a simple formula and the appearance of a superior commitment to peace. Yet Keith was the essential character in a welter of factionalism and recriminations that would cause any onlooker to depreciate the honesty of his expressions.

In Queen Anne's War, 1701–13, the Pennsylvania assembly once committed to supplying money in return for power, but reneged. Then in 1710–11, it levied a tax and granted the income to the war; the event became a *cause célèbre* at the time. The politics of the province was deeply divided between partisans of David Lloyd, often speaker of the assembly, on the one hand, and friends of the proprietor, on the other. Compounding that division were the Keithian partisans or schismatics, who were to be found predominantly in the political camp of David Lloyd. The putative issue of pacifism and the war tax got caught up in the partisanship. The Lloyd faction, recently bested in the assembly election of 1710, censured the tax and grant as contrary to Quaker pacifism and urged a boycott of the tax collector.[7] The most renowned penman on the Lloydian side, William Rakestraw, had an unmistakable record of partisanship, while ironically authoring one of the more honoured tracts on behalf of a more robust Quaker practice of peace. 'If war,' he wrote, 'be altogether contrary to the Law and Spirit of Christ, the maintaining of War by paying to it, is altogether contrary to the Law and Spirit of Christ.'[8] And moreover, as Keith had asserted in 1692, if Friends were not to be found in Caesar's 'camp' (army), they should not be in his 'court' (government). Those sentiments found a home in the consciences of mid-century Friends of immense rectitude and credibility, like John Woolman. But no known exponent of them in 1711 could boast of any such credibility; these messengers sullied the message.

The provincial government moved against taxpayers who refused to pay the 1711 levy and who could, if they so wished, dress their refusal in the respectable allegation of keeping their pacifist conscience. In Bucks County, Joseph Kirkbride, a Quaker minister and justice, prosecuted Henry Paxson for non-payment. Paxson had been a Lloyd partisan in the assembly for the unequalled term of six years. In 1691 he permitted his daughter to marry out of the Society, and the next year he followed George Keith out of the Society. In 1709, with others of the Lloyd party, Paxson worked to have the governor dismiss Kirkbride from the bench.[9] One can, if one wishes, assign him to the ranks of conscientious Pennsylvanians, exponents of a sturdier pacifism suggested by Keith. Or, equally well, one can assign Paxson to Lloyd party ranks and dismiss his boycott of the tax collector as mere partisanship. Paxson, Rakestraw, and undoubtedly other partisan Friends and ex-Friends were not credible apostles for peace; and their opposites in the Society were not even interested in expanding pacifism or its practice. The deleterious effects of schism and politics extended to pacifism as well as to many other aspects of Quaker life and reform.[10]

In sum, while they deserve credit for sheltering typical pacifist Pennsylvanians from the intrusion of war after 1689, Friends in public office so conspicuously mixed their pacifism with political partisanship and Whiggery that they made themselves unlikely apostles for peace.

War did not return until almost all the Friends from 1689–1711 were dead; their influence on their successors is improbable. When those successors violated pacifism – as they clearly and repeatedly did – the blame was largely their own. Unlike the first experience with war, the Society had a complement of conscientious members by the 1740s, whose commitment to pacifism was not mottled with prospects of personal advancement. In the 1740s and 1750s, Quaker assemblymen appropriated money for warfare and, as was their prerogative by that time, oversaw the expenditure of the revenue.[11] The censure they received was, however, inappropriately meagre, and was returned to them by few of their own brethren. Frankly, too few non-Quakers (as well as later historians) understood the ethic of rendering to Caesar to spot the Friends' deviation. And too many Pennsylvanians wanted a vigorous war against the French and Indians to pause and examine the ethical niceties of the Quakers. They *were* niceties, but grounded in scripture and very practical since they had preserved Friends' ability to stay in legislative offices while satisfying most of the demands for prosecuting war – that is, sending money to the Crown. But the sectarian niceties made for poor evangelism on behalf of peace. A clear pacifist testimony would attract notice and either convert others to it or arouse their disgust for Friends. Because after 1755 the Society got mostly disgust, they might just as well have practised a pacifism as robust as the impatient, bellicose critics credited them with.

The signal way to broadcast one's efforts for peace in these wars was to refuse to pay taxes for them and, if one had to raise money for war, indirectly or directly, then to resign from government. John Woolman and other Friends began to do just that or urge that upon others. It promised the end of Quaker dominance in Pennsylvania's government – a very sobering consideration. But the reformist, pacifist Friends found the Quaker presence meaningless, especially when the government commissioned the deaths of venerable Indian friends. A Holy Experiment with only nominal apostles for peace was not an experiment worth its salt.[12]

Government and Politics

Pennsylvania was renowned as the Quaker colony. In the seventeenth century, when Pennsylvania had a Quaker majority and proprietor, its Quaker identity was unmistakable. When those conditions disappeared, there remained that bastion of Quaker government, the robust, Wiggish Pennsylvania House of Representatives. By reason of Quakers' presence in the house, historians have usually dated Quaker influence to 1755, after which the withdrawal of sundry Quakers eliminated even that. Thereafter, whatever Pennsylvania was it should not be credited to Quaker oversight.

Recently historians have modified that picture by enlarging the strength and duration of Quaker influence in the province. In one of the most succinct and analytical investigations of Quaker leadership, Richard Ryerson found that the Quakers in the Pennsylvania house unmistakably qualified as an oligarchy. They showed themselves to be an extraordinarily durable elite, probably unique among all North American legislatures. Additionally, contrary to allegations that the Quaker influence died in the withdrawal of Quaker legislators in 1756, it persisted willy-nilly until 1775.[13] Whatever the quality of Pennsylvania's government and its promotion of peace, Quakers must be credited with a share of responsibility for it.

Because a case for elitism or oligarchy is not *ipso factor* a case for injustice or oppression, the examination of Pennsylvania's public life must proceed to the quality of government provided by the Quakers – although some democratic idealists have rested their case against Quakers without that examination. If government was not *of* the people, was it *for* the people?

Judgments upon the justice of government in Pennsylvania cannot escape reckoning with at least two events, the Paxton riot of 1763–4 and the overthrow of the 1682 provincial charter in 1776. Favourable judgments cannot escape the criticism of historians of the Progressive school who made much of the discontents expressed in 1763 and 1776. According to Progressive historians beginning with Charles H. Lincoln in 1901, Pennsylvania's government was dominated by a Quaker elite in its House of Representatives which was unresponsive to its western counties, to Philadelphia, and to its poorer citizens. Abetted by the small size of the house, misapportionment of representatives, and a property qualification for the franchise, the Quaker elite resisted change until it and the whole provincial constitution was overthrown in 1776 by a combination of urban radicals and frontiersmen.[14] This account of Pennsylvania history of course leads one to blame the Quakers for misgovernment that led not to peace or peaceful change but to upheaval and violence.

While innocent of Progressives' belief in the axiomatic frequency of conflict (rather than consensus) in America's past, several recent historians have lent support to the Progressive account. John Murrin describes the Pennsylvania house as uniquely Quaker, passive, and unresponsive to the needs of a major colony. Murrin indicts the Pennsylvania house for being the least active legislature in America, passing fewer laws per year than 'tiny and disorganized' Delaware, small New Hampshire, and other colonies. 'Pennsylvania constituents expected less from their legislature and got it,' Murrin inveighs. Robert Hohwald agrees; the Quaker legislature practised passive sovereignty, engrossing as much power as possible only so that rivals could not use that power against Quakers.[15] By the reckoning of these two historians, the victims were all Pennsylvanians and not just westerners. These authors are also, however, impatient with the deferential attitudes of the citizen victims.

George Franz studied the circumstances of the men who participated in the greatest collective expression of discontent in Pennsylvania before the revolution – the Paxton riot or march. He blames the legislature explicitly because its centralization of power deprived Paxton township and other local governments of their ability to fulfill the needs of their citizens. In such cases, riots and mobs became acceptable methods of solving one's problems. And yet Franz does not merely duplicate the Progressives' complaint. The Progressive 'contention that the Paxton boys were democrats of the west marching on the east for equal representation must be dismissed,' writes Franz. The complaint of unequal representation surfaced only after Philadelphia rivals of the Quaker party had talked to the Paxton protesters – presumably adding the misapportionment grievance to the Paxtonites' list.[16]

Other recent work tends strongly to refurbish the reputation of Quaker government for peace. No one has done more so in that respect than Alan Tully. In his book, *William Penn's Legacy*, Tully asserts that long periods of quiet and harmony characterized Pennsylvania's public life as much as the renowned episodes of conflict. He assigns part of the credit for the harmony to the Quakers' presence in Pennsylvania and its government. The provincial government, monopolized by Friends, did not aggrieve the voters. The polls were, moreover, a valid medium for voter discontent because of the franchise. The voting population included the new German population after 1718 and was not minimized by the franchise and the naturalization laws. Still, less than a third of the taxable persons voted, regardless of their ethnic group. Does that mean that the Quaker oligarchy connived at that outcome? No, Tully concludes, 'Many qualified Pennsylvanians failed to vote simply because they lacked interest ... The indifference of Pennsylvania's freeman was the indifference of the satisfied.'[17]

Turning to the western counties, Tully asserts that 'to emphasize this theme of western disenchantment [with the Quaker-run legislature] and alienation too insistently would be as misleading as to omit it.'[18] Albeit underrepresented in the house, when western voters elected representatives they did not choose rivals to the Quaker elite or Quaker party in the house; their choices worked with the party. Tully credits this cooperation especially to the continued good reputation of the minority Quaker population in western counties and to the Whiggish reputation of the Quaker party. The Quaker party was not unresponsive to the west, as befitted the west's support of it. Whereas inattention to local government and civil peace caused the Regulator rebellion in the Carolinas in the 1760s, Tully notes that in the same tumultuous decade the Quaker legislators provided for appellate courts in the western counties of Pennsylvania.[19]

Of the Paxton riot Tully writes that neither it nor the Indian attacks in the previous eight years really marked any realignment or any new departure in Pennsylvania's politics. For discontented Scotch-Irishmen from the west, the political alternative to the Quaker party was the proprietary party, rival to the Quaker party. But contrary considerations, like obnoxious proprietary quit rents, favouritism in the proprietary Land Office, and monopolization of premium western lands by the Penns kept westerners from switching allegiances to the proprietary party.[20] Westerners might not have been happy with their political options, but they invented no new ones.

Too many of the characterizations of Pennsylvania government and politics have depended on evidence from the uppermost level of government; judgments about the inadequacy of government, as well as the docility of voters, were not fully informed. Like Franz, Tully does not rest after looking at provincial government and politics, and he finds reasons to modify the earlier historical picture.

Lancaster and counties further west, without large numbers of Friends, had their own autonomous political organizations, free of the Quaker party control (which party they nevertheless supported). Local leaders' first obligation was to their county constituency and not provincial parties of either stripe; nor could the parties impose their will on the locals. The fact that the locals supported the Quaker party with few exceptions was the result of that party's policies on land and its occupation, taxes, and quit rents, as specified above.[21]

At the township level, Tully found government more vital than Franz. Township residents were not deferential, Tully believes, because they selected their own officers. While they could legally elect some, it appears that the non-elected officials were only nominally appointed by the proprietor. They were really chosen by their fellow townsmen and worked largely under their direction. The picture Tully paints is not one of an inert, mindless, and powerless citizenry.[22]

At least three other historians, Lucy Simler, Laura Becker, and Mary Schweitzer, have joined Tully in scrutinizing Pennsylvania government and society outside the capital.[23] In the provincial statutes, Simler finds the assembly consistently apportioning more authority and autonomy to the township, especially in the realm of taxation. 'To the colonists of southeastern Pennsylvania the township as a method of settlement brought orderly compact settlement and a government capable of maintaining the peace, supervising the highways, overseeing the poor, and of assuming an even greater role as the colonial world expanded and moved west.'[24] Were it not for the fact that Simler confines her generalization to the southeastern counties, her conclusion could hardly be more at loggerheads with that of Franz: the townships in Pennsylvania were not enfeebled, and the assembly was not guilty of it.

'From 1681 to 1755, power in Pennsylvania essentially was situated in the countryside,' writes Mary Schweitzer, where she means especially economic power. Credit for that belonged partly to the assembly – whose will, it seems, was not to cripple politically the countryside – but also to the initiative of the country population, which thwarted central authorities if they needed to.[25] Laura Becker studied Reading, Pennsylvania, where the population was predominantly German and immigrant, had little facility in English or prior participation in government, but still 'the percentage ... making use of the courts and voting in elections was impressive.'[26] The people they voted into office were inordinately from the English and wealthy minority.

The weight of the scholarship on provincial and local government favours the positive conclusion about its effectiveness and its value in the eyes of Pennsylvanians. That is most clearly the case in rural Chester, Bucks, and Philadelphia counties, but it seems true of the regions further west as well.

The Economy of Pennsylvania

'In America, almost every farmer lives on his own lands, and in England not one in a hundred does,' wrote Tom Paine, mostly from his experience in Pennsylvania.[27] Other Americans, visitors, and historians repeated the observation. Justice in America appeared in its large, agrarian, realty-owning population, especially in the eyes of Thomas Jefferson and other subscribers to republican political economy.[28] The economic self-sufficiency afforded to yeomen freeholders underlay their political independence and virtue. Equality before the law and one's governors followed from a widespread and fairly equal ownership of property. On the other hand, the injustice of slavery and the haplessness of slaves was obvious. Republicans fretted more over the danger of a large or increasing class of white agricultural tenants and urban wage-earners than they did over slavery. Jeffersonian presuppositions may have influenced historians, especially Progressives, who, in any case, researched the subject of land ownership, tenancy, and property distribution in early America. Some violent events, not surprisingly, were attributed to the inequitable ownership of land: the riots in the Hudson River valley in the 1760s, the New Jersey riots of 1745–54, as well as violence in Pennsylvania.[29]

Recent work in Pennsylvania's economic history shows some surprises of the 'good news, bad news' variety. Mary Schweitzer's 1987 book falls with the good news category. She found comparatively little reason for discontent in occupancy of land in Pennsylvania; indeed, practice there probably fulfilled the accolade of 'the best poor man's country.' 'Large tracts of [unoccupied] land were abhorred,' Schweitzer writes, 'and it did not take the colonists long to learn how to overturn the technicalities which might keep land out of cultivation.' Security in his or her occupation of the land was not difficult for the average settler in Pennsylvania to come by, moreover. Before 1760, obtaining a warrant and taking up the land was all that was needed. Even squatting, or 'quiet possession,' conveyed some security. The Scotch-Irish, notorious squatters, regularly benefited from that extra-legal custom.[30]

At first glance, Lucy Simler's intensive research into land occupancy in Chester County shows a less equitable situation than Schweitzer's. There had been prior cause for apprehension: Jackson T. Main, James T. Lemon, and Duane E. Ball had found evidence of a surprisingly large landless population in southeastern Pennsylvania.[31] Simler affirmed that such people indeed existed. They were either tenants or, secondly, inmates, also known as cottagers. Thirty to 40 per cent of taxed house-holders in some years were tenants. The inmates occupied a clearly lower status than the tenants. With their families, they lived with the resident landowners and provided seasonal labour to the owners. They began to appear at about 1740 and amounted to one in four Chester County families by 1760.[32] Together with the tenants the cottagers made up a sufficient part of the population to oblige historians to reassess the conventional wisdom of Paine, Jefferson, and others about landowner-ship, at least in the best poor man's country. Simler did that, of course, but also she has worked beyond the premises of Jefferson to enquire what in fact was the political economy in Pennsylvania.

What Simler discovers in the case of the tenants resembles the revel-ations from Sung Bok Kim's study on the tenants of the Hudson River valley.[33] In general, tenancy was not economically oppressive nor politi-cally disquieting in either place. Simler writes, 'Despite the rhetoric claiming that tenants were shiftless and landowners were tyrannical, in everyday life tenancy was widely seen as equitable and generally profit-able ... Clearly, too, not only individual tenants or landowners but soci-ety as a whole gained from tenancy in Chester.'[34] As for the cottagers, 'There is no evidence that either party to the arrangement [landowner or cottager] saw it as a system that would become permanently embedded ... The system worked to the convenience of both.' Men just out of inden-tured servitude, found in cottaging a means to some upward mobility; especially important, they might start a family and remain in the area.[35]

In sum, occupancy of land in Chester County approximated the alleg-edly undesirable situation that purportedly did not exist there or in much of America. Chester really represents an inversion of two cases, because, first, it supported many landless families, but, second, the fam-ilies found their situation unobjectionable. Whether the rest of Pennsyl-vania resembles Chester County is unknown and needs investigation.

Beyond the occupation and use of Pennsylvania's land, the provincial economy was affected by one of the most remarkable public economic institutions in colonial America, the Pennsylvania Loan Office. The office has long interested economic historians for various reasons, but Schweitzer additionally describes how it added to the equitability of life in Pennsylvania.[36] The office 'provided capital to people who would have been normally denied loans through the private sector,' did so at below-market interest rates, and in general operated more equitably and efficiently than private lenders. The recipients represented all landhold-ers, but, also, by connivance, included some first purchasers. The office's equitable purpose and operation, writes Schweitzer, reflected the Quaker origins and ethos of the government that created it.[37]

Finally, Schweitzer employs analytic techniques to take the overall measure of Pennsylvania's economy. With regard to growth in personal income, distribution of wealth, and efficiency of production, Pennsylva-nia did well, she believes. Inequities did exist, and time aggravated them. Yet compared with Europe, other American colonies, and later

Pennsylvania, the economy performed enviably to at least 1755. 'The stereotype of the colonial Pennsylvania countryside as a relatively equitable society before 1755 is not far from the truth.'[38]

The Administration of Justice

Nowhere is justice more the avowed objective of a community than in its laws and courts, and considering the premise of this essay, nowhere else should we expect to find peace more clearly nurtured. And our expectations of Friends should be all the higher in light of their particular religious profession. That is, Quakers distinguished themselves from their pacifist contemporaries by their engagement in government. While Anabaptists of various stripes avoided even voting, Friends protested when they were excluded from public life. Quakers' detractors periodically reviled them too for wielding public power, alleging since George Keith's time that sincere pacifists would decline all use of force, private, public, and international.[39] But no, said Friends, government was ordained by God and justifies its exercise of force by being 'a terror to evildoers.' Christians legitimately serve in domestic public office and wield force. It is force in pursuit of justice that makes all the difference; international war is forbidden because it is chaos and licentiousness, not justice. By reason of this Quaker distinction, we would do well to ask whether Friends provided justice in Pennsylvania and legitimated their own occupancy of office.

Compared with the histories of land occupancy, the economy, and the other agencies of government, the justice system has been a stepchild of academics. In his 1982 review of the literature on crime and justice in early America, Douglas Greenberg found only five works specifically on Pennsylvania.[40] The situation is improving.

The depiction of Pennsylvania's justice system we have for the first thirty years or so of the province is of disorder, or even chaos, hardly a system at all. William Penn, Governor Benjamin Fletcher, Anglican missionaries, and British officers of the customs and other services depicted Pennsylvania as lawless in varying degrees. Some few commentators said so sincerely, but others' motives are suspect. Historians believed one or more of them. Second, the unhappy picture obtains from the well-documented disorder within Pennsylvania's early politics: contention among proprietor, the Crown and other English authorities, the Church of England, and Pennsylvania residents. The Quakers themselves, Pennsylvania's possible leadership cadre, were obviously factious and schismatic. The inclination to extrapolate from this disorderly scene is almost irresistible. And some social theory may incline us to presume that stable systems are necessarily complementary. Greenberg concluded that Pennsylvania's criminal justice system suffered from 'near-anarchy' in its early decades and only later enjoyed regular justice and legitimate institutions. The problem was that Pennsylvania's nascent society had no acknowledged elite who would provide it with legitimate courts and justice; 'political wrangling' undercut the courts. Contrary to much 'conventional wisdom' about law enforcement, stable institutions of justice operate not from terrorizing evildoers and others, but by leaders persuading people that their society's interest is advanced by its legal institutions.[41]

Beyond the effect of having no elite, Pennsylvania society was otherwise deficient in the prerequisites for regular justice. The extant literature on all of the early American colonies indicates that 'a correlation existed between the effectiveness of law enforcement institutions and the willingness of those institutions to undertake morals prosecutions since only a smoothly functioning system of criminal justice could afford the time and energy necessary to regulate private morality.'[42] Pennsylvania prosecuted persons for morals crimes in its first thirty years, and very few later, but compared with such prosecutions in New England (especially New Haven), Pennsylvania did little at any time. And so, Pennsylvania appears unlikely to have had – and been able to have had – a smoothly operating criminal justice system. The enforcement of morals in turn depended upon a community's consensus on personal behaviour. The exclusive, homogeneous New England population afforded that consensus, but Pennsylvania, least of all the American colonies, had or desired that homogeneity. Presumably, it could never get efficient justice either.[43]

Another way of comparing New England and Pennsylvania society is that New Englanders put a premium on order and stability, whereas Pennsylvanians exalted liberty. Greenberg informs us that the sobering consequence of the difference is that 'where order thrived ... so too did oppression; where liberty prospered, so too did crime.'[44] Was crime then the price of freedom in Pennsylvania?

A recent peerless work on early Pennsylvania justice (in both the civil and criminal courts) is William Offutt's 1987 dissertation on the Delaware Valley, including New Jersey. Offutt addresses most of the issues Greenberg raised from the earlier literature and disproves more than he confirms of the conventional picture. William Penn's lament and others' accusations that there was a crime wave in Pennsylvania is not corroborated by the data from the courts.[45] The alleged symbiosis of politics and justice systems did not exist, for while undoubtedly politics and governments changed dismayingly often, a legal elite established itself surprisingly quickly, 'producing a legal system of great stability and public approval.' Also, most of the adult male public participated in the system.[46]

Whereas political stability was no prerequisite for the administration of justice, an elite may have been, for by Offutt's reckoning, one oversaw the justice system in the early Delaware Valley. That elite comprised mostly Quaker leaders, merchants, and high government officials. In civil cases, persons in these categories were most likely to be successful as plaintiffs. 'Failure to settle with a Quaker leader plaintiff led to almost certain defeat for the defendant,' Offutt found – but ordinary Quakers were no more successful than any other plaintiffs.[47] In the criminal courts, the defendants were representative of the general population as far as Offutt can tell. Defendants in the elite categories were found guilty at almost the same rate as the overall accused population, while the character of their crimes distinguished them as a social elite. Also, the wealth of the accused had little effect on the outcomes.[48]

Offutt leaves us with a picture of a system run by a surprisingly successful elite who used the system to secure their own status and legitimacy, but not inequitably. It is the elite that Greenberg did not find, doing what the claimed such an elite must do – persuade the people that their interest was advanced by this system. Judged by the Quaker standard of self-effacement, we may find the Quaker leaders in this elite deficient, but with a redeeming quality of not driving their rivals and inferiors so hard as to alienate them or to debilitate the justice system of early Pennsylvania.

By 1710, at the latest, Quakers were minorities in the grand and petit juries, writes Offutt, just as they were a minority in the province. Immigration that adulterated the Quaker concentration throughout the province might have supplied unhappy clients in the judicial system. With, among others, the question of immigrant discontent with the system in mind, Laura Becker studied the German immigrants and their progeny in Reading, Pennsylvania – where they comprised five-sixths of the married men. Rather than discovering discontent, her findings tend to confirm the situation that Offutt discovered.[49]

First, these Germans voluntarily employed the civil courts in large numbers between 1766 and 1775. In the criminal courts, few Reading men were accused, but 40 per cent performed some service or duty at court, 1766–75. Overall, two-thirds of the men had some involvement with the courts in the decade. These high rates of participation mean that the justice system was not removed from the people. The poor were included – the bottom 30 per cent of property owners sued more often than they were sued (reversing the trend in Offutt's study), but were average in the likelihood they would be accused of a crime. Their participation or even activism stood in clear contrast to their unhappiness with and their jeopardy in the courts of their respective German places of birth or family origin.[50]

In light of that record, the effect for Pennsylvania was likely a welcome one. Social scientists posit that popular involvement in government helps to promote acceptance of the system, increase satisfaction, and allay discontent and vigilantism; or, in other words, although involvement is not synonymous with justice, it promotes peace.

While quantitative studies of Pennsylvania justice are very few, historians have been more often attracted to extraordinary episodes of lawlessness and collective violence, usually riots, like the well-known Paxton riot, the Maryland boundary dispute, the Frederick Stump affair, and the Wyoming Valley 'war.' Trying to generalize about riots and violence rather than repeat narratives about Paxton and renowned riots, Thomas Slaughter recently examined the Lancaster County court records. 'Violence, anti-institutional ambitions, and intracommunal strife' were much more common in Lancaster than consensus historians have led us to believe, he summarizes.[51] While Slaughter supplies a few numbers from Lancaster criminal courts, there are no comparative data in his work and no data to substantiate his characterizations of his riots as anti-authoritarian – or of any other ilk.

A substantial number of Slaughter's Lancaster riot cases are from the Pennsylvania-Maryland border disputes of the 1730s. While Slaughter characterized them as anti-authoritarian, Charles Dutrizac looked at these events more intensively than Slaughter and found the rioters to have had various motives. Rioters could be mobilized because their victims were a different ethnic group – Germans or Scotch-Irish. They might riot because they were 'poor, often landless, laborers' and servants, who were sometimes enlisted in these 'riots' by the promise of land and pay from their superiors. Yet despite their use as mercenaries, anti-authoritarian sentiment mixed with their economic aspirations, for while enlisted by superiors to defy superiors from another colony, these people relished defying authority, denying deference to a class while doing so in the very limited arena of an intercolonial dispute.[52] How common were such discontents and ambitions among all Pennsylvanians and westerners? It would seem unlikely that they apply to inhabitants of the three original eastern counties, but among other westerners, possible refugees from the increasing cost of land in the east, the likelihood that they do grows. And yet it is difficult to conclude that dissatisfaction was prevalent without more information.

The Paxton march on Philadelphia was the largest and most famous expression of collective discontent and potential rebellion in Pennsylvania before 1776. Since 1970, at the latest, historians have not regarded the march as an expression of democratic discontent with an oligarchical Pennsylvania government and its insensitivity. Rather, it is the most conspicuous show of western discontent with the Indian policy of Pennsylvania, dating from the massacre of Conestoga Indians at the Lancaster jail in 1763 to near warfare in the Wyoming Valley in the 1770s. Some of the same riotous characters, like Lazarus Stewart, appear repeatedly in these disorders. Alden Vaughan bluntly states that the principal legacy of the Paxton march was an 'open season' on Indians.[53]

Three years after the Paxton march an aftershock occurred, the Frederick Stump affair. Stump stood accused of murdering ten Indians and was almost surely guilty, but he was never tried because a mob of Cumberland County men sprang him from jail, some contemporaries believed with the complicity of the county magistracy. The apparently abject inability of the justice system to bring Stump to trial enraged some of the principal men of the province from the governor on down. Historian G.S. Rowe comments that in Cumberland this 'Defiance of authority seems to have been endemic.'[54]

Finally, in the 1770s some Pennsylvanians repeatedly attacked and killed some Indians, other Pennsylvanians, and law officers in the Wyoming Valley (in Northumberland County), which lay in dispute between Pennsylvania and Connecticut. Like the Maryland border dispute, persons inclined and used to riotous behaviour used the dispute speciously to legitimate the violence.[55]

One means to test the hypothesis about the prevalence of riots in Cumberland as well as other counties is to learn what proportion of each county's recorded crime was riots and put it into the context of all crime. We would expect to find that Cumberland or similar counties contributed more cases of riots to the total for riots than Cumberland's total contribution of cases to the grand total for all counties. That is to say, we expect that Cumberland magistrates were more concerned about riots

Table 10.1. Indictments for riots and assaults, 1682–1800, as percentage above or below a county's percentage of all indictments
$(N = 29,845)^a$

County	Riot	Assaults
Bedford	1.5	0.5
Berks	4.0	0.4
Bucks	−2.8	0.0
Chester	0.6	−1.0
Cumberland	0.0	−0.1
Dauphin	4.8	0.6
Huntingdon	2.2	1.5
Lancaster	−3.0	−0.2
Mifflin	1.6	0.4
Northumberland	0.3	−0.3
Philadelphia	−0.5	0.4
Philadelphia City	−8.2	−1.8
Westermoreland	2.0	−0.4
York	−2.6	0.0

[a]The data were compiled by the author and Professor G.S. Rowe.

than they were with most other kinds of crime, when compared with other magistrates in the province. Table 10.1 lists for each of fourteen counties the *difference* between a county's percentage of all riot indictments (and for assaults too) in fourteen counties and its percentage contribution to the total indictments from those counties. Zero indicates a balance between riots and total crime, and a positive number indicates the preponderance of riots over all crime. Cumberland proves to be neutral by this index. Lancaster, containing Paxton Township and bordering Maryland, and York, also on the disputed border with Maryland, are comparatively 'deficient' in riots. However, five other western and northern counties are positive, Dauphin most clearly so. By this test the counties that were the scenes of notorious riots or the residences of notorious rioters did not have endemic rioting or pervasive interpersonal violence. We may do well to treat the famous outbreaks of disorder as isolated events that did not warrant the apocalyptic remarks of some contemporary observers.

Whereas the older literature on the westerners concluded that their participation in riots arose from widespread injustice done to them, mostly by the governments in Philadelphia or London, recent evidence tends to the conclusion that collective and interpersonal violence was not as common as earlier thought and, second, that not injustice and not the lack of institutions to provide justice, but the very *operation of justice* caused the westerners to become violent. The westerners did not want blind justice, they wanted the end of the Indian presence in the land they claimed, and not getting it constituted injustice in their eyes. Either the government in Philadelphia would commission the force to remove Indians, or the locals in the west would do it. And when and if the government brought the law down on them for their violence towards Indians, it was not riot or criminal conspiracy to stop the magistrates.

The fault was not solely the westerners'. Francis Jennings has spent most of a lifetime documenting relations between American colonists and Native Americans, especially in the Middle Atlantic region. In two long volumes published in the 1980s he displayed his unsurpassed knowledge of the events that turned the peaceful coexistence of Pennsylvanians with local Indians to violence.[56] Jennings leaves no doubt that eminent Pennsylvanians and Englishmen, including Quakers, shared the blame with westerners who more often committed the actual violent actions. Briefly, justice towards the Native Americans and peace commanded the highest respect from William Penn, but regrettably continued only during his lifetime. Beginning very shortly thereafter, persons he appointed – Lieutenant Governor William Keith, Provincial Secretary James Logan – as well as Penn's children, some English Friends, and others satisfied their appetite for private profit and public power by defrauding the Natives of land and furs. The Iroquois Confederation, jealous of their own power and eminence among Native Americans, collaborated in the fraudulent schemes, especially the infamous 'Walking Purchase.' The consequences of dishonesty would not appear to almost all Pennsylvanians until the Seven Years War, when to the astonishment of some concerned colonists, historically friendly Natives attacked and killed colonists. The French, rivals to the English for empire, were not innocent either, but yet, their enlistment of Pennsylvania's Natives in warfare was obviously facilitated by dishonest Pennsylvanians and English and overbearing Iroquois.[57]

It is a sobering realization that withal, violence where whites and Natives met in Pennsylvania appears close to inevitable. Had all the dishonesty miraculously disappeared from Pennsylvania's leaders and wealthy men and had the French disappeared, too, the exceptional growth of Pennsylvania's population – ironically in acknowledgment of its reputation as the best poor-man's country – would have led to clashes with Natives. It is the most intractable case of injustice in Pennsylvania's past, because government or well-intentioned private Friends could not remedy the needs of the westerners merely by doing more for them. The justice these whites demanded excluded justice to the Natives. In modern jargon, it was a zero-sum game. The mob that freed Frederick Stump in self-proclaimed justice as much as said that the Indians must have no justice.

Pennsylvania was a fair and equitable place for most men, it seems: for yeomen farmers, tenants, cottagers, pacifists, Anabaptists, German speakers, borrowers from the Loan Office, plaintiffs, and defendants. But how many of them could it invite and contain, despite its apparent spaciousness? How many could live peacefully with Native Americans? From the whole American experience, it seems that not even in all the trans-Appalachian west was there space enough for peace, save in eighteenth-century Pennsylvania. Should the epitaph of the peaceful experiment be 'died from success'?

Notes

1 The sentiment is not new. William Penn wrote essentially the same advice in his 1693 *Essay towards the Present and Future Peace of Europe, by the Establishment of an European Dyet, Parliament, or Estates.*

2 The premier example of Pennsylvanians' successful Whiggery was the unique ability of the Pennsylvania House of Representatives to raise and expend public funds without any reference to the executive officers of government. Neither Parliament nor any other colonial assembly enjoyed that power; it was contrary to all English constitutional practice. It was through the Loan Office, to be discussed later, that the Pennsylvania legislature amassed such power. James H. Hutson, *Pennsylvania Politics, 1746–1770: The Movement for Royal Government and Its Consequences* (Princeton, 1972), 6–16.

3 *Espistles from the Yearly Meeting of the People called Quakers, Held in London to the Quarterly and Monthly Meetings in Great Britain, Ireland, and Elsewhere; From the Year 1675, to 1759, inclusive* (London, 1760), 67. William Penn to Arthur Cook, J. Simcock, and others, 5 Nov. 1695, Gratz Collection, Governors, Historical Society of Pennsylvania. As early as 1660 eight English Friends protested paying taxes on the grounds that their taxes paid for war. The Society soon reprimanded them, and periodically thereafter repeated that Friends were obliged to pay their taxes even though the taxes paid for warfare. LF Spence Manuscripts, III, nos. 4, 100, 107, 118–19. LF Barclay Manuscripts, II, 165. Friends House, London. Somerset Records Office Manuscripts DD/SFR

8/2, 72. Tauton, U.K. For these references to the protestors, I am indebted to Richard Greaves and his unpublished paper, 'Shattered Expectations? George Fox, the Quakers, and the Restoration State, 1660–1685,' presented at the George Fox Commemorative Conference, Lancaster, U.K., 26 March 1991.

4 *Colonial Records of Pennsylvania: Minutes of the Provincial Council of Pennsylvania* (Philadelphia, 1852), vol. 1, 399–400. Hereafter *Col. Rec.*

5 Jack D. Marietta, 'The Course of Quaker Pacifism in the Colonial Wars: Pennsylvania's Legislatures, 1693–1748,' paper delivered at the conference of Quaker Historians and Archivists, 27 June 1980. *Col. Rec.*, vol. 1, 444, 451, 455, 457.

6 Ethyn Williams Kirby, *George Keith (1638–1716)* (New York, 1942), 59–60.

7 Marietta, 'Course of Quaker Pacifism.'

8 'William Rakestraw: Pacifist Pamphleteer and Party Servant,' *Pennsylvania Magazine of History and Biography* 98 (1974), 53–7. Hereafter *PMHB*.

9 William Rakestraw, *Tribute to Caesar, How Paid by the Best Christians, and to What Purpose. By Philalethes* (Philadelphia, printed by Jacob Taylor, n.d.), 26. Middletown Monthly Meeting minutes, 4–12 month-1691, 5–8 month-1692. Friends Historical Library, Swarthmore. *Votes and Proceedings of the House of Representatives of the Province of Pennsylvania* (Pennsylvania Archives, 8th series, Harrisburg, 1931–5), vol. 2, 855.

10 In a recent paper, J. William Frost adduced that the Keithian schism also forestalled anti-slavery reform in the Society in 1701. Conservatives were too anxious to restore order to the Society to advance abolition, or perhaps pro-slavery Friends used such anxiety expediently to stymie anti-slavery advocates. If abolition of slavery is justice to Afro-Americans, which few Friends would deny, then the Keithian schism delayed justice. 'George Fox's Ambiguous Antislavery Legacy,' paper presented at the George Fox Commemorative Conference, Lancaster, U.K., 27 March 1991.

11 Jack D. Marietta, *The Reformation of American Quakerism, 1748–1783* (Philadelphia, 1984), 138–42.

12 Marietta, *Reformation*, 156–8.

13 Richard Alan Ryerson, 'Portrait of a Colonial Oligarchy: The Quaker Elite in the Pennsylvania Assembly, 1729–1776,' in Bruce Daniels (ed.), *Power and Status: Officeholding in Colonial America* (Middletown, 1986), 109, 112–14, 119–20. Alan Tully, 'Quaker Party and Proprietary Policies: The Dynamics of Politics in Pre-Revolutionary Pennsylvania, 1730–1775,' in ibid., 84. Marietta, *Reformation*, 194–202.

14 Charles H. Lincoln, *The Revolutionary Movement in Pennsylvania, 1760–1776* (Philadelphia, 1901).

15 John M. Murrin, 'Political Development,' in Jack P. Greene and J.R. Pole (eds.), *Colonial British America: Essays in the New History of the Early Modern Era* (Baltimore, 1984), 439. Robert S. Hohwald, 'The Structure of Pennsylvania Politics, 1739–1766,' PhD dissertation, Princeton University (1978), 1–2.

16 George William Franz, 'Paxton: A study of Community Structure and Mobility in the Central Pennsylvania Backcountry,' PhD dissertation, Rutgers University (1974), iii, 41, 120, 122, 412–13, 417. And yet Franz qualifies his criticism of feeble local government by stating that if the Carolinas had had the county system that Pennsylvania did, there would have been no Regulator movement there. Franz was not the first to discredit the alleged democratic motives of the Paxton protesters, although no one did it better than Franz. See James E. Crowley, 'The Paxton Disturbance and Ideas of Order in Pennsylvania Politics,' *Pennsylvania History* 37 (1970), 321–2, and James Kirby Martin, 'The Return of the Paxton Boys and the Historical State of the Pennsylvania Frontier,' *Pennsylvania History* 38 (1971), 133.

17 Alan Tully, *William Penn's Legacy: Politics and Social Structure in Provincial Pennsylvania* (Baltimore, 1977), 92–4.

18 Tully, 'Quaker Party,' 88.

19 Ibid., 89.

20 Alan Tully, 'Ethnicity, Religion, and Politics in Early America,' *PMHB* 107 (1983), 511–12, 505–10, 512, 521, 529, 531, Tully, and 'Quaker Party,' 99–100.

21 Tully, 'Quaker Party,' 92–3.

22 Ibid., 99–103. Tully admits that his evidence of townsmen's activity comes from heavily Quaker townships, and practice may have been different elsewhere.

23 Franz, James T. Lemon, and Claire W. Keller belittled the importance of the township in public life, whereas Tully affirmed that the township was 'more than a handy unit of local administration' hauling water at the behest of the county and provincial officers. Franz, 'Paxton'; J.T. Lemon, *The Best Poor Man's Country: A Geographical Study of Early Southeastern Pennsylvania* (Baltimore, 1972), 111; C.W. Keller, 'The Pennsylvania County Commissioner System, 1712–1740,' *PMHB* 93 (1969), 382. Tully, *William Penn's Legacy*, 116.

24 Lucy Simler, 'The Township: The Community of the Rural Pennsylvanian,' *PMHB* 106 (1982), 66.

25 Mary M. Schweitzer, *Custom and Contract: Household, Government, and the Economy in Colonial Pennsylvania* (New York, 1987), 12.

26 Laura Leff Becker, 'The American Revolution as a Community Experience: A Case Study of Reading, Pennsylvania,' PhD dissertation, University of Pennsylvania (1978), 284–5.

27 Philip S. Foner (ed.), *The Complete Writings of Thomas Paine* (New York 1945), vol. 1, 203.

28 Robert E. Shallhope, 'Republicanism and Early American Historiography,' *William and Mary Quarterly* (hereafter *WMQ*), 3d ser., 39 (1982), 334–56, and 'Towards a Republican Synthesis: The Emergence of an Understanding of Republicanism in American Historiography,' *WMQ*, 3d ser., 29 (1972), 49–80.

29 Douglas Greenberg, 'The Middle Colonies in Recent American Historiography,' *WMQ*, 3d ser., 36 (1979), 405. Sung Bok Kim, *Landlord and Tenant in Colonial New York: Manorial Society, 1664–1775* (Chapel Hill, 1978). Thomas L. Purvis, 'Origins and Patterns of Agrarian Unrest in New Jersey, 1735–1754,' *WMQ*, 3d ser., 39 (1982), 600–27.

30 Schweitzer, *Custom and Contract*, 17, 109, 12, 98–100.

31 Jackson T. Main, *The Social Structure of Revolutionary America* (Princeton, 1965), 33–4, 180–2. Lemon, *Best Poor Man's Country*, 12, 94. Duane E. Ball, 'The Process of Settlement in Eighteenth-Century Chester County. Pennsylvania: A Social and Economic History,' PhD dissertation, University of Pennsylvania (1973), 78.

32 Lucy Simler, 'The Landless Worker: An Index of Economic and Social Change in Chester County, Pennsylvania, 1750–1820,' *PMHB* 114 (1990), 165. Lucy Simler and Paul G.E. Clemens, 'The "Best Poor Man's Country" in 1783: The Population Structure of Rural Society in Late-Eighteenth-Century Southeastern Pennsylvania,' *Proceedings of the American Philosophical Society* 133 (1989), 239. Lucy Simler, 'Tenancy in Colonial Pennsylvania: The Case of Chester Country,' *WMQ*, 3rd ser., 43 (1986), 569.

33 Kim, *Landlord and Tenant*.

34 Simler, 'Tenancy in Colonial Pennsylvania,' 569.

35 Simler, 'The Landless Worker,' 173–4. Simler and Clemens, 'The "Best Poor Man's Country" in 1783,' 239–40.

36 C.W. MacFarlane, 'Pennsylvania Paper Currency,' *Annals of the American Academy of Political and Social Science* 8 (1896), 50–75. Richard A. Lester, 'Currency Issues to Overcome Depressions in Pennsylvania, 1723 and 1729,' *Journal of Political Economy* 46 (1938), 324–75, and *Monetary Experiments, Early American and Recent Scandinavian* (Princeton, 1939). Leslie Van Horn Brock, 'The Currency of the American Colonies, 1700–1764: A Study in Colonial Finance and Imperial Relations,' PhD dissertation, University of Michigan (1941). Paton W. Yoder, 'Paper Currency in Colonial Pennsylvania,' PhD dissertation, Indiana University (1941). Theodore Thayer, 'The Land-Bank System in the American Colonies,' *Journal of Economic History* 13 (1953), 145–59.

37 Schweitzer, *Custom and Contract*, 139, 147, 151–5, 166. Alan Tully helps to explain the popularity of the Loan Office as well as add a political motive to its Quaker officers. He states that 'by midcentury numerous borrowers had

not made a payment in ten years.' *William Penn's Legacy*, 85. Schweitzer may have serendipitously answered Tully when she wrote that the problem at the Loan Office was not delinquent payments but poor record keeping of the repayments. *Custom and Contract*, 248.

38 Schweitzer, *Custom and Contract*, 80–7.

39 Marietta, *Reformation of Quakerism*, 263–4.

40 Douglas Greenberg, 'Crime, Law Enforcement, and Social Control in Colonial America,' *American Journal of Legal History* 26 (1982), 293–325.

41 Ibid., 309, 320–1.

42 Ibid., 316.

43 Jack D. Marietta, 'Law and the Enforcement of Morals in Early Pennsylvania,' paper delivered at the Organization of Americans Historians, 12 April 1980. Greenberg, 'Crime,' 304–9.

44 Greenberg, 'Crime,' 325.

45 William McEnery Offutt, 'Law and Social Cohesion in a Plural Society: The Delaware Valley, 1680–1710,' PhD dissertation, Johns Hopkins University (1987), 297–8.

46 Ibid., ii, 11, 460–1, 25, 27.

47 Quaker leaders are defined as meeting clerks, elders, overseers, treasurers, and representatives to quarterly meetings. High officials were justices, clerks, sheriffs, coroners, attorneys general, assemblymen, and councillors. Ibid., 179, 185.

48 Ibid., 59, 95, 357, 365.

49 Becker, 'The People and the System.'

50 Ibid., 139–40, 145, 148.

51 Thomas Slaughter, 'Crowds in Eighteenth-Century America: Reflections and New Directions,' *PMHB* 115 (1991), 28, 30–1.

52 Charles Desmond Dutrizac, 'Local Identity and Authority in a Disputed Hinterland: The Pennsylvania-Maryland Border in the 1730s, *PMHB* 115 (1991), 35–62.

53 See the citations at note 16. Alden T. Vaughan, 'The Frontier Banditti and the Indians: The Paxton Boys' Legacy, 1763–1775,' *Pennsylvania History* 51 (1984), 2.

54 G.S. Rowe, 'The Frederick Stump Affair, 1768, and Its Challenge to Legal Historians of Early Pennsylvania,' *Pennsylvania History* 49 (1982), 275.

55 Martin, 'Return of Paxton Boys,' 133.

56 *The Ambiguous Iroquois Empire: The Covenant Chain Confederation of Indian Tribes with English Colonies* (New York, 1984) and *Empire of Fortune: Crowns, Colonies, and Tribes in the Seven Years War in America* (New York, 1988).

57 *Ambiguous Empire*, 215–18, 243–4, 247–8, 262–74, 291–4, 306–7, 309–50, 388–97. *Empire of Fortune*, 10–11, 187–203, 278–81, 379–83.

11

Quaker Women and the Pacifist Impulse in Britain, 1900–1920

THOMAS C. KENNEDY

In late May 1918 John Henry Barlow, Clerk of the London Yearly Meeting, left this annual gathering of the Religious Society of Friends and made his way from Quaker Headquarters at Devonshire House, Bishopsgate, to the London Guildhall. Barlow wanted to be physically as well as spiritually united with three members of the Friends Service Committee (FSC) who were on trial there for violating the Defence of the Realm Act (DORA) by refusing to submit a pamphlet called 'A Challenge to Militarism' to the official censor.[1] After Barlow's dramatic departure, the presiding assistant clerk, Mary Jane Godlee, adjourned the business of the meeting so that those remaining might 'in reverent and prayerful silence' unite with their brothers and sister awaiting the heavy hand of the Warrior State. That moment, as she later recounted to her husband, an imprisoned conscientious objector, gave Esther Peet a sense of 'sharing in the … deep stand for truth in a way which I have not had a chance to do in public before.'[2]

At first glance, this riveting scene of faith and resistance would seem to be an authentic affirmation of two historic Quaker traditions: the defiant Friends in the dock witnessing to their testimony for peace and the female clerk symbolizing their traditional practice of sexual equality. But initial impressions can be misleading. Mary Jane Godlee was, in fact, the first woman ever to preside over the London Yearly Meeting and, until the twentieth century, the vaunted Quaker tradition of equality between the sexes had been observed largely in the breach.[3] Furthermore, despite the historic association of Quakerism with pacifism, it was not until the twentieth century, particularly during the Great War, that the Society of Friends as a corporate body promulgated the sort of radical and uncompromising peace testimony, reflected in the 'Challenge to Militarism' case, with which British Quakerism has subsequently become identified.

The purpose of this essay, beyond briefly pointing up some of the historical limitations of two vaunted Quaker traditions, is to discuss the role that women played during the first two decades of the twentieth century in formulating and witnessing to what became an all-encompassing Quaker peace testimony as well as to discern the relationship, if any, between Quaker feminism and the pacifist impulse that shaped this enlarged peace testimony.

Among the most radical teachings of Quaker founder George Fox was that the coming of Christ, with His gift of spiritual Indwelling or the Inward Light, had restored women to their original place of equality with men: 'For man and woman were helpsmeet, in the image of God and in righteousness and holiness ... before they fell ... after the Fall, in the transgression, the man was to rule over his wife. But, in the restoration by Christ, into the image of God and His righteousness and holiness again ... they are helpsmeet, man and women, as they were ... before the Fall.'[4] Accordingly, women were drawn to early Friends in fairly large numbers; and although Quakers always rejected the ministrations of 'hireling priests,' they did recognize the special spiritual gifts of certain lay preachers, male and female. Several women were among Fox's early preacher-followers, including a dozen of the so-called Valiant Sixty who began Quaker missionary activities during the 1650s.[5] Most prominent among these was Margaret Fell, who later married George Fox, and who emerges from the recent work of Bonnelyn Young Kunze as something like the co-founder of the Society of Friends.[6] According to Kunze, Fell's activities as well as her strong influence on George Fox were important reasons why 'women ... approached equality in the spiritual sphere in early Quakerism, probably to a greater extent than in other sectarian movements of the [seventeenth] century.'[7]

If Quaker women did, in fact, have something like spiritual equality, this condition did not carry over into the business of directing the day-to-day affairs of their Society. During the 1670s both the London Yearly Meeting, which would develop into the chief legislative organ of British Quakerism, and the Meeting for Sufferings, which became its working executive committee, were formed as exclusively male bodies. There were intermittent attempts to establish a parallel Women's Yearly Meeting, but these were quietly ignored or gently suppressed. As late as 1766, a proposal for a Women's Yearly Meeting was rejected on the ground that there were an insufficient number of women Friends with 'suitable abilities to carry on so weighty and important a work.'[8] Although a separate Women's Yearly Meeting was finally set up in 1784, it was endowed with no legislative functions; and, as one male Friend noted a few years later, the willingness of women Friends 'to be invested with greater power ... was somewhat limited by the prudence of the Men.'[9] Female Friends continued to make up a sizeable proportion of those who ministered at meetings for worship as well as to be represented among the non-preaching elders and overseers who guided the spiritual affairs of local meetings and supervised their ministry. With respect to the guidance and direction of their religious Society, however, the Men's Yearly Meeting remained authoritative until 1897, when the first women members were appointed to the Meeting for Sufferings. As Mary Jane Godlee, first acting female clerk, herself testified early in the twentieth century, the slow pace of meaningful female participation in the central governance of the British Society of Friends was 'very curious, and ... rather painful to those ... who may have believed in the theory that women Friends have always had an equal place with their brethren in the Church.'[10]

George Fox might have obtained an earlier release from Derby gaol, where he languished for more than a year in 1650–1, if he had accepted a proffered captaincy in the parliamentary army, but, as he recorded in his *Journal*: 'I told them that I lived in the virtue of that life and power that took away the occasion of all wars ... I told them I was come into the covenant of peace which was before wars and strifes.'[11] Fox's personal testimony was given corporate sanction in 1660–1 when, after a rising of Fifth Monarchy Men in which Quakers were allegedly implicated, the Society of Friends issued a 'Declaration from the Harmless and Innocent People Called Quakers ...': 'All bloody principles and practices ... we utterly deny ... all outward wars and strife, and fightings with outward weapons ... this is our testimony to the whole world ... the Spirit of Christ, which leads into all Truth, will never move us to fight and war against any man with outward weapons, neither for the Kingdom of Christ nor for the kingdoms of this world.'[12]

That seems clear enough. Certainly, this declaration was prominently cited by pacifist Quakers during the First World War. The citation was, however, a bit disingenuous. For, this particular seventeen-century document had had little to do with the 'historic' peace testimony of Friends, having been lost to posterity until it was culled out of obscurity during a surge of historical research inspired by the religious and intellectual stimulus of the late nineteenth-century 'Renaissance' of British Quakerism. In fact, the declaration appeared as an official Quaker document only in the 1911 edition of the Friends' *Book of Discipline*.[13]

This is not to say that in the intervening period Friends had failed to make known their general adherence to non-violence and non-resistance as a way of life. During the Restoration their passive response to the brutal enforcement of the Quaker and Conventicle Acts cost them, male and female, dearly in lives, limbs, and fortunes, as did their courageous refusal to give 'hat honor,' to recognize titles, to swear oaths, or to pay tithes.[14] The moral fortitude that enabled them to suffer stripes and imprisonments without retaliation arose, no doubt, from the belief, so artlessly expressed by ex-soldier William Dewbury, 'that the Kingdom of Christ was within, and the enemies was within, and was spiritual and my weapons against them must be spiritual, the power of God. Then I could no longer fight with a carnal weapon against a carnal man.'[15]

For all of this, however, the peace testimony maintained a low profile in the lexicon of essential Quaker beliefs for most of two centuries. Robert Barclay's *Apology* (1676), the classic exposition of seventeenth-century Quaker ideas and beliefs, deals only briefly with issues of peace and war (although what Barclay does say seems decisive),[16] and there was no specific pronouncement on the peace testimony by the London Yearly Meeting until 1730. When it was finally included among the 'Queries' directed by the Yearly Meeting to each Monthly Meeting to discover the 'state of the Church,' the peace testimony was, for some time, attached as a sort of appendage to the prohibition against the payment of tithes.[17]

During the two centuries following the death of George Fox (1691), Quakers maintained and even expanded their reputation as a peace-loving, if peculiar, people, but their public witness to the peace testimony waxed and waned. This is not surprising. Given the limited nature of most wars of the period and the fact that governments seldom troubled Quakers about their refusal to cooperate with military enterprises, it was difficult for Friends to make peace a burning political or even moral issue.[18] There was, of course, the public example of John Bright, particularly his courageous and politically costly opposition to the Crimean War and his resignation from Gladstone's Cabinet in 1882 because of the bombardment of Alexandria, but Bright's avowed support of the Unionist cause in the American Civil War and his refusal to condemn the use of violence in a contest between good and evil, pointed up his ambiguity concerning Quaker peace principles.[19]

Towards the end of the nineteenth century, in the course of the revitalizing spiritual renewal that has been called the Quaker Renaissance, some Friends, generally younger and well educated, did begin a serious search for the authentic source as well as the precise meaning of Quaker peace principles. Rejecting the biblical literalism of evangelical Friends who dominated the Society for most of the nineteenth century, they discovered in pacifist pronouncements of early Friends the concept of 'that which is of God' dwelling equally in every person and making every human life equally sacred. For them, this Inward Light was not only the chief means by which God revealed Himself and His message, but also the unimpeachable verification of their historic refusal to fight with carnal weapons.[20]

While the working out of the ideals of the Quaker Renaissance provided liberal-minded Friends with a challenging modern interpretation of their peace testimony and a higher level of rhetoric, there was, at the end of the nineteenth century, still no consensus as to what constituted an acceptable Quaker witness for peace. The war in South Africa provided a forum for testing that witness, but consensus remained elusive.

Quaker theologian and historian John Punshon has noted that in the twentieth century 'English Friends, for all their quiet demeamour and sweet reasonableness, are only happy at the extremes.'[21] Such a conclusion seems borne out by Quaker responses to the first major political cum theological event of this century, the Anglo-Boer War. The conflict in South Africa so divided British Friends, old and young, male and female, that five months after it began *Reynolds Newspaper* could feel safe in declaring that the Society of Friends was 'no longer to be regarded as a strenuous and united peace organisation.'[22] Female Friends certainly had a role in creating this impression. A few months after the outbreak of the war, the Cambridge classicist and anti-war Quaker J. Rendel Harris, recounting a meeting of the Cambridge Peace Society to one of his former students, noted, 'It was very sad to have our cause given away, as it was by Caroline Stephen ... There is no doubt in my own mind that we are betrayed in the citadel itself.'[23] Harris was disturbed not only because the war in South Africa had been publicly supported by a Friend but also because that particular Friend happened to be Victorian Quakerism's most illustrious recruit via 'convincement.' Caroline Stephen's description in *Quaker Strongholds* (1891) of the 'never-to-be

forgotten Sunday morning' when 'in a small company of silent worship-
pers,' she was delivered from despairing agnosticism into the 'most
soul-subduing, faith-restoring, strengthening and peaceful communion
... that I have ever known' had caused her to become, for much of the
reading public, the authentic voice of British Quakerism.[24]

Friends like Rendel Harris may have been annoyed and embarrassed
by Caroline Stephen's pro-war stance, but they should not have been
surprised. The publication of *Quaker Strongholds* has generally been
accounted a major event of the Quaker Renaissance, but a perusal of the
book reveals that Caroline Stephen's interpretation of the peace testimony might well give strict pacifists cause for concern:

It is commonly supposed that Friends have some special scruple about the use of
physical force ... This I believe by no means true of the Society at large, although
... very likely to be founded on fact as regards individuals ... I came to understand that the Quaker testimony against all war did not take the form of any ethical theory of universal application ... as to the 'unlawfulness' of war ... I
personally cannot but recognize that ... certain wars appear to be not only inevitable but justifiable ... I cannot, therefore, regard all war as wholly and unmiti-
gatedly blameable.[25]

Caroline Stephen's defection to the war camp pointed up the difficulties incumbent upon interpreting a peace testimony that had
remained a largely untested dictum for two centuries. Not only did this
ambiguity allow Stephen, as well as a number of other socially prominent Friends, to voice public support for the South African War but also,
in the words of one indignant anti-war Quaker, 'to plead that they must
be strictly regarded as very true Friends while they were doing so.'[26]

The proceedings of the Meeting for Sufferings in the spring of 1900,
seemed to bear out the view that Friends, divided and dispirited, had
surrendered moral leadership in the struggle against the war. The consensus of this body, effectively the executive committee for the London
Yearly Meeting, dominated as it was by elderly, cautious, and evangelical males, seemed to be that in light of the national mood, any attempt to
influence the government by condemning the war would be 'untimely'
and might weaken the Society's influence in the future. Still, this decision was far from unanimous. One of the Meeting for Sufferings' newly
appointed female members, Ellen Robinson (1840–1912), an educator
and recorded minister, was especially outspoken. Noting that influence,
like the war, should be of the present, Robinson reminded the meeting of

its obligation to provide leadership in witnessing to the peace testimony: 'If all war is wrong, this war is wrong, and we ought to say so ... instead of remaining passive spectators of the present fratricidal strife.'[27]

Ellen Robinson failed to carry the Meeting for Sufferings, but her personal campaign against the Boer War provided ample evidence that the pacifist impulse was very much alive among Friends. Robinson's public witness had begun in October of 1899 when she was appointed by the Women's Meeting of Lancashire and Cheshire Quarterly Meeting to visit the Men's Quarterly Meeting with a view to issuing a joint public statement of Friends' belief 'that war is wrong under all circumstances, irrespective of the ends to be accomplished,' including the possible improved treatment of Native races in South Africa. Declaring its intention to maintain a Christian witness against war 'with ... true spiritual vigour,' Ellen Robinson's Quarterly Meeting, at least, condemned the war as 'wholly contrary to the teaching of Christ.'[28]

When the London Yearly Meeting gathered in May 1900, without the guidance of a strong anti-war statement from the Meeting for Sufferings, to continue the debate over the South African conflict, Ellen Robinson presented her own striking personal message: 'The whole world seemed to be crying out for some one to deliver it from the monstrous yoke of militarism, which is crushing the life out of the nations. Let us be earnest and do our part.'[29] Many Friends agreed. One of these thanked her for having had the courage to condemn, as the Meeting for Sufferings had pusillanimously refused to do, 'the spirit of rampant militarism and the greed of land and gold' that had made war in South Africa possible.[30] And though Ellen Robinson's may not have been the decisive voice, the Yearly Meeting, after considerable wrangling, did finally issue a somewhat watered-down address on 'Christianity and the War' which incorporated at least a part of the message Ellen Robinson wished to deliver to the nation at war.[31]

Ellen Robinson was perhaps the most prominent among those female Friends who wished their Society to take an unequivocal public stand against the South African War. She never achieved that goal, but whatever her sense of failure about the less than decisive response of British Quakerism, she was undoubtedly an object of envy to those Quaker women who felt as strongly as she did about opposing the war, but who were constrained by domestic or other circumstance from any significant participation in anti-war activities. One of these was Dorothy C. Brown, the wife of a Manchester doctor, E. Vipont Brown, and the mother of small children, whose hand-written 'Journal' records her sense of frustration: 'It makes one weep to think of the suffering & misery there ... One can do so little, only sew garments & give what we can, it is such a drop in the bucket.'[32]

Dorothy Brown sewed garments as her contribution to the Friends South African Relief Fund Committee (FSARFC), which undertook a large-scale relief effort on behalf of war refugees, especially Boer women and children in British concentration camps. The FSARFC not only gave anxious home-bound female Friends some sense of participation, it also enlisted a number of them for service in the theatre of war.[33] These women, including Georgina King Lewis and Frances Taylor, visited South African refugee camps, dispensing clothing, powdered milk, and goodwill, but, in the end, even this activity became a source of division among Friends. For, in the wake of Emily Hobhouse's sensational revelation of 'loathesome and barbarous facts' about how incompetent adminstration of the camps had led to catastrophic death rates among Boer women and children, FSARFC representatives were accused, especially by their co-religionists, of kowtowing to military authorities and white-washing what Emily Hobhouse called the 'wholesale cruelty' of the camp system. Thus, even charitable activities meant to demonstrate Quaker adherence to their peace testimony became a basis for division.[34]

In the aftermath of the Anglo-Boer War, some Friends felt compelled to ask why the peace testimony was 'little more than a pious opinion ... almost independent of the other parts of Christian truth' to so many erstwhile Quakers.[35] Disturbed by this seeming lack of any strong sense of what the Society's witness for peace actually entailed, the Yearly Meeting in 1902 appointed a special deputation charged with visiting every Monthly Meeting in the Britain 'with a view to arousing our members to their responsibility ... of maintaining our testimony of peace.'[36]

The 1902 peace deputation had the effect of refocusing as well as re-emphasizing peace activities. During the Edwardian period Quakers were in the forefront of the struggle against the militarization of youth, the imposition of conscription, and the ascending arms race.[37] Friends, including Ellen Robinson, were also prominent in a series of widely publicized peace conferences that became a feature of the international diplomatic and even social scene. Perhaps the most famous female Friend to regularly participate in what one author has recently termed the European 'high-life peace circuit' was Priscilla Hannah Peckover (1833–1931). Sister of Lord Peckover of Wisbech and founder of the Local Peace Association Movement, which, from its founding in 1879 until it was over-

taken by events in 1914, enlisted thousands of British and other
European women in a worldwide campaign for world peace and goodwill, P.H. Peckover has generally been depicted as a model of late-Victorian Quaker pacifism.[38] But a recent Cambridge doctoral thesis by
Quaker historian Brian Phillips, 'Friendly Patriotism: British Quakerism
and the Imperial Nation, 1890–1910,' depicts P.H. Peckover and her
movement as a particularly egregious example of the sort of respectable
but superfluous and self-aggrandizing peace evangelism in which many
Quakers were engaged during the three decades prior to the First World
War. Peckover, Phillips claims, accomplished little except becoming a
surprisingly immodest superstar on the late-Victorian/Edwardian peace
congress circuit, hob-nobbing with royalty and heading up a movement
'positively drunk with its sense of amity and virtue.'[39] Even more dis-
turbing than the hollow superficiality of Peckover and other socially
prominent Quakers, says Phillips, is the uncomfortably ambiguous attitude towards British imperialism adopted by many Friends in the years
before 1914. Labour historian James Hinton has made the same point in
his *Protests and Visions*, noting that the British peace movement was
'deeply scarred by often unrecognized imperialist assumptions.'[40]

These arguments are sometimes persuasive, and they certainly serve
as correctives to the frequently hagiographic accounts written by Quakers about other Quakers. But if the pre-1914 Friends were as deeply sunk
in complacency and imperialist assumptions as Phillips believes they
were, it would be difficult, if not impossible, to explain the mentality
that persuaded at least some Quakers to risk public opprobrium, imprisonment, or worse in solemn, faith-driven resistance to the nation in arms
between 1914 and 1918. The roots of that resistance are obviously
diverse and complicated, but it seems clear that some of the strongest
strands of twentieth-century Quaker pacifism were produced during the
Edwardian period in which Phillips finds the peace testimony so wanting. One of these strands was woven through the idealism and *esprit de
corps* developed by a generation of men and women active in the Edwardian Young Friends Movement.[41] And this first strand was intertwined
with a second provided by the inspiring example of passive resistance
by early Friends as set out in the definitive histories of Quakerism published as part of the Rowntree Series just prior to the Great War.[42]

There is perhaps validity in Brian Phillips's emphasis on the too frequently complacent pride of a comfortable, middle-class, Late-Victoria
and Edwardian Quaker community that had inherited an admired legacy of resistance to Caesar without ever having faced the danger of

Caesar's wrath being visited upon it. Still, the peace testimony espoused by the pre-war Young Friends Movement would prove to be of a sterner variety than that of their parents' generation, or indeed, of any group of Quakers since the seventeenth century. Furthermore, William Charles Braithwaite's *Beginnings of Quakerism*, with its inspiring accounts of the courage, resourcefulness, and religious radicalism of early Friends, coming, as it did, into the hands of the best educated, most socially active generation in the Society's history, played a role in arousing a vital element of radical resistance among younger Quakers, female as well as male, during the First World War.

The beginning of the Great War came as a particularly devastating shock to most Quakers. Their usual world-view was shaped by a combination of liberal optimism as to the advancing state of civilization and Quaker sunshine as regards the benevolent propensities of human nature. The war seemed to be, in the words of the *Friend*, like 'some ghoulish terror of darkness' and, as one middle-aged member noted, 'Many Friends do not know where they are.'[43] Eventually, about one-third of Quaker males of military age decided that the armed forces were where they should be; probably a similar percentage of the 20,000 members of the London Yearly Meeting abandoned peace for the national cause and became 'war-Friends.' But however large a contingent, this group proved to be of little significance in the development of Quakerism's wartime position. Younger Quakers who marched away to the front thereby lost all control over the future direction of their Society and as for older Quaker home-front warriors, one female Friend summarized their wartime status by noting that 'one just did not listen to them.'[44] The opinions that were heard within the Society were, by and large, those of men and women who stayed at home to resist the war and conscription.

When British Quakers gathered at Llandudno in Wales in late September 1914 to consider, for the first time, what their Society's collective response to the war might be, a group of Quaker women gave its assessment to the assembled delegates: 'We believe that to us, too, a call has come ... It is the time for women to join hands as sisters. Do not let us wait till the darkness is over. This is the creative time in which we must draw together and unite in a conscious effort all the forces which have been entrusted to us.'[45]

These same women were instrumental in making the Llandudno Conference a launching pad for an organization that has been called

'Britain's most thoughtful pacifist society,' the Fellowship of Reconciliation.[46] Whatever form women's wartime activities took, aiding refugees, joining the Friends' War Victims Relief Committee in France, or throwing themselves into the anti-war, anti-conscription movement, their central thrust was to bear witness to their beliefs by 'doing work ... not being done elsewhere.'[47]

For all its traumatic impact and tragic consequences, the war was more than simply an unmitigated disaster for British Quakerism. However much Quakers might have deplored the war and struggled against it, for some of them, including and perhaps especially women, the conflict provided opportunities never previously imagined. It was a stimulating as well as radicalizing force, offering the opportunity to break free from the still stifling atmosphere of home and meeting and to become involved in activities that might somehow change the world. Among the changes the Great War brought to British Quakerism, probably the most radical was the transformation of the traditional Quaker peace testimony. The prolongation of the conflict made conscription, and Quakerism's first direct confrontation with the state since the seventeenth century, inevitable. Indeed, the longer the war lasted and the more horrible its destruction, both of human life and human liberty, the stronger was the tendency among Quaker pacifists to see it as an embodiment of all the dark forces their Society was pledged to overcome in its mission to establish Christ's kingdom on earth.

Militarism was, of course, the most familiar and consistent enemy. Pacifist Friends and their Liberal allies had been warning the nation of its implications and dangers for generations. But as the struggle against the war and its attendant horrors lengthened and escalated, new, hitherto less obvious, antagonists emerged. A number of Quakers, including women, began, for the first time, to discover an inexorable connection between the war and the social and economic system that had spawned it; others, especially women, came to associate the origins and prolongation of the war with the same principles of force and domination that had kept their sex in a state of perpetual subjection. For them, feminism and pacifism became inseparable weapons in the struggle for human emancipation.[48]

During the Great War Friends who added capitalism and the suppression of women to the list of moral, and mortal, enemies of both human progress and the establishment of God's kingdom on earth were concentrated in two radical Quaker organizations, the Socialist Quaker Society (SQS) and the Friends Service Committee (FSC), both of which were significantly, and for a time predominantly, influenced by women.

The Socialist Quaker Society was founded in 1898 with a view to revealing the close connection between the principles of Quakerism and the practice of socialism. Sexual equality was always one of the SQS's fundamental tenets, and women had consistently played a major role in its activities. But only with the growing disillusionment of many Quakers with the Liberal party after 1914 did the SQS become an important influence in helping to turn the social and economic views of a portion of the Society of Friends sharply to the left.[49]

At the Llandudno Conference in 1914, Mary Thorne, clerk of the Socialist Quaker Society, appealed to Friends to join in the search for 'such an economic system as shall help to liberate the spirit of man from his present thraldom.'[50] At the Yearly Meeting of 1915 a large 'Committee on War and the Social Order' was appointed 'to study and elucidate the causes of war, in so far as these might be found in the conditions of social and industrial life' and to apply their findings to the practical work of 'social and industrial reconstruction.'[51] The Socialist Quaker Society was strongly represented on this committee, which would in the course of the war introduce an element of economic and social radicalism into the official deliberations of the London Yearly Meeting that far surpassed even the most advanced pre-war social theories advocated by activist Friends.

One reason for this advancing influence was that Quaker socialists had the advantage of their own journal, the *Ploughshare*. This weekly paper had been published since 1912, but from February 1916 it appeared under a greatly expanded format (the result of financial support from wealthy anti-war Friends) as 'A Quaker Organ of Social Reconstruction,' with the goal of embodying 'in practical life an example of the testimony we hold, not only *against* all war, but *for* a new World Order.'[52]

The wartime *Ploughshare* makes fascinating reading, not only because of the generally high quality of the writing and artwork (especially a wonderful series of woodcuts) but, among other things, for the way in which it developed one of the chief radical preoccupations of Quaker feminists during the First World War, that is, the growing association of female emancipation not only with the necessity for the triump of absolute pacifism over the militarist state but also the victory of democratic socialism over capitalist materialism.[53] One female Friend, describing the atmosphere of the Yearly Meeting in 1916, which had gathered to consider the Society's response to general conscription, noted that 'the Society ... is about to be called again to renew and widen its peace testimony, its Social message, its attitude to (and of) womanhood ... After this war the triple Labour, Peace and Women's movement ... will surely find Friends concentrating their all to the task of human emancipation.'[54]

At the Yearly Meeting in 1915 a committee of twenty male Friends of military age was appointed with the charge 'to strengthen the Peace testimony among Friends of military age' and 'to oppose any move toward conscription.' This group named itself the Friends Service Committee and, eventually, with an expanded, and significantly female membership, it would become the chief vehicle for the establishment of a challenging, provocative, and radical new version of the traditional Quaker peace testimony.[55] It was of considerable significance that at least six of the original members of the service committee, including its only two officers, were also members of the Socialist Quaker Society.

One of the Friends Service Committee's first actions was to ask the 1915 Yearly Meeting to approve a minute recommending that in the event of conscription no exemption be given to Friends that was not equally applicable to non-Quakers.[56] The following November, as the danger of conscription began to loom large and well-placed older Friends worked feverishly to effect some compromise arrangement that would permit their younger counterparts to escape both military service and a head-on confrontation with the state, the FSC not only reiterated its opposition to any exemption that separated Quakers from other conscientious objectors, but also denounced 'any clause providing alternative service to military service.'[57] With these declarations the pacifist faction of the Friends Service Committee began to blaze the path that radical Quaker war-resisters would follow, leaving behind those cautious Friends of previous generations for whom the idea of the peace testimony appeared to be somewhat less all-encompassing.

A short time after the appointment of the Young Men's Service Committee a separate Women's Service Committee was also created, although, at the time, it seemed to be a sort of afterthought.[58] Following the imposition of conscription early in 1916, young male Quakers began to be arrested and imprisoned as conscientious objectors. As their numbers grew and the ranks of the FSC consequently thinned, Ester Bright Clothier, a granddaughter of John Bright, wrote to the chairman of the men's committee expressing extreme displeasure at the fact that the women's committee had been given little to do, despite the impending crisis, 'I think in Friends' things we ought not to exclude either sex ... After all, the work the Friends Service Com[mitt]ee is doing the great work of Friends at present and women have to share in the blessing that comes in such work – I am sick of being told Conscription is a man's question – it isn't – and I know you and probably all the Service Com[mitt]ee would agree.'[59]

Within a month of this feminist challenge, the service committee had become a single body – and, just in time. As more and more male Friends were consigned to prison or detention camps, Quaker women took an increasingly large and ultimately indispensable role in keeping their Society in the forefront of the struggle against conscription and the war.[60] For the last two years of the war, the radical thrust of Quaker pacifism, Quaker socialism, and Quaker feminism was to a considerable extent directed by radicalized female Friends whose views were significantly in advance not only of the larger wartime British society but of the consensus of their own religious society.

A prominent example of this sort of feminine leadership was Edith J. Wilson (1869–1953), a mother of four and an assistant clerk of the London Yearly Meeting (1915–21). Late in 1916, Edith Wilson addressed the question of Quakers and alternative service in an article for the *Ploughshare*.[61] Although, according to Wilson, it was quite natural for older Friends to try to work out some means by which younger members could avoid both the spiritual inconsistency of fighting and the physical unpleasantness of prison, it was, she concluded, not acceptable. Once an individual had determined to place his or her religious objections before the commands of a state which, as he or she believed, was engaged in an evil enterprise, that individual was no longer at liberty to compromise with that state and thereby, at least implicity, to condone its evil actions. By arranging schemes for alternative service, older Friends were, Wilson believed, smoothing the way for the conscientious objector to 'bargain with a thing he regards as essentially evil,' and, in effect, to become a defector from the battle against militarism: 'It is a tragedy of advancing years that wealth, and honours, and position, and comfort, gain such a hold upon us that it becomes well-neigh impossible to believe that young men are willing to sacrifice all these things, and life itself, in the pure joy of a quest for truth.'[62]

Edith Wilson continued to speak throughout the war for this uncompromising version of the peace testimony. With the younger leaders of the Friends Service Committee, she believed that any attempt by Quakers to gain exemption or concessions from the government was 'an acknowledgment that the laws of God are not really applicable in the Kingdoms of this world, and therefore it is no use trying to make them universal ... it [is] ... an unconscious yielding to the temptation to use a religious conviction as a plea for a political concession rather than as an inspiration to service and to sacrifice.'[63]

Like Edith Wilson, the Friends Service Committee, in its desire to ensure the purity of the Quaker peace testimony, went beyond rejecting government offers for alternative service and set about questioning Quaker alternatives as well. When local tribunals began assigning Quakers to the Friends Ambulance Unit (FAU) while denying that option to non-Friends, the FSC condemned the granting of 'preferential treatment' to Friends in violation of 'the spirit and concern of the Adjourned Yearly Meeting ... to unite ourselves to the fullest extent with all conscientious objectors.'[64] This was the beginning of a serious split between the service committee and the middle-aged leaders of the Friends Ambulance Unit, especially the unit's chief, Sir George Newman, who seemed to them entirely compromised by his close connections with government authorities.[65] For many middle-aged and moderate Quakers, the FAU was the crowning jewel of the Society's efforts to provide useful national service while avoiding open support for the war. The widening split between generations over the Friends Ambulance Unit was a further indication of the Friends Service Committee's role in pushing the Society towards a version of the peace testimony, that is, complete non-cooperation as well as non-resistance, that was beyond anything previously practised or even imagined by most Friends, at least since the seventeenth century.

The service committee militants, female as well as male, who may have comprised a bare majority within the FSC were intent on making their line of war-resistance *the* Quaker line, despite the fact that only a very few Friends took so extreme a position as that of the 145 Quaker absolutists who chose prison rather than any compromise with the wartime state. They were, of course, joined in this stand by over a thousand other non-Quaker absolutist conscientious objectors (COs), most of them socialists from the No-Conscription Fellowship (NCF). But, as a body, the Quaker absolutists went beyond the NCF and, indeed, divided with it over the question of how the anti-war movement should respond to the imprisonment of conscientious objectors that began in the spring of 1916.[66]

Quaker historian Jo Vellacott has, for one, noted that female members of the Friends' Service Committee, including its acting chair Edith Ellis, tended to take a hard and even intolerant line with respect to what constituted legitimate or faithful conscientious objection. Ellis and her supporters not only insisted that 'true' COs should refuse any form of alternative to military service and accept imprisonment as the logical result of their stand, but also rejected any attempts to mitigate the sufferings of those, non-Quaker as well as Quaker, who had been imprisoned.[67] If nothing else, this view certainly reveals that the militants maintained the courage of their convictions. Such inflexibility brought few new recruits into their camp. Bertrand Russell, as acting chairman of the No-Conscription Fellowship, admonished Edith Ellis for maintaining a stand that seemed to ignore the 'duty to human kindness' and to smack of 'the cruelty of fanaticism which is the very spirit that supports the war.'[68]

This sort of inflexible self-righteousness is not attractive, but it might be understandable in the context of the militants' vision of the struggle against the government and the war as a confrontation between the forces of good and evil; certainly, it made them far more troublesome to the powers that be than their minuscule numbers would seem to have warranted. Their faith in the righteousness of the struggle most assuredly gave Quaker pacifists the resolve to carry on, but so too did what they saw as the impeccable logic of their position. For if they were saying anything, FSC leaders like Edith Ellis were saying that it was *the war* rather than any single act or group of acts arising from the war that the peace testimony was about; the question, they said, was not: 'Do Friends refrain from fighting with carnal weapons?' but: 'Were Friends trying by every possible means to stop the war?' Most other Christian conscientious objectors, including the numerically larger Plymouth Brethren and Christadelphians, refused service because, as they saw it, the conflict in Europe was not their war. Quaker absolutists, however, would not perform even alternative service because the war emphatically *was* their war – the one their Society had been preparing to resist for two and a half centuries and the one from which it would emerge as a prophet society for transforming the world into the Kingdom of Christ.

The sort of radicalism represented in the ideas and activities of groups like the Socialist Quaker Society and the Friends Service Committee certainly added to the sense of drama involved in the Quaker wartime struggle against the militant capitalist state. The Friends Service Committee's hard-line stand effectively pushed the entire Society of Friends to adopt a far less cooperative stance *vis-à-vis* the government than many older and normally weightier Friends thought necessary or proper. To some extent, the wartime and postwar reports of the Committee on War and the Social Order also moved the Society of Friends in a more overtly leftward direction than the solidly Liberal pre-war Quaker leadership found comfortable.

In the longer term, however, after the crisis of the war had abated, and female citizens voted in national elections for the first time, the Society of Friends, if it did not revert to pre-war form, certainly adopted a less than revolutionary approach to the problems of the social order, including the question of female equality, both within Quakerism and in the larger society. To be sure, during the first worldwide Conference of All Friends, which met in London in 1920,[69] the point was made that the 'low estate of women has been shown to be always the direct fruit of warfare and a militant society' and that, by way of contrast, Quakers had from the beginning 'taken seriously the view that in Christ Jesus there is neither male or female' and, thus, they had a 'message and approach to the world that is peculiarly modern and timely.'[70] But, in the intervening decades, some female Friends have felt that the practical results of such pious phases were less than fully realized.[71]

The impact of wartime experience on the peace testimony was both more significant and more decisive. However tiny or isolated a group, the absolutists of the Friends Service Committee established and maintained sufficient influence within the monthly gatherings of the Meeting for Sufferings, the executive committee of the London Yearly Meeting, to ensure that the Society of Friends, as a corporate body, refrained from any agitation for the relief or release of imprisoned COs. Furthermore, their brand of resistance, in conscious imitation of the sufferings of seventeenth century Friends, became as Martin Ceadel has noted, the standard by which all subsequent pacifist war resistance has been measured.[72]

Thus, the peace testimony to which the London Yearly Meeting officially subscribed in 1918, and which was subsequently endorsed by the all-Friends conference of 1920, was not the vague adherence to peace principles endorsed by Friends until the end of the nineteenth century; nor was it the more refined and sophisticated version developed during the pre-1914 Quaker Renaissance. Rather, it was a radical pacifist doctrine, largely hammered out by younger Friends, female and male, many of them Christian socialists, inspired both by the example of the first generations of Quakerism and by the vision of how war resistance could transform Friends into 'a prophet Society, a body of moral pioneers, committed to the upholding of a truth which, though unpopular now, will one day be accepted by men.'[73]

Notes

1 The 'Challenge to Militarism' trial resulted from a deliberate decision by Friends to defy Regulation 27C (issued 26 Nov. 1917) of the Defence of the Realm Act: 'We ... intend to continue publication of such leaflets as we feel it our duty to put forth, without submitting them to the Censor ... in the interests of civil and religious liberty.' 'Minutes of the Peace Committee,' 6 Dec. 1917, MSS vol. CVI (1916–21), Library of the Society of Friends (LSF), London. Also see, 'Minutes,' Friends Service Committee (FSC), vol. 2, 1 May 1918, ibid. The Guildhall trial ended with the conviction of all three defendants. Arthur Watts and Harrison Barrow were each sentenced to six months, and Edith Ellis served out a three-month sentence in default of a fine. For the FSC's version of this incident, see *The Story of an Uncensored Leaflet* (London, [1918]).

2 Maude Robinson, "Lest We Forget": A Memory of the Society of Friends in the War Years, 1914–1918' (London, n.d.), 26, and E[sther] Peet to Hubert Peet, 4 June 1918, Peet Family Papers, seen by permission of Stephen Peet, London.

3 The overall question of the role and influence of women in British Quakerism awaits its historian. Since 1918, three other women, Maude Brayshaw, Jill Hopkins, and current clerk, Janet Scott, have served as the presiding member of London Yearly Meeting.

4 Quoted in William Charles Braithwaite, *The Second Period of Quakerism* (Cambridge, 1953, rev. ed.), 273.

5 See Phyllis Mack, 'Gender and Spirituality in Early English Quakerism, 1650–1665,' in *Witness for Change: Quaker Women over Three Centuries*, ed. Elizabeth Potts Brown and Susan Mosher Stuard (New Brunswick and London, 1989), 31–68. Also see Ernest E. Taylor, *The Valiant Sixty* (London, 1947), 43–4.

6 Bonnelyn Young Kunze, 'The Family, Social and Religious of Margaret Fell,' PhD dissertation, University of Rochester (1986); '"Walking in Ye Gospel Order," Margaret Fell and the Establishment of Women's Meetings,' paper read at the 7th Berkshire Conference on the History of Women, and '"Poore and in Necessity": Margaret Fell and Quaker Female Philanthropy in Northwest England in the late 17th Century,' *Albion* 21/4 (Winter 1989), 559–80.

7 Kunze, 'Gospel Order,' 11. Also see Mary Jane Godlee, 'The Women's Yearly Meeting,' in *London Yearly Meeting during 250 Years* (London, 1919), 97; and Braithwaite, *Second Period*, 273–4.

8 M.J. Godlee, 'Women's Yearly Meeting,' 106–7; Robert Barclay, *The Inner Life of the Religious Societies of the Commonwealth* (London, 1879, 3rd ed.), 528; and Rufus M. Jones, *The Later Periods of Quakerism* (London, 1921), vol. 1, 114–15. Braithwaite, *Second Period*, 286, claims that women's want of business training no doubt precluded their admission to important executive bodies such as the Meeting for Sufferings, but this view is disputed by Arnold Lloyd, *Quaker Social History, 1669–1738* (London, 1950), 107ff.

9 Joseph Wood to William Williams, 1787, quoted by Godlee, 'Women's Yearly Meeting,' 112.

10 Godlee, 'Women's Yearly Meeting,' 93–4. Also see Jones, *Later Periods*, vol. 1. 117–18.

11 *Journal of George Fox*, ed. John Nickalls (London, 1952) reprinted 1986, 65. Peter Brock believes Fox's words were a 'clear expression of pacifist conviction.' *The Quaker Peace Testimony, 1660–1914* (York, 1990), 14. Also see H. Larry Ingle, *First Among Friends: George Fox and the Creation of Quakerism* (New York, 1994), 66–7. Ingle believes that Fox and most other early Friends were ambivalent about the peace testimony until 1660.

12 The complete text is reprinted in Nickalls, *Journal of George Fox*, 398–404. Also see Brock, *Quaker Peace Testimony*, 24–7, and Horace G. Alexander, *The Growth of the Peace Testimony of the Society of Friends* (London, 1956, 2nd ed.), 3–5.

13 Richenda C. Scott, *Tradition and Experience* (London, 1964), 37–41. For the impact of historical research and writing on the Quaker Renaissance, see Thomas C. Kennedy, 'History and Quaker Renaissance: The Vision of John Wilhelm Rowntree,' *Journal of the Friends' Historical Society* 55/1–2 (1983–4), 35–56.

14 For the general background, see Ronald Hutton, *The Restoration* (Oxford, 1985), 210–90 passim, and John Punshon, *Portrait in Grey* (London, 1984), 82–92.

15 William Dewsbury's *Works* (London, 1689), 55.

16 See *Barclay's Apology in Modern English*, ed. Dean Freiday (Newberg, 1991), 391, 425–35. Quaker supporters of the First World War made much of Barclay's apparently cursory treatment of the peace testimony. One of these, Howard Sefton-Jones, noted that 'our foremost Quaker theologian ranked war with cock-fighting, bull-baiting, may-pole dancing ... and other popular amusements of his day, and so far less offensive in the sight of God than Hirling Ministry, Oaths, or Payment of Tithes.' 'The Eight Query,' *Friends Quarterly Examiner* (FQE) 51 (April 1917), 222. In reaching this conclusion, Sefton-Jones chose to ignore some powerful admonitions against violence, for example: 'It is impossible to reconcile war and revenge with Christian practice' or 'War is absolutely unlawful for those who would be disciples of Christ.'

17 This reference to the peace testimony was included in the *General Epistle* of
    1730. These epistles were issued annually by London Yearly Meeting for the
    guidance of members; reference to the peace testimony was repeated in 1742,
    1744, 1746, 1757, and 1760. From the 1790s the standardized 'Eight Query'
    read: 'Are you faithful in maintaining our Christian testimony against all
    War, as inconsistent with the precepts and the spirit of the Gospel?' From the
    Quaker *Book of Discipline* (London, 1834, 3rd. ed.). For the Queries, see Rufus
    M. Jones, *The Latter Periods of Quakerism* (London, 1921), vol. 1, 134–40. Scott,
    Tradition and Experience, 40–1, maintains that it was only in the early nineteen
    century, with the growth of humanitarian ideals, that Friends, in general,
    adopted the view that the taking of human life was positively evil under all
    circumstances.

18 Peter Brock, *Quaker Peace Testimony*, 24–46, provides a detailed examination
    of this period as well as a discussion (257–64) of Jonathan Dymon's 'Essay on
    War,' a section of his *Essays on the Principles of Morality* (1829) and one of the
    surprisingly few Quaker anti-war classics.

19 For Bright and the American Civil War, see Keith Robbins, *John Bright* (Lon-
    don, 1979), 124–30, and G.M. Trevelyan, *The Life of John Bright* (London, 1913),
    230–52. For a Quaker view of Bright's public witness to Quaker ideals, see
    Howard Gregg, 'John Bright: Called to the Lord's Service,' *Quaker Religious
    Thought* 24/3 (Summer 1990), 8–30. Bright's refusal to condemn all violence
    had reference to the Indian Mutiny. Also see Sefton-Jones, 'Eight Query,' 219.

20 Elizabeth Isichei, 'From Sect to Denomination among English Quakers,' in
    Patterns of Sectarianism, ed. Brian R. Wilson (London, 1967), 175–6, and *Victo-
    rian Quakers* (Oxford, 1970), passim. For an overview of the impact of the
    Quaker Renaissance on the peace testimony, see Thomas C. Kennedy, 'The
    Quaker Renaissance and the Origins of the Modern British Peace Movement,
    1895–1920,' *Albion* 16/3 (Fall 1984), 243–72. Also see, Hirst, *Quakers in Peace
    and War*, 41, 114–15, 522, and passim, and 'Historical Introduction,' *The Peace
    Testimony of the Society of Friends* (London, 1920), 1–2.

21 Punshon, *Portrait in Grey*, 205.

22 Quoted by Richard A. Rempel, 'British Quakers and the South African War,'
    Quaker History 64 (Autumn 1975), 77. Hope Hay Hewinson's *Hedge of Wild
    Almonds: South Africa, the Pro-Boers and the Quaker Conscience* (London and
    Cape Town, 1989), 105–47, provides a dense but useful summary of Quaker
    differences concerning the Anglo-Boer War.

23 J. Rendel Harris to Margaret Clark, 23 Feb. 1900, 'Quaker Principles,' Box 3,
    Woodbrooke College Library (WCL), Birmingham.

24 *Quaker Strongholds* (London, 1891), 3. Also see Jones, *Later Periods*, vol. 2, 967–
    70.

25 *Quaker Strongholds*, 122, 130, 15, 139. Immediately after the publication of *Quaker Strongholds* some Friends did express serious concern about Stephen's apparently slight regard for the importance of the peace testimony in the spiritual witness of Quakerism. See, for example, William Edgerton, 'Have Friends a Testimony against War?,' *Christian Worker* 21/14 (2 April 1891), 212–31.

26 Shipley N. Brayshaw to the *Friend*, 9 March 1900, 153–4. Prominent pro-War Friends included, besides Caroline Stephen, the noted lexicographer, publisher, and philanthropist, John Bellows, and Thomas Hodgkin, banker, historian of Italy, and probably the most distinguished public Friend of his day. For a discussion of the debate within the Society, see Hewinson, *Hedge of Wild Almonds*, 127–47.

27 *British Friend (BF)*, May 1900, 111, and the *Friend*, 26 Jan. 1900, 58–9. There is no biography of this important Quaker minister, educator, feminist, and peace activist, but see the brief sketch in *Biographical Dictionary of Modern Peace Leaders*, ed. Harold Josephson (Westport and London, 1984), 811–13.

28 'Minute' 1 and 'Minute' 8, Lancashire and Cheshire Women's Quarterly Meeting, 19 Oct. 1899, 65–6, 67, Lancashire Record Office, Preston, and *BF*, Nov. 1899, 300.

29 *BF*, 8 June 1900, 156–7.

30 Frederick Sessions to the *Friend*, 9 March 1900, 154–5.

31 'Minutes and Proceedings of London Yearly Meeting.' 1900 (LYM), 64–9, and *BF*, July 1900, 188–90.

32 'Journal of Dorothy Crowley Brown, 17 Jan. and 20 June 1901, seen by permission of her daughter, Elfrieda Vipont Foulds, Yealand Conyers, Lancashire.

33 See FSARFC, 'Minutes,' 1899–1908, LSF. Also see LYM, 1901, 23–4, 115.

34 For the controversy see *BF*, July 1901 to May 1902, passim; Hewinson, *Hedge of Wild Almonds*, 205–24; and Rempel, 'British Quakers,' 90–1, 91N.

35 John Stephenson Rowntree, 'Memorandum on the Peace Committee, LYM 1902,' BOV H1/12, LSF.

36 *BF*, June 1902, 154.

37 See Thomas C. Kennedy, 'Opposition to Compulsory Military Service in Britain before the Great War,' *Peace and Change* 8/4 (Fall 1982), 7–18.

38 The papers of the Wisbech Local Peace Association, including some personal correspondence of P.H. Peckover and the entire run of *Peace and Goodwill*, the quarterly journal she edited from 1882 until her death in 1931, are housed in the Swarthmore College Peace Collection, Sarthmore, Pa. There is no biography, but see the sketch in *Biographical Dictionary of Modern Peace Leaders*, 736–8.

39 Brian David Phillips, 'Friendly Patriotism: British Quakerism and the Imperial Nation, 1890–1910,' PhD dissertation, Cambridge University (1989), 193, 200.

40 Phillips, 'Friendly Patriotism,' 5–9, and James Hinton, *Protests and Visions* (London, 1989), viii, 2, 29.

41 For Young Friends during the Edwardian period, see A[lfred] N[eave] B[rayshaw], 'The Young Friends' Movement,' *Swanwick, 1911* ([London, 1912]), 5–10, and J. Omerod Greenwood, *Quaker Encounters*, vol. 1, *Friends and Relief* (York, 1975), 172–7. Also see, Kennedy, 'Quaker Renaissance,' 248–51.

42 The pre-war volumes were Rufus M. Jones's *Studies in Mystical Religion* (1908) and *Spiritual Reformers in the 16th and 17th Centuries* (1914), but most important was William C. Braithwaite's *Beginnings of Quakerism* (1912). The Rowntree series was named for both John Wilhelm Rowntree, who conceived the idea for the series but died in 1905 at age thirty-five before the project was well underway, and his father Joseph, who provided the necessary financial support for researching and publishing the volumes. See Thomas C. Kennedy, 'History and the Quaker Renaissance: The Vision of John Wilhelm Rowntree,' *Journal of the Friends Historical Society* 55/1–2 (1983–4), 35–56.

43 *Friend*, 7 Aug. 1914, 575–6, and Ernest E. Taylor, 'Diary, 1914–,' 27 Aug. 1914, Temp. Box 23/3, LSF.

44 For examples of articles and letters by Quakers who supported the war, see the *Friend*, 20 Aug. 1915, 652–4; 3 Sept. 1915, 687; 10 Sept. 1915, 707; 5 Nov. 1915, 84–5; and 19 Nov. 1915, 871–3.

45 From the published proceedings of the Llandudno Conference, *Friends and the War* (London, 1914), 131.

46 Martin Ceadel, *Pacifism in Britain, 1914–1945: The Defining of a Faith* (Oxford, 1980), 35. Extensive material relating to the Llandudno Conference and the origins of the Fellowship of Reconciliation may be found in the Herbert M. Hodgkin Papers, Temp. MSS. 355, LSF.

47 A. Neave Brayshaw, *Friends and the Inner Light* (London, [1915]), 70.

48 For an illuminating discussion of the growth of the view that the historical relationship between militarism and misogynism made pacifism a necessary aspect of the feminist struggle, see Jo Vellacott's Introduction to *Militarism versus Feminism: Writings on Women and War*, ed. Jo Vellacott and Margaret Kamester (London, 1987), 1–34. Also see H.M. Swanwick, 'The World after the War ... Franchise Reform,' *Ploughshare*, 1/9 n.a. (Oct. 1916), 278: 'The war has revealed to many anti-suffragists that their political philosophy was precisely the doctrine which ... all ... execrate as Prussianism.'

49 The Socialist Quaker Society *Minute Book*, 2 vols. (1898–1909; 1910–13) and a scrapbook of collected SQS publications are in the LSF in London. The best

account of the pre-1914 activities of the SQS is Peter d'A Jones, *The Christian Socialist Revival, 1877 1914* (Princeton, 1968), 367–89; a more partisan view, as well as some new and interesting material is provided in Tony Adams's *A Far-Seeing Vision: The Socialist Quaker Society (1898–1924)* (Bedford, n.d.), which summarizes his MA dissertation (1985) on the Socialist Quaker Society at Leicester University. Also see the *Ploughshare*, 1/1 ns. (Feb. 1916), 35 for a summary of SQS ideals and objectives.

50 *Friends and the War*, 124–5.

51 Of the original thirty-six members appointed to the War and Social Order Committee, eleven were female, and at least that many were also members of the SQS; see Minute 118, LYM, 1915, 274–5. Also see the *Ploughshare*, 1/1 n.s. (Feb. 1918), 1; William H. Marwick, 'Quaker Social Thought,' *Woodbrooke Occasional Papers* 2 (London, 1969); and Herbert H. Horwill, 'A Quaker Socialist Movement,' *Constructive Quarterly* 1/2 (June 1921), 318–31.

52 J. Edward Hodgkin, 'The "War and Social Order" Committee' *Ploughshare*, 1/1 n.s. (Feb. 1916), 33–4.

53 See, for example, Louie Bennett, 'The Allies of Feminism,' *Ploughshare*, 2/12 n.s. (Jan. 1918), 360–2, who argued that the feminist movement had no validity unless it was allied with democracy and pacifism.

54 L[ucy] F. M[orland], 'Impressions of Yearly Meeting: The Society in Unity and "Under Conviction,"' *Ploughshare*, 1/6 n.s. (July 1916), 169–70. Also see, 'The Adjourned Yearly Meeting: A Churchman's Impressions,' ibid., 1/1 n.s. (Feb. 1916), 41: There were others who looked upon the State as an alien, anti-social, and certainly anti-religious organization, leagued with all the powers of evil.'

55 The Friends Service Committee manifesto and a list of original members are in the FSC 'Minutes,' vol. 1, 78, LSF. Also see Kennedy, 'Quaker Renaissance,' 256–9, and 'Fighting about Peace: The No-Conscription Fellowship and the British Friends' Service Committee, 1915–1919,' *Quaker History* 69/1 (Spring 1980), 3–22.

56 See LYM, 1915, 193–4. For the FSC manifesto and the list of original members, see FSC 'Minutes, Records of Work and Documents Issued,' 3 vols. June 1915–May 1920, LSF. Also see the recollections of Horace Alexander, an original member, in *Quaker History*, 70 (Spring 1981), 48, and Henry T. Hodgkin to Rufus M. Jones, 31 May 1915, Box 9, RMJP, Haverford College Quaker Collection.

57 FSC 'Minutes,' vol. 1, 'Proceedings of the Friends Service Committee Meeting at Devonshire House,' 3 Nov. 1915, 21, and 'Memorandum Re. Conscience Clause,' 18 Nov. 1915, 22, Friends Service Committee Files, Box IV, LSF.

58 LYM, 1916, 36, and John W. Graham, *Conscription and Conscience* (London, 1922), 161n.

59 Esther Bright Clothier to Robert O. Mennell, 11 and 20 June 1916, FSC Files, LSF. Also see Kennedy, 'Quaker Renaissance,' 261–2.

60 LYM, 1917, 170, lists only thirteen female members, including Esther Bright Clothier, on the service committee out of a total of thirty-six, but by early 1917 most of the committee's male members were in prison or some other type of detention.

61 "'Alternative Service": Friends and a Perplexing Problem,' *Ploughshare*, 1/7 n.s. (Aug. 1916), 203–4. Edith Wilson also wrote 'The Absolutists' Case Against Conscription,' a shortened version of which was the basis for the 'Challenge to Militarism' pamphlet for which Edith Ellis and two male Friends were tried at the Guildhall in 1918 (see above). See entry for Edith Jane Wilson, 'Dictionary of Quaker Biography,' LSF.

62 Wilson, "'Alternative Service,"' 204–5.

63 Edith J. Wilson, 'Law-Abiding Citizens,' *Ploughshare*, 2/2 n.s. (March 1917), 62–3.

64 Robert O. Mennell and Hubert W. Peet to Friends of Military Age, 22 March 1916, Temp. MSS, Box 31, LSF. This letter is apparently a much toned-down version of one of the same date which accused the FAU of compromising the position of Friends 'in direct opposition to the pronouncements of the Meeting for Sufferings and the spirit of the Yearly Meeting,' FSC, 'Minutes,' 2, vol. 1: FSC to members, 22 March 1916, FSC Files; and Hubert W. Peet to Herbert Corder, 18 March 1916, ibid.

65 Sir George Newman (1870–1948), an influential birthright Friend who was both editor of the *Friends Quarterly Examiner* (1900–43) and literary advisor to *Friend* (1912–32). A medical doctor, knighted in 1911 for his pioneering work in children's medicine, including his book on *Infant Mortality* (1906), Newman was, in addition to being president of the FAU, in government service, as chief medical officer and principal assistant secretary to the Board of Education, before, during, and after the war.

66 For a discussion of the divisions this approach caused both within the peace movement and among Quakers, see Kennedy, 'Fighting about Peace,' 8–19.

67 See Jo Vellacott, *Betrand Russell and the Pacifists in the First World War* (Brighton, 1980), 196–7, and private information. Also see Kennedy, 'Fighting about Peace,' 16–18.

68 Bertrand Russell to Edith Ellis, 11 Sept. 1917, and Ellis to Russell, 22 Sept. 1917, FSC Files, LSF. For the same argument earlier advanced by a female Quaker, see E[dith] J. B[igland], 'Our Own Ruthlessness: A Warning That We Need,' *Ploughshare*, 1/8 n.s. (Sept. 1916), 232.

69 See *All-Friends Conference, Official Report* (London, 1920) and Thomas C.

Kennedy, 'Why Did Friends Resist? The War, the Peace Testimony, and the All Friends Conference of 1920,' *Peace and Change* 14/4 (Oct. 1989), 355–71.

70 Quotes from Report of Commission II (National Life and International Relations), Henry T. Hodgkin, 'The Quaker Movement and the Modern World,' 7, and Report of Commission III (Personal Life and Society), Introduction, 5, in *The Peace Testimony of the Society of Friends* (London, [1920]).

71 When Yearly Meeting met at Exeter in 1986, the annual Swarthmore Lecture on the history and role of Quaker women was a collective and radical feminist critique of the Society's failure to measure up, in either the present or in past generations, to George Fox's admonition: 'The Lamb of God ... is but one in all His males and females, sons and daughters, and they all are one in Christ, and Christ one in them all.'

72 Ceadel, *Pacifism in Britain*, 60 and passim.

73 'The Life of the Society of Friends,' in *The Peace Testimony of the Society of Friends* (London, [1920]), 21–2.

12

The Quaker Peace Testimony and the Nobel Peace Prize

IRWIN ABRAMS

When the Norwegian Nobel Committee announced on 31 December 1947 that the peace prize would go to the Friends Service Council of London (FSC) and the American Friends Service Committee (AFSC) of Philadelphia, the Oslo *Dagbladet* told its readers that 'the Quaker religion consists of relief work.'[1] What of the peace testimony? Were the Quakers given the prize simply for their good works? This essay will seek to ascertain the part played by the Quaker peace testimony in the thinking of the Norwegian Nobel Committee, in the attitude of the Quakers towards the prize, and the public interpretation of it by the Quakers, and in public opinion. The research was mainly carried out at the Norwegian Nobel Institute in Oslo and the AFSC Archives in Philadelphia.[2]

The earliest Quaker nomination recorded in the archives was in 1912, when a member of the Danish parliament proposed the Peace Committee of the Society of Friends in London. Then in 1923 and 1924 the Quakers were nominated by the well-known professor of international law, Walther Schücking, and members of the German interparliamentary group, apparently as a consequence of the large-scale Quaker postwar food relief program in Germany.[3] The next nominations for the Quakers were in 1936, 1937, and 1938, and since in each of these years the committee placed them on its short list, we can see what the committee advisers reported.

In 1936 two members of the Norwegian parliament, Nils Lavik and Jakob Lothe, and a number of professors, including four from Vienna and one from the Netherlands, submitted nominations for 'the Society of Friends.' The committee adviser in political economy and sociology, Wilhelm Keilhau, who had himself been active in the peace movement, prepared a scholarly six-page report that was very positive. Referring to the nominations, he wrote; 'No reasons have been cited. The proposers probably thought it unnecessary. For anyone who has participated actively in peace work knows that the Society of Friends can be seen in a way as the oldest peace organization in the world. It is actually somewhat surprising that the first proposal took until 1936 to be made [sic], especially as the Quakers have not made any particularly significant contributions in recent years. Actually, here we have a candidacy that can be supported as a century-long activity that could be brought forward at any time.'

Keilhau went on to give the historical background of the Society and its humanitarian and peace activities, basing this on the standard work of the time by Margaret E. Hirst, which demonstrated how the peace testimony had always been an integral part of Quaker religious belief and practice. Keilhau pointed out, however, the practical problem of giving a prize to the Society of Friends, since there was no central organization of the international movement, and it would hardly be possible to share it between the different yearly meetings. The best way would be to divide it between the FSC of London, representing the peace efforts of English and Irish Friends, and the AFSC. This had been the suggestion of Keilhau's Quaker friend Ole Olden, when Keilhau had written him a confidential letter asking to what legal entity a possible award could be given. But Keilhau questioned whether this would be appropriate, since it was the 'Society of Friends' that had been nominated for the prize.[4]

This problem was resolved in 1937, when the long-time committee member Bernhard Hanssen, a shipowner who had been associated with the peace cause for many years, specifically proposed the FSC and the AFSC, referring to the Keilhau report. The adviser's report this time was written by Ragnvald Moe, secretary of the Nobel committee, who briefly updated Keilhau, emphasizing the philanthropic work of the two Quaker committees. In 1938 Hanssen repeated his nomination, and the report by Professor Frede Castberg, adviser in international law, again stressed the humanitarian nature of Quaker activity while referring as well to the traditional peace position. This was currently evidenced in Quaker opposition to British rearmament, he said, noting that it was expressed in writing, not political agitation.[5]

The committee made no awards during the war years, and in 1945 gave two prizes, for 1944 to the International Red Cross Committee and for 1945 to Cordell Hull. In 1946 the committee divided the prize between two other Americans, the International YMCA official John

Mott and Emily Greene Balch, the successor to Jane Addams as head of the Women's International League for Peace and Freedom. Balch's opposition to the First World War had cost Balch her teaching position at Wellesley College. Later she had joined the Society of Friends. In the Second World War, however, with great anguish, she had decided to support the war effort to vanquish Hitlerism.[6]

On 15 November 1946, the very day after the announcement of the prize for Mott and Balch, Christian Oftedal, a member of the Nobel committee who was a liberal editor, wrote to his Quaker friend Wilhelm Aarek, asking for information about the Society of Friends in case of 'a possible prize.' Unaware of the Keilhau report, he asked whether it could go to 'the head church?'[7] Aarek relayed the request to Friends House in London. There then ensued a number of Quaker committee meetings and exchanges of letters with the AFSC before Friends agreed that the FSC and the AFSC would be the appropriate recipients of a possible prize, just as Keilhau had recommended ten years before.[8] At one point the executive committee in London wrote Aarek that there was 'hesitation at accepting the suggested prize if it should be offered,' and there was question as to whether the Society of Friends 'could rightly accept nomination for a prize for work undertaken under religious concern.'[9]

At the AFSC there was no such hesitation. The board asked the staff to send the requested information to Oslo, but to make no special efforts to win the prize. It was not felt inappropriate to ask both Eleanor Roosevelt and Herbert Hoover to write to Oslo, and Mrs Roosevelt wrote a good letter. Hoover was in touch with the AFSC about overseas relief at this time, but apparently he did not comply with the request.[10]

The AFSC persuaded London Friends to give up their objections. Clarence Pickett, AFSC executive secretary, wrote that he agreed with them that 'the Society of Friends is a religious body, and not a peace organization.' But if its service agencies were to be recognized by the Nobel committee as having made 'a distinctive contribution to the ideals in the charter of the Nobel Peace Prize ... should we categorically refuse in advance? We as Friends believe that we should appeal to that of God in every man. If the response is to recognize our way of life and peaceful spirit, we have some responsibility to let the Nobel Committee and the general public acknowledge their recognition.' Such recognition, Pickett thought, could have the effect of winning others to Quaker ideals.[11]

Meanwhile, months earlier, before the 1 February deadline for submitting nominations, the two committees had already been nominated. It was probably Oftedal who inspired proposals from at least two eligible nominators, Erling Wikborg, a parliamentary deputy of the Christian Folk Party and an Oxford Grouper, and Ole Olden, who could nominate in his capacity as a member of the council of the International Peace Bureau in Geneva. As a Quaker himself, Olden had some reservations, but remembering the earlier nomination and having heard that there would be others, he finally submitted his proposal for the FSC and the AFSC. Wikborg some months later told Myrtle Wright, the English Friend who had lived in Norway since the beginning of the occupation, that he had made the nomination after 'he was given a wink by the Nobel Committee that they wished Friends to be proposed for the prize.' The other nominators were the deputies Lavik and Lothe, who had proposed the Society of Friends in 1936.[12]

The other nineteen nominees included former Soviet ambassador to Sweden Alexandra Kollontai, by herself and also paired with Eleanor Roosevelt by nominators who wished to symbolize Soviet-American friendship, Governor Herbert H. Lehmann, who had directed the United Nations Relief and Rehabilitation Administration (UNRRA), and President Beneš of Czechoslovakia. The strongest candidate was Mohandas K. Gandhi, who had won independence for India by the methods of non-violence. The Nobel committee has often been reproached for failing to recognize him, but as I have explained elsewhere, the timing was unfortunate. War was raging between India and Pakistan, the news reports about Gandhi's attitude were unclear, and most probably the committee decided to postpone a decision until the next year. In 1948, however, Gandhi was assassinated.[13]

In any case, the committee's decision for the Quakers was unanimous, so their representatives were told in Oslo. At that time the committee announced its awards without giving its reasons, as it does today. But Chairman Gunnar Jahn, who was director of the Bank of Norway, told the press that the Society of Friends had been selected because of its great humanitarian work. 'This reason is so obvious,' he said, 'that further comment ought to be unnecessary.'[14] As we shall see, in his speech at the award ceremony later, he provided a good deal of thoughtful comment.

The old question about how to give the prize to the Society had come up once more. Committee member Herman Smitt Ingebretsen, a prominent Conservative deputy also influenced by the Oxford Group, told in a newspaper article how, 'when the Nobel Committee decided to give the prize to the Society of Friends, the Committee was presented with the difficulty that there was actually no authority that could receive the prize on behalf of the Society.' So it was divided between the two committees.[15] Myrtle Wright was later told by Oftedal that his interest was in, as she put it, the 'wider aspect of our Society and our message.' She later wrote 'the more I hear about the motives of the Committee, the more I am clear that it is Quakers and Quakerism which they wish to recognise and not merely the work of any two committees.'[16]

The news of the prize came as a complete surprise to the AFSC. The staff knew the organization was being considered, but they thought it was for 1948. Clarence Pickett recorded his reaction in his journal: 'It is very humbling to have so much attention centered on the Society of Friends, and I hope it will give us a new sense of responsibility for the way in which we conduct our lives and our affairs, home and abroad, so that we may not too seriously disappoint those who long for another way of meeting the world than that of violence.'[17] The statement to the press made by the AFSC Board included the lines, 'Our humanitarian service is based on religion. It is inseparably connected with a refusal to sanction the method of war.' Clarence Pickett did have the opportunity to give this Quaker message to the world when the Voice of America asked him to record a statement to be translated and broadcast to twenty-four countries, but while the choice of the Quakers was greeted with universal approval by the media, the emphasis was generally upon humanitarian service in the spirit of brotherly love, with little reference to the testimony against war.[18]

The press coverage was extensive. The AFSC public relations office noted: 'Editorials in dozens of papers across the country, including all the major ones in New York and Philadelphia ... feature stories all over the country ... good Negro press coverage ... foreign press in the United States and European press.' Commenting on all this, the public relations director wrote to a friend, 'The winning of the Nobel Award certainly gives us an excellent news peg, and I want to take advantage of it as humbly as possible.'[19] In Philadelphia the editorial in the *Inquirer* commended the AFSC for working 'incessantly to alleviate the horrors of war and its aftermath,' but there was no specific mention of its efforts to prevent war. But the *Evening Bulletin* declared that the AFSC 'has demonstrated that the ancient testimony against war is not a purely negative principle' and discussed its 'healing missions.'[20] The *New York Herald Tribune* sent a feature writer to spend a day at the AFSC, and her story gave the best account of its current activities, but there was no reference to the peace testimony. The *New York Times* editorial declared that for three hundred years the Friends had 'practiced the principles of brotherly love. They will not fight or bear arms. They hate war, but they do not shun or quake before danger wherever acts for mercy are required.'[21]

The editorial in *Collier's* called the Friends 'real peace workers,' who had been at it ever since George Fox 'laid down the principles that war is an egregious crime.' It was placed next to a Cold War editorial advocating expelling American Communists to Russia. The *Christian Century* celebrated Quaker religious motivation, but did not explicitly refer to the peace testimony.[22] *Newsweek* had a short article referring to the relief of suffering by the Quakers, but *Time* printed a photograph of 'Friend Pickett' and quoted Fox's declaration that he 'lived in the virtue of that life and power that took away the occasion of all wars,' going on to say that the Society of Friends 'has done its sober best to take away the occasion for war by refusing to bear arms.'[23]

In Norway almost all the editorials were favourable. Even the *Dagbladet*, which characterized Quaker religion as consisting of relief work, had kind words for the Friends but felt that the prize had been established for individuals who had made great contributions to peace and should not be given to organizations as a reward 'for a warm heart, good relief work, and beautiful words.'[24] The Labour Party newspaper *Arbeiderbladet* had supported the candidacy of Kollontai but approved of the Quaker prize. It did state, 'It is a sensitive question that Quakers from a religious viewpoint are opponents in principle to military service,' but it pointed out that in the First World War Quakers had done significant civilian work and important work related to the war, and in the Second World War many Quakers had enlisted in the armed services. When Quakers refuse to bear arms, the editorial declared, they engage in humanitarian service and work for reconciliation. Ursula Jorfald, a long-time peace activist, in commenting in the Oslo *Dagbladet* on this editorial, wrote that she was grateful that the Nobel committee had overlooked this 'sensitive question' in its decision. She generally approved of the Quaker prize, but she did raise the question as to whether war relief humanized war and might actually make it more possible.[25] Myrtle Wright reported that an outspoken article in the conservative *Aftenposten* had attacked all pacifists, especially the Friends, 'an attack that puts me in real fighting trim and shows that fortunately we are able to stir up a section of the population who ought to feel us as a danger if we are of any worth at all!'[26]

In several articles there was mention that the Quakers did not take up arms but had served bravely as ambulance drivers and stretcher-bearers on the battlefields. This had been the work of another Quaker organization, the Friends Ambulance Unit (FAU), which had been founded by English Friends in the First World War, with no formal ties to the Society of Friends. In 1940 Oslo had served as a staging area for the members of the FAU who served briefly on the Finnish front in the Winter War with the Soviet Union and then helped the Norwegians when Germany invaded.[27]

After the war Norwegians knew of the Quaker workers helping with reconstruction in the scorched earth areas of Finnmark in northern Norway and perhaps had heard of the similar work they were doing in northern Finland. It was not surprising that the Norwegian press concentrated on the relief work. The Norwegian Quakers were a small group of about one hundred, and little was known about their religion, although several articles describing the Society of Friends were published at the time of the prize.[28]

Myrtle Wright felt that it was most important 'to use the opportunity to drive home the deeper motives and experience which lie behind the outward activities.' When she was interviewed about the prize, she tried to explain how 'relief work is the positive side of the pacifistic philosophy of life.' In her letters to London and Philadelphia, she urged the Quaker representatives coming to Oslo to accept the prizes to emphasize the religious basis of the Quaker work in the their speeches.[29] These were Margaret Backhouse, who chaired the FSC, a former faculty member and warden of Westhill Training College in Birmingham, and Henry J. Cadbury, chairman of the AFSC and one of its founders in 1917, who was a biblical scholar and Hollis Professor of Divinity at Harvard University.

Before these representatives arrived, Myrtle Wright and the Norwegian Friend Sigrid Lund went to see August Schou, the secretary of the Noble committee who was making the arrangements for their hotel and for the customary banquet held on the evening of the award ceremony. They explained to Schou about the Quaker tradition of simplicity and asked whether this might be observed. He agreed to cancel the reservations he had made at the fashionable Hotel Bristol, so that Margaret Backhouse and Henry Cadbury could stay with the Lunds, but Myrtle Wright reported that 'the idea of a dinner without wine was an impossible thought to him.' They did not insist, recognizing that, as Myrtle Wright put it, 'If we make ourselves too "odd" we shall be classed with the pietistic and fundamentalist movements which would also give an

entirely wrong picture of that for which we stand.'[30] Margaret Backhouse and Henry Cadbury did attend the banquet in evening clothes, as
was expected, but Henry wore a second-hand coat of tails borrowed
from the AFSC clothing storeroom, which was destined to cross the
Atlantic again with a shipment of used clothing and eventually to outfit
a member of the Budapest symphony orchestra. The next morning
Henry Cadbury was to be seen sweeping the snow away from the
Lunds' doorstep.[31]

As for the award ceremony in the great hall of the University of Oslo,
traditionally held on 10 December, Henry Cadbury was pleased to find
it very simple, 'no pomp and circumstance.' The king and his retinue
were there, along with foreign diplomats and Norwegian dignitaries,
but the program consisted only of an opening orchestral number, Han-
del's 'Samson' overture, the presentation speech by Chairman Jahn, his
handing over of the scrolls and the medals to the two Quaker representatives, who made brief speeches of acceptance, and the concluding
playing of the Norwegian national hymn. The king and crown prince
then came forward to offer their congratulations, and when they left the
hall the ceremony was over.[32]

Jahn's speech was all that the Friends present could desire. Jahn surprised them by showing, as Henry Cadbury reported, 'a very good com-
prehension of the history and characteristics of Quakerism.' He had
obviously put to good use all the materials the Quakers had sent and
more. It should be said that Jahn was regarded very sympathetically by
Norwegian peace activists, much more so than any of his successors as
committee chairman.[33] Jahn began by saying, 'The Nobel Committee of
the Norwegian Parliament has awarded this year's Peace Prize to the
Quakers, represented by their two great relief organizations.' Jahn's
phrasing seemed to confirm what his fellow members of the committee,
Ingebretsen and Oftedal, had indicated, and what Myrtle Wright
believed about the committee's motives, that the prize was intended primarily for the Society of Friends, not the two committees. Moreover, as
Jahn traced the history of the Society, the peace testimony was an important theme of his speech. He told how George Fox and his followers
were 'opposed to all forms of violence. They believed that spiritual
weapons would prevail in the long run – a belief born of inward experience.' 'The Quakers have always been opposed to violence in any form,'
Jahn declared, 'and many considered their refusal to take part in wars
the most important tenet of their religion. But it is not quite so simple.'
Jahn quoted the Declaration of 1660 and explained that 'it goes much

further than a refusal to take part in war. It leads to this: it is better to
suffer injustice than to commit injustice. It is from within man himself
that victory must in the end be gained.'

Jahn told how the Quakers had taken part in founding the first peace
society and subsequently had participated in all active peace movements as well as in other efforts for social justice. 'Yet it is not this side of
their activities – the active political side – which places the Quakers in a
unique position. It is through silent assistance from the nameless to the
nameless that they have worked to promote the fraternity between
nations cited in the will of Alfred Nobel.' Jahn recounted examples of
Quaker relief work, pointing out that it was not the extent of this work,
but the spirit in which it was performed that was so important: 'The
Quakers have shown us that it is possible to translate into action what
lies deep in the hearts of many: compassion for others and the desire to
help them ... which, translated into deeds, must form the basis for lasting
peace. For this reason alone the Quakers deserve to receive the Nobel
Peace Prize today. But they have given us something more: they have
shown us the strength to be derived from faith in the victory of the spirit
over force.'

In their acceptance speeches, Margaret Backhouse and Henry Cadbury made it clear that they were representing Quakers all over the
world and that their work was made possible by the support of thousands who were not members of their small society. Margaret Backhouse
emphasized that Quakers were very ordinary people and that 'it was the
strength given to the group' that had enabled them to maintain their testimonies for three hundred years. Henry Cadbury referred to the Quaker
traditions of 'renunciation of all war' and 'practical pacifism.' Margaret
Backhouse explained that the Quaker protest against war springs from
'their basic faith in the potential of Christ-likeness in every man resulting in an attitude to life that makes peace a necessary and natural outcome ... Love is very infectious and if Quakers have started the infection,
they will rejoice.' Henry Cadbury stressed the role of the ordinary individual in another way:

If any should question the appropriateness of bestowing the peace prize upon a
group rather than upon an outstanding individual we may say this: The common people of all nations want peace. In the presence of great impersonal forces
they feel individually helpless to promote it. You are saying to them here today
that common folk, not statesmen, nor generals nor great men of affairs, but just
simple plain men and women like the few thousand Quakers and their friends, if

they devote themselves to resolute insistence on goodwill in place of force, even in the face of great disaster past or threatened, can do something to build a better, peaceful world. The future hope of peace lies with such personal sacrificial service. To this ideal humble persons everywhere may contribute.'

Henry Cadbury concluded by calling upon the Norwegians and other Europeans not to take sides with the United States or the Soviet Union, but to serve as a bridge of understanding between the two. For this he was later 'severely eldered' by the senior American diplomat in Oslo, whose major objective, after all, was to keep the Norwegians on the American side.[34]

In their Nobel lectures two days later, both Quakers once again underlined the religious basis of Quaker work. Henry Cadbury declared that foreign relief efforts had been directed as a means of conciliation: 'It is intended to illustrate the spirit that takes away the occasion of war.' He said that Quakers were so naive as to say, 'If war is evil, then I do not take part in it.' This means that in every war some Friends had suffered. William Penn summed it up briefly, 'Not fighting, but suffering.' 'Not all can follow this course, not all Quakers every time follow this course. We recognize that there are times when resistance appears at first to be a real virtue, and then only those most deeply rooted in religious pacifism can resist by other than physical means.' 'The greatest risk of war,' he declared, 'is in the minds of men who have an unrepentant and unchanging view of the justification of past wars.'

Henry Cadbury admitted that holding the Quaker position brought much searching of heart, especially with modern total war. Friends have had to consider whether their position means disloyalty to the state, 'and they have had to learn to distinguish loyalty to the policy of a government in power from loyalty to the true interests of a nation.' Quakers held that wars could mostly have been prevented, that few wars can be justified by their results, and that the moral distinction commonly claimed by both belligerents between defence and aggression was rarely objective or complete. Once war began, nobler standards tended to be degraded to match those of the enemy. Quaker pacifism was not passive or negative, but led to efforts to prevent war and to the international service for which Quakers were known. 'This international service is not mere humanitarianism; it is not merely mopping up, cleaning up the world after war. It is a means of rehabilitation and is aimed at helping the spirit and giving hope that there can be a peaceful world.'[35]

Neither before nor since in a Nobel prize lecture has the moral and practical case for religious pacifism been presented so forthrightly. It took courage to do this before an audience of Norwegians who had so recently been liberated by force of arms, yet these were people whose spirit had never been broken by German power and whose non-violent resistance to the German occupation had been effective in many ways.

Henry Cadbury had only five days in Oslo and then had to hurry back to Cambridge to resume the classes that Harvard University, by formal action of the president and fellows, had permitted him to reschedule for a week. He brought with him the scroll, the gold medal, and a cheque for $20,251.36, AFSC's share of the prize, and a sheaf of clippings from the Oslo newspapers. At least their photographs, Henry Cadbury said, were not flattering.[36]

How were the prize funds to be used? The AFSC had been negotiating with the Soviets hoping to be able to announce at the award ceremony that the money would be used for feeding children in orphanages in the Minsk area, but agreements were not reached. There has long been a misconception that the funds were used in the AFSC purchase of $25,000 worth of streptomycin for the Soviet Union. This money had been contributed when the AFSC had made known its interest to use the Nobel funds to improve American-Soviet relations, but the Nobel funds were actually used for a number of peace projects, including a film, the expenses of the working party that published the AFSC pamphlet on the United States and the Soviet Union, and a Quaker mission to the Soviet Union in 1955. A small portion went to cover the expenses of Henry Cadbury's trip to Oslo to receive the prize.[37]

A few days after the announcement of the award, Clarence Pickett wrote to all Friends meetings in the country, notifying them of the award and declaring that the AFSC 'arose out of the religious life and concern of the Society of Friends,' and that 'the life and work of the whole Society has been recognized in this award.'[38] It was only partly understood in public opinion about the Quaker peace prize how the peace testimony and the relief work both proceeded from 'the religious life and concern of the Society of Friends.' The world prefers to honour the Quakers for their good works, but does not always consider work for peace to be among them. Despite all the kind words about the Quakers when the prize was announced, it did not take very long for the AFSC's efforts for reconciliation with the Soviet Union during the Cold War to elicit what the Quaker poet Whittier once called 'the public frown.'

As we have seen, the intention of nominators and of the Nobel committee in making its grant was to honour the Society of Friends as a whole, just as Clarence Pickett conceived of it, and not just its service organizations. The award was not given just for the relief work and certainly not for the peace testimony as such, although in the remarkable speech of Chairman Jahn there was full recognition that the relief work was a translation in deeds of the inner life of the Society and that the peace testimony was an integral part of the Quaker way of life.

There could be no greater appreciation of Quaker peacemaking than Jahn expressed in his concluding remarks. As a 'salute' to the Quakers, he quoted the lines of Norway's poet, Arnulf Overland, which he said had been so important to Norwegians during the war:

Only the unarmed
    can draw on sources eternal.
To the spirit alone will be the victory.

Notes

1 *Dagbladet* (Oslo), 1 Nov. 1947. Newsclippings Scrapbooks, Norwegian Nobel Institute, Oslo (hereafter cited as NNI Scrapbooks). This comment by the *Dagbladet* begins the short account of the Quaker prize in my book, *The Nobel Peace Prize and the Laureates* (Boston, 1988), 148–50. See also my article, 'Clarence Pickett, the AFSC, and the Society of Friends,' *Friends Journal* (April 1991).
2 I am very grateful for the generous assistance of Anne C. Knelling, Head Librarian, Norwegian Nobel Institute, and Jack Sutters, AFSC Archivist.
3 Det Norske Stortings Nobel Komité, *Redegjorelse for Nobels Fredspris*, vols. 1–39 (Kristiania [Oslo], 1901–39), Archives of the Norwegian Nobel Committee (hereafter NNC Archives). The references to the Quaker nominations are in vols. 12, 23, and 24. These yearly volumes, printed only for the eyes of the committee, included the reports of the advisers on those nominees selected for special consideration. Unfortunately for this research, these reports and nomination materials are accessible only up to 1941, in accordance with the Nobel fifty-year rule.
4 Wilhelm Keilhau, 'Vennenes Samfund (Kvekerne),' *Redegj.*, vol. 36, 86–92; Margaret E. Hirst, *The Quakers in Peace and War: An Account of Their Peace Principles and Practice* (London, 1923), reprinted with Introduction by Edwin B. Bronner (New York and London, 1972); Ole Olden to Henry J. Cadbury, 7 Feb. 1948, AFSC Archives. Olden sent Cadbury, as an historian of the Society of Friends, his account of the origins of the Quaker prize. Most of the materials on the Nobel prize in the AFSC Archives are in two boxes filed under 'General Administration 1947.'

5 Ragnvald Moe, 'American Friends' Service Committee og Friends' Service Council,' *Redgj.*, vol. 37, 73–4; Frede Castberg, 'American Friends Service Committee og Friends Service Council,' *Redgj.* vol. 38, 36–7.

6 Abrams, *Nobel Peace Prize*, 142–6.

7 Christian Oftedal to Wilhelm Aarek, 15 Nov. 1946, Aarek Papers, in possession of Hans Eirik Aarek, Stavanger, Norway.

8 This correspondence is filed in the folder, 'Proposal Friends Receive Prize,' AFSC Archives.

9 Lewis Headley, Clerk, Meeting for Sufferings, to Wilhelm Aarek, 21 Jan. 1947; Stephen J. Thorne, Recording Clerk, Central Offices of the Society of Friends, to Clarence Pickett, 23 Jan. 1947; AFSC Archives.

10 Clarence Pickett's introduction to 'Report on the Nobel Award 1947,' an AFSC mimeographed collection of documents, including the speeches in Oslo and the report of Henry Cadbury; Pickett to Herbert Hoover, 22 July, to Mrs Franklin D. Roosevelt, 18 Aug. 1947; Mrs Franklin D. Roosevelt to Wilhelm Aarek, 23 Aug. 1947. Pickett reported to the AFSC staff that Hoover had written to Oslo (Ruth Smith's report of staff meeting of 3 Nov. 1947), but there is no evidence in the Hoover papers at the Herbert Hoover Library in West Branch, Iowa, the Hoover Institution at Stanford University, or the NNC Archives, Oslo, that he did (Dwight M. Miller, Senior Archivist, Herbert Hoover Library, to Irwin Abrams, 17 Oct. 1990; Anne Van Camp, Archivist, Hoover Institution, to Irwin Abrams, 11 Oct. 1990). The AFSC materials are in the AFSC Archives; a copy of Mrs Roosevelt's letter is also in the Aarek Papers. Pickett asked that the letters of support be sent to Aarek, wrongly assuming that he was a member of the Norwegian parliament; ordinarily such recommendations sent so late in the selection process would go directly to the Nobel committee.

11 Clarence Pickett and Henry J. Cadbury to Stephen J. Thorne, 14 April 1947; Pickett did not think that the prize should be given to the Society of Friends for its 'definite pacifist testimony' because 'our showing in the recent war had been so weak' (Pickett to Harry Silcock, 15 Jan. 1947); AFSC Archives.

12 Henry Cadbury wrote in his diary in Oslo, 'Mrs Oftedal said that her husband had worked hard to get us the prize' (Oslo Notebook, 1947); Olden to Cadbury, 7 Feb. 1948; Myrtle Wright to Cadbury, 12 Jan. 1947; Myrtle Wright to Pickett, 9 Feb. 1947; (all above in AFSC Archives); Wilhelm Aarek to Erling Wikborg, 25 Jan. 1947, Aarek Papers; Geir Lundestad, Director, Norwegian Nobel Institute, to Irwin Abrams, 11 Oct. 1990.

13 Abrams, *Nobel Peace Prize*, 137. Stephen Hay quotes in his essay in this collection what Gandhi actually said at the prayer meeting of 26 Sept. 1947, and he has kindly referred me to Gandhi's protest on the very next day that journal-

ists 'have given the headlines that I wanted war' (*Collected Works of Mahatma Gandhi*, vol. 89, 252).

14 'Report by Henry J. Cadbury,' in 'Report on Nobel Award,' AFSC Archives; *Philadelphia Evening Bulletin*, 1 Nov. 1947. The folder, 'Magazine Articles and Publicity,' in the AFSC Archives contains most of those referred to here.

15 Herman Smitt Ingebretsen, 'Vennes Samfun' (Religious Society of Friends), *Morgenbladet*, 1 Nov. 1947. NNI Scrapbrooks. References to Norwegian press are to Oslo newspapers, unless otherwise indicated.

16 Myrtle Wright to Pickett, 9 Feb. 1948, AFSC Archives.

17 Clarence Pickett, 'Journal,' 21 Oct. 1947, AFSC Archives; Clarence Pickett, *For More Than Bread* (Boston, 1953), 305–6.

18 'Statement by Board of Directors of American Friends Service Committee, Nov. 5, 1947,' in 'Report on Nobel Award,' AFSC Archives.

19 Memoranda, John Kavenaugh to AFSC Branch Offices, 26 Nov. 1947; undated memorandum, 'The following publications carried stories ...'; John Kavenaugh to David Hinshaw, 7 Nov. 1947; AFSC Archives.

20 'A Most Fitting Award,' *Philadelphia Inquirer*, 1 Nov. 1947; 'Honor to the Friends,' *Philadelphia Evening Bulletin*, 31 Oct. 1947; AFSC Archives.

21 'Quakers Humble at Nobel Prize,' by Dorothy Dunbar Bromley, *New York Herald-Tribune*, 9 Nov. 1947; 'The Nobel Peace Award,' *New York Times*, 2 Nov. 1947; AFSC Archives.

22 'Real Peace Workers Rewarded,' *Collier's*, 20 Dec. 1947; Kavenaugh to Branch Offices, 26 Nov. 1947; 'An Award Richly Deserved,' *Christian Century*, 12 Nov. 1947; AFSC Archives.

23 *Newsweek*, 10 Nov. 1947; *Time*, 10 Nov. 1947.

24 *Dagbladet*, 1 Nov. 1947, NNI Scrapbooks.

25 *Arbeiderbladet*, 1 Nov. 1947; Ursula Jorfald, 'Tanker omkring fredsprisen' (Thoughts about the peace prize); *Dagbladet*, 17 Nov. 1947; Myrtle Wright deplored that even such a friend of peace as Jorfald was ignorant of 'our positive work for peace, removal of causes of strife and injustice,' Wright to Cadbury, 18 Nov. 1947; AFSC Archives.

26 Charles B. Middlethon, 'Pacifismen gjor forhandsarbeidet for nye undertrykkere' (Pacifism prepares ground for new oppressors), *Aftenposten*, 19 Nov. 1947, NNI Scrapbooks; Wright to Cadbury, 22 Nov. 1947, AFSC Archives.

27 A. Tegla Davies, *Friends Ambulance Unit: The Story of the FAU in the Second World War, 1939–1946* (London, 1947), 13–29; John Ormerod Greenwood, *Quaker Encounters*, vol. 1, *Friends and Relief* (York, England, 1975–8), 282–3. The FAU worked on battlefields in the First World War and was revived in 1939 to undertake wartime medical work. Its members served in Europe, the Middle East, India, and China, where their China Convoy worked under

most dangerous conditions. AFSC workers joined the convoy as soon as pacifists drafted during the war into Civilian Public Service were released, and in 1946 AFSC took over the responsibility for the renamed 'Friends Service Unit (China),' while British Quakers headed the joint operations in India, where FSC and AFSC had both been involved.

28 In Finnmark AFSC work-campers joined the rebuilding efforts in which Norwegian and other Scandinavian Friends took part. In Finnish Lapland the AFSC organized work camps. I visited all these projects in the summer of 1946. Among the articles published about the Quakers were the following: Ingebretsen, 'Venneness Samfunn'; Louise Bohr Nilsen, 'Om "Vennenes Samfunn" (Kvekerne),' *Arbeiderbladet*, 3 Nov. 1947; 'Hvem er kvekerne som fikk fredsprisen?,' (Who are the Quakers who got the peace prize?), *Arbeiderbladet*, 12–13 Nov. 1947, based on an article by Rufus Jones; 'Kvekerne pa valplassene uten vapen' (Quakers on battlefields without weapons'), *Kongsberg Dagblad*, 4 Nov. 1947; Theo Findahl, 'Hos kvekerne i Philadelphia' (Among Quakers in Philadelphia), *Aftenbladet*, 22 Nov. 1947, by the paper's New York correspondent, who visited the headquarters; NNI Scrapbooks.

29 Wright to Pickett, 3 Nov. 1947, AFSC Archives; *Morgenbladet*, 1 Nov. 1947, NNI Scrapbooks.

30 Wright to Cadbury, 11 Nov. 1947, AFSC Archives.

31 Mary Hoxie Jones, 'Henry Joel Cadbury,' in Anna Brinton (ed.) *Then and Now: Quaker Essays Historical and Contemporary* (Philadelphia, 1960), 52–3; Margaret Bacon, *Let This Life Speak: The Legacy of Henry Cadbury* (Philadelphia 1987), 147–51.

32 'Cadbury Report'; Program, Nobel Fredspris 1947, 10 Dec. 1947; Cadbury noted in his Oslo notebook that the Warsaw Pact diplomats did not attend the ceremony; AFSC Archives.

33 Gunnar Jahn's speech of presentation is printed in Norwegian and French in *Les Prix Nobel en 1947* (Stockholm, 1948), 58–69, and in English in 'Report on Nobel Award' and in Frederick W. Haberman (ed.), *Nobel Lectures: Peace*: (Amsterdam, London, and New York, 1972), vol. 2, 373–9; Cadbury, 'Report'; interview with Johanne Reutz Gjermoe, Nesbru, Norway, 23 April 1983, a veteran champion of women's rights and peace, who praised Gunnar Jahn and told me his wife was a member of the Women's International League for Peace and Freedom.

34 The acceptance speeches by Backhouse and Cadbury are in *Les Prix Nobel*, 69–72; 'Report on Nobel Award'; Cadbury, 'The Nobel Peace Prize: A Personal Perspective,' *Friends Journal* (1 April 1974), 202; Cadbury's remarks about Norway not taking sides were reported in the *New York Times*, 11 Dec. 1947.

35 Backhouse's lecture, 'The International Service of the Society of Friends,' and Cadbury's, 'Quakers and Peace,' are in *Les Prix Nobel*, 237–48, 'Report on Nobel Award,' and Haberman, vol. 2, 380–7, 391–401.
36 Cadbury, 'Report'; Bromley, 'Quakers Humble,' *New York Herald-Tribune*.
37 Memorandum, Stephen Cary to Regional Office Executive Secretaries, 30 Dec. 1960, AFSC Archives.
38 Pickett: 'To all Friends Meetings throughout the United States,' 7 Nov. 1947, AFSC Archives.

PART III:

GANDHI AND
THE INDIAN TRADITION
OF NON-VIOLENCE

NO VOLUME DEALING WITH THE PACIFIST IMPULSE in history could possibly omit the figure of Mohandas Karamchand Gandhi (1869–1948) and his contribution to the theory and practice of non-violence. The literature on Gandhi is vast. The four essays in this section deal with selected aspects of his non-violence and its background in Indian and Western traditions. Gandhi always emphasized that he was a Hindu, and his thinking and lifestyle remained embedded in Hinduism, whatever Western accretions he acquired over his lifetime. From early times the Hindu religion preached ahimsā, or non-violence, but at the same time, as did Christianity, it also evidenced violent impulses. The two interacted with one another throughout the centuries. Klaus K. Klostermaier, utilizing literature in Sanskrit and Hindi, examines the ancient teaching and relates it to modern Hinduism as represented by the militant Hindu Mahasabha, on one side, and by Gandhianism, on the other. At present, he sums up, 'The advocates of non-violence are not entirely missing, but they seem to be in a minority.'

Though Gandhi's knowledge of Buddhism was indirect (that religion had disappeared from India many centuries ago), the early Buddhists' witness for non-violence, like that of their contemporaries the Jains, was more uncompromising than that of the Hinduism from which Buddhism had emerged. Roy C. Amore, on the basis of classical south Asian texts, surveys 'Peace and Non-violence in Buddhism' at the time of its beginnings, roughly 500 BCE. He traces its developing non-violence within the sociopolitical and cultural settings and discusses the non-violent ethic of King Ashoka, the royal convert to Buddhism, and the evolution of Buddhism in Sri Lanka.

The degree of influence exerted on Gandhi by Western pacifism and Indian non-violence continues to be a matter of debate among Gandhian scholars. But alongside Gandhi's reading of the New Testament it was certainly his subsequent acquaintance with Tolstoy's *The Kingdom of God Is within You* that was to bring the young Indian into contact with the Western tradition of pacifism. James D. Hunt, in his essay on 'Gandhi, Tolstoy, and the Tolstoyans,' looks first at Gandhi's knowledge of Tolstoy and then at various persons, publications, and organizations that deepened Gandhi's knowledge of the Tolstoyan ethic during his South African years.

The final essay in this section, by Stephen Hay, deals with Gandhi's non-violence on a more theoretical level. Hay first examines the metaphysical bases for Gandhi's non-violence and then proceeds to various moral, political and international aspects. He emphasizes the distinction made by Gandhi between the non-violence of a coward and the non-violence of a courageous individual. In Gandhi's view, Hay tells us, 'Courageous violence could be a stepping-stone to courageous non-violence, although not a necessary one.' Hay analyses Gandhi's growing opposition to British rule, the test to Gandhi's principles that emerged in Pakistan, and compares Kant's and Gandhi's views on how humanism can achieve lasting international peace.

13

Himsā and Ahimsā Traditions in Hinduism

KLAUS K. KLOSTERMAIER

For many Westerners Mahatma Gandhi (1869–1948) was the true representative of the essence of Hinduism. He embodied the spirit of non-violence (*ahimsā*) and the faith that truth/God (*satya*) will ultimately prevail.[1] His lessons of non-violent resistance were taken up by the leaders of the American civil rights movement and praised, belatedly, by some recent popes. Those who have studied Indian thought under the guidance of the statesman-philosopher Sarvepalli Radhakrishnan (1888–1975) will have learned from his writings that Hinduism is the religion of peace and tolerance, which neither has the need nor the ambition to employ violence in any form. Hinduism is pure spirituality transcending all those conflicts that have drawn other religions into wars of faith with each other or with themselves.[2]

Observers of the Indian contemporary scene must have noticed that fundamentalist political Hindu organizations have been instrumental in provoking a great number of violent confrontations with non-Hindus over such mundane issues as the repossession of the Rāma and Krṣṇa janmabhūmīs in Ayodhyā and Mathurā. They openly advocate militant and aggressive Hindu policies *vis-à-vis* non-Hindus. Unsettling and ominous as their speeches and actions might be, threatening the very existence of a free and democratic, pluralistic and secular India, they reflect as genuine and historical a tradition of Hinduism as did Gandhi and Radhakrishnan.

In the following a brief sketch will be provided of six tributaries to the Ganges of Hinduism, some freighted with vessels of war, others carrying messages of peace – some doing both.

Vedic Warriors and Their God

The basic Indian creation myth, fully developed already in the *Rgveda*
and forming the preamble to the authoritative *Manusmrti*[3] presents the
origin of humankind from a primordial 'person' in terms of caste society: *brahmans, kṣatriyas, vaiśyas,* and *śudras* emerge simultaneously, each
with well-defined roles and duties, cooperating for the welfare of society
as a whole. Not only are the respective caste duties well marked off
against each other, they are exclusive means to attain salvation.
Although the pursuit of learning, meditation, and tranquility is the
means through which a *brahman* can reach individual perfection, it
would be disastrous for anyone else to follow that path. Not only would
society suffer for lacking an essential ingredient, that person herself
would not find fulfilment and liberation. Birth is destiny. The means to
win ultimate felicity for the warrior is fighting a war in defence of
dharma. Society as a whole cannot exist without the strong arm of the
custodians of *dharma,* who, if necessary, will use force to make sure that
adharma will not win out.

Vedic society, as it is reflected in the *Rgveda* and the *Brāhmaṇas,* did not
subscribe to *ahiṁsā* as its highest ideal, as did later Buddhist and Jain traditions. It not only sanctioned the killing of animals, sometimes in large
numbers, for the purpose of the all-important *yajna,* it also gave high
standing to its warriors, whose duty it was to kill the enemies of the
Vedic religion. The most often invoked deity, Indra, has the attributes of
a warrior himself, being praised as 'destroyer of enemies,' 'devastator of
cities,'[4] and 'Vrtra-killer.'[5]

For long it was believed that the battles the *Rgveda* refers to were reminiscences of the 'Aryan invasion,' the movement of nomadic fair-
skinned 'Aryans' from the steppes of southern Russian or inner Asia
into the area of today's Punjab. When the first ruins of the Mohenjo-
Daro/Harappa civilization were discovered, they were used as evidence
to support the theory: here were the 'mighty forts' and the 'vast cities'
that Indra helped to defeat. It has been established meanwhile beyond
doubt that the so-called Indus civilization was not brought to an end
through the violence of invaders, but through climatic changes. It also
has recently been found that the Sarasvatī, the river along which most
Rgvedic settlements seem to have sprung up and which is eulogized in
the *Rgveda* as the mightiest of rivers, had dried out by 1900 BCE. This
indicates a much earlier presence of the 'Vedic Aryans' in India than
hitherto assumed. Scholars who have worked up the archaeological,

geological, and linguistic evidence that has accumulated over the past decade, have come to the conclusion that the Vedic Indians did not know any other home but north-western India and that, contrary to conventional scholarship, the movement of populations was not from west to east but from east to west. The wars, then, that are reported in the *Ṛgveda*, would have been wars between different clans of the same people, battles between those who considered themselves orthodox and those who had fallen away from Vedic orthodoxy.[6]

Vedic society did not know conscription or total war. Fighting wars was the exclusive business of kṣatriyas. Brahmans were explicitly forbidden to engage in warfare.

The Smṛtis, the law books that codified rather early what must have been traditional practice of the Aryans, encourage kings to wage wars against neighbouring kings: to conquer another kingdom brings as much merit as good administration of one's own realm. And being killed in battle of this nature secures heaven.[7]

Peace Thoughts in the *Upaniṣads*

The *Upaniṣads*, as can easily be notice, differ radically in their outlook and orientation from the ritual-and-war dominated *Saṁhitās* and *Brāhmaṇs*. They too are considered *śruti*, revealed sacred word, providing humans with guidance in this life. They are in letter and spirit close to early Buddhist and Jain texts (many of which may be in fact contemporary with the later Upaniṣads) seeking liberation of the spirit from the fetters of rebirth rather than conquest of territory. They were composed by sages who had reached the last of the four brahmanical stages of life: *samnyāsa*, renunciation, dedicated to finding the Self and the All. Violence and greed had no place in this search. Nor had ritual and sacrifice. *Ahiṁsā*, the refusal to kill animals for the sake of sacrifice (and for the sake of consumption of meat) became a cornerstone of their practice and teaching: if all life was one, if your own soul once dwelled in the body of an animal, and if the animal was possibly a parent reincarnated, how could you kill it? How would killing animals (or humans!) further your spiritual life? If meditation was the way to reality, if one found the highest fulfillment in one's own heart in an act of spiritual rapture, what purpose would it serve to kill another ensouled being? It only brought bad *karma* and had to be atoned for in later births. Becoming free from the necessity of being reborn, however, was the real aim of life.[8]

The communities of ascetics, who later became known as Buddhists and Jains, apparently originated from the circles of these Upaniṣadic for-est-sages and shared many of their practices, even if they developed dif-ferent ideas of what ultimate liberation consisted in and how it was to be reached. They certainly insisted on *ahiṁsā*,[9] the avoidance of killing of animals for sacrifices, and they emphasized the futility of the ritual-sac-rificial complex. As ascetics (though they came from different caste back-grounds) they maintained brahmanic ideals: they were not to engage in wars, not to resist violently, and they had to be prepared to be tortured and killed in the process of promulgating the true *dharma*. Many indeed were. It is from this Upaniṣadic, Buddhist, Jain tradition that modern Hindu notions of *ahiṁsā*, as entertained by Mahatma Gandhi, originated.

'The Mother of All Battles': The *Mahābhārata*

The longest and most famous of all epic poems in the world, the *Mahā-bhārta*, deals with a war: the most destructive war ever fought, according to Hindu tradition, the war which initiated the Kaliyuga, the age of strife in which we now live.[10] Its description of the eighteen days of battle, which brought to ruin an empire and death to millions of warriors, is the longest and most graphic of its kind. However, the longest of its eigh-teen *parvans* (books) is called *Śāntiparvan*, Book of Peace. It deals with a great many issues not related to the battle and has been used throughout Indian history as an important source for ethics.

In another section, the *Bhiṣmaparvan*, it reports about a 'covenant made between the Kurus, the Pāṇḍavas and the Somakas ... regarding the different kinds of combat.'[11] This probably repeats what was consid-ered traditional conventions of warfare. Battle was to be between equals. One had to give notice and not attack someone in surprise. People not armed should not be fought. Many similar texts can be found in later *smṛti* works which bespeak a tradition of chivalry and of limitation of warfare to the professionals. Under no circumstances were civilians to be brought into the war, and it would have been unthinkable to kill women and children as part of the planned operations. The kind of indiscriminate and total war that is advocated today as 'just war' would have been termed 'demonic' by the ancient Indians.[12]

The *Rāmāyaṇa*, the oldest and most beloved of India's *kāvyas*, deals with many wars and warlike situations – its climax is the invasion of Lanka. It portrays Rāvaṇa as demon-king, but he is not without noble qualities, which are duly acknowledged.

The Purāṇas, reflecting the life and thought of India from between ca.

400 BCE to 1200 CE better than any other type of literature, treat war as something quite common and normal. Wars of conquest fought by legitimate rulers designed to increase their realm were an honourable matter: the conquered kingdom was not to be devastated or occupied, but to be brought into vassalage. By today's standards these 'conquests' were rather tame events – comparable to today's hockey or football matches (with casualties usually lower than at many soccer matches in Europe). The conquering princes went about their enterprise in a rather leisurely manner.[13]

It was understood that the code of ethics accepted in ordinary life would also apply in times of war. The wholesale destruction of towns and villages, the mass murder of civilians, the raping and looting that are the norm in modern warfare (notwithstanding the idealistic Geneva conventions) would have been unacceptable to traditional Indian society. The kind of warfare introduced by the Muslim conquerors was something totally new to India – it was warfare no longer inspired by the warrior's ambition to win fame and to subdue rival princes, but warfare motivated by religious reasons. It was warfare no longer controlled by a knightly code of war but it was either/or, life and death for all the population of the country, the kind of total war that can only be waged by people who know that God is only with them and not with the enemy, who are unable to see anything but the devil in the faces of their opponents.

War *and* Peace in the *Bhagavadgītā*

Technically, the *Bhagavadgītā* is a part of the *Mahābhārata*. It is however, not considered a mere interpolation in the text, but has been for centuries treated as an independent work: It contains God's revelation imparted as advice to Arjuna at the eve of the great war.[14]

Arjuna is a member of the warrior caste – so are his opponents, members of the same family feuding over succession to the same kingdom. In the beginning Arjuna states his case for non-violence, for not entering the war, whose terrible outcome has been indicated to him in nightmares and omina. One could call him a 'conscientious objector' in today's terms: he is described by Sanjaya, the uninvolved narrator of the story, as 'being completely overcome by compassion' (*kṛpayā paramaviṣṭo*).[15] He exhibits signs of physical abhorrence of war, such as paralysis of movement, drying out of his mouth, shaking and aching all over his body.[16] He points to the absurdity of war and the imbalance between the suffering caused by war and the advantages expected. He finds this particular war religiously and morally objectionable too: fighting it will not only rob him of his peace of mind, it also will cause the loss of fulfilment in the beyond, since he is about to kill relations and teachers. War, he maintains, is motivated by greed – an action based on greed cannot be morally right. War is hell and leads to hell. Rather than enjoy kingship won through such a war he would renounce all claims to status and wealth altogether and become a beggar-hermit.

Krṣṇa, the voice of God and the protector of *dharma*, states the case for war. He does not deny the truth of what Arjuna has said – but he declares it as relative in the face of an absolute truth that he is going to reveal. On the basis of traditional arguments, Krṣṇa declares Arjuna's decision not to fight as militating against the traditions of the race (it is called *anārya*, which would be the Indian equivalent to 'Un-American Conduct'), as unprofitable (*ajuṣṭam*), as not designed to gain him heaven (*asvargyam*), 'heaven' being the highest aspiration and reward of warriors, and, finally, as dishonourable (*akirtikāraṇam*), 'honour' being understood to be the ultimate value for a warrior. On the level of profoundest insight, Arjuna's arguments simply do not apply: since birth and death are necessary corollaries of life, and since souls continuously return after the bodies die (by whatever means), death does not really matter, and the truly wise do not grieve for either past or future. The activity of the war concerns just these mortal bodies – they are not worth more than a garment that one picks up and drops again. At the centre of reality there is no activity: there is, in reality, neither slaying nor being slain. In addition, from a standpoint of ultimate reality, the war has already been fought, the killing has already taken place, the battle anticipated by Arjuna is only a stage demonstration of a play already complete, reflecting an unchanging law of God-created nature and God-maintained world order.

To confirm this and to convince Arjuna that he has to fight this war Krṣṇa grants him a vision of his divine form, the *viśvarūpa*, which contains all beings and all history. Arjuna, the warrior, is only an instrument executing a divine plan: *Deus lo vult* – God is with him![17]

The Hindu thinkers, who made Krṣṇa convince Arjuna that he had to fight and that he himself would guide his chariot into battle, were fair enough to realize that the other side was also receiving divine help in the form of Krṣṇa's army. God fights his wars on both sides. It would be a lowly human delusion to consider one of two opponents exclusively associated with God and the other not. God's immanence is absolute and total, the polarities leading to wars are relative and partial.[18] *Dharma* demands that the war be fought to its bitter end. *Dharma* does not leave Arjuna the choice to renounce his station in life so as to avoid war. *Dharma* is about justice and retribution, but the Lord of Dharma is the Lord of all, just and unjust, killer and killed.

Peace, however, is also taught in the *Bhagavadgītā*: the warrior must reach in his heart the peace that nobody can rob – he must rid himself of greed and anger, which (as Arjuna had said) vitiates any and every activity of war, he must fight as if he did not fight, he must act as if he did not act, he must do everything with a heart free from desire (*niṣkāma karma*). Then, in the midst of the tumult of battle, he will have peace, the only real peace there is. If he retired to a cave in the Himālayas he would not find peace of mind, because he would have abandoned his duty, betraying the cosmic divine plan through which alone he can find personal fulfilment.

The *Bhagavadgītā*, we have to remind ourselves, is not just *a* book among countless others, it is for many Hindus *the* book: God's own word, divine counsel to follow in times of inner and outer turmoil. The choice between peace and war, violence and non-violence is not ours: our *dharma* places us in specific positions, God's inscrutable plans make wars happen and cease.

Non-violence as Unconditional Prerequisite for Seekers

In Patañjali's Yoga, *ahiṁsā* figures as the first of the five *yama* – together with *satya* (truthfulness), *asteya* (non-stealing), *brahmacarya* (sexual continence), and *aparigraha* (freedom from covetousness), it constitutes the virtues (habits) necessary for a person wishing to reach inner peace and personal perfection.[19] (It should be noted here that the idiom as well as the praxis of Patañjali Yoga is reminiscent of Buddhism and that it has been seriously suggested that the *Pātañjala Yoga Sūtras* were originally a Buddhist work.)

Since the cultivation of the *yama* is essential as preparation of the higher meditation practices of Yoga, the *sūtras* not only mention their importance but also teach the adept how to acquire them. The classical commentaries go into great detail explaining what is meant by *ahiṁsā* and how to acquire it.[20]

The Indian fondness for classification is at work also in the schematic demonstration of the varieties of *hiṁsā/ahiṁsā*. *Hiṁsā* (violence) as a vice can be either perpetrated by the violent person herself, caused by her, or permitted by her. In all these cases it arises out of anger, greed, or delusion. Each of these forms of violence can occur in a mild, medium, or strong form. Altogether, then, we have twenty-seven different forms of *hiṁsā* to be eradicated and counteracted by twenty-seven different forms of *ahiṁsā*.

The *Yoga Sūtras* insist that the vow of *ahiṁsā* (as of all other *yamas*) is 'universal, and not limited by life-state, space, time and circumstances,' that is, it insists that it is not sufficient to observe *ahiṁsā* in just certain areas or with regard to certain places or times.[21] *Hiṁsā* is defined as any violation of living beings – by contrast *ahiṁsā* would be the habit of not inflicting any pain on any living being whatsoever. The *Yoga Sūtras* describe as the result of *ahiṁsā* that 'hostilities are being given up in the presence (of the practitioner).'[22] This statement provided inspiration for Gandhi: he firmly believed that the mere presence of a genuinely non-violent person would be sufficient to stop a violent person from proceeding with violence.

Ahiṁsā is *one* of five 'universal habits' that have to be practised together to make a person fit to enter the path of liberation. If a person practised *ahiṁsā* alone and would not be truthful or honest in her dealings with other people, she could not claim to qualify for Yoga. For Gandhi too, *ahiṁsā* and *satya* were the two pillars of moral life upon which all activity, public and private, had to rest.

The Extension of Ahiṁsā to Premā: The Vaiṣṇava Contribution

From the fifth century onwards Hinduism, properly speaking, developed largely in reaction against Buddhism and Jainism, which at that time were the majority religions of India. Hinduism nominally maintained its Vedic base and insisted on the performance of rituals, but it appropriated many (probably indigenous) elements like temples, images, and a large number of new, revealed scriptures, the *Purāṇas*, *Āgamas*, and *Tantras*. It also became sectarian in the sense that groups of devotees rallied around a particular deity, such as Śiva, Viṣṇu, Śakti, Surya, and Gaṇeśa, who for their followers became the Supreme, identified with the Upaniṣadic *brahman*. Large numbers of professional priests and theologians catered to the needs of the people in this sectarian context, developing impressive and extensive systems of religious theory and practice. Śaivism and Śāktism continued the practice of animal (and even human!) sacrifices (possibly they not only preserved the ancient Vedic practice but took over such atavistic customs from indigenous populations) and of frenzied orgies in honour of their deities. Vaiṣ_ṇavism, on the other side, seemed to have absorbed not only many former Buddhists but also much of the ethos of Buddhism, with its emphasis on non-violence. There are no animal (or human) sacrifices in Vaiṣṇavism, and Vaiṣṇavas are vegetarians as a matter of religious principle. Their abhorrence of violence also shows in their more gentle forms of asceticism: there is no self-mutilation of the type often found among Śaivas and no self-decapitation as practised by some Śāktas as the supreme act of devotion. Vaiṣṇavas honour Viṣṇu with flowers, fruit, incense, and hymns. They practice fasting and meditation and aim not only at not violating other living beings but at embracing all of them with love. Viṣṇu, as the 'friend of all living beings,' is immanent in all that lives. It was especially the movement around Caitanya in sixteenth-century Bengal, later called Gauḍiā-Vaiṣṇavism, which saw in Kṛṣṇa the 'archetype of love' and in religion the way to reach that state of being where everything appears as an expression of this divine love.[23] It is quite evident that each and every action – in deed, word, or thought – that would violate love would be prohibited.

It was probably as much under the influence of Vaiṣṇavism as under that of the Christian gospels, that Mahātmā Gandhi began translating the word ahiṁsā as love: a positive engagement on behalf of living beings rather than a mere refraining from injury, as the word originally meant.

The path to this universal love is a kind of 'imitation of Kṛṣṇa': his loves as depicted especially in scriptures like the Bhagāvata Purāṇa are to be studied and followed and practised in mind, till the devotee's heart becomes one with Kṛṣṇa's and views all beings with the same affection as Kṛṣṇa does.

It may appear as not a little ironic that followers of this tradition have, in our time and age, become fairly violent proponents of a kind of militant political Hindu fundamentalism. In the name of love for the cow they have provoked riots designed to pressure state governments into forbidding the slaughter of cattle. In the name of their gentle faith they have organized aggressive demonstrations to liberate Kṛṣṇa's traditional birthplace in Mathurā from Muslim encroachments.

These events do not reflect so much on the ethos of Vaiṣṇavism as on the ethos of our time, in which violence has become so commonplace and so commonly expected in connection with the voicing of grievances that nobody apparently even sees anything wrong with a 'religion of love' (Hindu or Christian) inciting the masses to murder and mayhem for its own political aims.

Conclusion

Hinduism in our time – like other mass religions – is polarized in its attitudes to peace and war. For a time it seemed that Gandhi's interpretation of Hinduism (as of all religion worth its name) as an expression of *satya* and *ahiṁsā*, truth and love would prevail, and that Hinduism would become a major pacifist force in the world. Christians joined the Gandhian movement and Westerners became Hindus in the belief that here was a religion that took seriously not only Jahwe's commandment 'thou shalt not kill' but also Jesus' injunction of brotherly love extended to all humankind. Not all those who were attracted by Gandhianism stayed with it. Some resented what they saw as a certain disregard for the human individual, who was to become an instrument for the realization of an abstract ideal. Gandhi obviously did not mind the suffering and death of millions, as long as it was in pursuit of the ideal of non-violence. Martyrdom for the sake of a distant *Rāmarājya* was something to be sought for; ordinary life with its ordinary human satisfactions did not count much in the scheme. Gandhi's interpretation of Hinduism as a religion of non-violence and truth brought forth the Hindu opposition. Today we see the reawakening of a form of traditional Hinduism that perceives in militancy for the sake of Bhārat Mātā the genuine expression of the Hindu spirit.[24]

Modern militant Hinduism began with Dayananda Saraswati and his Ārya Samāj: it was first directed against Christian missions and Muslims in India. It broadened its base with the emergence of the Hindu Mahāsabhā a generation later, in protest against what some Hindus perceived to be the surrender of the Indian Congress to Muslim pressure. It was intended to be a militant Hindu political party that uncompromisingly strove for a Hindu-dominated independent India. The Hindu Mahāsabhā had found in Vir Savarkar its greatest and most strident ideologue. A contemporary of Gandhi and Nehru, he relentlessly attacked both the Gandhian principle of *ahiṁsā* and Nehru's idea of a pluralistic secular state. He maintained that 'the belief in absolute non-violence ... evinces no mahatmaic saintliness but a monomaniacal senselessness' and that 'the militarization and industrialization of the Hindus must constitute our immediate objective.'[25] The Rastria Swayamsevak Sangh, a Hindu Mahāsabhā front organization, built up from the 1930s onward a kind of private army in the service of militant Hinduism. It has grown and been amplified by private Hindu armies under other names, most of them under the umbrella of the Hindu Viśva Pariṣad, which was formed in 1964 in Bombay to counteract what was perceived as a Christian missionary threat in connection with the World Eucharistic Congress in Bombay.

Nobody who has followed events in India since independence can be unaware of the many brutal and large-scale communal riots. While certainly not the only culprits, Hindu militants have openly advocated violence and incited their followers to aggression against non-Hindus in the name of Hinduism. The advocates of non-violence are not entirely missing, but they seem to be in a minority nowadays. It does no longer seem possible idealistically to argue with Gandhi that *ahimsā*, understood as universal love, is the central truth of Hinduism. Today's militant Hindus have all the arguments of the late twentieth-century real world on their side: large numbers of followers, the power to coerce events in their direction, the will to use any means in pursuit of their interests, and the disregard for minorities who are too weak to resist with force.

I do not wish to end on such a pessimistic note. Could we then, by way of a somewhat more positive conclusion, suggest a concept made popular by Kaka Kalelkar, a devoted Gandhian, but also reflecting much of the spirit of traditional India as well, namely, the notion of *samanvaya*.[26] *Samanvaya* means harmonization, it designates the method of resolving contradictions and conflicts. The term was used by Śankara as the title to the first section of his commentary on the *Brahmasūtras*, where he shows that the various apparently contradictory Upaniṣadic statements about *brahman* can be reconciled with an in-depth understanding of *brahman*. The surface meaning of various scriptural statements may appear to differ and disagree, but there is a common intentionality of all scripture that is found through a depth hermeneutics. Kaka Kalelkar, following Gandhi, applied the principle of *samanvaya* to the plurality of religions that, in the course of history, has not only led to intellectual exclusivism and spiritual absolutism, but also to violent conflict and to mutual destruction. *Samanvaya* does not dissolve the differences that characterize the different traditions of humankind, but it allows us to recognize their family resemblance and to come together in a 'familyhood of religions.' That might be the best we can do at present in order to activate the potential for inner and outer peace, which Hinduism no doubt possesses.

Notes

1 Gandhi's major utterances on peace are collected in the anthology *For Pacifists* (Ahmedabad, 1949).

2 See, for instance, his *The Hindu View of Life* (London, 1927) (many reprints).

3 The Puruṣasūkta is found in Ṛgveda X:90. On the origin of caste and the system of *varṇāsramadharma*, see K. Klostermaier, *A Survey of Hinduism* (Albany, 1994, 2nd ed.), 333–44.

4 Ṛgveda IV: 42, 1: 81.

5 The oldest version is in Ṛgveda I:32. The event is a major motif in Hinduism and has been treated extensively in much of the later Hindu literature. For more information, see K. Klostermaier, *Mythologies and Philosophies of Salvation in the Theistic Traditions of India* (Waterloo, 1984), 12–39.

6 See N.S. Rajaram and D. Frawley, *Vedic Aryans and the Origins of Civilization: A Literary and Scientific Perspective* (St Hyacinthe, 1955).

7 *Manusmṛti* VII: 89.

8 On the Upaniṣads and their teaching, see *A Survey of Hinduism*, 193–220.

9 Jains consider *ahiṁsā paramo dharma*, that is, the highest religion.

10 On the *Mahābhārata* and *Rāmāyaṇa*, see *A Survey of Hinduism*, 81–98.

11 *Bhīṣmaparvan* I:27–32. P.V. Kane in *History of Dharmaśāstra* (Pune, 1946) vol. 3, 209–10, has collected many other references to similar conventions observed by warring parties.

12 The *Ārthaśāstra* of Kautilya calls war in which the conventions of chivalry are not kept and women and children and other non-combatants are slain 'demoniac' war, against the 'fair' war in which the rules are observed.

13 J. Auboyer, *Daily Life in Ancient India* (London, 1965), 283–7, graphically describes under the heading 'War and Victory' the methods of warfare in ancient India.

14 On the *Bhagavadgītā* and its history of interpretation, see *A Survey of Hinduism*, 94–107.

15 *Bhagavadgītā* II:1.

16 Ibid.

17 *Deus lo vult* was the battle-cry under which the crusaders assembled to fight the 'infidels.'

18 According to Vedānta all polarities (*dvandva*) are expressions of relative reality, and only relative reality exhibits such *dvandva*.

19 On Patañjala Yoga, see *A Survey of Hinduism*, 397–407.

20 For a summary of such commentaries, see Brahmamitra Avasthi, *Pātañjalayogaśāstra* (in Hindī) (Delhi, 1978), 100–6.

21 *Yogasūtra* 11:31.

22 *Ibid.* 11:35

23 See K. Klostermaier, 'The *Bhaktirasamṛtasindhubindu* of Viśvanātha Cakravarti,' *Journal of the American Oriental Society* 94/1 (Jan.–March, 1974), 96–107. Also, 'A Universe of Feelings,' in E. Weber and T.R. Chopra (eds.),

Shri Krishna Caitanya and the Bhakti Religion (Frankfurt am Main, 1988), 113–33.

24 For more detail, see *A Survey of Hinduism*, 461–76.

25 *Hindu Rashtra Darshan* VI (Pune, 1964), 424, 427.

26 Sri Kakasaheb Kalelkara, in *Samanvaya* (in Hindī) (Bodhgaya, 1965), 6–14, 23–62, 83–104.

14

Peace and Non-violence in Buddhism

ROY C. AMORE

Non-violence Values along the Ancient Ganges

An ethic of non-violence was central to Buddhism from its inception. Buddhism, as we know it, arose in the Ganges region of northern Indian approximately twenty-five hundred years ago. To the people of the day this area was known as the Middle Region, lying between the oceans of the Jambu Continent (Jambudvipa) – jambu are a fruit still to be found in the markets of India. During the seventh and sixth centuries BCE this Middle Region had undergone political transformation in the form of a consolidation from a region with numerous small kingdoms and republics to a region consisting of four large kingdoms. The rapid changes had been set in motion by a population explosion based upon the introduction of iron technology, especially the iron ploughshare, into the area.[1] Each kingdom had as its capital a major city in which the various sciences of the day thrived. These included both economic staples such as metal working, textile manufacturing, medicine, nutrition, and writing, as well as the sciences characteristic of ancient cities such as mathematics, logic, astronomy/astrology, and political science.

The economy of the Middle Region thrived because of the interplay of three sectors: (1) a rich, expanding agricultural base[2] with large estates owned by a ruling-class of landlords and worked by commoners and slaves, (2) a newly formed trade business conducted along a caravan route that crossed the region from east to west, and (3) an emerging banking industry complete with money lending and coinage.[3]

The emergence of the large kingdoms created great wealth as well as power among the ruling kshatriya class, and the thriving trade business created wealth among the merchant class. Furthermore, some members of the brahman class held wealth in the form of land and especially cattle, the traditional form of wealth.[4] Upper-class males had a strong grip on power and prestige, but some upper-class women were well educated and enjoyed wealth and prestige.[5]

The Buddhist texts normally only mention the kshatriyas when speaking about the republics, as opposed to the kingdoms. The republics were ruled by an aristocracy of kshatriya clans, it seems.[6] Another matter that emerges in the Buddhist texts in a way curiously different than what we would expect from reading brahmanical literature is that the vaishya, merchant class, is seldom mentioned. Instead, the picture of social life in ancient India that one gets from the Buddhist texts is that of a brahman class of landowners/priests; a ruling house in the kingdoms or a ruling, kshatriya class in the republics; a householder class; and various service occupations.[7]

Hidden beneath the peace and prosperity were serious social and ideological divisions, however. There were tensions between the upper classes and the commoners, as we would expect, but the new money economy had created a large urban merchant class whose wealth and financial power outstripped its social status.[8] The brahman class, being more conservative, was critical of money lending, and the ruling class looked down upon the merchants as landless. Furthermore, brahmans and kshatriyas took pride from the Purusha creation hymn in the Rig Veda, which gave them high status as, respectively, the mouth and arm of the sacrificed primordial 'person' (purusha). The ruling-class writers of the law books sometimes went so far as to group the merchant, vaishya class together with the commoner, shudra class.[9]

In addition to the tension between the new urban rich and the traditional landed rich, the region had undergone an infusion of Aryan culture in recent centuries. The kshatriya and brahman classes were the elite of an Aryan culture that had entered the region from farther west. It introduced new languages, marriage customs, political norms, and social conventions to the Middle Region. Important everyday things such as new forms of pottery[10] and metal working were introduced as well.

For our analysis of non-violence, the most important cultural tension was between the brahman priests and the traditional spirituality of the region. It is very difficult to prove that a distinct regional religious tradition did exist, because the written sources we now have are the products of the brahman elite. However, there are linguistic and archaeological data that lend support to the claim that the religion of the brahmans had been superimposed upon the traditional spirituality of the region. It seems worthwhile to reconstruct this traditional religion, for it forms the basis of two for the world's living religions that have non-violence at the heart of their teachings, Buddhism and Jainism.[11]

Along the Ganges were camps that served as the centres for various religious teachers. Many of the teachers were brahmans, but these open-air seminaries admitted non-brahman students (*shramana*) as well. Normally, only males were admitted, it seems, but the Jain leader Parshva founded an order for females as early as the tenth century BCE according to Jain tradition.[12] And Shakyamuni Buddha, somewhat reluctantly we are told, instituted a monastic order for women as well as men. Each camp had its spiritual master, who laid down a discipline (*vinaya*) and a set of teachings (*dharma*). There was a fierce rivalry among the masters as they competed for students and respect. Like university students today, the students of ancient India checked out the various teachers, looking for one whose combination of teachings and discipline suited the student.

There were areas of general agreement among the masters. With regard to discipline, all the teachers required the students to take a vow of celibacy. There were always dietary restrictions, the most common one being the avoidance of meat eating on the grounds that killing animals caused them suffering. Most masters required their disciples to rise quite early and to spend many hours working to sustain the camp as well as at meditating and learning. These religious training camps were the forerunners of the later monastic movement of India, and perhaps beyond.

Students were expected to engage in ascetic practices, denying themselves bodily pleasures for the sake of spiritual development. Some of the ascetic practices were relatively mild, by *their* standards, such as standing or sitting in a fixed posture for several hours at a time, or fasting during full moon days, or sleeping on the ground. Other practices were quite severe; such as exposing oneself to rain for long periods in the cool season, or standing nude in the sun for hours during the hot season, or piercing one's skin with metal objects, or going without food or water for very long periods.

The ethical values of the masters were rooted in the concept of *ahiṁsā*, which literally means non-harming. It was this issue that most seriously divided the brahmans from the non-brahman teachers who represented the traditional values of the Middle Region. The differing value systems came into sharpest focus over the issue of performing the animal sacri-

fices required in the brahmanical tradition. The brahmanical definition
of the unethical person was one who was not a sacrificer, whereas the
Ganges masters defined the unethical person as one who harmed living
beings. One value system required animal sacrifices, while the other
condemned them.

The tension between the brahman sacrificers and the Ganges masters
is apparent in one of the animal stories included in the Buddhist Jataka
collection. The story tells about a brahman who ordered his servants to
bathe and garland a goat in preparation for a sacrifice. While being
washed in the river, it suddenly laughs, then cries. When asked to
explain the laughter, the goat tells the brahman that it laughed with
delight when it realized that this was its last rebirth as a goat, and that
its next birth would be as a human. As for the crying, the goat explains
that in further reflecting about its past rebirths, it recalled that the reason
it had been condemned to hundreds of rebirths as a goat was because in
its last human rebirth it had been a brahman who committed the bad
karma action of killing a goat as part of a sacrifice. It cried when it
thought about the suffering its current brahman owner would have to
endure in his own future rebirths! Needless to say, the brahman decided
not to sacrifice that goat, and to adopt the value of *ahiṁsā*.[13]

Another Buddhist scripture satirizes the brahman sacrifice, and in the
typical style of the Buddha, gives an alternate explanation of the elements of a 'true sacrifice.'[14] According to the story a brahman named
'Sharptooth,' which is not meant to be taken as a real name, came to the
Buddha to ask about the proper use of the sacred implements of the sacrifices – which is about as likely, historically, as a Jewish temple priest
asking Jesus about how to use the fire tongs at the Jerusalem temple! The
Buddha responded by telling the story of a past king named Wide-realm
who abandoned his plan to sponsor a Vedic sacrifice of hundreds of animals in favour of a more modest, egalitarian offering dedicated not to
the gods, but to the welfare to all living creatures. Unlike the brahmanical sacrifices, no commoners were forced to provide labour for the sacrifice. As a follow-up to his sacrifice, King Wide-realm set up food and
medicine distribution places throughout his kingdom in order to provide the basic welfare of all and to eliminate the poverty that breeds
crime. The brahman Sharptooth got the message and went forth to do
likewise.[15]

The Buddhist disciples, or 'renouncers,' had to set themselves apart
from the world of the householder, but those who were of brahman
background had to renounce that as well. They gave up their cooking

pots, the tuft of hair at the back of their heads, and the utensils used in carrying out the Vedic sacrifices.[16]

The most zealous proponents of *ahiṁsā* wore masks over their faces and strained their drinking water to avoid unintentionally killing insects. The Jain leader Mahavira advocated these extreme forms of *ahiṁsā*. Sakyamuni Buddha did not advocate these practices, but did encourage his disciples to avoid stepping on earthworms, and so forth.

The attempts to live one's everyday life according to the principle of *ahiṁsā* was not limited to those who had taken religious vows. Some lay-people, or 'householders,' gave up hunting or fishing as occupations. Others even shied away from farming because ploughing involved killing insects. Most householders seemed to have continued to eat meat, even if they did not kill the animal, but one group took *ahiṁsā* to an interesting level. They lived as vegetarians most of the year, but once a year a group of the males killed one elephant for a communal feast. The idea was that they got nutrition from the animal while limiting their bad karma to that generated by a single act of harming, and that bad karma was shared by a group!

Buddhist Social Ethic

What effect did this strong personal *ahiṁsā* ethic have on the Buddhist social ethic? Before addressing that question, however, we should respond to the criticism that Buddhism may not actually have a social ethic. It is true that the emphasis of Buddha's teaching was on one's personal behaviour and the goal of purifying one's mind (*citta*). Most Buddhists are familiar with the following Dharmapada verse, which is cited as a summation of Buddhist thought:

The avoidance of all evil,
The cultivation of wholesome consciousness,
The purification of the mind,
This is the teaching of the buddhas.[17]

This is an individual ethic. Indeed, it has been argued that the modern understanding of the individual first appeared in Buddhist texts. The Buddhist project was to improve society at large by purifying the motives of individuals. Basing their approach on what appeared to work in the real world, as we might say, they held that a cadre of tranquil, generous, non-violent persons could be the catalyst for social transformation.

Although the pacifist impulse in early Buddhism was focused on individuals, there was a drive towards social reform as well. The reforms centred upon the abuses of the brahmans and the responsibilities of the kshatriyas. In contrast to our era, the business class does not come under serious criticism.

Shakyamuni Buddha was critical of the privileges assumed by the brahmans as a social class and as an hereditary priesthood. With techniques such as the following, he challenged the idea that social status could or should be derived from birth status rather than personal achievement: 'Ask not about a person's birth status (*jati*, caste), ask about a person's character.' A whole chapter of the Dharmapada, one of the most popular of the Buddhist scriptures, is dedicated to the claim that the 'true brahman' is one who has purified the mind, as opposed to one who is merely born into the priestly class. In this way, the Buddha argued that the real brahmans were those who had made progress on the spiritual path. To put the matter in terms of our topic, the true 'holy ones' are those who live by the principle of *ahimsā* and not those who officiate at the animal sacrifices. The *ahimsā* ethic thereby led to a challenge to the theoretical underpinnings of the Indian social order. The implication was that the Rig Veda's Purusha hymn, which has its counterparts in other ancient Indo-European cultures,[18] was wrong to lay down sacrifice as the model spiritual activity and wrong to legitimize a hereditary class system.

As for the kshatriyas, the ethic of non-violence led Shakyamuni Buddha to criticize their practice of undertaking wars to expand one's territory. The main object of the wars of aggression during the Buddha's time was to gain control over strategic points on the banks of the Ganges.[19] Such territorial wars were as old and well established in Indo-European culture as animal sacrifices. The cattle raid carried out by the third of the three legendary heros in Indo-European mythology legitimized, even idealized, wars of aggression by the ruling kshatriya class.[20] One time, according to the Buddhist texts, Shakyamuni Buddha was staying in the vicinity of a battlefield on which the armies of the kingdoms of Magadha and Savatthi were fighting. The king of Magadha had started the war to expand his territory, and he had decisively won the battle and forced the other king into retreat. When Buddha's disciples reported the battle to him, he explained that the Magadhan king was evil, and the Savatthi king was good. The good king had been defeated, but only temporarily, Buddha predicted. His point was not so much a prediction of the future but rather an expression of the basic *ahiṁsā* teaching that 'conquest leads only to more fighting.' In the words of the Dhammapada,

> Hatreds are never ended or calmed by hate,
> Hatreds are only calmed by non-hate.
> This is an everlasting principle.[21]

Buddhist thought speaks against poverty on the grounds that it directly causes suffering to the poor and indirectly causes crime, which brings suffering to others. This means that the Buddhist condemnation of poverty is linked only indirectly to the ethic of *ahiṁsā*.

Early Buddhism had two very different approaches to poverty. In the first it called upon the king to set up food stations to provide rice and curries for the poor. The obligation of the government to provide such rice kitchens is found throughout the early Buddhist literature, but I cannot find in the Buddhist texts any standards given for who qualifies to receive the free food. There *seems* to be no concern that the welfare rolls would grow too big. Was there so little concern because the food was second rate? Perhaps, but certain kings who are especially virtuous made a point of eating at their own rice stations, and the texts stress that the food should be of a good variety. It would seem that in ancient India, as in modern southern Asia, it is considered an insult not to serve a variety of curries with the rice.

In the second approach to poverty, Buddhism put the onus upon government to alleviate poverty. A king who fails to rule by righteousness (*dharma*) allows poverty and, therefore, crime to increase.[22] Another cause of poverty is a government that over-taxes the people to build up the royal treasury. Whether the taxes take the form of goods or of services – a common form of taxation in traditional India – the result is that the people have less time and money to use for their own basic needs.[23] One Buddhist sutra makes the very modern-sounding point that the hoarding of wealth by the wealthy few causes poverty among the disadvantaged.[24]

Most references to giving in the Buddhist texts refer to donations to the Sangha, and in Buddhist karma theory such gifts to worthy persons are the most meritorious. However, as Lily De Silva rightly notes, Buddhist thought also strongly endorses charity to the poor. Besides recommending gifts to the monks, Buddhist texts 'also speak of *Kapanas*, "destitutes," *addhikas*, "wayfarers," *vanibbakas*, "vagabonds," and *yacakas*, "beggars," to whom also should be given.'[25]

The *ahiṁsā* ethic also led to a critique of abuse against women and female infants. The Buddha even dared, according to the text, to chastise a king for his improper attitude of disappointment at the birth of a daughter.[26] Shakyamuni's admonition to him tried to put a positive twist to the birth of a daughter, by pointing out that a daughter might be better than a son. She might, he suggests, be very wise and virtuous. Unfortunately, from our perspective, the reasons given for preferring a baby girl are definitely of a pre-feminist nature – such as, she may be outstanding at virtues such as being a good wife and honouring her mother-in-law, and she many make the king a proud grandfather by bearing sons who do great things. But whatever the cultural standards may be for taking pride in one's children, the point remains that the non-violence impulse in Buddhism made some progress in correcting the age-old social preference for male offspring. The Buddhist teaching is in sharp contrast with brahmanical prayers, offered on behalf of the sponsor of the Vedic sacrifice, 'for sons and long life' as a reward for undertaking the ritual.

Unlike early Christianity, Buddhism enjoyed royal patronage from the start, for the Buddha himself converted several regional kings. As in other matters, Buddhists took a middle position on the matter of law and order. They sanctioned the use of punishment, even capital punishment, for the control of crime, but at the same time they condemned the use of unjust or unnecessarily cruel punishments. Their ethic of non-violence was considered applicable to the king's personal and judicial behaviour and to the nature of the laws he proclaimed. In short, the king was not considered an absolute authority in Buddhism, but was required to operate within the confines of *dharma* as understood by the Buddhist tradition.

The famous king known in the West as Ashoka is known to Buddhists as Dharma Ashoka. This title has several connotations. Besides distinguishing him from another Indian king named Ashoka, the name implies both the sense of 'Ashoka, who was concerned with Dharma' and 'Ashoka, the Righteous.'

The story of Dharma Ashoka is so well known that for our purposes it is necessary only to call attention briefly to the role he plays in the institutionalization of the Buddhist ethic of non-violence. Having inherited the throne from his father and grandfather, who had driven the Macedonians out of central India, Ashoka had annexed even more territory to the south and west, such that he ruled an empire that included most of modern India. The Buddhist histories claim that as a result of Ashoka's reflection on a particularly bloody war with the east coast kingdom of Kalinga, he underwent a conversion to Buddhism and began promoting the ethic of non-violence. Probably his family had previously been supporters of *ahiṁsā* traditions, such as Jainism, and so his conversion to Buddhism was not a major shift.

Ashoka called, according to his famous rock edits, for a *dharma* conquest, as opposed to further military conquests. In the message posted in the Kalinga area, he expresses remorse at having been responsible for the death and suffering of so many people. His government's ideals include security, self-control, impartiality, and cheerfulness for all living creatures in his empire. Ashoka spells out his 'conquest by *dharma*' and claims that it is spreading within the Indian continent and among the Alexandrian kingdoms, whose kings he names. Ashoka states that real satisfaction in ruling over people comes only from inducing them to follow *dharma*.

Ashoka juxtaposes his own pledge to be just and moderate in punishment with a warning to his Kalinga subjects and the nearby tribal people that he will not hesitate to deal firmly with rebels and criminals, despite his commitment to non-violence. Ashoka's promotion of *dharma* becomes a model for later Buddhist rulers. Wars of aggression and cruel or unjust punishments were considered to be against *dharma*, but the government was thought to have the duty to punish criminals and rebels. By the end of Ashoka's reign, the new Buddhist sociopolitical order had spread to governments beyond India. Our analysis now turns to one such country for which we have the evidence of chronicles, Sri Lanka.

Buddhist Non-violence and the History of Sri Lanka

How does the pacifist impulse manifest itself in the ongoing history of countries where Buddhism remains the majority religion? Trevor Ling, in his book *Buddhism, Imperialism, and War*, has described the various wars fought by Buddhists in the modern history of Burma and Thailand.[27] He concludes that, although Buddhist teaching has stressed the suppression of aggression on the part of individuals, it has not suppressed aggression by kings. This aggression has led to several wars between Buddhist kingdoms. Ling summarizes his study as follows: 'We return therefore to the point from which we began this closer inspection of the South-East Asian Buddhist nations' record in peace and war, namely that loyalty to the state has come first and common interest with Buddhist co-religionists a poor second.'

The suppression of individual aggression among Theravada Buddhists has not necessarily been a good thing, Ling argues. Drawing upon Herbert Phillips's study, *Thai Peasant Personality*, Ling holds that some Buddhists have internalized their aggression in ways that are not conducive to mental health.[28] For men whose aggressive tendencies have been kept down by Buddhist *ahiṁsā* teachings, such as non-hatred and non-anger, service in the royal military can provide a release of pent-up feelings, Ling suggests. He further speculates that this may explain why Buddhist troops were sometimes described as 'cruel in victory.'[29]

How has the pacifist impulse worked out in the history of Sri Lanka, where Buddhism has been the majority religion since the time of Dharma Ashoka?

The Buddhist teaching of non-violence did not keep the Sinhalese from carrying out capital punishment and other severe punishments on criminals. Milder punishments such as a fines, exile, or imprisonment were used by the kings and other officers of justice in traditional Sri Lanka, but sentences of dismemberment and beheading seem to have been common as well. In some cases, the prisoners were tortured before being beheaded.[30] And the seventeenth-century prisoner Robert Knox claims to have known of a heinous case in which a mother was made to eat the flesh of her dead child.[31]

The gentler side of Sri Lankan values, on the other hand, was expressed in practices such as the granting of amnesty or reduction of their sentences to prisoners on special Buddhist occasions or on the occasion of a royal coronation. Also, those on death row were given a final meal[32] and the chance to make merit by giving something to a monk. The latter was a custom that had Indian antecedents. We learn that Sri Lankans sometimes escaped punishment by taking sanctuary in a monastery. One king who violated this sanctuary had to make amends for his indiscretion.[33]

The current strife between Tamils and Sinhalese on the island is easily traceable back as far as the victory, celebrated in Sinhalese history, of the Sinhalese King Dutthagamani over the Tamil King Alara.[34] The chronicles credit Alara with ruling justly and justify the war which overthrew him on the basis of restoring rule over the island to its 'rightful' Buddhist protectors. The Buddhist view that destiny and divine purpose were on the side of Dutthagamani is suggested in the Great Chronicle's narration of how the god Sakka (Indra) sent an attendant to make bricks for Duttahgamani's post-victory project of building the Great Stupa (Mahathupa). Later, Sakka also sent an attendant to decorate the island for the ritual of enshrining the relics in the stupa.

The Sri Lanka described by the historical chronicles was governed not by a 'kingship' but a 'Buddhist kingship.' The British-style government of independent Sri Lanka, which emerged in 1948, was a fairly adequate replacement for the 'kingship' part of Buddhist kingship. The problem that Buddhists in Sir Lanka have been struggling with since 1948 is: what will replace the 'Buddhist' part of the old Buddhist kingship?

The first significant attempt to deal with this issue came in 1951 when a group of leading Buddhists presented to the prime minister a twenty-six-page paper entitled 'Buddhism and the State.' This germinal paper was quite critical of the British for failing to support the Buddhist religion and culture during their colonial rule, and it called upon the Sri Lankan government to do what the British had not; namely, support Buddhism. The Buddhists who wrote this paper and approached Prime Minister Senanayake in 1950 and 1951 requesting state support of Buddhism were calling for the restoration of the classical Theravada pattern of Buddhist kingship. Senanayake's response, 'The Buddha has pointed out the path of development, and no state aid can take man there,'[35] did not take into account the traditional role of the Buddhist king as protector of the pacifist impulse and related values in Buddhism.

When the government refused these Buddhists' request to form a commission to inquire into the reasons for the neglect, the Buddhists formed their own 'Buddhist Committee of Inquiry.' Though it was without legislative power, it was taken to be very important by the people, and the forces of Buddhist revival in Sri Lanka centred upon it. The commission's report, in its English edition, was entitled 'The Betrayal of Buddhism' in order to stress the explanation that the decline of Buddhism was caused by the British betrayal of their Kandyan Convention commitment. The accusation was not that the British were bad or exploitive overlords, but that they had not fulfilled their function as protector of Buddhism. When the British negotiated the take-over of Kandy, the last holdout of indigenous rule, they had found it necessary to consent to the now famous provision that 'the religion of the Boodhoo ... is declared inviolable and its Rites, Ministers and Places of Worship are to be maintained and protected.' The governor who had to sign the agreement, Sir Robert Brownrigg, and the British back in England were embarrassed by this. Siriwardane describes the conflict:

Brownrigg confessed to the Earl of Bathurst, in a bulletin dated the day after the signing of the Convention, that he included the article only because it was a *sine qua non* of the cession.

It was distasteful to Brownrigg, an ardent Christian who considered the spreading of Christianity in Ceylon to be part of his official duties. To the chiefs, on the other hand, it was not conceivable that Buddhism could exist separate from the state.[36]

With their hearts not in it, the British gradually betrayed the agreement: 'At first, a British Resident in Kandy undertook the necessary official function in lieu of the Kandyan monarch who had been displaced. But in the 1830's, under pressure from the Christian missionary organizations in England, the London government decided it was inappropriate for a British official to bear responsibility for maintaining property, confirming officers, and generally overseeing the affairs of Buddhist temples.'[37]

As a corrective to the situation, the Buddhist Committee of Inquiry recommended the establishment of a Buddha Sasana Council, modeled after the Burmese one, 'to which may be entrusted all the prerogatives of the Buddhist kings as regards the Buddhist religion assumed by the British Crown in 1815.'[38]

Why is it that these modern Buddhists were so eager to have someone function as king? The first reason that occurs to the observer, and which is implicit in the Buddhists' statements, centres around the fact that colonialization robbed the Buddists of their role as the leaders of the culture.[39] It was reasoned that if there were someone in power who was officially charged with protecting Buddhism, the island could return to something like its old pattern. The role of the protector, surrogate Buddhist king, in this line of reasoning was mainly negative. It should protect Buddhism against the onslaught of Christian missionaries and civil laws that favoured non-Buddhists and should protect the Sangha against being downgraded by fake monks who put on the robe as a cover-up for their evil practices. Such functions as these had indeed been the responsibility of the Buddhist king, and there was a need for their being carried out in modern Sri Lanka.

I suggest that besides these rather political and negative reasons, there was a positive, religious reason for wishing to reinstate the institution of the Protector of Buddhism. This reason is that in Theravada tradition the merit-doing king is the head of the laity. This understanding of merit theory is quite clear in the Mahavamsa's treatment of the conversion of Sri Lanka under King Devanampiya Tissa.

As the ideal Buddhist king, Devanampiya Tissa is the lay complement to the Thera Mahinda. The Mahavamsa presents Tissa as Mahinda's most important convert. He is the beginning point for the conversion of the island. Tissa is the example of both the pious layman's conduct and of proper Buddhist kingship.

As an outstanding example of lay conduct Tissa is said to have engaged in numerous meritorious acts. He interrupts his hunting expedition to listen to Mahinda preach the *Dhamma* and immediately takes the triple refuge. When Mahinda accepts his 'invitation to come to Anaradhapura, Tissa receives him as an honoured guest and serves Mahinda food by his own hands. The next day he gives the Mahamegha Park to the Sangha. He also gives the Sangha his verbal and mental support. These are precisely the meritorious acts described in the early texts.

Tissa sets the ideal for Sinhalese Buddhist kingship as it is understood in the Mahavamsa. Following his standard, the Mahavamsa judges kings according to their meritorious or demeritorious acts and their diligence in maintaining justice. Tissa himself is presented as completely meritorious, as is made clear by the account of his many great meritorious acts read at the hour of this death.

The Mahavamsa's concept of the meritorious king has as its background two opposite views of kingship. Dumont, following Kane, has distinguished these two views on the basis of how each sees the origin of kingship. One, in which 'kingship is in some manner a divine institution,'[40] is similar to the ancient Near Eastern conception of kingship. Here, kingship is a gift of the gods to mankind for its own good. This concept, seeing the king's functions as being divinely ordained, leads to an identification of the king with an appropriate god and to the attribution of magical power of the king.

The other conception of kingship that provides a background to the Mahavamsa is more modern in tone. Dumont describes it as having an entirely different character, because it describes kingship as having originated from a contract between the future subjects and the future king. The clearest exposition of this view is found in the Digha Nikaya's story of the Great Elect, which describes the origin of kingship without reference to gods. Dumont writes, 'What strikes one immediately in this tendency, in contrast with the other, is the quite profane notion of kingship it exhibits: the king is just someone who is put in charge of the maintenance of public order, in exchange for which service his subjects leave to him a part of the crops they harvest.'[41]

These two views of kingship are combined in the Mahavamsa's conception of Buddhist kingship. Its notion of the king as the layman giver who represents the whole island introduces into Buddhism some of the magico-religious aspects of kingship, drawing heavily on the current of Indian thought that viewed kingship as a divine institution.

Besides using his power of merit to avert plagues and droughts, the Buddhist king had as one of his most important functions the duty of promoting *Dhamma*. This understanding of the king's role has as its background both the general Indian concept of occupational *Dhamma* and the particular stress given to the promotion of *Dhamma* by Asoka. To some extent the *Dhamma* the kings were to promote was not peculiarly Buddhist. The Mahavamsa does not hesitate, for example, to praise the diligence in meting out justice of the non-Buddhist King Elara – the very king who was slain by the Buddhist hero, Dutthagamini. It reports that when rain came out of season, Elara blamed himself, thinking, 'the king who promotes *Dhamma* gets rain only in the proper season.'[42] By his magical power (*tejas*), the gods were compelled to send rain at the proper time. The Mahavamsa's position is that the Buddhist king should promote *Dhamma* both in the general sense of justice and in the sense of the Buddhist teachings.

The conception of a Buddhist kingship which arose during the Asokan era led in Sri Lanka to the idea that the king ought to be subordinate to some extent to Buddhism. This is especially evident in the Mahavamsa's account of the bringing of a branch of the Bo-tree to Sri Lanka (chapters 18 and 19). According to this account King Asoka first engaged in a Rite of Truth in which he pronounced the facts that the south branch of the tree was destined to go to Sri Lanka and that he would stand unalterably firm in the doctrine of the Buddha. Then he ritually bestowed his kingship on the Bo-tree three times. Later the Naga kings bestowed their kingship on the tree, and at the climactic arrival of the tree in Sri Lanka, Tissa likewise ritually made it the king of his island. This ritual clearly expresses the post-canonical Buddhist idea that the ideal king exercises his power in service of the religion.

When Prime Minister Senanayake said that no state aid could take persons along the Buddhist path of development, he just was not taking into account that part of traditional Buddhist teaching that holds that the lay ruler sets the standard of Buddhist behaviour for all lay Buddhists by thought, word, and deed. The ruler's behaviour is more than mere example; according to Buddhist tradition it activates the power of merit throughout the island, making for peace, welfare, and morality. The prime minister saw Buddhism as a matter of individual achievement, but there has been a complementary social dimension of Buddhist achievement also. The nature of this social dimension is relevant to the consideration of the Buddhist revival movement.

Perhaps the various reasons that the Buddhists gave in the 1950s for the revival of Buddhism and Buddhist culture on the island can be summarized under the common call to give Buddhism its 'rightful place.' Arasaratnam makes the interesting distinction between Sinhalese and Ceylonese: 'The political aim of the new nationalism was to separate the Sinhalese element in the Ceylonese nation and seek to establish it above all other sections.'[43]

In the first few years of Sri Lanka's independence, religious interests were seldom openly discussed in politics, and it was possible for many groups of Sri Lanka to participate in the rise of Ceylonese nationalism. But after 1955, and especially during the election campaign of 1956, there emerged a Sinhalese nationalism, perhaps one could even say a Buddhist nationalism, centred around the issues of Sinhala only and Buddhist dominance of the island's politics and culture.

The arguments for Sinhalese rather than English were often practical ones aimed at giving Sinhala speakers more opportunity for government jobs. But the call for the return of Sinhala as the main language of the island was also a part of the revival of the Buddhist culture. Arasaratnam has summarized the motive of the revival well:

The justification for the emphasis on Buddhism was that Ceylon was the historic island of the Buddha Dhamma, an early receipt of the message of Buddhism which it has since carefully treasured. They felt that the state should come forward more forcefully to fulfill its function as the protector of Buddhism and reestablish the historic connection between the state and the Buddhist Church ... They wanted the state to use its resources and power to help Buddhist institutions to their feet, to put its various houses in order, and to lead the Buddhist revival that was taking place.[44]

Referring to those who like himself were calling for the revival of Buddhism along lines expressed in 'The Betrayal of Buddhism,' Malalasekera said that such Buddhists 'have no desire to make Buddhism the State religion – in spite of the cry raised by self-seeking politicians – but they want the State to help them rehabilitate themselves and undo some, at least, of the injustices perpetrated against them during the days of their subjection.'[45]

Other Buddhists were not so modest in their expectations, especially during the celebration of the Jayanti, the 2500th anniversary of Buddhism. Smith observes that 'the identification of Buddhism with the state on this occasion was all but complete, and a precedent was established for massive intervention by the government in religious affairs.'[46] There was a movement towards pro-Buddhist schools, the news media carried many articles giving instruction in Buddhism, the monks were extremely active in politics instructing the people on which party to vote for in order to promote Buddhism, and the laymen were being constantly reminded that Sri Lanka was important to the world precisely because it was the homeland of pure Buddhism.

I suggest that besides the more immediate reasons that are usually given by Buddhists and Westerners, the desire for a state Buddhism in Sri Lanka was in part caused by the resurgence of the social dimension of Theravada's ethics. Recent writers have tried to correct the view that Buddhist ethics are solely individualistic by identifying a social dimension in Buddhist ethics centred around the theory and practice of merit. In a previous article I suggested that an important part of very early Buddhism's project was the transformation of a society from a harming to a giving orientation.[47] One important means for achieving the reformed social order was that of achieving a Buddhist consensus.

The idea was that of a society in which people of outstanding moral character, whether ordained or lay, used their thoughts, words, and actions to influence the people in a proper lifestyle. The misdirected ('uprooted') person who praises the unpraiseworthy, blames the unblameworthy, appreciates that not worthy of appreciation, and shows displeasure to that deserving appreciation is said to generate demerit, which means that person and the society will suffer. On the other hand, the person who uses influence for the good, generates merit. This person's influence leads to the happiness of the people, and the power (merit) of the good actions brings happiness as well.[48] Theravada laypeople are familiar with this teaching through the following Dhammapada verses: 'If one does evil, do not let them do it again and again! Do not consent to it! Suffering follows from evil. If one does a meritorious deed, let them do it again and again! Consent to it! Happiness follows from merit.'[49]

This belief that public figures have a Buddhist role to play, besides that of being pious individuals, shaped Buddhism in India under Ashoka and subsequently in Sri Lanka from Devanampiya Tissa onward until colonialization. It is the belief that a consensus for the Buddhist ethic should be developed and maintained by education of the youth, by state ceremonies and festivals, by political leaders publicly giving both monetary and verbal support to the Sangha, by the monks' model living and *Dhamma* teaching, and by the maintenance of pilgrimage places. Every one of these traditional means of public Buddhist influence was revived during the upsurge of Buddhism after 1955. The debate centred around the degree and manner in which each should be undertaken in a modern state, while the underlying belief that public or state promotion was integral to Buddhism was seldom challenged.[50]

The symbolic culmination of the Buddhist revival in Sri Lanka came when the British Christian governor general was replaced with a Sinhalese Buddhist governor general. At the installation ceremony the new governor general took on his new responsibility and then sat at the feet of a Thera who reminded him that even though he was now the highest ruler in the land he was still subordinate to the Buddhist *Dhamma*. If the Buddhist histories are to be followed with reference to Ashoka, it could be said that he carried out the social dimension of the Buddhist *Dhamma* without giving offence to non-Buddhists. In Sri Lanka the Tamil minority has resented the Sinhalese attempts to make the country more Buddhistic.

Conclusion

The pacifist impulse in Buddhism is rooted in the ethic of non-violence that was the characteristic spiritual value along the ancient Ganges. This *ahiṁsā* ethic gave rise to a personal ethical system that encouraged non-harming occupations, vegetarianism, and kindness to all living creatures. On the political level, the *ahiṁsā* ethic gave shape to ethical guidelines for rulers which discouraged wars of aggression, hunting, and cruelty towards enemies and criminals. It recognized a need for the punishment of crimes and wars of defence.

The history of the pacifist impulse in Buddhist-dominated Sri Lanka suggests that the *Buddhist* value of non-violence sometimes came into sharp conflict with the *Sinhalese* desire to control territory held by Tamils. The *ahiṁsā* ideal applies to all levels of human endeavour, from the family to government, but in practice Buddhists have made compromises with the *ahiṁsā* ideal on both the personal and political levels.

Notes

1 Romila Thaper, 'Ethics, Religion, and Social Protest in the First Millennium BC in Northern India,' *Daedalus* 54 (Spring 1975), 120.
2 Uma Chakravarti, *The Social Dimensions of Early Buddhism* (Delhi, 1987), 16.
3 Thapear, 'Ethics, Religion, and Social Protest, 129–32.
4 A Deva once claimed superiority for cattle as a means of livelihood. 'In his reply, the Buddha favours agriculture as against pastoralism, and in this he was clearly reflecting the new values of the period. Consequently, the possession of fields become an extremely valuable asset and is frequently reflected in the Buddhist texts. Chakravarti, *Social Dimensions of Early Buddhism*, 19.
5 L.S. Dewaraja, *The Position of Women in Buddhism* (Kandy).
6 Chakravarti, *Social Dimensions of Early Buddhism*, 13, points out that 'the use of the clan name was a prerogative only of the *khattiyas* [kshatriyas] and it was never used for other inhabitants of the *ganasangha* [republics], such as the artisans and the brahmanas.'
7 Chakravarti, *Social Dimensions of Early Buddhism*, ch. 3, has well described the Buddhist use of the term 'householder' (*gahapati*) in the Pali texts.
8 N. Wagle, *Society at the Time of the Buddha* (Bombay, 1965).
9 Charles Drekmeier, *Kingship and Community in Early India* (Stanford, 1962), 85.
10 See H.N. Singh, *History and Archaeology of Black and Red Ware* (Delhi, 1982), and Hyla Stuntz Converse, 'The Agnicayana Rite: Indigenous Origin?,' *History of Religions* 14/2 (Nov. 1974), 81–95.
11 Chakravarti, *Social Dimensions of Early Buddhism*, notes that S. Dutt in *Early Monastic Buddhism*, 56, was among the first to call attention to the connection between the partial aryanization of Eastern India and the rise of Buddhism.
12 J.C. Jain *Life in Ancient India as Depicted in the Jain Canons* (Bombay, 1947), 22–4.
13 This story is no. 18 in the Pali Jataka collection. See also Roy C. Amore and Larry D. Shinn, *Lustful Maidens and Ascetic Kings* (New York, 1981), 100–1.
14 For a discussion of the satirical nature of this and other Buddhist stories, see T.W. Rhys Davids's Introduction in *Dialogues of the Buddha*, vol. 1, which has been reprinted in *Kutadanta Sutta: On True Sacrifice* (Kandy, 1968), 1–6.
15 The story is told in the Kutadanta Sutta, which is no. 5 in the Digha Nikaya.
16 Chakravarti, *Social Dimensions of Early Buddhism*, 37.
17 Author's translation of verse 183 of the Pali Dhammapada.
18 Bruce Lincoln, 'The Indo-European Creation Myth,' *History of Religions* 15/2 (Nov. 1975), 121–45.
19 Chakravarti, *Social Dimensions of Early Buddhism*, 9.

20 Bruce Lincoln, 'The Indo-European Cattle-Raiding Myth,' *History of Religions* 16/1 (1976), 42–65.

21 Author's translation of Pali Dhammapada no. 5.

22 See the sutra on the duties of the Wheel-turning Ruler, the Cakkavattisihana-dasutta, no. 26 of the Digha Nikaya of the Pali canon.

23 This view is expressed is some of the Jatakas. For a discussion of the issue, see Lily De Silva, 'Teachings of the Buddha and the Liberation of the Poor,' *Dialogue*, 15/1–3 n.s. (1988), 38.

24 See the Aggannasutta of the Digha Nikaya, and the discussion of it in De Silva, 'Teachings of the Buddha,' 38.

25 Ibid., 44.

26 Samyutta-nikaya, i.84. For an English translation see Mrs Rhys Davids, trans., *The Book of the Kindred Sayings*, vol. 1 (London, 1971), 110–11.

27 Trevor Ling, *Buddhism, Imperialism, and War: Burma and Thailand in Modern History* (London, 1979). See esp. ch. 6, 'Buddhists at War,' 135–47.

28 Ibid., 146–7.

29 Ibid., 147.

30 Wilhelm Geiger, *Culture of Ceylon in Mediaeval Times* (Wiesbaden, 1960), 147.

31 Robert Knox, *An Historical Relation of Ceylon* (Dehiwala, Sri Lanka, 2nd ed., 1966), 63. Reprint of 1681 edition.

32 Geiger, *Culture of Ceylon*, 147.

33 Ibid., 148.

34 The Sri Lankan chronicles use the spelling *damila* for the modern Tamil.

35 Cited by D.E. Smith in 'The Sinhalese Buddhist Revolution,' *South Asian Politics and Religion*, ed. Donald Eugene Smith (Princeton, 1966), 457.

36 C.D.S. Siriwardane, 'Buddhist Reorganization in Ceylon,' in *South Asian Religion and Politics*, 539.

37 W. Howard Wriggins, *Ceylon: Dilemmas of a New Nation* (Princeton, 1960), 186.

38 Ibid., 199.

39 Smith, following Mendis, notes that the report of the Buddhist Committee of Inquiry 'ignored the doctrine of kamma as the Buddhist explanation of the present condition of an individual or a society.' He means that it gave Western-style, historical rather than Karmic explanations for the Buddhist problems in Ceylon, yet there remains one very old motif which runs through the report – meritorious Buddhist kingship.

40 Louis Dumont, 'The Conception of Kingship in Ancient India,' *Contributions to Indian Sociology*, no. 6 (Dec. 1962), 58.

41 Ibid., 59.

42 MV, 168.

43 S. Arasaratnam, 'Nationalism, Communalism, and National Unity in Cey-

lon,' *India and Ceylon: Unity and Diversity*, ed. Philip Mason (London, 1967), 265.

44 Ibid., 267.

45 *Times of Ceylon*, 15 Jan. 1956.

46 Smith, 'Sinhalese Buddhist Revolution,' 460.

47 Roy C. Amore, 'Giving and Harming: Buddhist Symbols of Good and Evil,' in *Developments in Buddhist Thought: Canadian Contributions to Buddhist Studies*, ed. Roy C. Amore (Waterloo, 1979), 93–103.

48 See Anguttara Nikaya, book ii, no. 1.

49 Author's translation of verses 117–18.

50 It would be interesting to compare the less doctrinally precise Buddhist feeling that state support is necessary with the Muslim doctrine of *Dar-ul Islam*.

15

Gandhi, Tolstoy, and the Tolstoyans

JAMES D. HUNT

In June 1910 Mohandas K. Gandhi created Tolstoy Farm, a rural community outside Johannesburg, South Africa, as a vehicle for his struggles
against racial legislation. The name was not a casual homage to a
famous writer; it was the acknowledgment of a powerful presence in
Gandhi's life. Tolstoy, who not only advocated non-resistance to evil but
also a wide range of initiatives in individual ethics and social reform,
was a major and prophetic voice among those who were disturbed by
the trends evident in modern industrial societies.

Gandhi's relation with Tolstoy has been examined many times, most
notably by Dr Peter Brock,[1] but his involvement with some admirers of
Tolstoy also needs exploration. This essay will look first at Gandhi's
knowledge of Tolstoy and proceed to the persons, organizations, and
books that enlarged and enriched Gandhi's knowledge of Tolstoyan
values.

Tolstoy

By the 1880s Tolstoy's new teachings of moral perfectionism were
becoming known not only in Russia but throughout the world. Gandhi
at this time was in his adolescence (he would be twenty in 1889). His
earliest references to Tolstoy suggest that his knowledge came through
vegetarian literature,[2] but he was not deeply moved until reading *The
Kingdom of God Is within You* in 1893, which impressed him with its independent thinking, profound morality, and truthfulness.'[3]

The great theme of that book is the failure of Christians to acknowledge 'the law of non-resistance to evil by violence,' particularly with
regard to war and legalized state violence, and also the hypocrisy of jus-

tifying war and injustice in the name of Christ. At the end Tolstoy called for a personal decision to look within and see the truth: 'You need only free yourself from falsehood and your situation will inevitably change of itself. There is one and only one thing in life in which it is granted man to be free and over which he has full control – all else being beyond his power. That one thing is to perceive the truth and profess it.'[4] Gandhi later wrote of this book, 'Its reading cured me of my skepticism and made me a firm believer in *ahinsa*.'[5]

Ten years pass before we find another reference to Tolstoy in Gandhi's writings. In 1904 he mentioned Tolstoy as one of the moral guides governing the establishment of his Phoenix settlement, a land colony organized around a newspaper and print shop. His weekly *Indian Opinion* printed a few references each year, showing that Tolstoy remained on his mind. Several visitors observed that he kept a picture of Tolstoy in his law office. In 1905 he introduced Tolstoy's ideas in simplified form for the Indian merchants who were his supporters, foreshadowing many of the familiar ideas of his own mature philosophy:

1 In this world men should not accumulate wealth;
2 No matter how much evil a person does to us, we should always do good to him. Such is the commandment of God, and also His law;
3 No one should take part in fighting;
4 It is sinful to wield political power, as it leads to many of the evils in the world;
5 Man is born to do his duty to his Creator; he should therefore pay more attention to his duties than to his rights;
6 Agriculture is the true occupation of man. It is therefore contrary to divine law to establish large cities, to employ hundreds of thousands for minding machines in factories so that a few can wallow in riches by exploiting the helplessness and poverty of the many.[6]

While in London in October 1909 Gandhi wrote to Tolstoy for the first time, not to discuss philosophy but to ask permission to translate and publish a letter Tolstoy had written to an Indian revolutionary, advising that India would become free only through rejecting violence and obeying the law of love. Gandhi printed 20,000 copies under the title *A Letter to a Hindu*. On the return voyage to South Africa, he wrote his most Tolstoyan work, *Hind Swaraj, or Indian Home Rule*.[7] This was the first of several exchanges which continued until Tolstoy's death in November 1910. During this year Gandhi established Tolstoy Farm, his second rural retreat, and actively courted Tolstoy's support for his work. He sent copies of his biography and of *Hind Swaraj* and received the endorsement, 'Your activity is the most essential work, the most important of all the work now being done in the world.'[8]

Despite his admiration for Tolstoy, and his consistent citation of Tolstoy as the greatest proponent of non-violence, there were significant differences between them. Peter Brock has identified them: 'Gandhi differed from Tolstoy both in his much more positive attitude toward the state and the nation ... and in his belief in the need for active resistance to evil.'[9]

Tolstoy taught absolute non-resistance. He believed that all coercive action was forbidden by Jesus, and this included almost all actions of government, not only war. He believed that as religion was based on the Law of Love, and the state was based on violence, they were incompatible. Tolstoy also believed that the power which would undermine the state and permit a return to true religion was consistent with individual refusal to cooperate. Such individual action could lead to the formation of small voluntary communities of non-resistants living the new life and spreading the doctrine.

Gandhi taught non-violent resistance. While asserting, with Tolstoy, the ethical primacy of non-violence, he believed in taking purposive action to remove evils and to establish a better society. Unlike Tolstoy, Gandhi did not see non-violent action as simply the refusal to participate in state violence, but as a means of inducing the state to change its policies. Gandhi took a more political route, seeking not to supplant the state with a perfectionist society, but to transform it by the efficacy of non-violent means of social reform. Thus, Gandhian non-violence is not non-resistance, it is non-violent resistance or non-violent transformation. A Gandhian community would not only be an exemplification of a better way of life; it would be the centre of activities intended to cause government to change its ways.[10]

There was more to Tolstoy than his doctrine of non-resistance. To quote Brock again, the Tolstoyan impulse 'combined uncompromising nonviolence with unrelenting criticism of society.'[11] Gandhi once acknowledged three debts to Tolstoy: first, he practised what he preached; he exemplified truth. Second, he was the greatest apostle of non-violence of our age, and third, his doctrine of 'bread-labour,' namely, that 'everyone was bound to labour with his body for bread.'[12] In referring to bread-labour, Gandhi pointed towards all the exploitive structures of society and highlighted the moral imperatives of a more egalitarian social order. As his secretary and biographer Pyarelal recalled, 'Tolstoy brought home to Gandhiji the social implications, particularly in the economic sphere, of the law of love as perhaps none else ... Nobody before Tolstoy had clearly divined or stated that the cause of the poverty of the poor was the idleness of the rich, and therefore really to help the poor and put an end to "the slavery of our times" the privileged class had first to get off their backs and learn to live by their own industry.'[13]

Gandhi did not read Tolstoy's great novels, but he did know a number of the short stories, and he read many of Tolstoy's later works on religion and ethical reform. In the Appendix to *Hind Swaraj*, he cited *The Kingdom of God* ..., *What Is Art?*, *The Slavery of Our Times*, *The First Step*, *How Shall We Escape?*, and *Letter to a Hindu*. At one point his newspaper was selling copies of *War and Peace*, *Anna Karenina*, *Hadji Murad and Other Stories*, *Tales and Parables*, and *A Letter to a Hindu*.[14] Gandhi's reading included *The Gospels in Brief*, *The Four Gospels Harmonized and Translated*, *What to Do?*, *On Life*, *My Confession*, *Thoughts on God*, *The Relations of the Sexes*, and *Christianity and Patriotism*. Among the stories he read were 'God Sees the Truth, but Waits,' 'Ivan the Fool,' and 'The Death of Ivan Ilyich.' He also read Aylmer Maude's *Life of Tolstoy* and Ernest Crosby's *Tolstoy as a Schoolmaster*. He translated into Gujarati for his newspaper *Letter to a Hindu*, 'God Sees the Truth,' and 'Ivan the Fool.' Clearly Gandhi had a good knowledge of Tolstoy's religious and confessional writings, some acquaintance with his didactic stories, and had read some of the secondary literature on Tolstoy's work.

The Tolstoyans

In addition to his reading of Tolstoy and direct correspondence, Gandhi moved in a milieu in which Tolstoy's ideas and works were highly valued. Tolstoyans were in his household, among his supporters, and all about him. In South Africa Gandhi's two closest European friends were fans of Tolstoy. The journalist Henry Polak first met Gandhi as a vegetarian, but in the conversation mentioned his admiration for Tolstoy. 'I have a shelf full of his books in my office. Come and look at them,' Gandhi replied.[15] The architect Herman Kallenbach, with whom Gandhi lived from 1908 through 1912, was also a vegetarian and a Tolstoyan, though an inconstant one. It was Kallenbach who was the owner of Tolstoy Farm.

'The history of Tolstoyism as a world-wide movement still remains to be written,' wrote William B. Edgerton in 1968,[16] and it is true even today. In Russia some of Tolstoy's disciples were peasants, particularly peasant leaders, often strongly religious but unorthodox. Others were aristocrats, including princes and former military officers who, like the Tolstoys, owned vast estates together with whole villages of peasants. Notable among these was Vladimir Chertkov (1854–1936), a member of the court nobility and an army officer. Retiring from the army, he set up many progressive enterprises on his own estates before he met Tolstoy in 1883, and thereafter became his closest business and personal companion.[17] Though many of Tolstoy's own religious and ethical writings were proscribed by the Russian censors, Chertkov's connections enabled him to establish a Tolstoyan publishing house named Posrednik (The Intermediary) to distribute good literature cheaply to the common people.[18] Under such influences, Tolstoyan agricultural colonies began to emerge in various parts of Russia. These encountered the usual difficulties to be expected when idealistic but unskilled intellectuals attempt to take up farming and community living. It was Brook Farm all over again.[19]

Outside of Russia, Tolstoyan groups began to emerge in Western Europe, America, Japan, Bulgaria, Austria-Hungary, and elsewhere. Books and pamphlets by Tolstoy that were forbidden in Russia were translated into other languages, and the Russian originals were also printed to be smuggled back into the country.

In 1897, after Tolstoy took up the cause of the Dukhobors (Wrestlers of the Spirit), an anti-militarist Christian sect, his leading Russian colleagues were exiled. Chertkov, who had often visited England in his youth and had friends among the British aristocracy, chose to go there and remained for eleven years, devoting his time to publicizing Tolstoy's ideas and publishing his works in both English and Russian. His arrival coincided with the emergence of the greatest wave of English Tolstoyism. According to Michael Holman, who has been examining the British Tolstoyans, 'Nowhere, outside Russia, was Tolstoy's popularity greater in the last twenty years of his life than in England ... His moral fervour, his penetrating analysis of the ills of contemporary society and his combination of a very basic, personalised Christianity with what can best be called anarcho-populism, accorded well with the prevailing anti-establishment mood.'[20]

The strongest Tolstoyan group in England was the Croydon Brotherhood Church, established in 1894 under the leadership of John Coleman Kenworthy (1863–1948), a socialist influenced by Emerson, Ruskin, and

Henry George before encountering Tolstoy's ideas in 1890. At the Brotherhood Church Kenworthy established a news-sheet first named the *Croydon Brotherhood Intelligence,* later the *New Order.* There was a Brotherhood Publishing Company and a Brotherhood Trust Store, which obtained its goods from cooperative societies. Late in 1895 Kenworthy went to Russia to meet Tolstoy and was encouraged to establish a cooperative agricultural community. In 1896 land was found near Purleigh, Essex, some thirty miles northeast of London. The colony had some fifteen members by the end of 1897; a major split occurred in July 1898, and this experiment was effectively finished by the end of 1899, although a few settlers lingered until 1904. During its brief life Purleigh was a thriving centre of Tolstoyanism. Chertkov came and rented a house in the town to set up a press for his work, and other Russians came and went. At Tolstoy's suggestion, Aylmer Maude, an English businessman who translated his work, also moved nearby with his family and became a major financial supporter for the colony.[21]

Other, smaller, Tolstoyan communities were established at Leeds, Blackburn, and two other locations in Essex. The group that broke away from Purleigh in 1898 established a new colony in Whiteway, Gloucestershire. This one survived longer than any of the others, mainly by abandoning the doctrinaire Tolstoyan approach in order to create new modes of action by which the cooperative community could overcome its characteristic difficulties, whereupon it was regarded by many, including Gandhi, as a failed Tolstoyan experiment. This was the only Tolstoyan colony that Gandhi actually visited; indeed the only one in existence in England by the summer of 1909.[22]

Though Gandhi was not in London during the peak of Tolstoyan organizational activity between 1895 and 1900, the work of the London Tolstoyans had some significance for him. He developed connections with a number of these people, and his library was full of their publications.

Tolstoyan Publications

When Vladimir Chertkov arrived in Croydon in 1897 at the beginning of his eleven-year exile, he immediately began publishing banned Tolstoyan materials in Russian, and also established the Free Age Press as an outlet for cheap, uncopyrighted English translations of Tolstoy's newer works, on the model of his Posrednik publishing operation in Russia. Early in 1900 he asked Arthur C. Fifield, a Brotherhood Church member with whom he had frequently discussed the publication and distribution of books, to manage the latter.[23]

The Free Age Press then consisted of Arthur Fifield and Chertkov, and a few translators such as Aylmer Maude. Fifield was an 'assistant translator,' improving the English of Chertkov and other Russians. He also did all the office work and made arrangement with printers. 'I was publisher, manager, joint editor, joint translator, publicity agent, advertising expert, warehousemen, porter, packer, clerk, bookkeeper, office boy and stamp licker, all in one,' he wrote.[24] Free Age publications included books, such as the novel *Resurrection* and *The Slavery of Our Times*, or *Christian Martyrdom in Russia*, leaflets with two or more pages, and pamphlets of various sizes. All were designed to sell for minimum prices and were distributed widely through commercial booksellers.

Fifield worked with Free Age for only three years, from early 1900 to the middle of 1902, in that time bringing out forty-three publications. He left after a dispute with Chertkov (the aristocrat quarrelled with practically all his associates) and soon thereafter started his own publishing house, the Simple Life Press, later using his own name, A.C. Fifield, Publisher. In this new form he produced many volumes on Tolstoyan themes, including a few by Tolstoy himself. His books spanned the concerns of the London Tolstoyans: works by and on Tolstoy himself, simplicity in living (the Simple Life Series seems to have been his first set of publications, with over twenty volumes), vegetarianism, protests against exploitation, and affirmations of the hope of human brotherhood. He published Emerson, Edward Carpenter, *The Horrors of Sport*, *Facts about Flogging*, *The Imitation of Christ*, the fairy tales of George MacDonald, and Ernest Howard Crosby's anti-militarist satire, *Captain Jinks*, *Hero*.

Five of the twenty titles cited by Gandhi in his *Hind Swaraj* were from Fifield. There were two essays by Thoreau, 'On the Duty of Civil Disobedience'[25] and 'Life Without Principle,' and Godfrey Blount's *A New Crusade*, calling for simplicity in lifestyle, the revival of traditional crafts, and the renewing of country life. The fourth was *The Fallacy of Speed*, by Thomas Taylor, a sweeping critique of modern civilization, questioning the presumed benefits of improved transportation. Gandhi admired Taylor's work enough to translate it into Gujarati for the readers of *Indian Opinion*. R.H. Sherrod's *The White Slaves of England* surveyed dangerous and unhealthy conditions in industry. Eleven Fifield titles were found in Gandhi's ashram library,[26] including *Sayings of Tolstoy* (1911), Crosby's *Tolstoy as a Schoolmaster* (1904), and Percy Redfern's *Tolstoy – a Study*

(1907). Salome Hocking (Mrs Fifield) was represented by her novel of Tolstoyan communities, *Belinda the Backward: A Romance of Modern Idealism* (1905). Three were by the vegetarian Henry Salt, including *Animals' Rights* (1905).

The second major publisher of Tolstoyan reform literature was Charles W. Daniel (1871–1955), who happened to find a job in a publishing firm whose manager, Fred R. Henderson, was a member of the Croydon Brotherhood Church and chiefly interested in publishing Tolstoy. Daniel was soon convinced and became a principal organizer of the London Tolstoyan Society. In 1902 he began his own publishing business and also distributed Free Age books, eventually supplanting Fifield as the leading publisher of unorthodox books with a Tolstoyan ambience. In 1904 he started a monthly, first called the *Crank*, and later the *Open Road*. The first name was suggested by Mary Everest Boole, one of its regular contributors. 'A crank,' she said, 'is little thing that makes revolutions.'[27] The magazine provided a vehicle for all sorts of reformers, 'anarchists, pacifists, Georgists, vegetarians, diet reformers, anti-vaccinationists' and brought Daniel to the attention of Tolstoy, whom he visited in 1909. As his nephew Jeremy Goring recalled, 'He wanted to attack exploitation in all its forms: the exploitation of animals by the food and fur trades, by the world of entertainment, and by medical research; the exploitation of the soil by artificial fertilizers; the exploitation of men by the machinery of modern society.'

Daniel's publications reflected his eccentric mixture of ideas. 'There were books on child psychology by Mary Everest Boole, Eleanor Cobham and other educational pioneers. There were books on health by Josiah Oldfield, Valentine Knaggs, and A. Rabagliati, who were among the first fully qualified medical men to advocate Nature Cure. There were books on vegetarianism and diet reform by ... Edgar J. Saxon.' His wife, Florence Daniel, wrote on many subjects, but especially diet and health. The firm published a pamphlet series called *People's Classics*, offering cheap editions of the thoughts of great writers, a series of *Christian Mystics*, and one called *Pearls from the Poets*.

Gandhi cited only one Daniel publication, a Tolstoy essay, in *Hind Swaraj*, but twenty-nine Daniel titles were found in the ashram library. Mrs Boole, Isabella Fyvie Mayo, and the health writers Valentine Knaggs and Arnold Eiloart[28] were each represented by three titles. Mrs Florence Daniel's *Healthy Life Cook-book* was there also, as were many issues of the *Open Road*.

Daniel was imprisoned in 1917 for publishing pacifist literature, and in 1918 was fined for an anti-war novel that included homosexuality. He continued to produce unorthodox publications and a succession of small magazines, finally concentrating on health books. He liked to tell of overhearing a man say, 'That's Daniel, the publisher. Nice chap, but a damn fool at business.'[29]

Aylmer Maude

The greatest wave of Tolstoyan enthusiasm in England had passed when Gandhi became personally involved in 1909, but he became acquainted with two persons who had significant knowledge of the movement, the translators Aylmer Maude and Isabella Fyvie Mayo. Though their attitudes towards Tolstoy and the movement differed, each contributed to Gandhi's understanding of it.

Aylmer Maude (1858–1938) was surely the person closest to Tolstoy of any that Gandhi actually met (save for his meeting with Tolstoy's daughter Tatiana Sukhotina in Rome in 1931, long after his ideas had matured). He was an English businessman who went to Moscow in his youth and eventually became a director of the Anglo-Russian Carpet Company. After meeting Tolstoy in 1888 and holding long talks with him, he became 'Tolstoy's closest English friend.'[30] At the age of forty he retired to England with his Russian-born wife Louise and their four sons. He bought a house in Essex, within walking distance of the Tolstoyan colony at Purleigh, and became, with his wife, one of the best of Tolstoy's English translators. He continued to visit Russia, assisted Tolstoy in a number of projects, and devoted the next forty years to the production of high-quality translations of Tolstoy in English.[31] However, Maude had experienced only what has been called a 'temporary conversion to the principles of Tolstoyism.'[32] While retaining a great admiration for Tolstoy, he began to articulate strong criticisms of Tolstoy's views on perfect non-resistance, sexuality, and government, which are clearly set forth in his two-volume *Life of Tolstoy* (1908, 1910), the manuscripts of which were read by both Tolstoy and his wife. In his conclusion to the biography, Maude wrote, 'It has been my task to point out that though Tolstoy is sincere and wise, he, like all mortals, makes mistakes – and does so just because he, too, oversimplifies and would solve the very complex problems of property, sex, and Government, by the all too simple method of utterly condemning and rejecting those things.'[33]

When Gandhi first wrote to Tolstoy, 1 October 1909, Maude was visiting at Tolstoy's estate Yasnaya Polyana and was asked to contact Gandhi on his return to England. No record remains of their conversation, but Gandhi's note of 10 November 1909 indicates that there was discussion of Tolstoy's concept of non-resistance, for Gandhi informed Maude that 'Ballou's books' were in the British Museum.[34]

In *The Kingdom of God Is within You* Tolstoy had written of his joy upon discovering the non-resistance beliefs of the American Unitarian minister Adin Ballou (1803–1890). Nevertheless, when he quoted long passages from Ballou's writings, Tolstoy omitted those in which Ballou disagreed with absolute non-resistance. Ballou allowed the use of 'noninjurious physical force' for correction, restraint, or defence, and made this very clear in letters he exchanged with Tolstoy in 1889 and 1890. Tolstoy wrote to Ballou, 'A true Christian will always prefer to be killed by a madman, than to deprive him of his liberty.'[35]

Maude likewise objected to Tolstoy's assertion that 'no physical force must be used to compel any man to do what he does not want to do, or to make him desist from doing what he likes.' He declared that Ballou 'thought the question out much better.'[36] Since Gandhi's satyagraha accepted something like Ballou's 'noninjurious physical force' on that point he probably would have agreed with Ballou, whose works he never read, though he affirmed Tolstoy as the prophet of non-violence.

Herman Kallenbach visited Maude two years later and reported, 'He believes that Tolstoy has done more work than any other reformer during the last century. He essentially believes in his writings on religion, morality and art, but he considers his non-resistance doctrine and his wholesale condemnation of existing Governments and institutions, are not justified.[37] Responding to this letter, Gandhi said, 'I am not surprised that Maude has impressed you. He is a fine man but his reasoning is bad ... His rejection of the doctrine of non-resistance to evil takes away everything from the praise he bestows on Tolstoy. If Tolstoy was the greatest reformer of his age in Europe, he owed it to his doctrine of non-resistance ... I think I told you that I honoured Maude as a true man, i.e., a man who tried to act up to his beliefs – but I do not accept his qualified acceptance of Tolstoy's teaching.[38]

On another subject, Maude and Gandhi could find greater agreement. Maude had strong views on the failure of the Tolstoyan communities to sustain themselves and to accomplish their goals. He had heard much about the early colonies in Russia and lived adjacent to Purleigh, where he played a large role.

Kallenbach, having had a year's experience on Tolstoy Farm, discussed communes with Maude and wrote to Gandhi, 'He considers this

Tolstoyan Settlement [Purleigh] and all other movements started on similar lines, entire failures, as he thinks that human beings cannot work
and co-operate together unless actual rules are laid down for guidance.
He does not doubt their good intentions, but says that he has invariably
found that the enthusiast who has nothing to risk and is not able to do
actual work, is the first to accuse the man, who has to make a thing
somehow pay, in order to find food and shelter for such settlers, of
immoral intentions, and is probably the greatest hindrance to the actual
worker.'[39] Gandhi responded, 'Of course there must be rules for the
guidance of voluntary associations. Only it must be borne in mind that
Tolstoyan belief does not contemplate huge settlements in states.'[40]

At the time Gandhi established his first community in 1904, he
unknowingly showed more agreement with the critic Maude than with
the Purleigh pioneers; Phoenix was to be a brotherhood of equals, but
with certain powers reserved to Gandhi, who owned the land and the
industry (the press), and retained a veto over major decisions such as
membership and finances. Gandhi maintained similar control over all of
his communities or ashrams.[41]

Isabella Fyvie Mayo

If Gandhi's relationship with Maude proved disappointing, this could
not be said of the other Tolstoyan who entered the Gandhi circle soon
after. Isabella Fyvie Mayo (1843–1914) was the most consistent Tolstoyan
in communication with Gandhi. Her relationship with him began with
Tolstoy's final letter to Gandhi, written only two months before his
death. Tolstoy asked Chertkov to translate the letter into English. When
transmitting the letter, Chertkov added that he would ask his friend Mrs
Mayo to enter into communication with Gandhi and that she might be
able to write an article on his work for an English journal.[42] Gandhi then
asked Kallenbach, with whom he was living on the farm, to carry on the
correspondence.

Mrs Mayo was born of Scottish parents in London. Her father, a baker,
died when she was eight, leaving a large business debt. At seventeen,
Isabella determined to pay off this debt and made a living doing secre-
tarial work and other business writing (including addressing envelopes
at the rate of 1500 per day). She began to publish poems and stories
under the pseudonym Edward Garrett and at twenty-four was asked to
write for a Sunday magazine a series of articles on the sick, the lonely,
and the outcast. She decided to do it in story form so that it would

become a novel. This proved to be the key to financial success. *The Occupations of a Retired Life* (1868) was the first of some twenty-two novels written over the next thirty-two years. Married at twenty-seven to a solicitor, John Mayo, she was widowed at thirty-four and move to Aberdeen. Her novels, while popular, have been described as 'beneath the notice' of reviewers.[43] Not until she was thirty-nine, with nine novels behind her, did she publish under her own name.

'I first knew Tolstoy's works about the year 1887, and *at once* found that I had entered into a sympathy which I had found in *no other* modern writer,' she wrote.[44] Although *War and Peace* had been published in 1869 and *Anna Karenina* in 1877, none of Tolstoy's works were known in Western Europe until after 1885. Thus, his radical works on religion and society became known to anglophones simultaneously with his novels,[45] and Mrs Mayo shared in the excitement. It gave her life a new direction. She was active in anti-vivisection societies, promoted cooperative societies and international brotherhood, abhorred racism, protested military conscription, and became a Labour member of the Aberdeen School Board.[46] An opponent of the South African (Boer) War, her house was stoned by patriots.[47]

'We are vegetarians, dispensed with all *personal* service, and refuse all "going to law" etc. or any "righting of wrongs" in a way requiring *force* of any kind,' she explained to Kallenbach.[48] In time, she began to assist in the translation of Tolstoy's works by improving the English of Russian translators in England such as Chertkov and his associate Alexander Sirnis (1881–1918), and published many articles on Tolstoy and on Tolstoyan themes.[49] In 1893 she and others founded a 'Society for the Recognition of the Universal Brotherhood of Man,' which published 'a little paper' called *Fraternity* from July 1893 to February 1897. The journal sought corresponding relationships with other magazines, including the *Afro-American* and *India*.[50] Soon after its closing, she was invited to write for *New Age*, 'A Weekly Record of Christian Culture, Social Service and Literary Life.' Later Florence and Charles Daniel used her writings in the *Open Road*. Mrs Mayo also wrote for the *Millgate Monthly*, published by the Co-Operative Press of Manchester, for *Our Circle*, a juvenile paper for the Co-Operative Societies, also in Manchester, and for *Fellow Mortals*, an anti-vivisection paper.

In her initial letter to Kallenbach, Mrs Mayo stated that she had written on Indian matters and even on Gandhi in *Fraternity* perhaps around 1897, and was a regular reader of *India*, the *Indian Spectator*, the *Punjabi*, and other Indian papers.[51] On reading Gandhi's *Hind Swaraj, or Indian*

Home Rule, she was 'lost in admiration,' and added, 'I have long felt that the Future of India, if it is to have a Future worth having, is wholly in Indian hands.'[52] On receiving documentary materials from Gandhi and his London agent Lewis Ritch, she published articles on his work in three papers early in 1911.[53] In these she emphasized Gandhi's relationship to Tolstoy, saying that 'something like "apostolic succession" connects this man with the great Russian teacher.'[54] Her weekly correspondence with Kallenbach lasted until her death in May 1914. Over a hundred letters survive.[55]

A year after Gandhi and Kallenbach opened Tolstoy Farm, Kallenbach toured Europe and visited Mrs Mayo in Scotland. She provided him with introductions to fellow Tolstoyans in Britain. These were Maude, Sirnis (Chertkov had returned to Russia), Daniel, Mr J. Hope Allen, who was a friend of Edward Carpenter, and a Mr G.D. Laurie, the traffic manager at the Carlisle Railway Station, who had become interested in Gandhi through Mrs Mayo's articles. The list is rather small and suggests the decay of the British Tolstoyan movement by this time. Kallenbach met all he could find and reported on them to Gandhi.

Mrs Mayo's commendation of Aylmer Maude was highly qualified, to say the least. She told Kallenbach, 'I have corresponded with him, argumentatively, but never have met him. He *repudiates* Tolstoy's ideal of "Non-resistance to evil by Violence" – which I think should have disqualified him from being Tolstoy's biographer, as he cannot help writing with a *bias*.'[56] Kallenbach was more attracted to Charles and Florence Daniel, with whom he then corresponded almost as frequently as with Mrs Mayo.[57] This energetic, gracious, and high-minded lady was a soul-mate to Gandhi. In the three years of their correspondence, they shared many concerns, both political and personal, and she did much to reinforce Gandhi's already well-developed Tolstoyan interests. He wrote that she was a 'truly noble soul ... She was one of the few true interpreters of Tolstoy's teachings.'[58]

These then are the cast of Tolstoyans around Gandhi: Polak and Kallenbach, who lived with him; the Tolstoyan publishers and their books, in which he and his entourage read deeply; the experimental communities of Purleigh and Whiteway, which preceded his own experiments at Phoenix and Tolstoy Farm; and two significant figures in the Tolstoyan circle, Aylmer Maude, who was dedicated to presenting Tolstoy's works but disagreed with him often, and the principled believer Mrs Mayo.

Gandhi's encounter with Tolstoy led him into an international network of Tolstoyan idealists whose conception of an ethical and peaceful society transcended the single dimension of non-resistance. Their attempt to embody Tolstoy's later philosophy led to experiments in education, economics, diet, and modes of resistance and social change. Gandhi's attention to their work is evident in correspondence, diaries, and in publications circulating among his circle of friends.[59] Some, like Charles Daniel and Mrs Mayo, followed Tolstoy more literally than he, as when they opposed wars in which Gandhi himself served.[60] They provided support, inspiration, and companionship as he experimented with the new vision of *satyagraha*, but while Gandhi revered Tolstoy he was determined to move beyond non-resistance to non-violent social transformation.

Notes

1 The most authoritative treatments are William B. Edgerton, 'The Artist Turned Prophet: Leo Tolstoj after 1880,' in *American Contributions to the Sixth International Congress of Slavists*, vol. 2, 61–85 (The Hague, 1968), and Peter Brock, *Pacifism in Europe to 1914* (Princeton, 1972), and most recently his *Freedom from War: Nonsectarian Pacifism, 1814–1914* (Toronto, 1991).

2 Mohandas K. Gandhi, 'Guide to London' in *The Collected Works of Mahatma Gandhi* (hereafter *CWMG*) (Delhi, 1958–1984), vol. 1, 89, and Gandhi, *An Autobiography* (London, 1949), 65.

3 *Autobiography*, 114.

4 Leo Tolstoy, *The Kingdom of God and Peace Essays* (London, 1936), 442.

5 Speech on the birth anniversary of Tolstoy, 10 Sept. 1928, *CWMG*, vol. 37, 260.

6 *Indian Opinion*, 2 Sept. 1905 (in Gujarati), in *CWMG*, vol. 5, 56–7.

7 This incident has been examined in my *Gandhi in London* (New Delhi, 1978), 152–5, and in my 'Gandhi, Thoreau, and Adin Ballou,' *Journal of the Liberal Ministry* 9/3 (Fall 1969), 32–52.

8 Tolstoy to Gandhi, 7 Sept. 1908 (o.s.); translation by Vladimir Chertkov, as cited by Isabella Fyvie Mayo, in *The Open Road* (London, March 1911), 197. Quite different translations are given by R.F. Christian in his *Tolstoy's Letters* (New York, 1978),vol. 2, 706, by A. Maude in Tolstoy, *Recollection and Essays* (London, 1937), 438, and by Pauline Padlushak in *CWMG*, vol. 10, 513. See the discussion of this correspondence in Kenneth Rivett, 'Gandhi, Tolstoy, and Coercion,' *South Asia* (Australia), 54 n.s. (Dec. 1988), 29–56, esp. 33ff.

9 Brock, *Pacifism in Europe*, 468. Cf. Edgerton, 'Artist Turned Prophet,' 83.

10 Following Rivett.

11 Peter Brock, *The Roots of War Resistance: Pacifism from the Early Church to Tolstoy* (Nyack, 1981), 75.

12 *CWMG*, vol. 37, 260.

13 Pyarelal, *Mahatma Gandhi I: The Early Phase* (Ahmedabad, 1965), 707.

14 Books for Sale, *Indian Opinion*, 10 June 1914.

15 Henry S.L. Polak, 'Some South African Reminiscences,' in Chandrashanker Shukla (ed.), *Incidents of Gandhiji's Life* (Bombay, 1949), 231.

16 As cited in Brock, *Pacifism in Europe*, 539.

17 Martin Green, *The Origins of Nonviolence: Tolstoy and Gandhi in Their Historical Settings* (University Park, 1986), 193–201; see also Aylmer Maude, *The Life of Tolstoy: Later Years* (New York, 1910), 512–17, and William Edgerton, 'Vladimir Grigoryevich Chertkov,' in Harold Josephson (ed.), *Biographical Dictionary of Modern Peace Leaders* (Westport, 1985), 162–3.

18 Martin Green, *Tolstoy and Gandhi: Men of Peace* (New York, 1983), 185.

19 Their troubles have been keenly observed in Maude, 309–18, 417–19, and in Edgerton, 'Artist Turned Prophet,' 64–5.

20 Michael J. de K. Holman, 'The Purleigh Colony: Tolstoyan Togetherness in the Late 1890s,' in Malcolm Jones (ed.), *New Essays on Tolstoy* (Cambridge, 1978), 194–5.

21 Ibid. On the Purleigh colony, see also W.H.G. Armytage, *Heavens Below: Utopian Experiments in England, 1560–1960* (Toronto, 1961), 342–58, and Dennis Hardy, *Alternative Communities in Nineteenth Century England* (London, 1979), which provides maps and photos of all the Tolstoyan communities, 172–209. A sympathetic fictional view of these communities may be found in Salome Hocking, *Belinda the Backward: A Romance of Modern Idealism* (London, 1905).

22 Gandhi to Polak, 26 Aug. 1909: 'Whiteway was at one time a Tolstoyan Colony. The settlers have not been able to live up to the ideal. Some have gone, others are living there, but not carrying out the ideal,' in *CWMG*, vol. 9, 369. On Whiteway, see Hardy, 199–207, and Nellie Shaw, *Whiteway: A Colony in the Cotswolds* (London, 1935).

23 The account of Fifield is drawn largely from Michael J. de K. Holman, 'Translating Tolstoy for the Free Age Press: Vladimir Chertkov and his English Manager Arthur Fifield,' *Slavonic and East European Review* 66/2 (April 1988), 184–97. I have as yet little information on Fifield's later career.

24 Memoir by Fifield (1936) quoted in Holman, 'Translating Tolstoy,' 188.

25 This edition introduced the longer (and incorrect) title for 'Civil Disobedience,' which has been widely copied. Thoreau did not know of it, but then he may not have known the phrase 'civil disobedience' either. His title was 'Resistance to Civil Government.' See my 'Gandhi, Thoreau, and Adin Ballou,' 36–7.

26 Data on Gandhi's ashram library are from an examination of the pre-1915 titles in the donation of Satyagraha Ashram books to the M.J. Library in Ahmedabad, India, following the closing of the ashram in 1930. The core of this library consisted of books brought by Gandhi from South Africa in 1914.

27 Data on Daniel's career are drawn almost entirely from a pamphlet by Jeremy Goring, *The Centenary of a 'Crank' Publisher: Charles William Daniel (1871–1955)* (Ashingdon, Essex, 1971), and from Nicolas Walter, 'C.W.Daniel: The Odd Man,' *The Raven: Anarchist Quarterly* 9 (1989?), 69–83. For these I am indebted to Jane Miller, who with her husband Ian is carrying on the C.W. Daniel Company Ltd. line of unorthodox health books. Subsequent quotations on Daniel are taken from Goring unless otherwise specified.

28 Arnold Eiloart was a member of the Tolstoyan colony at Purleigh, and he was among those who moved to Whiteway to establish a new colony.

29 Goring, 16.

30 R.F. Christian, 'The Road to Yasnaya Polyana: Some Pilgrims from Britain and Their Reminiscences,' *Slavonic and East European Review* 66/4 (Oct. 1988), 551.

31 Holman, 'The Purleigh Colony,' 204ff. and his 'Half a Life's Work: Aylmer Maude Brings Tolstoy to Britain.' *Scottish Slavonic Review* 4 (1985), 39–53. Maude disapproved of the politics of the Free Age Press, complaining that 'instead of paying due attention to the quality of its versions, and delaying publication until that has been properly attended to, it made the great mistake of being in a hurry, and issuing inferior translations, which subsequently blocked the way for better translations.' Maude, *Life of Tolstoy*, vol. 2, 556.

32 Holman, 'Purleigh,' 204.

33 Maude, 584–5.

34 Gandhi to Maude, 10 Nov. 1909. *CWMG*, following a handwritten letter, mistakenly prints 'Ballow's books,' vol. 9, 527.

35 Maude, 356. The correspondence was edited and published by Lewis G. Wilson. 'The Christian Doctrine of Non-Resistance,' *Arena* (Boston) 3 (Dec. 1890), 1–12. Since Wilson abridged the texts and altered Tolstoy's English, one should compare the text of the two final letters with Frederic I. Carpenter, 'A Letter from Tolstoy,' *New England Quarterly* 4/4 (Oct. 1931), 777–82. An account of the exchange from Ballou's side may be found in his *Autobiography* (Lowell, 1896), 508–11. Maude's description of this correspondence is severely abridged in his revised edition of 1930. See also Brock, *Freedom from War*, 91–9.

36 Maude, 353 and 362.

37 Herman Kallenbach to M.K. Gandhi, 30 Aug. 1911.

38 Gandhi to Kallenbach, 23 Sept. 1911.

39 Kallenbach to Gandhi, 30 Aug. 1911. Aylmer Maude, reflecting on the Tolstoyan colonies and the Dukhobors, observed, 'To hold a commune together requires either a great identity and immutability of life-habits, or a stereotyped religious tradition: so that the members, from force of habit or from religious hypnotism, may not wish to do anything that runs counter to the communal customs. The only other thing, apparently, that renders communism possible is a very strong leadership dominating the entire group. In the case last mentioned, rapid collective material progress is quite possible, so long as the strong and capable leader is there to sanction changes and decide what changes shall be tolerated, and when they shall be introduced,' Maude, *A Peculiar People: The Doukhobors* (London, 1905), as cited in Armytage, 354.

40 Gandhi to Kallenbach, 23 Sept. 1911.

41 See my 'Experiments in Forming a Community of Service: The Evolution of Gandhi's First Ashrams,' in K.L. Seshagiri Rao and Henry O. Thompson (eds.), *World Problems and Human Responsibility: Gandhian Perspectives* (Barrytown, 1988), 177–203.

42 Chertkov to Gandhi, ca. 7 Sept. 1910 (o.s.), *CWMG*, vol. 10, 511.

43 *Longman Companion to Victoria Fiction* (London, 1989), 425–6. This entry seems to be the first notice she has received since her death in 1914. A search for her personal papers has been without fruit.

44 Isabella Fyvie Mayo to Herman Kallenbach, 25 Aug. 1911.

45 Edgerton, Artist Turned Prophet, 61–3.

46 William Diack, 'Isabella Fyvie Mayo,' *Millgate Monthly* (June 1909), 551–4.

47 Mayo to Kallenbach, 4 Dec. 1913.

48 Ibid., 25 Aug. 1911.

49 For instance, 'Tolstoy: His Works and How to Read Them,' *East and West* (Bombay), April 1911, and a reference to a pamphlet she wrote on Tolstoy, ca. 1903. No bibliography has been found, and her memoirs, *Recollections of … more than fifty years …* (London, 1910), say nothing of her Tolstoyan phase. She confided to Kallenbach that her *Recollections* were to make clear that she had 'faced practical life,' and that in only a future volume (which unfortunately she did not live to write) would she record her convictions. Mayo to Kallenbach, 1 March 1912.

50 Ibid., 3 May and 17 June 1912.

51 Ibid., 3 Nov. 1910. In 1897 Gandhi had already begun to attract notice in London papers, especially following the mob scene at Durban harbour. See 'The London Deputation of 1897,' in my *Gandhi in London*, 41–6.

52 Mayo to Kallenbach, 3 Feb. 1911.

53 Mayo, 'The Hard Lot of Certain British Subjects,' *Millgate Monthly* (Manches-

ter) 6/66 (March 1911), 362–9, reprinted soon after in the *Daily News* (London), and a three-part article 'Another Wise Man From – The East,' with photos, in the *Open Road* (London) 8/3, 4, and 5 (March, April, and May 1911), 196–204, 262–76, and 319–32.

54 Mayo, 'Another Wise Man,' 197.
55 Kallenbach's letters were not preserved, but Mrs Mayo's were kept by the recipient and now are in the National Archives of India.
56 Mayo to Kallenbach, 25 Aug. 1911.
57 Kallenbach's diaries record his weekly correspondence with relatives and friends. The Daniel letters seem to have been entirely lost.
58 Gandhi, 'The Late Mrs Mayo,' *Indian Opinion*, 20 May 1914, in *CWMG*, vol. 12, 415–16.
59 This was not the only European reform circle in which Gandhi moved. The support he received from Protestant clergy and lay leaders has been examined in my *Gandhi and the Nonconformists*. Another group which was significant for him was the women's suffrage movement, described in *Gandhi in London*, 101–3 and 137–42, and at somewhat greater length in 'Suffragettes and Satyagraha,' *Indo-British Review* (Madras) 8/1–2 (June 1981), 65–77.
60 Gandhi's military service has been closely examined in Peter Brock, *The Mahatma and Mother India* (Ahmedabad, 1983), 50–74.

16

Gandhi's Non-violence: Metaphysical, Moral, Political, and International Aspects[1]

STEPHEN HAY

Mohandas K. Gandhi's rationale for courageous non-violent action, or *ahiṁsā*, was complex, and to comprehend it fully we must first grasp his four most basic assumptions about the nature of God and human souls. They were: that God was immanent, rather than transcendent; that souls, in each of which a part of God resided, were immortal and passed through many reincarnations, into higher or lower forms of life; that souls could be enmeshed by their karma in three constituent elements or qualities of character – one bad, one intermediate, and one best; and that *moksha*, or release from endless rebirths, was both possible and highly desirable.

These four presuppositions can help us understand the high value Gandhi placed on courageous non-violence, his toleration of courageous violence, and his intense dislike of cowardly non-violence. I will show how he applied this hierarchy of values in times of both peace and war and how his metaphysical assumptions strengthened his capacity for suffering and loving service on behalf of others. In my conclusion I will indicate how his ideas about democracy and international peace overlap as well as complement those of Immanuel Kant.

Four Metaphysical Bases for Gandhi's Non-violence

Gandhi often spoke of God as an immanent, indwelling power or force in all that lives. 'But who is God?' he once asked. 'God is not some person outside ourselves or away from the universe. He pervades everything ... Being immanent in all beings, He hears everything and reads our innermost thoughts. He abides in our hearts and is nearer to us than the nails are to the fingers.'[2] He embraced the idea put forward earlier by Swami Vivekananda, that God is the 'sum total of all souls.'[3] Because of this conviction, Gandhi believed the quickest way to find Him was to reach out to others. 'The ocean is composed of drops of water, each drop is an entity and yet it is part of the whole ... In this ocean of life we are all little drops. My doctrine means that I must identify myself with life, with everything that lives, that I must share the majesty of life in the presence of God. The sum total of this life is God.'[4]

A second central assumption about human beings was that their bodies contained undying souls ensnared in a potentially endless series of births and deaths. 'The soul,' Gandhi wrote, 'is immortal, unchangeable and immanent. It does not perish with the physical body but journeys on from one mortal frame to another till it completely emancipates itself from earthly bondage.'[5] Faith in the immortality of his soul strengthened his civic courage in opposing injustices as he encountered them, and gave him the fortitude to endure the bodily hardships – such as numerous imprisonments and fasts – this opposition often entailed.

A third assumption Gandhi accepted was the common Hindu belief that there is a cause and effect relation between a person's thoughts, feelings, words, and actions during his or her soul's past and present incarnations and its situations in future ones – the so-called law of karma. 'I am a believer in previous births and rebirths,' he wrote. 'All our relationships are the result of the samskaras we carry from previous births'[6] (samskaras being 'impressions on the mind of acts done in a former state of existence'[7]). According to this theory, one's karma determines the relative strength of each of the three constituent elements or qualities called the gunas (literally, 'the strands') that keep souls entrapped in successive bodies. The worst of these qualities is tamas, the 'darkness' that envelops souls ignorant of their true nature. Souls dominated by it wallow in ignorance and sloth and, if in human bodies, risk being reborn in lower forms of life. A better quality, although not the best, is rajas, restless 'passion,' which, when it predominates, shackles the soul to the pleasures of the body, the emotions, and incessant physical activity.

The highest quality or strand of the three is sattva, 'goodness,' etymologically related to satya, Gandhi's favourite name for God, and also present in the word satyagraha.[8] Sattva purifies the soul through spiritual activity and prepares it for its highest state, liberation from the three gunas, and therefore from all future incarnations. Depending on which of these three strands prevails in them, the souls of humans, animals, reptiles, fish, insects, and plants progress through body after body, going up or down the scale of life or remaining at the same level.

As far as I can discover, Gandhi seldom wrote or spoke about these three qualities apart from his two translations of and commentaries on the Bhagavad Gita, his favourite scripture. Yet it is plain that he knew them well, for they appear many times in that text, with the emphasis always on the beneficial effects of *sattva*.[9] In one of his two commentaries Gandhi observed, 'The only way of rising to this state beyond the three *gunas* is to cultivate the *sattvik* quality, for in order to rise to that state one is required to cultivate the virtues of fearlessness, humility, sincerity, and so on. So long as we live in the body, there is some evil, some violence. The most, therefore, that we can do is to be *sattvik* in the highest degree possible.'[10]

On the basis of the fourth assumption, the possibility and desirability of final release from rebirth, Gandhi yearned to become so pure and good that his soul could then transcend the qualities that bound it to successive bodies. 'I once thought,' he said to a British friend who had known him well in South Africa, 'that I could finish the wheel of rebirth in this incarnation. I know now that I can't, and that I shall have to return to it. We cannot escape it, but I hope it will only be once more that I come back to it.'[11] And in 1921 he affirmed, 'The only thing dear to me is *moksha*. My whole effort is to attain *moksha* at the end of this very life.'[12]

Cowardly versus Courageous Non-violence

Now let us look at Gandhi's practical applications of these four assumptions – God within all, the reincarnation of souls, the three karmically determined qualities or strands that bind each soul to bodily existence, and the possibility of liberation from the round of repeated births and deaths. How did they inspire him to act and urge others to act in various situations?

First we must understand that situations, for Gandhi, included the inner conditions of individuals souls. The non-violence of a cowardly individual, bogged down in spiritual ignorance and sloth, was totally unacceptable to him. Great courage was needed to withstand abuse from those who relied on brute force to perpetrate and defend their injustices, and Gandhi much preferred courageous, even violent resistance to such wrongs to their cowardly acceptance.

Here is what he said in 1920 about that priority: 'I do believe that where there is only a choice between cowardice and violence, I would advise violence. Thus when my eldest son asked me what he should have done, had he been present when I was almost fatally assaulted in

1908, whether he should have run away and seen me killed or whether he should have used his physical force which he could and wanted to use, and defended me. I told him that it was his duty to defend me even by using violence ... But I believe that non-violence is infinitely superior to violence.'[13]

In 1921 when Muslim fanatics in southwest India slaughtered and forcibly converted Hindus, Gandhi wrote, 'I want both the Hindus and Mussulmans to cultivate the cool courage to die without killing. But if one has not the courage, I want him to cultivate the art of killing and being killed rather than in a cowardly way flee from danger.'[14] In a 1924 article on 'Hindu-Muslim Tension: Its Cause and Cure,' he advised, 'Between violence and cowardly flight, I can only prefer violence to cowardice. I can no more preach non-violence to a coward than I can tempt a blind man to enjoy healthy scenes.'[15] Courageous non-violence remained his ideal, but when violence 'is offered in self-defence or for the defence of the defenceless,' he said in 1946, 'it is an act of bravery far better than cowardly submission.'[16]

Courageous violence could be a stepping-stone to courageous non-violence, although not a necessary one.[17] Here are two of his statements to that effect, both made in the 1920s: 'Cowardice is wholly inconsistent with non-violence. Translation from swordsmanship to non-violence is possible and at times even an easy stage. Non-violence, therefore, pre-supposes ability to strike. It is a conscious deliberate restraint put upon one's desire for vengeance. But vengeance is any day superior to passive, effeminate and helpless submission. Forgiveness is higher still ... A man who fears no one on earth would consider it too troublesome even to summon up anger against one who is vainly trying to injure him.'[18] 'My creed of non-violence is an extremely active force. It has no room for cowardice or even weakness. There is hope for a violent man to be some day non-violent, but there is none for a coward.'[19]

These three alternatives – cowardly non-violence, courageous violence, and courageous non-violence – may be viewed in light of the Bhagavad Gita's assumption that the soul rises or falls according to which of the three qualities or 'strands' it allows itself to be most tethered by. Cowardly non-violence is a reflection of the quality of *tamas* – that strand of 'ignorance and delusion' that, in Gandhi's translation of the Gita 'makes one negligent and indolent.'[20] Courageous violence stems from the predominance in the soul of *rajas* – the intermediate quality that expresses itself in the 'passion and craving' that commonly motivate physical action.[21] Courageous non-violence correlates especially well with *sattva*, the highest of the three qualities in human nature, English equivalents of which are 'goodness, virtue, excellence,' and 'purity.'[22] We might add a fourth level below these three, the use of violence in a cowardly manner, for instance, when a person with a weapon uses it aggressively, rather than in self-defence, to harm someone who is unarmed. Gandhi maintained that 'it is not a sign of strength but of weakness to take up the pistol on the slightest pretext.'[23]

Cooperating with and Opposing British Rule over India

Gandhi's thought also extended to three sorts of external circumstances: those where individuals or groups dealt with other individuals or groups, those in which the Indian people either cooperated with or resisted British rule, and those where independent nations were poised to wage or were actually engaged in warfare.

Several peculiarities of India's situation before 1947 facilitated the use of non-violent methods in opposing foreign rule. Within that 80 per cent of the population directly controlled by the British, rather than in what they called 'the princely states,' individuals were not allowed to possess firearms. Although Gandhi, who had spent his childhood and youth in two of those semi-autonomous principalities ruled by martial Rajput clans, denounced this as emasculation,[24] it did create a more favourable environment for non-violent action than might otherwise have been the case. In addition, the Indian judiciary's independence from the executive branch and its protection of such civil rights as freedom of speech and assembly and trial by jury created opportunities for non-violent activity against British rule that would have been impossible under a dictatorship.

Until 1920 Gandhi believed the people of India to be too ignorant and disorganized – shall we say too dominated by *tamas*? – to be ready for national self-government. He therefore judged them in a position to benefit from British rule. This attitude first began to take shape in South Africa, when in 1898 he debated helping the British colonists in their war against their Boer attackers. 'I felt that, if I demanded rights as a British citizen, it was also my duty, as such, to participate in the defence of the British Empire. I held then that India could achieve her complete independence within the British Empire.'[25] He felt a similar duty in 1914 when he arrived in Britain just after it entered the First World War. He organized an ambulance corps from among Indian residents there, as he had done twice in South Africa, and reasoned that both he and his countrymen would gain moral and political strength though non-violent war service:

I had hoped to improve my status, that is, of my people through the British Empire ... If I desired to retain my connection with the Empire and to live under its banner, one of three choices was open to me: I could declare open resistance to the war and, in accordance with the law of satyagraha, boycott the Empire until it changed its military policy; or I could seek imprisonment by civil disobedience of such of its laws as were fit to be disobeyed; or I could participate in the war on the side of the Empire and thereby acquire the capacity and fitness for resisting the violence of war. I lacked this capacity and fitness, so I thought there was nothing for it but to serve in the War.[26]

In 1918, for like reasons, and to persuade the British that Indians were not cowards but deserving of greater self-government, he tried to recruit Indian civilians to join the army. He even considered doing so himself. To a British friend who questioned him about this he replied, 'I see that my countrymen are not refraining from acts of physical violence because of love for their fellows, but from cowardice, and peace with cowardice is much worse than a battlefield with bravery. I would rather they died fighting than cringing in fear.[27] Mrs Polak added, 'Indeed it was with great difficulty that some of his friends, including my husband, prevailed upon him not to offer himself as a combatant soldier, as an example to others.'[28] It would be even better, he wrote another British friend, if his recruits 'with hearts of love lay down their guns and challenge the Germans to shoot them – their fellow men – I say that even the German heart will melt.'[29]

In an important 1920 article, 'The Doctrine of the Sword,' Gandhi wrote, 'I would rather have India resort to arms in order to defend her honour than that she should in a cowardly manner become or remain a helpless witness to her own dishonour ... I am not pleading for India to practise non-violence because it is weak. I want her to practise non-violence being conscious of her strength and power. No training in arms is required for realization of her strength ... I want India to recognize that she has a soul that cannot perish and that can rise triumphant above every physical weakness and defy the physical combination of a whole world.'[30]

From 1920 on Gandhi no longer tolerated the British Empire's governance of his country, but in 1928 he defended his prior participation in its wars when replying to the Dutch pacifist, Barthelemy de Ligt. One of his arguments ran, 'I could not, it would be madness for me to, sever my connections with the society to which I belong' and to which he was indebted for many facilities and privileges. 'My position regarding that [Empire's] Government is totally different today and hence I should not voluntarily participate in its wars.'[31]

When, however, in 1942 it came to the defence of his country against an anticipated invasion from Japan, he proposed that Indian rather than non-Indian soldiers be called on to fight. 'Now we have promise of a never-ending stream of soldiers from America and possibly China. I must confess that I do not look upon this prospect with equanimity. Cannot a limitless number of soldiers be trained out of India's millions? Would they not make as good fighting material as any in the world? Then why foreigners?'[32]

He was ready, as before, to see courageous fighting in battles by men of one country against those of another, even though he much preferred his countrymen to resist Japanese aggression non-violently. But in all his twenty-seven years of opposition to British imperial rule he never praised the use of brute force, even by the bravest, as superior to non-violent resistance. 'I firmly believe that freedom won through bloodshed or fraud is no freedom,' he wrote in 1928.[33] And it has been his leadership of non-violent movements of satyagraha, or 'soul-force,' against unjust rule over his countrymen that has inspired similar movements in the United States under Martin Luther King, Jr, and more recently in Eastern Europe. In all three cases courageously non-violent opposition by large numbers of people has moved their governments to cease repressing or allowing the repression of their own citizens – or, in British-ruled India, their subjects.

The failure of the students' massive sit-in at Peking's central square in 1989 was perhaps due partly to China's still strong tradition of authoritarian government and partly to absence among those students of the kind of leadership Gandhi provided in the satyagraha movements he led. Gandhi's condemnation of the similar blocking by students of a much smaller passageway at the University of Calcutta could also be applied to the Peking situation: 'There must be no impatience, no barbarity, no insolence, no undue pressure. If we want to cultivate a true spirit of democracy, we cannot afford to be intolerant. Intolerance betrays want of faith in one's cause.'[34]

As for the outcome of his own country's freedom movement, in the last months of his life Gandhi felt severely disappointed that the All-India National Congress and the All-India Muslim League had agreed, at the latter's insistence, to partition it into two sovereign nations, one where Muslims were in the majority, the remaining one where Hindus predominated. Before and after this denouncement on 15 August 1947 large-scale rioting and killing broke out between the two communities. He was reported as concluding that 'the so-called non-violent non-co-operation of India was not really non-violent. It was the passivity of the weak and not the non-violence of the stout in heart who would never surrender their sense of human unity and brotherhood even in the midst of conflict of interests, who would ever try to convert and not coerce their adversary ... He had all along laboured under an illusion. But he was never sorry for it. He realized that if his vision were not covered by that illusion, India would never have reached the point which it had today.'[35]

Should India Wage War against Pakistan?

In the weeks after independence, news reached Gandhi of the persecution and murder of Hindus and Sikhs in Muslim-dominated Pakistan. He voiced his anguish over such cruelties at his 26 September prayer meeting:

If we were convinced that we could never expect justice at the hands of the Pakistan Government and if they did not admit their mistakes then we had our own Cabinet which included Jawaharlal [Nehru], Sardar Patel and many other good men. If even they cannot stop the Pakistan Government for indulging in these things, then ultimately they would have to resort to war ... We should not take the offensive. But we must be ready to fight ... But we have to choose the path of justice. I would not bother if all the Hindus and all the Muslims have to die following that path [of war] ... But I fight not with the sword, but with the weapons of truth and non-violence.[36]

Here we have a somewhat confused statement by Gandhi of a just war theory. The government of India may have to 'resort to war' but 'not take the offensive' in order to try to prevent the perpetration of injustices in a neighbouring country. He personally preferred a higher way.

War between India and Pakistan broke out soon after over a different issue. On 23 October 1947, when Kashmir's Hindu maharaja still delayed in deciding whether or not to join one or the other nation, frontier Muslim tribesmen crossed from Pakistan into his state. The maharaja appealed to the government of India to send troops, which it agreed to do. Gandhi approved the decision, saying, 'I shall dance with joy even if everybody in Kashmir has to die in defending his land ... All this is the play of God [the Hindu conception of God's actions in the visible world, or *lila*]. But we have always to make the right effort and that consists in dying while doing the right thing.'[37] On 11 November 1947 he clarified his position: 'If I could have my way of non-violence and everybody listened to me, we would not send our army [to Kashmir] as we are doing now. And if we did send, it would be a non-violent army. It would be a non-violent fight if our people went there and gladly met their death at the hands of the Afridis [i.e., the invading tribesmen].'[38] And in the last month of his life, when both Pakistani and Indian forces battled each other in Kashmir, he said, 'Let us pray to God that He may spare us the threatened strife, but not at any price. All that we may pray to God is to grant that we may either learn to live in amity with each other or if we must fight to let us fight to the very end. That may be folly, but sooner or later it will purify us.'[39]

It may seem rather odd to a Western audience to think of death in violent combat as purifying, but it does appear consistent with his ranking of courageous violence in a just cause as much more beneficial to the soul than cowardly surrender or flight.

Courageous Non-violence and Loving Service Aid the Soul's Movement towards God

This brings us back to Gandhi's assumptions that the soul migrates through many incarnations and can ultimately win release from corporeal existence and achieve proximity to God. Death was only a temporary cessation of life and therefore not to be dreaded. It was not the dissolution of the body, much less physical suffering, that was to be feared, but rather this quagmire of potentially ceaseless bondage of the soul to an unending succession of bodies. 'A satyagrahi [one who offers satyagraha],' he wrote in 1940, 'is dead to his body even before the enemy attempts to kill him, i.e., he is free from attachment to his body and only lives in the victory of the soul.'[40] This faith made it considerably easier for him to cheerfully face life-threatening situations, compared with persons who believe they enjoy but a single lifetime.

In an important 1940 article entitled, 'The Non-violence of the Brave,' Gandhi stressed the spiritual utility of dying courageously and nonviolently:

Just as one must learn the art of killing in the training for violence, so one must learn the art of dying in the training for non-violence ... He who has not overcome all fear cannot practise ahisma [courageous non-violence] to perfection. The votary of ahisma has only one fear, that is of God. He who seeks refuge in God ought to have a glimpse of the *atman* [soul] that transcends the body; and the moment one has a glimpse of the Imperishable *atman* one sheds the love of the perishable body ... Violence is needed for the protection of things external, non-violence is needed for the protection of the *atman*, for the protection of one's honour ...

The bravery of the non-violent is vastly superior to that of the violent. The badge of the violent is his weapon – spear, or sword, or rifle. God is the shield of the non-violent.[41]

Whatever the external circumstances, the ideal for Gandhi remained the non-violence of the courageous and *sattvik* person, a living example of goodness and purity and a channel of spiritual power. 'Non-violence [of the brave] is an active force of the highest order,' he remarked in 1938. 'It is soul force or the power of the godhead within us.' 'Even an infinitesimal fraction of it, when it becomes active within us, can work wonders.'[42] Cowardice, on the other hand, he described as 'impotence worse than violence.'[43]

He also equated soul-force with the force of love. 'If I could popularize the use of soul-force, which is but another name for love-force, in place of brute force, I know that I could present you with an India that could defy the whole world to do its worst.'[44] His 'love-force' was not soft and sentimental, but unselfish identification with the divine core in the souls of others. It aimed to make an unjust opponent more conscious of that spiritual reality within, helping him or her to become more just, more truthful, and less violent.

More generally, Gandhi's striving towards his goal of release from rebirth meant living a prayerful, disciplined, and selfless life of loving service to all who needed it. Here the influence on him of New Testament teachings is evident. They had been impressed on him by his readings of them, church services he attended as a law student in London,[45] Protestant missionaries in South Africa, and the later writings of Leo Tolstoy.[46] But his ethic of love differed from the early Christian one by not proscribing violence in all situations. This came about because his ethic was grounded in a different set of metaphysical assumptions, including an eschatology in which souls were judged by the 'law' of karma, separately and a potentially infinite number of times, rather than all together on a single and final judgment day. The unjust were thus not damned to eternal hellfire but in need of a helping hand, so that they could also move up the path towards moral-spiritual perfection and ultimate release from rebirth. (I use the word 'moral-spiritual' because these two words were closely linked in Gandhi's thinking; he once declared, 'I use the adjective moral as synonymous with spiritual.'[47]) By helping others one helped oneself: 'I believe that if one man gains spiritually, the whole world gains with him and, if one man falls, the whole world falls to that extent. I do not help opponents without at the same time helping myself and my co-workers.'[48]

A Coda: Kant and Gandhi on How to Progress towards World Peace

Immanuel Kant and Mohandas K. Gandhi make an interesting and important pair of thinkers to compare on ways to achieve lasting peace among nations. For both earnestly wished humanity to reach this goal, and their recommendations partly coincided and partly complemented each other. We might say that while Kant thought on the macro-level of political philosophy in his cogitations on how world peace could eventually be established, Gandhi worked daily on the micro-level of interpersonal relations. 'I am not built for academic writings,' Gandhi once wrote. 'Action is my domain. What I understand, according to my lights, to be my duty and what comes my way I do.'[49]

Both saw representative governments as their ideal. Gandhi's political goal throughout most of his life was an autonomous and democratic India. Kant's farseeing eyes viewed the establishment of such governments as only the first of three steps in his 1795 plan for 'perpetual peace.' His first of three 'definitive' articles in this plan stipulated that 'the civil constitution of every State should be republican.' He anticipated that in order to gain security against each other's antisocial tendencies, men would increasingly form republics, for 'the republican constitution is the only one entirely fitting to the rights of man.' Under it the legislative, executive, and judicial branches are separated, and all citizens – whether in or out of government – live equally free and equally subject to laws restraining them from harming one another.[50]

These same protections of individual liberties presumably led Gandhi to conclude that 'democracy disciplined and enlightened is the finest thing in the world.'[51] Characteristically, he added the proviso that 'true democracy can only be the outcome of non-violence.'[52] Freedom and equality were also attainable only on that basis: 'My notion of democracy is that under it the weakest should have the same opportunity as the strongest. That can never happen except through non-violence.'[53]

Whereas Kant saw purely selfish interests activating men to organize for peace among themselves, Gandhi held aloft the altruistic ideal of courageous and loving non-violence and its application in the ardent pursuit of justice. For as we have seen, he viewed both as speeding his and other souls towards their final release from bodily existence. And inasmuch as 'the first condition of non-violence is justice all round in every department of life,'[54] a truly non-violent society had first to be a just one. Only then would it be a peaceful one: 'All the world over a true peace depends not upon gunpowder but upon pure justice.'[55] He worked strenuously for justice and domestic peace both in South Africa and India, using the power of his voice and pen and such measures as satyagraha, sarvodaya ('the flourishing of all,' his village self-improvement program), his efforts to remove untouchability, and the struggle for national self-government. In international disputes, as well, he supported the nation with justice on its side. He wrote in September 1939, 'My non-violence does recognize different species of violence – defensive and offensive ... A non-violent person is bound, when the occasion arises, to say which side is just. Thus I wished success to the Abyssinians, the Spaniards, the Czechs, the Chinese and the Poles, though in each case I wished that they could have offered non-violent resistance.'[56]

So these three – democratic government, the non-violence of free citizens, and justice – may be seen as forming in Gandhi's mind a kind of pyramid, with justice as its foundation, a society composed of courageously non-violent and loving individuals resting upon that base and ever strengthening it, with perfect democracy as its apex. A democratic government of that kind could then work with other nations to build a peaceful world, an outcome Gandhi implied when he said, 'My task as a lover and promoter of peace ... today consists in unflinching devotion to non-violence in the prosecution of the campaign for regaining our liberty. And if India succeeds in so regaining, it will be the greatest contribution to the world's peace.'[57]

Apart from his personal example and testimony to the efficacy of courageous non-violence in the pursuit of justice, Gandhi's greatest gift to international peace lay in showing how non-democratic governments could be transformed into democratic ones without recourse to violence. In cases of international aggression, he advised applying the same economic penalties he urged against British rule over India: 'It may be long before the law of love will be recognized in international affairs ... Yet ...

we can see how the world is moving steadily to realize that between nation and nation, as between man and man, force has failed to solve problems, but that the economic sanction of non-co-operation is far more mighty and conclusive than armies and navies.'[58]

Kant relied on practical reason rather than selfless love to diminish the temptation to start wars. 'If the consent of the citizens is required in order to decide that war should be declared ... nothing is more natural than that they would be very cautious in commencing such a poor game, decreeing for themselves all the calamities of war. Among the latter would be: having to fight, having to pay the costs of war from their own resources, having painfully to repair the devastation war leaves behind, and, to fill up the measures of evils, load themselves with a heavy national debt' (which is exactly where the United States has landed itself today). An autocratic ruler, however, may readily 'resolve on war as on a pleasure party for the most trivial reasons' and suffer no personal hardship therefrom – a generalization no longer true in this age of bombs and long-range missiles.[59]

In surveying the causes of modern wars Ivor Thomas similarly concluded: 'Democracy is certainly one of the greatest safeguards of peace and, conversely, autocracy may be reckoned among the causes of war. Bismarck saw clearly at the outset of his career that he would not have been able to carry out his plans if he had to get parliamentary sanction each time [he launched a war]. The existence of a free parliament imposes many salutary checks on the pursuance of an aggressive policy. Unfortunately [in 1914] there were no such checks in Austria, Germany, and Russia, where the caprice of a ruler or minister could plunge the whole nation into the misery of war.'[60] Public opinion may support one or more elected governments' military efforts to restore the independence of a victim of an aggressive autocracy, as in the cases of Belgium in 1914, Poland in 1939, or Kuwait in 1991, but not an attack on another democracy, whose people enjoy the same liberties that their own citizens wish to see preserved and universally honoured.

Surely it is not a coincidence, and it is a source of great hope for the future, that since their establishment in modern times, no freely elected independent democracy has ever waged war against another. (Britain's government was not yet freely elected when it attacked the United States in 1812, and the Boer republics were not fully independent when they invaded the British colonies of South Africa in 1899.) This fact has been ably demonstrated in an article by Dean V. Babst,[61] but demands more attention than it has thus far received. In an important two-part article, Michael W. Boyle also noted the peaceful relations that have been maintained among a growing number of democracies during the past two centuries and showed how prescient Kant was in foreseeing this outcome.[62]

If past precedent continues to prevail, the more democracies there are in the world, the fewer will be the chances of war breaking out. And as informed publics see these dangers lessen, they will doubtless press their governments to reduce still further their tax-financed weaponry and thus their potential for armed conflict.

After the establishment of representative governments, the second of Kant's 'definitive articles for perpetual peace among states' stated that 'the law of nations shall be founded on a federation of free states.' Kant foresaw that the rule of law and constitutional rules for law-making in republican nations would eventually lead them for their own security to establish a steadily expanding 'league of nations,' 'league of peace,' or 'federation of states which has for its sole purpose the maintenance of peace.' He predicted that as this federation 'gradually spread to all states,' they would 'secure their freedom under the idea of the law of nations,' which would govern their relations with one another but not supersede each nation's domestic laws.[63]

Was there room in Gandhi's mind for a global federalism similar to Kant's? The answer is yes, but he couched his endorsements of it in several different ways. As early as 1924 he believed that 'the better mind of the world desires today not absolutely independent States warring against one another, but a federation of friendly inter-dependent States … I see nothing grand or impossible about our expressing our readiness for universal inter-dependence rather than independence.' In 1942 he suggested that 'the structure of a world federation can only be raised on a foundation of non-violence, and violence will have to be totally abjured from world affairs.' He also described the paramount path to peace in terms that went beyond Kant by advocating, not just laws and treaties, but 'the law of love' as the energy that would some day bind humanity together. 'Mutual love enables Nature to persist. Man does not live by destruction. Self-love compels regard for others. Nations cohere because there is mutual regard among the individuals comprising them. some day we must extend the national law to the universe, even as we have extended the family law to form nations – a larger family.[64]

Kant's third proposal for the spread of peaceful relations among nations would guarantee individuals the freedom to trade and to travel in other countries under a cosmopolitan 'law of world citizenship,' which 'shall be limited to conditions of universal hospitality.' Through trade, 'the spirit of commerce, which is incompatible with war, sooner or later gains the upper hand in every state. As the power of money is perhaps the most dependable of all the powers (means) included under the state power, states see themselves forced, without any moral urge, to promote honourable peace and by mediation to prevent war wherever it threatens to break out.'[65] And the mind-broadening effects of travel, along with the value of study in foreign countries, confirm the merit of this 'definitive article.' Although Kant never went farther than sixty miles from his home town, Gandhi would probably never have learned many of his ideas and methods had he not studied for two and a half years in London and worked for twenty more in South Africa.[66]

To conclude: Kant, the more realistic thinker, expected human reason coupled with self-interest to play the major role in achieving world peace. For Gandhi, the more idealistic reformer, it was non-violence and love that would one day unite humanity. The thoughts of these two remarkable men complement each other in a most harmonious way. Together they should guide human minds and hearts towards that long-desired goal expressed by Abraham Lincoln: 'a just, and a lasting peace, among ourselves, and with all nations.'[67]

Notes

1 I must acknowledge my debt to Peter Brock for his pioneering work on Gandhi's apparently ambiguous attitude towards participation in war. His article, 'Gandhi's Non-violence and His War Service,' published in *Gandhi Marg* (New Delhi), no. 23 (Feb. 1981), 601–16, in *Peace and Change* 7/1–2 (1981) 71–84, as well as in his *The Mahatma and Mother India* (Ahmedabad, 1983), 50–74, encouraged me in my own efforts to understand why Gandhi valued so highly such military virtues as disciplined performance of duty, physical courage, and willingness to suffer, if not die, for a worthy cause. A penetrating analysis of Gandhi as a pacifist by Rashmi-Sudha Puri, 'The "Pacifist," in Gandhi,' *Gandhi Marg*, no. 20 (July 1976), 175–86, also helped me to better grasp Gandhi's position and alerted me to the small anthology of Gandhi's thoughts, *For Pacifists*, comp. Bharatan Kumarappa (Ahmedabad, 1949), from which some of the quotations in this article have been drawn.

2 Mohandas Karamchand Gandhi, *The Collected Works of Mahatma Gandhi* (hereafter *CWMG*) (New Delhi, 1958–84), vol. 50, 203.

3 Vivekananda's formulation is quoted in Surendra Verma, *Metaphysical Foundations of Gandhi's Thought* (New Delhi, 1970), 6, who cites as his source Hari-

das Bhattacharya, *The Cultural Heritage of India* (Calcutta, 1956), 4.699. Bhattacharya does not give the original source of this sentence he attributes to Vivekananda: 'The only God in whom I believe is the sum total of all souls, and above all, I believe in my God the wicked, my God the miserable, my God the poor of all races.'

4 *CWMG*, vol. 48, 180. Note also vol. 60, 106, 'We are all sparks of Truth. The sum total of these sparks is [the] indescribable, as-yet-Unknown Truth.' And vol. 69, 88, 'The sum total of all that lives is God.'

5 Ibid., vol. 46, 73.

6 Ibid., vol. 72, 354.

7 Monier Monier-Williams, *A Sanskrit-English Dictionary* (Oxford, 1899), 1120c.

8 He frequently used the worth 'Truth' in speaking of *satya* in English. See the short anthology of his remarks, *Truth Is God*, comp. R.K. Prabhu (Ahmeda-bad, 1955), and the chapter on 'Religion and Truth,' in *All Men Are Brothers: Life and Thoughts of Mahatma Gandhi as Told in His Own Words*, comp. Krishna Kripalani (Chicago, 2nd ed., 1972). He calls God 'the Supreme Good' in *CWMG*, vol. 37, 349, which better conveys his meaning. (I assume that this same passage is incorrectly printed as 'the Supreme God' in *All Men are Brothers*, 32.)

9 In G.A. Jacob, *A Concordance to the Principal Upanishads and Bhagavadgita* (Delhi, [1891] 1963), their appearances in the Devanagari script, mostly in chs. 14, 17, and 18, are listed at 333–4, 399, 781, and 957 – *guna* thirty-two times, *tamas* thirteen times, *rajas* eleven times, and *sattva*, eighteen times.

10 *CWMG* vol. 32, 320.

11 Millie Polak, *Mr Gandhi: The Man* (London, 1931), 185.

12 *CWMG*, vol. 20, 53. See also vol. 39, 3–5 and 401–2, in the introduction and conclusion to his autobiography.

13 Ibid., vol. 18, 132.

14 Ibid., vol. 21, 321–2.

15 Ibid., vol. 24, 142.

16 Ibid., vol. 85, 483.

17 Gandhi said in 1918 that 'the ability to use force [but not its actual use] is nec-essary for a true appreciation of satyagraha,' and later that year wrote, 'one need not assume that heroism is to be acquired only by fighting in a war. One can do so even while keeping out of it ... We can cultivate manliness in a blameless way.' Ibid., vol. 14, 454, vol. 15, 52.

18 Ibid., vol. 31, 292–3.

19 Ibid., vol. 34, 3.

20 Ibid., vol. 49, 140.

21 A fine Sanskrit-English dictionary defines the *guna* of *rajas* as 'the cause of the

great activity seen in creatures.' V.S. Apte, *The Practical Sanskrit-English Dictionary* (Bombay, [1890] 1924), 792.

22 Ibid., 952.

23 *CWMG*, vol. 24, 141.

24 For example, in ibid., vol. 48, 109. Gandhi said in 1917 that he regarded the absence of 'military science' in Indian education as 'an accidental gain,' but added that those who wanted 'to learn the use of arms ... should not be denied the opportunity.' Ibid., vol. 14, 29. See also vol. 15, 16, and vol. 72, 415.

25 Ibid., vol. 39, 173 and 493, n.T3 and n.T4.

26 Ibid., vol. 39, 279 and 502, n.T4. He offered a similar argument in his reply to a 1929 criticism by Tolstoy's disciple, Viktor Chertkov. Ibid., vol. 39, 423–4.

27 Polak, *Mr Gandhi*, 177.

28 Ibid.

29 *CWMG*, vol. 14, 477.

30 Ibid., vol. 18, 132–3.

31 Ibid., vol. 37, 270.

32 Ibid., vol. 76, 49.

33 Ibid., vol. 37, 271.

34 Ibid., vol. 19, 313.

35 Ibid., vol. 89, 62. The report of this conversation with the African-American educator, Stuart Nelson, in Gandhi's weekly newspaper *Harijan* ('the children of God') for 31 Aug. 1947, has 'ever try,' whereas *CWMG* has 'even try,' I believe mistakenly.

36 Ibid., vol. 89, 246–7, translates this speech from the Hindi book, *Prarthana pravachan* (prayer discourse), which gives it in much greater length than the third-person summary in *Harijan* (5 Oct. 1947), 362. Each omits points made in the other: *Harijan*, for example, leaves out the crucial proviso that India should not take the offensive.

37 *CWMG*, vol. 89, 434. As before, *Harijan* (9 Nov. 1947), 406, carries a briefer report.

38 *CWMG*, vol. 89, 480–81.

39 Ibid., vol. 90, 357. See also *Harijan* (11 Jan. 1948), 509.

40 *CWMG*, vol. 72, 383.

41 Ibid., vol. 72, 416. For excellent collections of his sayings on non-violence, see *All Men Are Brothers*, and the much fuller anthology, *The Mind of Mahatma Gandhi*.

42 *CWMG*, vol. 68, 29.

43 Ibid., vol. 85, 281.

44 Ibid., vol. 39, 357.

45 See my 'The Making of a Late-Victorian Hindu: M.K. Gandhi in London, 1888–1891,' *Victorian Studies* 33/1 (Autumn 1989), 82–3.

46 For his reflections on the teachings of Jesus, see *The Mahatma and the Mission- ary: Selected Writings of Mohandas K. Gandhi*, ed. Clifford Manshardt (Chicago, 1949), and M.K. Gandhi, *What Jesus Means to Me*, comp. R.K. Prabhu (Ahmed- abad, 1959).

47 *CWMG* vol. 75, 216.

48 Ibid., vol. 25, 390.

49 Ibid., vol. 83, 180. The punctation in this source has been changed from that in *Harijan* (3 March 1946), 28.

50 Immanuel Kant, *Perpetual Peace*, ed. and trans. Lewis White Beck (Indianapo- lis, 1957), 10 n1, 29, 10–11, 14.

51 *CWMG* vol. 47, 236. For Gandhi's views on democracy, see Kripalani, *All Men Are Brothers*, 338–48, and esp. the pamphlet collecting his remarks on *Democ- racy: Real and Deceptive*, comp. R.K. Prabhu (Ahmedabad, 1961).

52 *CWMG* vol. 76, 388.

53 Ibid., vol. 72, 60.

54 Ibid., vol. 72, 29.

55 Ibid., vol. 15, 285.

56 Ibid., vol. 71, 10–11.

57 Ibid., vol. 39, 424.

58 Kripalani, *All Men Are Brothers*, 455, wrongly attributed to a non-existent 23 June 1919 issue of *Young India*.

59 Kant, *Perpetual Peace*, 12–13.

60 Ivor Thomas, 'War and Its Causes,' in E.F.M. Durbin et al., *War and Democ- racy: Essays on the Causes of Prevention of War* (London, 1938), 213–14.

61 Dean V. Babst, 'A Force for Peace,' *Industrial Research* (April 1971), 55–8. Babst studied all 116 major wars involving 438 countries between 1789 and 1941 and found none between freely elected and independent democracies.

62 Michael W. Boyle, 'Kant, Liberal Legacies, and Foreign Relations,' *Philosophy and Public Affairs* 12/3 (Summer 1983), 205–35, and 124 (Fall 1983), 323–53. I am grateful to Peter Brock for informing me of the existence of this important two-part article.

63 Kant, *Perpetual Peace*, 16, 18, 51, 18, 19.

64 *CWMG*, vol. 25, 481–2, vol. 76, 388, vol. 22, 489.

65 Kant, *Perpetual Peace*, 20, 32.

66 See these books by James D. Hunt: *Gandhi in London* (New Delhi, 1978) and *Gandhi and the Nonconformists: Encounters in South Africa* (New Delhi, 1986).

67 Abraham Lincoln, 'Second Inaugural Address,' in *The Collected Works of Abra- ham Lincoln*, ed. Roy P. Basler, Marion Dolores Pratt, and Lloyd A. Dunlap (New Brunswick, 1953), vol. 8, 333.

PART IV:

PACIFISM AND PEACE MOVEMENTS IN THE MODERN WORLD, 1890–1955

FROM THE EMERGENCE OF AN INTERNATIONAL PEACE MOVE-
MENT IN 1815 the history of pacifism became in many areas closely
intertwined with the history of the broader movement advocating
world peace. This movement included peace advocates who were not
absolute pacifists alongside those who could be considered pacifists in
the stricter meaning of that term. The last section of this book considers,
therefore, various aspects of this interrelationship between pacifists and
internationalists of various kinds who, under certain conditions, were
ready to support war. The book ends in the mid-1950s when, with the
launching of the first broadly based anti-bomb campaigns, a new era in
the history of peace began.

The 'pacifists' of Sandi Cooper's essay entitled, 'The Re-invention of
the "Just War" among European Pacifists before the First World War,'
are the European peace advocates in France, Germany, Italy, and Russia, who, during the quarter century before the First World War, had
wrestled with the question: under what conditions would war be justified? When hostilities finally broke out in 1914, they viewed the conflict as a justified one insofar as their own side was concerned, and they
were ready to fulfil their military obligations if called upon for active
service. Leaders of peace societies in these countries now engaged in
controversy over such issues as war guilt. Peace advocates in Italy were
among those who urged that their country intervene on the side of the
Entente, which indeed took place in May 1915. Cooper shows how such
attitudes were rooted in the previous history of the peace movements of
the countries she deals with. In each case these movements reserved the
right of national self-defence while at the same time believing that warfare had by then become an outmoded method of resolving international disputes. When war broke out in 1914 the only dissent from such
'patriotic pacifism' came from certain women's groups hitherto centring
their activities on peace as much as on social and feminist issues.

Michael Lutzker's essay covers roughly the same period as Cooper's.
But the 'themes and contradictions' he perceives in the American peace
movement during the twenty-two years before the United States's entry
into war in 1917 differ in some respects from those present in the contemporary peace movements of the European continent. Lutzker characterizes almost all the American peace organizations of that era as elitist.
He has chosen two contrasting peace leaders as case studies here: the
internationalist educator, Nicholas Murray Butler, and the anti-militarist and anti-imperialist journalist, Oswald Harrison Villard. Lutzker
sees both men, for all their differences in outlook, as 'each ... in his own

way, prophetic in their fears of what the Great War would do to *their* world, once it was unleashed.'

The Russian revolutions of 1917 opened a new era in the history of humankind. The attitude of pacifists to the new Russia that emerged after the fall of tsardom, and especially to the ultimately triumphant Bolshevik regime, varied. In his essay, 'Pacifism and Revolution: Bertrand Russell and Russia, 1914–18' Richard Rempel studies the changing response to events in Russia of Russell, then active in Britain's Non-Conscription Fellowship. Russell argued that the first (March) Russian revolution was a pacifist one and an example of passive resistance to tyranny, despite an element of violence present in tsardom's fall. After tracing Russell's views on war from 1901 to 1917, Rempel outlines his gradual disillusionment with the Russian revolution as an instrument of peaceful change over the winter of 1917–18. Russell eventually came to regard the March Revolution as a lost opportunity, first as a result of Kerensky's continued prosecution of the war and then of the increasingly authoritarian character of the Bolshevik experiment.

Among the most consistent and energetic opponents of war during these years of conflict and reconstruction we find various women's groups. In '"Transnationalism" in the early Women's International League for Peace and Freedom,' Jo Vellacott examines the genesis and early activities of the most important of these groups, the Women's International League for Peace and Freedom (WILPF). She centres on the 'transnationalism' displayed during the immediate postwar period by the WILPF, a factor that has led to the organization often being neglected in both feminist and peace history when 'written nationally rather than internationally' (as has usually happened). The WILPF activists then committed themselves to what proved to be, as Vellacott writes, 'both a vision and a practical way of life.'

This vision, this commitment to both feminism and peace and to the consequent implications for life, as a whole, emerges in the campaign engaged in by the English writer and pacifist, Vera Brittain, during the Second World War for sending food relief to Nazi-occupied Europe. Y. Aleksandra Bennett's essay on this episode in Brittain's career is based largely on the latter's papers at McMaster University. The author entitles it 'A Question of Respectability and Tactics.' Brittain's efforts, which some pacifists regarded with suspicion, among other reasons as an attempt to humanize – and possibly prolong – the war, were met, on the other hand, with support from a number of 'respectable' persons like George Bell, Bishop of Chichester. All this formed part of Brittain's 'tactics' to present the food-relief campaign – in the form of the Famine Relief Committee headed by Bishop Bell – to government and public alike as one based on far broader support than the 'unrespectable' pacifist community by itself was providing. True, Brittain did not succeed in her objective. She and her pacifist and non-pacifist fellow campaigners, as Bennett points out, 'nevertheless succeeded in making a signal contribution to keeping the nineteenth-century tradition of moral protest alive in wartime.'

The wartime record of France's small community of Christian pacifists, most drawn from the (Protestant) Reformed Church, has gained widespread respect. Courageous help given to Jews in face of Nazi persecution by Pastor André Trocmé and his wife Magda at Le Chambon is the subject of a striking book by Philip P. Hallie, *Lest Innocent Blood Be Shed* (1979). The same cannot be said of the ambiguous wartime conduct of French secular pacifists. Some of the leading 'integral' pacifists of the pre-war era were indeed accused of collaborationism and of pro-Vichy sympathies. Such accusations overshadowed the postwar pacifist movement and weakened it, for instance *vis-à-vis* the communist-inspired peace movement. In his essay, 'Ambivalence in the Post–Second World War French Peace Movement (1946–52),' Norman Ingram discusses attempts of French 'integral' pacifists to regroup and the difficulties they encountered from being widely regarded as defeatists and Pétainists. He also deals with the fate of the dwindling number of old-style liberal internationalists who had survived from the pre-war period. Ingram, in conclusion, points to 'ongoing balkanization' as a potent factor in the continuing weakness of the non-communist French peace movement.

The final essay in the book, by Thomas P. Socknat, deals, like Ingram's, with the immediate postwar years and the onset of the Cold War and is titled, 'The Dilemma of Canadian Pacifists during the Early Cold War Years.' It is devoted to the quandary of Canadian pacifists in face of the nuclear threat and at their inability to avert an impending Third World War in which Canada would inevitably be involved. As Socknat writes, 'Under such circumstances the moral relevance of pacifism was seriously questioned.' This circumstance greatly undermined the small Canadian Fellowship of Reconciliation, which eventually ceased to function altogether. Socknat also examines the role at this time of the controversial United Church minister James G. Endicott, a non-pacifist and supporter of the communist peace position, in creating a politicized peace movement with ties to the Moscow-based World Peace Council. This new movement succeeded for a time in gaining considerable popular support, including that of some – though by no means all – pacifists. Indeed, disenchantment with Endicott on the part of Canadian pacifists increased during the Korean War, when Endicott charged the Americans with carrying on bacteriological warfare, preparations for which, he claimed, were being made on Canadian soil. Endicott's close ties with the Soviet Union discredited him not only with Canadians in general but also with the country's moral and religious pacifists. But these were now left in disarray until the late 1950s. Then a campaign for nuclear disarmament developed in Canada, as in many other countries outside the Soviet bloc, and Canadian pacifists now returned to a more active political role.

17

The Reinvention of the 'Just War' among European Pacifists before the First World War

SANDI E. COOPER

In 1914, as the peace in Europe fractured, nearly two decades of friendship and collaboration among European pacifist leaders, forged in twenty-one international congresses, ruptured as well.[1] Gaston Moch (1859–1935), president of the Délégation Permanente des Sociétés françaises de la Paix, Ludwig Quidde (1858–1941), head of the Deutsche Friedensgesellschaft, and Ernesto Teodoro Moneta (1833–1918), president of the Unione Lombarda per la pace and editor of Italy's most influential pacifist newspaper, *La Vita Internazionale*, ended their relationships, not because of government censorship, but because each viewed the war as defensible and necessary.[2] Official policy positions and military logic submerged the pacifist impulse. In 1914 peace activists did not challenge official assertions that their nation had been attacked and, therefore, was engaged in an unavoidable, just war.[3] As the First World War began, few pacifists – and few socialists – rose to protest the mobilizations or disputed the claim that the fight was essential to national sovereignty and survival.

Gaston Moch, who resigned his captaincy in the French artillery in 1893 to join the peace movement, resumed his military status in 1914 without any apparent reluctance – apart from general anguish that the war had begun. In a remarkable letter to Ludwig Quidde sent via the International Peace Bureau at Berne, he compared the mood in France during August 1914 to the spirit of the great days of the French revolution: 'August 4th (funeral for Jaurès and a meeting of the Chamber) and 21 and 22 (sign-up of foreign volunteers) are the noblest and most uplifting days which I have seen. More than 40000 foreigners from everywhere ... arrived in good order ... on the Invalides to sign up: Italians, Russians, Swedes, Swiss, Romanians, Russian Jews, Poles, etc. (I only describe the ones I saw) marching in regular columns with French flags alongside their own flags ... It is like the volunteers of 1792 but not because 'la patrie est en danger' ... it is humanity that is in danger because of the Prussian regimes and the two military-feudal camarillas.'[4] Moch reported that his colleagues among the French pacifist community had either volunteered for regular service or joined a reserve unit. He personally requested an assignment on the Belgian front as an artillery specialist.

Another long-time French peace activist, Charles Richet (1850–1935), and André Weiss, an eminent international law specialist, toured Italy in September to persuade their Latin sister to abandon neutrality and take up arms in the crusade against Prussian aggression.[5] German behaviour, Richet asserted, ignored the rules of war, reintroduced barbarism in Europe and forced the French to fight 'to protect the rights of all nationalities oppressed by Germans – Italians, Poles, Alsatians, Danes' and to liberate Belgium.[6] The war crimes of the Germans, Richet maintained, ought not be matched by French reprisals in kind but, rather, 'When the struggle will end [we must act] with great sympathy for the unfortunate victims of two sinister rulers ... In this colossal struggle, we stand for the freedom of peoples, liberty, the future and the definitive pacification of the world.'[7] For these continental pacifists the war in 1914 was undertaken in defence of national sovereignty in France; to liberate occupied Belgium whose international rights as a neutral had been trampled; and on behalf of the Serbians, who had been attacked despite European diplomatic efforts to call a conference to negotiate a settlement between Vienna and Belgrade.

Ludwig Quidde who believed that the Central powers did not bear the sole responsibility for the war, produced a pamphlet which asserted: 'Since the question of war or peace has now been removed from the realm of what we want, and our nation, threatened in the East, North and West, is engaged in a fateful struggle, every German friend of peace will have to fulfil his duty toward the fatherland as any other German. He will not be outdone in patriotic devotion by those who had nothing but derision and scorn for the idea of peace when it was still time. We share the general duties with all our compatriots.'[8] Instead of fruitless examination of the causes of the war and who was responsible, Quidde urged pacifists to concentrate on planning for a postwar world. Along with Alfred Fried (1864–1921),[9] the well-known Austrian peace leader and editor of *Die Waffen Nieder*, Quidde wanted the Berne headquarters of the International Peace Bureau to convene its executive committee so that pacifists could assert a common position on the world that would emerge from the peace table.[10] He began to work closely with Dutch neutrals to design proposals for pacific organization, a move that troubled Henri Golay (1867–1950), the newly appointed director of the peace bureau. (Golay feared that the headquarters of the international movement would become an irrelevant organism if initiatives were developed elsewhere.[11]) Personally, Golay, while publicly neutral, believed that French pacifists were correct. German aggression against Belgium had violated a fundamental premise of the pre-war movement, and the war in self-defence was justified. Quidde seemed to treat the invasion of Belgium as a sideshow and a diversion.

Quidde's position enraged the French and Italian peace community. In a 'Letter to a German Pacifist,' the president of La Paix par le Droit, the philosopher Theodore Ruyssen asserted, 'In 1792, the Legislative Assembly declared that the Revolution would wage war not against Peoples but against Kings. A similar feeling animates us today.'[12] There was no interest in planning for a postwar world as long as German soldiers occupied Belgian and French soil. Ruyssen's view was echoed by the French senator known for his pacifism, the Baron Paul Henri d'Estournelles de Constant (1852–1924),[13] who pleaded with his friend, Nicholas Murray Butler, to head off any overture for a ceasefire by the American president until German troops left occupied soil. Bluntly, d'Estournelles de Constant asserted, 'better to die, better to lose everything, than to let ignoble German militarism win.'[14] French pacifists were adamant against Quidde's proposal for a meeting on neutral ground.

In Italy, neutrality was the official policy in 1914 since Rome was not obliged to follow its Triple Alliance partners unless they had been attacked first. Pacifists were relieved. 'The Italian people want war with no one,' asserted Edoardo Giretti (1864–1940)[15] at a public meeting which roared its approval: 'In the present crisis [we] do not wish the State to undertake any action that is not one of peaceful mediation among the peoples being sucked into the whirlwind of a struggle which is the utter negation of civilization and humanity.'[16] Rosalia Gwis-Adami (1880–1930), Italy's leading woman pacifist who usually shared the point of view of her mentor, E.T. Moneta, applauded the neutrality of the government, urged defensive preparations, and hoped that Rome 'would not let itself be drawn into using the army except for the defense of national integrity.'[17]

By the end of October, however, a substantial portion of the Italian pacifist community reversed itself and demanded that Italy intervene on the side of the Entente. At a meeting of 7 November 1914 the Unione Lombarda requested that the government 'intervene at the opportune moment ... employing its moral as well as material forces' to end the war.[18] Italian pacifist arguments favouring intervention – which appeared a month before the ex-socialist Benito Mussolini made the same call – were based on a variety of reasons, the primary being 'respect for liberty and nationality' inscribed in the principles of the Milanese peace society.[19] Increasingly, pacifists published inflammatory articles labelling the Germans as Teutonic barbarians or Huns, crusaders for a world empire.[20] Women pacifists alerted Italian women to the new economic and societal roles that they would have to play if war came.[21] Indeed, before the Italian government actually declared itself on the side of the Entente in May 1915, its peace movement had prepared the way. In Berlin, Ludwig Quidde published an angry essay in the *Tageblatt*, arguing that this war had nothing to do with Italian interests. Enraged, Moneta published the most biting document of the entire pacifist repertoire, 'Dear Ex-Friend,' which he ran over four issues of *La Vita Internazionale*. In it, Moneta spat forth complaints against both Quidde and Germany that might have provoked a duel under other circumstances. Beginning with a comparison of how Germany and Italy were unified, Moneta recited a litany of German barbarisms against the international civil order – its efforts to wreck the Hague peace conferences, its refusal to support arbitration, its unwillingness to recognize the nationality rights of oppressed groups under its thumb, and its failure to abide by international law by the violation of Belgian neutrality. A final crusade against Prussian feudalism to make Germany a fit member of the European republic was entirely appropriate.[22] A profound 'duplicity in the national psyche' of Germans, asserted Moneta, had to be rooted out to assure the future peace of Europe. Only a war of the peoples in favour of liberty could attain this precondition for organized peace.

As the war unfolded, the leadership of the British peace movement, too, concluded that neither a meeting of the central executive board of the International Peace Bureau nor a public appeal to President Wilson to intervene would be advisable. While they preserved a discreet silence and avoided public polemics, British pacifists and internationalists saw their movement overwhelmed, once Belgian neutrality was violated and His Majesty's Government entered the war.[23] By October 1914 British pacifists began to think in terms of long-run strategies, the reconstitution of the postwar world. They even suspended their long-standing public crusade against military training in the schools.[24]

Nonetheless, because Quidde managed to gather ten signatures on a petition to convene the executive committee of the Berne bureau, Golay and Henri La Fontaine (1854–1943),[25] its president, were forced to hold it. La Fontaine, an exile from his native Belgium, opened the meeting on 6 and 7 January 1915. French delegates refused to come and gave their proxies to La Fontaine and Edoardo Giretti. British delegates came reluctantly, supporting the French, Italian, and Belgian positions. Quidde and Fried controlled the Austrian, German, Dutch, and part of the Swiss delegations, refusing to accept French-Italian arguments that the violation of Belgian neutrality had to be rejected in a public statement if the international movement were to preserve any credibility.

Giretti, who moved the resolution, pointed out that he had once been the lone butt of patriotic fury in Italy when he denounced the invasion of Libya in 1911.[26] It was clear that he was challenging Quidde to stand up for unpopular principles. After two days of intense discussions, the meeting was adjourned without any public statement. A stalemate emerged, neither side able to muster a majority favouring a common position by the whole movement. La Fontaine bid the group farewell: 'What we can hope for, as we separate, is that these sad circumstances will soon change. As much as I am ... an internationalist, I am also ... Belgian. But here, permit me to express the hope that our friends from German and Austrian nations will acknowledge the wrong that they have done to us.'[27] They did not. Quidde's hope that a meeting of the Berne executive board would produce a joint statement on the war backfired. In many ways, the meeting was the epitaph of the peace movement in Europe that flourished in the nineteenth century.[28]

Admittedly, the First World War taxed the commitment and capability of pacifists from belligerent nations to preserve their national movements, not to speak of a peace movement which had functioned across boundaries. Without question, the German march into Belgium and France in August and September 1914 altered the circumstances for international cooperation in ways profoundly different than pre-war crises such as the Moroccan affairs, for instance, had done. Nonetheless, among continental pacifists, specific arguments and beliefs had developed during the second half of the nineteenth century that provided a foundation for much of the pro-war support of 1914 and after.

Unlike Great Britain and the United States, where initially most pacifists in the nineteenth century came from religious communities or reform-minded Free Traders, most of Italy's peace activists were shaped by the *Risorgimento*, the resurgence of the peoples of the Italian peninsula from 1815 to 1871 into a modern nation state. The first generation of Italian activists who created peace committees in the late 1860s and 1870s had participated actively, some on battlefields, in the national liberation movement of the fifties and sixties.[29] In the entourage surrounding Giuseppe Garibaldi was a young adjutant named E.T. Moneta whose political initiation as a teenager had been throwing stones at Austrians during the glorious five days of Milan in 1848. After the Austrian reoccupation of northern Italy, he joined the underground and Garibaldi's staff. The cause of Italian liberation – and that of the other oppressed peoples of Europe – was a sacred obligation and a precondition of international peace.

Progressive Europeans who supported the 'renaissance of nations,' as Victor Hugo called it, hoped it would occur with a minimum of violence. Indeed, Hugo optimistically wrote to Garibaldi: 'The renaissance of nations is unavoidable. As for me, I am profoundly convinced that when the time comes, very little blood will be spilled; the Europe of peoples *will make itself*. Revolutions, the best and most necessary of them, must be responsible and you, like me, are one of those who dread spilling one extra, unnecessary drop of blood to lift the enormous weight. No blood at all would be the best way.'[30] Hugo saw no contradiction in calling Garibaldi 'one of the heroes of peace who traversed war; the just sword.'[31] A decade later when the Italian unification was complete, Hugo described Garibaldi as 'the glorious sword of light, truth and justice' – who created the possibility of European peace.[32] Garibaldi was invited to preside over the opening congress of the Ligue Internationale de la Paix et de la Liberté in Geneva in 1867 where he received a tumultuous welcome. He remained honorary president for several years afterwards, and his name attracted a vast outpouring of support for the group which was curtailed with the Franco-Prussian War. In the young Italian state, created through several brief wars between 1859 and 1870, the association of military heroism, justice, and peace was an automatic equation.

Garibaldi hoped that the new nation for which he risked his life repeatedly would create a wholly different military system than was typical of Europe. In 1859–60, his adjutant, Stefan Türr, recommended plans for a national guard and volunteer corps, plans that were totally rejected by the king and ministers who took control of the new state and created a professional army. 'The armed nation' terrified the ruling elites as well as the diplomatic community. Türr believed that had the nation been organized in that fashion, Italy would have had a formidable military capable of liberating the Tyrol from Austrian control but, more important, a force which would never permit 'unjust wars, capricious enterprises, but only struggles for the supreme, legitimate goal, that of the independence of the nation. From such a war, no citizen is exempt. In the organization of national armies, the principle of compulsory service, required of everyone without distinction ... will put a final end to the grievous divisions which exist in so many nations between the military and the people.'[33] Türr's and Garidaldi's vision of a citizen army was historically based in the French experience of the 'great revolution' – precisely what terrified governing elites. To Garibaldi and Türr, the armed nation was not responsible for imperial expansion, but democratic liberation.[34] This kind of force required military training in schools, something for which Moneta campaigned all his life. The abolition of permanent, standing professional armies with an officer corps drawn from aristocrats who detested and mistreated enlisted men was a basic belief of nineteenth-century progressives. It was enshrined in the program of the Ligue Internationale de la Paix et de la Liberté and in that of most Italian peace societies. A proper force, a citizen militia, would be democratic and defensive. If warfare for nation-making was justified because of the higher good of human liberation and rights, then certainly war to reserve the state was equally justified.

Moneta and the Milanese progressives who created the Lombard Union for Peace and Arbitration in 1887–8 proceeded to develop the peace movement in *fin de siècle* Italy on these premises. In 1889 at a national congress of peace activists in Rome, Moneta commented in a speech on arms reduction and disarmament: 'The only war which modern civilization will agree to fight is defensive war which requires that all citizens act to take up arms and enter the battlefield ... [but] because of lingering ancient prejudices from days gone by armies organized for wars of conquest.'[35] Türr, who became a leading figure in international peace circles when the central office of the movement was organized in Berne (after 1891), represented this point of view regularly at congresses. As chair of the seventh international peace congress which sat in Budapest, in 1896, Türr noted 'over the centuries, wars and revolutions were essential to destroy obstacles which arose against liberty and progress. Today the task which remains to us is to develop the progress of civilization ... and not to apply progress to our own destruction.'[36] One of the ways in which this might be attained was by the transformation of the standing European armies into productive organizations, an idea proposed sporadically in the nineteenth century[37] and reintroduced to pacifists in the mid-1890s by Virginie Griess-Traut and Frédéric Bajer.[38]

The view that war was justified to create independent national states, the embodiment of the popular will, was an axiomatic truth to Italian pacifists, though hardly accepted across the pacifist spectrum. When a Polish nationalist demanded pacifist support at a Berne congress, moderates led by Frédéric Passy and British religious participants, rebuffed this request. 'We are not,' Passy observed, 'a congress of diplomats charged ... with re-designing the map of Europe.'[39] Deputies at this congress from Polish, Slavic, Serbian, and Italian groups agreed that war ought to be abolished but reserved that 'the right of insurrection by the Poles was not only certain, it was sacred.'[40]

In 1910 Moneta commented to the national peace congress in Como: 'The pacifist idea is the product of free nations. Only where government is the creation of peoples who have conquered their own freedom *even by force* [italics added] do citizens have the possibility of instilling in others the love of the Good and the hatred of arrogance ... [as well as] communicate through speech and the press to a wider public.'[41] To Moneta, there would be no peace movement without democratic states, and no democratic states were ever born in Europe – or elsewhere – without violent upheaval. There were just and necessary wars. Peace in the Garibaldian tradition was not peace for its own sake but peace with justice, observed another Italian peace activist.[42] Consequently, when the First World War erupted, Italian support for the Entente was 'entirely natural,' said Moneta, 'since our society and journal in its twenty years of life have always promulgated peace worthy of free peoples; and since we have always argued for the necessity of a civilian-military education including the school years [so that] ... our Italy would be prepared in case of war; and for the same reasons, we have proposed a European federation in the tradition of Carlo Cattaneo who first had the idea ... Our pacifism always had the practical content of a vision which now the masses are beginning to understand.'[43]

Besides the Garibaldian inspiration, the Italian and, sometimes, the continental peace movements recognized Giuseppe Mazzini among their inspirations. Though Mazzini himself refused to support the 1867 congress in Geneva where Garibaldi presided, the program contained the central argument to which he had devoted his life – 'whether the essential condition of permanent peace does not require liberty ... and the establishment of a confederation of free democracies making up the United States of Europe?'[44] Personally, Mazzini thought the moment was inauspicious to discuss peace questions when so many European peoples remained tethered to old monarchies, but his eventual object was to remake the map of Europe. With the First World War, it appeared as if such a moment was possible. After the American entry, which included Woodrow Wilson's Fourteen Points, Italian pacifists joyously welcomed *wilsonismo* as the triumph of Mazzini.[45] Thus, for pacifists, the First World War represented the last crusade for democracy, freedom, and peace and the triumph of realistic, not Quaker, pacifism.

Certain French pacifists provided a second formulation that justified or at least accepted and excused the use of war under restricted circumstances in the modern world. Self-defence was the common denominator. In his very definition of pacifism, itself, one author wrote that it was a 'profound love of peace' but added,

It does not follow that we must want peace always and inspite of everything. Pacifism is not cowardice; indeed, the opposite. No one has the right to let justice die because of fear of struggle. A man of courage never provokes a quarrel with his neighbor, but if the latter attacks ... he defends himself with all means at this disposition. If the attack was brutal and violent, he will certainly confront his aggressor in a [like] manner, fight or be beaten, kill or be killed. That is war, the triumph of force which serves the interests of law or that of injustice.[46]

Besides an a priori belief in the right of self-defence, French and other European writers who studied the role of war throughout history maintained that a few political justifications for its use in the present still remained. Liberal thinkers, economists, sociologists, and philosophers such as Gustave de Molinari, Emile de Laveleye, Jacques Novicow, Gugliemo Ferrero, and Théodore Ruyssen, among others, believed that war had exercised significant, often positive influence in social and cultural development. Theirs was a utilitarian, instrumental analysis. None considered war inevitable. Indeed, Novicow, a Russian sociologist whose life work was devoted to studying the issue, campaigned energetically against the fatalistic Darwinian view that captured so many contemporaries in public life and scholarly communities.[47]

Novicow drew careful distinctions between war and struggle (*guerre* and *lutte*), commenting that the forms of conducting struggle and competition did not necessitate annihilation.[48] His paradigms of the ways in which earlier civilizations used war and violence concluded that modern civilization no longer needed such forms of political action to attain viable ends. None of the material or spiritual requirements of complex international economic and cultural relations that modern Europe had evolved could possibly be served by extermination.

On the other hand, while admitting the occasional value of warfare in the past, Novicow noted that in the millennia between 1500 BC and AD 1860, there had been 230 years of peace. (He did not state what cultures and peoples he had studied.) Between the fifteenth and nineteenth centuries, 286 wars of all sizes occurred in Europe. What legacy did all this conflict leave, he asked? Many of those wars were to redress grievances from previous conquests. Did the results prove the superiority of the victor over the vanquished? Was peace or stability an outcome? Based on the record, Novicow concluded that yet another European war would not be the final use of this murderous tool that produced nothing but instability.[49] Scathingly he denounced sociologists, historians, and popularizers whose messages communicated the inevitability of warfare and the celebration of violence as a given of human nature and social organization: 'Conquest hypnotizes us. The desire for aggrandizement has been foremost for so many centuries ... that it relegates all other social preoccupations to the realm of the unconsious.'[50] These intellectuals provided respectability for the persistent power of retrograde social groupings whom Novicow loosely termed 'Junkers.' He feared that such classes, tied to archaic instincts of brutality ... deeply rooted in ... the immense majority of the human species' would unleash the worst war humanity had ever seen if they felt overly threatened.[51] The solution was to muster opposing political forces in a vast coalition, including feminists, socialists, and pacifists in order to strengthen the waffling liberal centre that Novicow feared could not prevent the 'frightful holocausts' that modern weaponry would permit.[52] The political combination for which Novicow pleaded was the only hope for future peace, and here he echoed an idea expressed half a century earlier by Victor Considérant, a Fourierist, who feared that the counter-revolution of 1849 would permanently derail European evolution towards freedom and peace.

Théodore Ruyssen, president of La Paix par le Droit from 1898 to 1948, argued that warfare occasionally produced unintended benefits. The Crusades, he noted, 'opened Christian ports to oriental civilization. The Italian wars, disastrous for our armies, expedited the maturation of the Renaissance in France; the Thirty Years War brought religious peace to Europe; Valmy and Jemappes opened Germany to the [French] Revolution.'[53] He rejected the idea, however, that the recent flowering of economic prosperity in Germany was a result of the Franco-Prussian War, since indicators of German development were evident before 1871. Gustave de Molinari, editor of the *Journal des Economistes*, whose career spanned the second half of the century, also argued the value of war in antiquity, for agrarian tribes, for the preservation of settled communities against nomadic depredation, and finally for the creation of the state. However, the last development transformed warfare into an imperial experience, requiring vast state resources to support a new bureaucracy. With the disappearance of barbarian threats, warfare had no real justification, and Molinari bitterly attacked it as an excuse to sustain a special class which perpetuated warfare in order to control a majority of state revenue. War and arms races benefited 'the military hierarchy by accelerating advancement in grade and pay ... the politician by increasing his power and influence, and ... officials, for it enlarges the scope of their activity.'[54] The result, he argued, was that despite all revolutions and social change, the control of the state remains in the hands of people whose interests are opposite to those whom they govern.[55]

Similar arguments were advanced by the Italian industrialist and peace activist, Edoardo Giretti, who was bitterly opposed to protectionism, to the close ties between generals and steel industry owners, to the use of scarce resources in underdeveloped Italy for armaments, and especially to the support of a military class that contributed nothing to social and economic growth.[56] Giretti largely avoided the question of the historic value of war, but his compatriot, Gugliemo Ferrero, explored it thoroughly in his study of militarism.[57] Ferrero used a comparative anthropological approach, contrasting the social role of violence and war among the Sudanese dervishes with modern Western society. The 'childlike' faith that happiness can emerge from destruction characterized earlier, primitive societies, observed Ferrero; it survives among matured societies in the form of warfare. Beyond this psychological explanation, Ferrero damned the continued resort to war as a symptom of the limited inventiveness of modern mankind, which ought to use its intellectual and physical energy for the creation of capital and the employment of labour. Absent the ingenuity needed to absorb lazy segments of the population, modern nations turn to warfare to acquire territory as a method of growth.[58] It did not work any longer. For Europe it was an atavistic catastrophe; for the contemporary Ottoman Empire, it might be a necessity – at least, until the oligarchy was replaced by groups 'more desirous of progress and civilization ... [willing to remedy] the present evils and rehabilitate that portion of Asia.'[59]

Among peace activists, the historic value of warfare was generally accepted, but its value for contemporary Europe was calculated as zero. Most agreed with Jean de Bloch, whose study of war became the gospel for the pre-war peace movement, that a war between the two well-armed alliances of Europe, the Triple and the Dual Alliances, would end in the destruction of European monarchy, vast rivers of blood and no victory, the likelihood of socialist revolution, and the destruction of Europe's global role.[60] Bloch spent little time on the past; his six-volume study emphasized the technological revolution of the new weaponry; the drastic changes in the battlefield since the American Civil War and the Russo-Turkish War; the revolution in ship construction, ordinance, and armaments; the implications of a long, stalemated war for the European social order; and concluded that war would be suicidal. With such a powerful central vision, Bloch did not discuss the right of defensive warfare. To his death in 1902, he campaigned to communicate the horrible new truths to those in power. Little concerned with popular opinion,[61] Bloch preferred outreach to ministers, generals, strategists, politicians, kings, presidents, and editors of established media.

War might be an anachronism; its probable consequences would likely end European prosperity to the advantage of the Americans and Japanese; its human toll was unimaginable. Nevertheless, under some circumstances it was essential. To Gaston Moch, the peace movement had to admit and face up to this nasty reality. From his earliest involvement with the Ligue Internationale de la Paix et de la Liberté, he struggled to persuade French and European colleagues that the movement absolutely had to take a stand on the legitimacy of warfare which was concomitant with principled containment of force and pacifist determination to reduce the arms race. In part, argued Moch, history provided the answer – the levée en masse of the French Revolution, which illustrated the amazing ability of trained, mobilized citizen-soldiers to defend a territory. This military formation and not professional armies was superior for national defence. Contemporary experience in Switzerland demonstrated how well it worked. There, a popular militia composed of all able-bodied males, trained from the schoolyard up, defended the nation. It was democratic and inexpensive.[62] Moch's analysis paralleled August Bebel's study, *Nicht stehendes Heer, sondern Volkswehr.*[63] Both argued the obvious – if governments seriously meant that all their weaponry was intended for defensive purposes only, then a popular militia was all that any nation needed. The campaign that pacifists and socialist allies had to wage, Moch observed, was one to eliminate the professional forces and substitute armed populations led by democratically trained officers. There would be no need for three-year conscriptions, as every continental nation would possess an army of reservists.

Besides his insistence on the feasibility of the militia, an idea usually associated with Jean Jaurès in France,[64] Moch campaigned vigorously at universal peace congresses for an endorsement of his arguments. He wanted pacifists at the Monaco meeting in 1902 to endorse a resolution which stated

a) that permanent armies ... be replaced by the system of the armed nation; and b) that ... in each nation, a constitutional law be passed stating that the army exists only for national defence.[65]

For different reasons, German and British delegates protested, and Moch exploded at peace activists who were so out of touch with reality that they refused to discuss the most dangerous institution of the civilized world – the conscripted, professionally controlled army and the eternal arms race.[66] Eventually, his proposals were incorporated into the international movement by Emile Arnaud, who drew up the *Code de la Paix* of the movement that was passed by the Stockholm Congress of 1910. In this multi-articled project for international order, the right of self-defence was tacitly accepted as a justification for warfare. The code insisted on the right of nationalities to govern themselves and on the rights of nations to defend themselves. German and British delegates remained very unhappy.

By 1910 the Italian insistence on sacred warfare for national liberation and nation-making had begun to wane. In their own congresses, pacifists began to debate ways to help Italian compatriots who still lived under Austrian rule (the so-called unredeemed provinces of the eastern Alps) to attain measures of ethnic and cultural freedom short of political liberation by warfare.[67] French pacifists, similarly, began to debate measures for Alsatian autonomy within the German federation, recognizing that war for the 'liberation' of Alsace-Lorraine was wanted by no one. Moreover, the international movement entertained recommendations that would lead to the peaceful separation of colonies from mother countries in the twentieth century[68] in an effort to invoke the newly formed Hague Tribunal in novel ways.

Thus, when the war in 1914 broke out, continental pacifists – notably French, Belgian, and Italian, usually supported by Scandivanians – had evolved a qualified position on warfare. The sad necessity of bloodshed on behalf of sovereignty, freedom, and the sanctity of *la patrie* was accepted. Non-violent resistance was not an option in 1914, and few pacifists from the pre-war movement were even sympathetic to private decisions for conscientious objection. Despite the patriotic support of the war by French and German pacifists, police surveillance remained tight.

The only dissent from the pro-war position of the patriotic pacifists that took an organized and vocal form arose from groups of women whose pre-war public lives had not been centred on the international peace movement. Rather, these women had created the feminist-suffragist movement or laboured as social workers, teachers, or doctors. They were the women who heeded the calls of Dr Aletta Jacobs in The Netherlands, Jane Addams in the United States, and Chrystal Macmillian in Great Britain to come to The Hague in 1915 and discuss ways in which women could re-weave the peace. That meeting was a signpost pointing to the formation of a very different kind of peace movement that grew after the war ended.

Notes

1 For a study of secular continental pacifism in the last century, see Sandi E. Cooper, *Patriotic Pacifism: Waging War on War in Europe, 1815–1914* (Oxford, 1991); also see, Werner Simon, 'The International Peace Bureau, 1892–1917: Clerk, Mediator, or Guide?' in Charles Chatfield and Peter van den Dungen (eds.), *Peace Movements and Political Cultures* (Knoxville, 1988) 67–80; Verdiana Grossi, *Le Pacifisme Européen, 1889–1914* (Brussels, 1994).
2 Biographies of peace activists are in Harold Josephson et al. (eds.), *Biographical Dictionary of Modern Peace Leaders* (Greenwood, 1985); Warren Kuel (ed.), *Biographical Dictionary of Internationalists* (Greenwood, 1983); Helmut Donat and Karl Holl (eds.), *Die Friedensbewegung: Organisierter Pazifismus in Deutschland, Österreich und in der Schweiz*, with an Introduction by Dieter Lattman (Düsseldorf, 1983).
3 Victor Basch, *Bulletin du Ligue des Droits de l'Homme* 15/3 (1915), 200.
4 Letter to Ludwig Quidde, 20–4 Aug. 1914, in Bureau International de la Paix, Archives (United Nations Library, Geneva), file 'Crise de 1914, 11.
5 *La Vita Internazionale* 17 (5 Oct. 1914), 548.
6 Ibid., 549–50.
7 'Les Représailles,' *La Paix par le Droit* 14 (Aug.–Sept. 1914), 443–4.
8 'Zweites Kriegsflugblatt der Deutschen Friedensgesellschaft' (15 Aug., 1914), reprinted in Quidde, *Pazifismus im Weltkrieg*, quoted in Brigette Goldstein, 'Ludwig Quidde and the Struggle for Democratic Pacifism in Germany, 1914–1930,' PhD dissertation, New York University (1984), 56–7.
9 Biography in Josephson et al. (eds.), *Biographical Dictionary*.
10 'Crise du 1914' in Bureau International de la Paix, Archives.

11 Werner Simon, 'International Peace Bureau,' 73–4.

12 *La Paix par le Droit* 14 (Aug.–Sept., 1914), 450–1.

13 Biography in Josephson et al. (eds.), *Biographical Dictionary*. Also, Adolf Wild, *Baron d'Estournelles de Constant (1852–1924): Das Wirken eines Friedens-nobelpreisträgers für die deutschfranzösische Verständigung und die europäische Einigung* (Hamburg, 1973).

14 Letter to Christian Lange, 10 Aug. 1914, arrived Oct. 1914, in Letters of Lord Weardale, Archives, Interparliamentary Union (Geneva), box 28.

15 Biography in Josephson et al. (eds.), *Biographical Dictionary*.

16 Quoted in *La Vita Internazionale* 17 (5 Aug. 1914), 412. A study of Italian pacifism in 1914–15 is in Sandi E. Cooper, 'The Guns of August and the Doves of Italy: Intervention and Internationalism,' *Peace and Change* 7 (Winter 1981), 29–43.

17 *La Vita Internazionale* 17 (5 Aug. 1914), 412. See also *Giovine Europa* 2 (9 Sept. 1914), 138.

18 *La Vita Internazionale* 17 (20 Nov. 1914), 601.

19 Article I, *Statuto ed Regolamento dell'Unione Lombarda per la Pace e l'Arbitrato Internazionale* (Milan, 1887).

20 E.T. Moneta, 'Terminando l'Anno: il germanesimo e i nostri doveri,' *La Vita Internazionale* 17 (20 Dec. 1914), 645–6; Rosalia Gwis-Adami, 'Germania e Inghilterra,' *Giovine Europa* 2 (Nov. 1914), 150.

21 'Che faremo in caso di guerra?' *Giovine Europa* 3 (Jan. 1915), 8.

22 *La Vita Internazionale* 18 (20 June–5 Aug. 1914), 305–69, passim.

23 Letter of Frederick Green to Henri Golay, 22 Aug. 1914, Bureau International de la Paix, Archives, no. 7281.

24 National Peace Council (Great Britain), Minute Book, entries of 2 Sept. to 7 Oct. 1914, 299–304, in Library, London School of Economics.

25 Biography is in Josephson et al. (eds.), *Biographical Dictionary*.

26 'Crise de 1914' in Bureau International de la Paix, Archives, Stenographic record of the meeting of 6–7 Jan. 1915, 6–8.

27 Meeting of 7 Jan. 1915, 32.

28 For a contemporary description, see A. de Morsier, *La paix par le droit et la guerre: Abrégé historique et documents* (Geneva, 1915).

29 Sandi E. Cooper, 'Patriotic Pacifism: The Political Vision of Italian Peace Movements, 1867–1915' in Udo Heyn (ed.), *Occasional Papers Series*, no. 14, California State University, Los Angeles, (1985), 9–14, passim.

30 Hugo to Garibaldi, 20 Dec. 1863 in Papers of Giuseppe Garibaldi, Istituto per la Storia del Risorgimento Italiano (Rome) B242 (CCXLII) no. 36(1).

31 *Ibid.*

32 Hugo to Garibaldi, 10 Feb. 1871, ISRI B927 no. 35, 1, 2.

33 Türr to Garibaldi, Paris, 20 Jan. 1867, ISRI B52 no. 2(59), 4 pp., handwritten.

34 Napoleon perverted the mission of the people's army which originally (1793) claimed that it would make war on the castles but bring peace to the cottages.

35 E.T. Moneta, 'Del disarmo e dei modi practici per consequirlo per opera del governi e dei parlamenti,' in *Congresso di Roma per la Pace e per l'Arbitrato Internazione (12–16 Maggio, 1889)*, ed. C. Facelli and L. Morandi, Città di Castello, 1889, 63–4.

36 General Stefan Türr, opening speech, *Bulletin officiel du VIIe Congrès Universel de la Paix*, Budapest, 17–22 Sept., 1896 (Berne, 1896), 21.

37 Ferdinand Durand, *Des Tendances pacifiques de la société européenne et du rôle des armées dans l'avenir* (New York, [1845], 1972), with an Introduction by Dennis Sherman.

38 Virginie Griess-Traut (1814–98) proposed that European forces be made over into groups for public works development, and Bajer (1837–1922) brought her idea to the Budapest meeting of the international movement. *Bulletin officiel* (1896), 68.

39 *Bulletin officiel* (Berne, 1892), 125.

40 Ibid., 84.

41 Speech to VI National Peace Congress, Como, Sept., 1910, in *La Vita Internazionale* 10 (20 Sept. 1910), 411.

42 G. Casazza in *La Vita Internazionale* 21 (20 Feb. 1914), 64–5.

43 *La Vita Internazionale* 21 (5 Jan. 1918), 1.

44 Congrès International de la Paix, *Projet de Réglement et de Programme* (Geneva, 1867).

45 Felice Momigliano, 'Dal nazionalismo all'internazionalismo,' *La Vita Internazionale*, 21 (20 March 1918), 109–10.

46 Barraute de Plessis, *La Patrie Blanche* (Paris, 1909), 5–6.

47 Biographies are in Josephson et al. (eds.), *Biographical Dictionary*. Novicow's summary of his anti-Darwinian position is in *La Critique du Darwinisme sociale* (Paris, 1910).

48 *Les Luttes entre sociétés et leurs phases successives* (Paris, 1893), reprinted in Garland Library of War/Peace, with a new Introduction by S.E. Cooper (New York, 1971).

49 *War and Its Alleged Benefits* (London, 1912, with an Introduction by Norman Angell; reprinted New York, 1971, with an Introduction by S.E. Cooper), 16–18. This was his only work translated into English; the original was *La Guerre et ses prétendus bienfaits* (Paris, 1894).

50 *Conscience et volontés sociales*, (Paris, 1897) 284–5.

51 *La Critique du darwinisme sociale*, 3.

52 *War and Its Alleged Benefits*, 115; *L Affranchissement de la femme* (Paris, 1903), 339.
53 'De la méthode dans la Philosophie de la Paix,' in *Morale Générale*, vol. 2, Bibliothèque du Congrès International de Philosophie (Paris, 1903) 342.
54 *The Society of Tomorrow: A Forecast of Its Political and Economic Organization*, trans. P.H. Lee Warner, Introduction by Hodgson Pratt (London and New York, 1904; reprinted New York, 1971), 13–14.
55 *Grandeur et décadence de la guerre* (Paris, 1898), 126.
56 Speech, *Atti del congresso nazionale delle società per la pace in Torino* (29–31 maggio e 2 giugno 1904) (Turin, 1906) 67.
57 *Il militarismo* (Milan, 1898). The English version, *Militarism*, reworked after the Spanish-American War, appeared in London (1902), reprinted New York (1972), with an Introduction by S.E. Cooper.
58 *Militarism*, 87–8.
59 Ibid., 166.
60 The six-volume study of war appeared first in Russian and Polish; a French edition, *La Guerre* appeared in 1898; the last volume only, containing conclusions, was translated into English as *The Future of War*. *La Guerre* and *The Future of War* are available (New York, 1972). An important study of Bloch's influence is Peter van den Dungen, *The Making of Peace: Jean de Bloch and the First Hague Peace Conference* (Los Angeles, 1983), ed. Udo Heyn.
61 Bloch left an endowment to create a museum of war and peace at Lucerne which opened after his death but did not survive serious financial difficulties in the following years.
62 His arguments were developed in *L'Armée d'une Démocratie* (Paris, 2nd ed. 1900).
63 Published 1898. Moch's original appeared in 1898 also.
64 Jaurès' *L'Armée nouvelle*, part of his *L'Organisation socialiste de la France*, appeared in 1910 and drew heavily on Moch's arguments without attribution.
65 *Bulletin officiel*, Monaco, 1902, 10.
66 *Bulletin officiel*, Rouen and Le Havre, 1905, 143.
67 Speech of Angelo Ghisleri, Como, 1910.
68 See esp., proposals of François Nicol to the Universal Peace Congress, 1910; Speech of the Egyptian delegate to the Universal Peace Congress, Geneva, 1912.

18

Themes and Contradictions in the American Peace Movement, 1895–1917[1]

MICHAEL A. LUTZKER

The First World War, that 'dark scar across the history of Europe,' as Michael Howard has called it, continues to haunt us.[2] In its wake have come many of the most formidable problems with which the statesmen of the twentieth century have had to grapple – the Russian revolution, the Nazi revolution, and the disintegration of vast colonial empires.

This fascination with the war has led many historians to view the early years of this century as essentially the overture to that conflict, strikingly expressed in the title of Barbara Tuchman's book *The Proud Tower* (from which death looked down). The focus on the war's origins has seemed an imperative to many. So, too, the immediate crisis of July 1914, and the failure of diplomats to contain it, has never ceased to absorb us. 'All Europe has gone crazy,' wrote one American witness to the first days of the conflict. For many Americans the war's outbreak gave powerful meaning to the term 'entangling alliances.'[3]

Yet this virtual fixation with the 'root causes' of the war and the failure of diplomacy during the last days of peace, leads to a tendency to dismiss those contemporaries who viewed the decade before the war as heralding an almost unparalleled opportunity for the peaceful resolution of disputes.

In the United States, between 1905 and 1914, peace organizations were founded and drew to themselves men of power and influence. Large donations of private money to establish peace foundations attracted public attention. Financiers, lawyers, industrialists, educators, and former diplomats devoted considerable effort to the pursuit of world peace. Such practical men of affairs (as they often styled themselves) were not accustomed to associating themselves with 'lost causes.' What attracted them to this most challenging of tasks? This essay examines some of the strands of thought among peace advocates in the decade before the war and considers their responses to that conflict.

The founding of new peace organizations after the turn of the century was concurrent, broadly speaking, with the emergence of the United States as a major industrial power and the pre-eminent protector of the Western Hemisphere. These groups were established following the victory over Spain in 1898, and the annexation of Hawaii and the Philippines that helped make the United States a competitor for trade and influence in East Asia. They drew encouragement from the process of Anglo-American rapprochement. The peace movement gained public attention from the Hague conferences of 1899 and 1907, although there was a tendency to exaggerate the accomplishments of these gatherings. The movement was diverse enough to encompass advocates of the 'Large Policy' as well as anti-imperialists, for all could agree that the United States could provide both leadership and an example that the rest of the world might follow.

Between 1899 and 1914 a substantial number of new organizations identified with the peace movement were founded; they included the Intercollegiate Peace Association, the New York Peace Society, the American Society for International Law, the American School Peace League, the Cosmopolitan Clubs, the American Association for International Conciliation, the World Peace Foundation, the Carnegie Endowment for International Peace, the American Society for the Judicial Settlement of International Disputes, and the Church Peace Union. In addition, the venerable American Peace Society added chapters in several states.

Virtually all were elitist in character. They made little or no attempt to appeal to industrial workers or farmers, established no real links to the women's suffrage movement, and were composed almost entirely of old-stock Protestants. After the outbreak of the First World War the movement underwent a dramatic change. New organizations emerged, and their activities highlighted the differences between the pre-war and wartime movements.[4]

Instead of trying to discuss the many organizations that can be found under the peace rubric, I have selected two individuals who may be considered exemplars of the movement, ideal types, if you will, and by examining their lives and careers, will suggest the diversity of ideas, strategies, and responses to issues that could dwell in the house of peace. These two are among several that could be chosen, but both were not only recognized leaders admired by their colleagues and berated by their critics, but also fascinating characters in their own right: Nicholas

Murray Butler, educator, political strategist, and a leading spokesman
for the cause of international amity; and Oswald Garrison Villard, journalist, editor, and outspoken anti-militarist.

In the public mind each was considered a leader of the peace movement. Although their views were strongly at odds, there are some common elements in their backgrounds that set them apart from most
Americans. Both came from the upper middle class, each had the benefit
of a college education, including graduate studies. Both lived in Europe
for a time as young men and travelled there often. Each possessed a
strong interest in public affairs, while many of their fellow students did
not. Both men had their formative experiences in the late nineteenth century and began as Manchester liberals with strong beliefs in free trade
and a limited sphere for government.

The differences between them are no less significant. Butler traced his
heritage to Britain, while Villard was proud of his family's roots in Germany. Butler was a stalwart of the Republican party and favoured its
expansionist policies overseas. Villard, a latter-day Mugwump, described himself as an independent Democrat and a committed anti-imperialist. Yet both men became deeply involved in the peace movement,
this despite a multitude of other commitments. In retrospect each
proved to be something of a prophet. They represent, perhaps as well as
two individuals can, some of the major themes and contradictions
within the peace movement of the early twentieth century.

Nicholas Murray Butter

It would be difficult to name another American of the twentieth century
who made so great an impact upon as many diverse fields of endeav-
ours as did Butler, long-time president of Columbia University. He
wielded extraordinary influence in education, domestic politics, and
international relations. A recital of his career, while impressive in itself,
gives little indication of the enormous range of his personal relationships with statesmen and men of letters the world over. His personal
influence is difficult to measure. It must be assessed in part at least from
Butler's own accounts[5] and weighed against a rather marked tendency
to immodesty. There can be no doubt, however, that his acknowledged
leadership in the field of education served Butler well. It in no way prevented his playing an important role in the high circles of the Republican party, and it seems to have been of considerable advantage in his
efforts at unofficial diplomacy, an avocation to which Butler increasingly devoted his talents earlier in this century.

The future president of Columbia University was born in 1862 to a moderately well-to-do family, his father a carpet manufacturer and a leading citizen of Elizabeth, New Jersey. Butler Sr was of English ancestry, his kin including a distinguished jurist. It was through his father's cousin, Lord Chief Justice Coleridge, that the young Nicholas Murray was first presented to Gladstone. In later years Butler noted that such introductions to highly placed individuals, as a youth, had made it possible for him to come to know intimately the leaders of Europe.

While an undergraduate at Columbia he attracted the attention of then President Frederick A.P. Barnard, who was largely instrumental in the young man's decision to pursue a career in education. After receiving his doctorate in 1884 Butler embarked on a year of travel and study at the universities of Berlin and Paris. He immersed himself in the academic life of Berlin, but there were other rewards as well. Invited to the home of Eduard Zeller, his distinguished philosophy professor, Butler and his fellow students listened to noted scholars holding forth. Upon occasion more worldly gentlemen, including Chancellor Bismarck, discussed the affairs of the day. Butler was struck by the presence of some 20,000 soldiers stationed in Berlin at the time, not, it seems, to parade but having to do with what Butler calls the 'Socialist agitation' of that time.

He found Paris no less fascinating and, for a busy graduate student, seems to have been remarkably observant of the political scene. He found the figure of General Boulanger still troubling the political waters, which were stirred as well by radical and socialist oratory, and he notes that even the quiet precincts of the Sorbonne were shaken by the fall of Jules Ferry from power in 1885.[6]

Upon his return to the United States he began a teaching career at Columbia in philosophy and education, rising rapidly in rank. A man of enormous energy, Butler involved himself in numerous educational reform movements. In 1891 he founded and, for twenty-nine years edited, the influential *Educational Review* and was elected president of the National Education Association in 1894.

It is not clear whether Butler's talents came to the attention of the business community as a result of his work in education or his activities in the Republican party, but he was offered several high-level corporate positions. Instead, Butler put his administrative talents to work for Columbia. When he succeeded to the presidency of that institution in 1902, his close relationship with numerous business leaders proved exceedingly helpful; endowments were increased enormously. Such wealth was beneficial in attracting noted scholars and building new facilities. It also established Butler as one of the foremost figures in New York.[7]

Oswald Garrison Villard

Villard came from a similar social stratum, but unlike Butler he traced his heritage to a family of notable reformers.[8] The abolitionist and pacifist William Lloyd Garrison was his grandfather, and his mother Fanny Garrison Villard kept the flame of pacifism and women's rights burning brightly. Henry Villard, his father, was a German immigrant who first worked as a journalist covering the Lincoln-Douglas debates, and many of the famous battles of the Civil War, but he was best known as the builder of the Northern Pacific Railroad. Born in 1872, Oswald grew up in comfortable circumstances. When his father faced bankruptcy the family moved to Berlin where they lived from 1884 to 1886 surrounded by many relatives. There at age fifteen Oswald experienced the strict discipline of German schools and saw first-hand the militarization of German youth. Thenceforth, he became a strong critic of the German military system. However, young Villard also saw the other side of Germany. The Villard home in Berlin was often filled with eminent leaders of science and academe whom Oswald came to admire.[9]

After the family returned to the United States Villard entered Harvard, where his studies with its distinguished faculty left him memories that he treasured all his life. As a graduate student Villard was chosen by the noted historian Albert Bushnell Hart to be his teaching assistant. Hart later confided to him that the appointment was due less to his scholarship than to his social standing and well-tailored appearance. As a junior instructor Villard lunched regularly with the luminaries of the faculty who, when they were not good-naturedly teasing him, impressed him by their deep concern with public issues.

His pacifist forebears notwithstanding, Villard enjoyed studying military science, drilled with a Harvard military unit, and served for a time with a Massachusetts artillery company. As he relates it, he was slow to come to his reformist, pacifist position. He approved, for example, of President Cleveland's use of federal troops to break the Pullman Strike of 1894, and it was not until the Spanish-American War and the American conquest of the Philippines that Villard embraced pacifism. He denounced the war with Spain as an unnecessary evil and was outspoken in his condemnation of President McKinley. The adoption of Spain's dreaded 'reconcentration' tactics by United States forces in the subsequent Philippines campaign convinced Villard of the power of war to brutalize Americans and drove him to active membership in the Anti-Imperialist League. By this time he had left Harvard determined to be a journalist and was enjoying his role as editor of the venerable *New York Evening Post* and the *Nation*.[10]

The Philippine issue also concerned Butler who, unlike Villard, was a 'strongly convinced expansionist.'[11] Writing to President McKinley regarding the Islands, Butler urged that the United States retain the entire archipelago. But here, as in other instances, his thinking went beyond the immediate issue. He had a grander plan in mind, namely, to use possession of the islands, as he put it, 'in the interest of the final solution of the eastern question, and for the promotion of the world's peace.' This 'solution' was to capitalize on Germany's desire for a foothold in the Philippines by offering her one in return for substantial trade concessions that would allow the United States to greatly increase its exports to Germany and her colonies. Butler recognized that the presence of the German fleet in the waters nearby the Philippines had exasperated many Americans, but 'in the course of time, perhaps after a few months only' such a quid pro quo could be accomplished.[12]

Unlike Butler, Villard combined his anti-imperialism with a lively interest in domestic reform. He opposed the corrupt political machines through his involvement with the Citizens Union. To the literary radicals of the *Masses*, Villard was too respectable to be counted among them; but in fact his later role as a founder and treasurer of the National Association for the Advancement of Colored People (NAACP), coupled with his strong support for the education of African-Americans in the South, put him in the forefront of patrician reformers. Indeed, the ridicule he faced for his participation in the interracial public events of the NAACP, as well as his appearance in women's suffrage campaigns, no doubt prepared him for the bitter attacks he was later to encounter for his wartime pacifism. In some respects, he was more outspoken than his fellow editors on the *Evening Post* and the *Nation*.[13] Meanwhile, Butler's continued interest in international affairs found expression through the Lake Mohonk conferences on international arbitration. These annual gatherings, begun in 1895 by the Quaker entrepreneur Albert Smiley, were by invitation and drew businessmen, lawyers, and jurists as well as educators and clergymen. Military leaders (often retired) were also invited. Discussions were wide ranging and demonstrated an effort to achieve some perspective on the changing relationship between the United States and the other powers. Out of the meetings came the planning that produced the American Society of International Law and the New York Peace Society, both of which were formed in 1906.[14]

Butler's energies were directed towards the formation of a different group. In 1899 the Columbia president had met a French senator, Baron Paul d'Estournelles de Constant, who founded Conciliation Internationale in 1905. The baron believed in the value of private initiatives to improve international relations. Such efforts, conducted by influential men of affairs, who enjoyed the confidence of their governments, could be particularly useful in resolving international disputes. While unofficial channels of diplomacy were conducive to flexibility in negotiations, they had the added advantage of being easily disavowed by any government that did not wish to carry them forward. In 1906 the baron urged Butler and Congressman Richard Bartholdt of Missouri to found a branch in the United States, the American Association for International Conciliation (AAIC). Andrew Carnegie, who had helped finance several peace organizations, agreed to provide substantial support. Its work was to be done by an executive committee of seven.[15]

The time was auspicious, for the second Hague Conference was to gather in 1907. Butler and his colleagues resolved to put the AAIC at the disposal of the Roosevelt administration. The organization, Butler wrote the president, would advance the cause of international conciliation by 'such instruction of public opinion' as was necessary to win support of whatever proposals the United States delegates brought to the Hague Conference. The AAIC would work 'without flourish of trumpets ... and entirely in accord and harmony with the wishes and purposes of yourself and [Elihu] Root.'

Following the executive committee meeting to outline a program, Butler proposed to submit it to Roosevelt and Root for their approval. Butler assured the president that he wanted to stay clear of 'a certain type of peace propaganda which really discredits and interferes with the whole wise movement to promote better and more intelligent relations between nations.'[16]

This was something of a departure. Unlike the peace societies of the nineteenth century that had little access to power but could be sharply critical of government, the AAIC would act, in Butler's view, as an unofficial agency of the administration to propagandize for its policies, as yet unstated.[17]

Both Butler and Villard held fast to the belief that United States' friendship with both Britain and Germany was necessary and desirable. They recognized as well that the growing naval rivalry between the two great Anglo-Saxon nations constituted a danger to world peace.

American peace advocates who closely followed European affairs were increasingly disturbed by the naval arms race. When it showed no signs of abating by 1909, Butler made what was for him a rare public criticism of Britain. Addressing the Mohonk Conference he regretfully noted that Britain, which had contributed so mightily to world civilization, seemed to be possessed of the spirit of militarism. He found the nub of the problem to be Britain's insistence on the two-power naval standard. It was to be expected that with her far-flung empire she would have the world's largest fleet. But how, Butler wondered, could the British argue that their naval fighting strength must be greater than the next *two* most powerful navies combined, when this included nations such as France and Japan, with whom she was on friendly terms? 'In other words,' contended Butler, 'unless all such treaties of alliance and comity are a fraud and a sham, these nations at least should be omitted from the reckoning.'[18]

Despite these concerns, Butler remained optimistic about the prospects for peace. He described an incident he had witnessed in 1908 following an international conference of the Interparliamentary Union held in Berlin. Germany's imperial chancellor had afterward offered his official residence to the hundreds of parliamentary delegates from many nations.[19]

Standing under the spreading trees of his own great gardens, surrounded by the leaders of German scholarship and of German political thought, Prince von Bülow was approached by more than two score members of the British Parliament with Lord Weardale at their head. In a few impressive, eloquent and low-spoken sentences Lord Weardale expressed to the Chancellor what he believed to be the real feeling of England toward Germany, and what he felt should be the real relationship to exist between the two governments and the two peoples. In words equally cordial and quite as eloquent, Prince von Bülow responded to Lord Weardale with complete sympathy and without reserve.

Butler, deeply impressed, felt that such expressions represented a 'final refutation of the widespread impression' that the two nations were hostile and were drifting towards armed conflict.[20]

The arms race in Europe disturbed Villard, but the attempts of the United States to build a larger peacetime military establishment were of more direct concern, and Villard addressed this issue in his usual direct manner.

In 1910 President Taft's secretary of war dispatched a sensational secret report to Congress declaring that both coasts were defenceless and large naval appropriations were necessary. The story was quickly leaked to the press and headlines screamed, 'A War Scare in the Capitol.' Congressional partisans of the 'Yellow Peril' filled the air with stories of how 200,000 foreign troops could land on the Pacific Coast, blow up mountain passes, and strangle communication with the East. Congressional opponents were quick to denounce the 'secret' report as a transparent effort to stampede the lawmakers into voting for larger appropriations, and Taft quieted the furor by reassuring the country and disavowing his war secretary's report.[21] Villard, writing in the *Evening Post*, was scornful of those who called American defenceless. He caustically observed that the 'annual war scare' over military appropriations had not been up to the level of those in the past. 'How many times,' he asked, 'had naval increases been voted following predictions of doom, only to have the military return the following year pleading that the nation's plight was more desperate than ever before.'[22]

When Villard was named a director of the New York Peace Society in 1910 he wrote a letter sharply attacking those in the organization who belonged to the Navy League. He refused to work with those who gave only lip-service to the cause of peace while at the same time favouring increased armaments. Nevertheless, Villard refrained from criticizing the organization publicly. As yet the divisions within the peace movement lay just beneath the surface.[23]

Meanwhile, Butler had taken new steps to enlarge his influence within the movement. In 1910 peace advocates everywhere hailed the crowning achievement of the age: the gift by Andrew Carnegie of ten million dollars to establish the Carnegie Endowment for International Peace.[24] A century earlier the pioneers of the peace movement had been sustained in their efforts by religious faith but little in the way of resources or influence on government policies. By contrast, the Carnegie Endowment and the World Peace Foundation (established earlier the same year) were amply funded and led by men whose views commanded the respect of government leaders. Butler, who had originally wanted to name the organization the Carnegie International Institute, had the largest influence on Carnegie's choice of trustees. Butler's friend Lord Weardale, a leader of the Interparliamentary Union, sent a glowing message of congratulations to Carnegie while confiding to the Columbia president that the business leaders, former diplomats, and conservative statesmen who would head the foundation were an assurance that the fund would be wisely administered.[25]

Villard's *Evening Post* was among the few dissenters. The newspaper paid tribute to Carnegie's generosity, but expressed its disappointment that the trustees did not include 'a single radical opponent of war ... but many who, like Mr Joseph H. Choate ... express an interest in peace, but are hot for battleships too.'[26]

It soon became clear that Carnegie's past support of several peace groups, often in spontaneous response to a specific project, would henceforth be the province of the foundation, which would apply its own careful set of standards. As Butler put it to one of the first executive committee meetings, 'We are necessarily going to disappoint a great many of the more vocal – if I may use that word – applicants for money under the Endowment, and I thought it would be good policy at the outset to let slip these dogs of peace a little, so that these people would not turn on us when we settle down to the more serious study of the problems we have to face.'[27]

Elihu Root, former secretary of state and president of the endowment, intended to use much of its resources to undertake a large-scale scientific study of the causes of war instead of, in his words, treating its symptoms. This meant supporting scholarship rather than opposing manifestations of militarism.

Of all the endowment's trustees Butler was probably the one who had given the most thought to its work. The division he headed, that of 'Intercourse and Education,' was given the broadest mandate. He envisioned the endowment as an international information center that would sift facts and separate them from the passions of national politics. Since one of his greatest fears was the misrepresentations of one government's policy by the sensationalist press of another, Butler sought to make the foundation nothing less than an authoritative repository of facts to which governments and the press could turn to correct sensationalist distortion.

By the end of 1913 Butler announced with obvious pride that 'through trained and highly competent correspondents, the Division is kept informed regarding international policies and conduct everywhere. It is probably no exaggeration to say that the most accurate and detailed information to be found in any one place regarding the conduct of international affairs ... is to be found in the archives of the ... Education Division of the Carnegie Endowment.'[28]

The near war with Mexico in April 1914 offers a striking contrast in political tactics by the two peace leaders. President Wilson, while refusing to recognize the dictator, General Victoriano Huerta, had resorted to a variety of diplomatic pressures to depose him. Butler, fearing United States intervention, persuaded the Carnegie Endowment to embark upon a private initiative, after first clearing the idea with the State Department.[29] With $20,000 in endowment funds, Butler dispatched former assistant secretary of state Francis Loomis to Paris to confer with influential Mexican diplomats and former Cabinet officials from the deposed Diaz regime. The idea was to open the way for a new provisional government representing several factions involved in the ongoing civil war. The documentation is not complete, but it is clear that the proposed regime was heavily weighted on the conservative side, and subsequently the plan fell through.[30]

The crisis culminated when Wilson inflated a minor incident and a refusal by Huerta to apologize by firing a salute to the American flag – the famous 'Affair of Honor.' The president used this as a pretext to land American troops at Vera Cruz. The Mexicans resisted, a bloody battle followed, and all factions in the Mexican civil war denounced Wilson's interference, in the process attacking American consulates in various cities. The press of both countries assumed that war was imminent as Mexico broke diplomatic relations.[31]

Villard hastened to Washington to lobby for peace. He sought out members of Wilson's Cabinet only to find Treasury Secretary William McAdoo insisting (to Villard's disgust) that the nation's honour had to be upheld, and Commerce Secretary William Redfield, who had just returned from a tour of the Midwest, convinced that the American people were overwhelmingly behind the president. When Villard talked to the army commanders he found them less enthusiastic than the political leaders. They foresaw little glory from what would be a prolonged conflict. Villard's indignation was divided between the Wilson administration and the New York Peace Society. He complained to Carnegie about its lack of public pressure in the crisis. 'A thousand telegrams a day should be going ... to members of the Cabinet.'[32]

Following the battle at Vera Cruz, Butler confided to a friend that the whole situation resembled a political opera bouffe: 'It would be exceedingly amusing if it were not so appalling.'[33] But there is no record of a protest from him.

The European War

The outbreak of war in the summer of 1914 left those who had laboured to prevent it with their faith in reason deeply shaken. A few years earlier Butler had dared to imagine the possibility of Britain and Germany going to war: 'What could more surely lead to conviction of high crimes and misdemeanors at the bar of history than for two culture-peoples, with political and intellectual traditions in their entirety unequaled in the world's history in this twentieth century to tear each other to pieces like infuriated gladiators in a bloody arena? The very thought is revolting, and the mere suggestion of it ought to dismay the civilized world.'[34]

Initially, it seemed quite clear that little could be done while the first great battles were fought. The few voices that cried out otherwise were quickly stilled. As the German armies poured across the Belgian borders, Henri La Fontaine, Belgian senator and president of the International Peace Bureau, cabled Carnegie with a frantic request for additional funds to keep the peace forces together. La Fontaine was particularly distraught that the Carnegie Endowment trustees had seen fit at that time to cut in half the funds allocated to the international organizations.

Actually, the endowment leaders had remained consistent with their original principles. If they had declined to play a partisan role in peacetime they were scarcely likely to do so with the advent of war. Accordingly, they immediately stopped the funding of any publications in foreign countries. As Butler explained: 'No other course was possible. To continue ... peace propaganda in the face of the war that raged was to make ourselves ridiculous, while nothing was clearer than that the advent of war and its issue would completely alter our program of work.'[35]

Such was the shock of the war that for a brief time Villard and Butler stood side by side in the same organization, the League to Limit Armaments, organized by Villard in December 1914. Butler chaired the opening meeting, and according to Villard, 'No one could have made a better or more powerful antipreparedness speech.'[36] Soon those individuals favouring a military build-up by the United States began to form their own organizations. They received increased support following the sinking of the *Lusitania* in May 1915. A few months later Butler began to speak out for the 'Higher Preparedness.' Armies and navies were only means, not ends. The key to the somewhat obscure language in this address is to be found in Butler's assertion that the nation was 'crying out for leadership.' This could only be read as a thinly veiled attack on Wilson.[37]

Gradually, it became unmistakably clear that far from being decided swiftly, the struggle in Europe was settling down to a mighty test of endurance. This fact signalled the beginning of an effort by the bellligerents to mobilize vast reserves of energy and power that each nation was, as yet, only dimly aware it possessed. Moreover, the contending alliances increased their efforts to win neutral nations to their side. Attempts to mediate the conflict were not encouraged as long as either side believed that victory was possible. Another obstacle became apparent as the war progressed. The very success of each belligerent's war propaganda directed at its own civilian population made a compromise peace less likely. In the process of arousing hatred of the enemy (in order to intensify the war effort), a peace short of victory would become politically hazardous.

Inevitably, the war sharpened differences among American peace advocates that had been largely ignored or glossed over during the prewar years. Those who felt that the work of peace societies must begin in earnest with the threat of war took a dim view of their passivity following August 1914.

One of the sharpest attacks came from Villard. In 1915 he resigned from the New York Peace Society and followed this with an outpouring of speeches and articles opposing any military build-up by the United States.[38] Shortly before America entered the war he made a scathing attack on the conservative pre-war groups titled, 'What Is Wrong with Our Pacifists?'[39] He found the cause 'cursed by the adherence of innumerable men and women who gave it the merest lip-service, who avowed themselves believers in peace but invariably coupled their avowal of faith with some compromising phrase, that immediately removed the danger of their being called unpatriotic or impractical or fanatical.'

Villard recalled that before the war it had been 'quite the fashion' to join a peace society just as one might join groups to prevent cruelty to children and animals.[40] He singled out the Carnegie Endowment's quiescence as incomprehensible in the face of the most destructive of wars: 'Its income is $639,000 during the current year. It might as well have had nothing. Read its latest year book – ... not one reference to the moral iniquity of what is going on, not one single evidence of a profound passion for peace ... A thousand studies on international law, a thousand inquiries as to the history of the war, a thousand banquets to visiting foreigners, will not stir a single soul to rise in protest at any cost.'[41]

To the assertion by some that a radical anti-war position would drive away 90 per cent of the peace society's membership, Villard's answer was simple. The peace movement would be infinitely stronger, and its work far more meaningful, if its ranks held only those willing to go to jail for their beliefs. Harking back to his radical abolitionist ancestors Villard asserted that the movement to liberate the slave had progressed most rapidly when it began to count its martyrs. He foresaw a growth of the peace movement because its followers, too, were beginning to be persecuted.[42]

Butler, as might be expected, pursued a different path. Like his colleagues on the board of the Carnegie Endowment he was strongly favourable to Britain and the Entente, but he had been too extravagant in his praise of the kaiser shortly before the war to make so rapid a public turnabout. With characteristic aplomb, the Columbia president turned this seeming handicap to advantage. He confided to Lord Weardale that instead of allowing himself the luxury of publicly declaring his views on the war, he would remain free from controversy and would therefore be able to exercise more effective influence in the future.[43]

It was under a pseudonym, 'Cosmos,' that he published a lengthy analysis of the war, in late 1916, along with proposals for a possible peace settlement. This appeared serially in the *New York Times*, and shortly afterward in book form, stirring considerable discussion. Butler cited public declarations of war aims by Viscount Grey and Chancellor von Bethmann-Hollweg in which each talked about a future peace that protected the rights of small nations. From the high-sounding generalities each leader had made to his respective countrymen (to assure them that their cause was just) Butler extrapolated the view that it was possible to find a peace formula that would satisfy both belligerents. Instead of a negotiated peace based upon stalemate, however, he called upon the Germans to acknowledge that they could not win and, therefore, to accept an Entente victory of limited proportions. The war could then be ended by international agreement in which the United States would be a participant in restoring the rights of small nations. Furthermore, Germany would retain a significant role in the international community, though compelled to dismantle her military system, and lower her tariff barriers. Based on a worldwide adoption of 'the open door policy of international trade,' Butler foresaw a lessening of antagonism.[44]

It was with commendable restraint that a critic pointed out that the German chancellor's speech was inspired by the idea of peace with a German victory, while the British statement presumed an Entente triumph. Moreover, Butler's plan showed remarkably slight appreciation of the gigantic emotional forces stirred by the war. Certainly, the German people, as well as their leaders, were far from believing themselves incapable of victory, and as the war weariness in the French army made itself felt, the possibility grew that the Entente might suffer defeat.[45]

Ten months after the outbreak of the war in Europe, Villard assumed the role of Washington correspondent for the *Evening Post*. The newspaper, long owned by the Villard family, did not have a large circulation, but its editors had enjoyed considerable respect, and its readership included many influential people. The sinking of the *Lusitania* deeply shocked Villard. He denounced it as a 'violation of the fundamental decencies of civilization,' but cautioned against too hasty a response. His use of the phrase 'too proud to fight' was picked up by Wilson in an impromptu speech and brought the president a hail of criticism. Wilson's calm but firm handling of the crisis deeply impressed Villard, though he continued to urge the administration to be more even-handed and press the British harder for their seizures of American ships bound for neutral ports. When the German government announced that it would not sink passenger ships without giving warning, Villard hailed it as a magnificent vindication of diplomacy over force. He broke a 114-year precedent at the *Post* by printing a large picture of Wilson on the front page with the caption, 'The man who, without rattling a sword, won for civilization.' For a time Villard was credited as having more influence with Wilson than was actually the case. There is no doubt that he enjoyed his presumed role. However, when the president determined to get out in front on the military preparedness issue and undertook a western speaking tour, Villard accused Wilson of frightening people into support for a larger military force.[46]

Villard never approved of Henry Ford's ill-fated Peace Ship, but in trying to give Ford some advice he became linked in the public mind to the auto magnate's foolish promise to get the boys 'out of the trenches by Christmas.'[47] Villard's stature as a journalist suffered a decline. During the 1916 presidential campaign Villard refused to join his fellow peace activists in the American Union against Militarism when they supported Wilson's re-election. The president's embrace of military preparedness isolated Villard, and the final declaration of war turned him from a courageous critic of militarism to a defiant seeker after scapegoats. Wilson became his *bête noire*.[48]

The United States Enters the War

When war came to America the Carnegie Endowment for International Peace turned over part of its office to the Committee on Public Information, the government-sponsored group charged with rousing the American people to their wartime duties.[49] No zeal could match Butler's. He cast aside the role of private diplomat and of 'Cosmos' in favour of the kind of single-mindedness he had found so objectionable on the part of 'sentimentalists' among the peace advocates. After summarily dismissing two Columbia professors for questioning the wisdom of the war, he embarked upon a bold crusade to impeach Senator Robert LaFollette for his anti-war statements. Butler told the American Bankers Association that 'you might just as well put poison in the food of every American [soldier] as to permit that man to talk as he does.'[50] Some were unkind enough to remind the Columbia president that he had once been an extravagant admirer of the kaiser and that he had more recently attacked Germany's academic community for their blind obedience to the German state.

Something had happened to the 'international mind,' a phrase widely proclaimed by Butler just a few years before: 'that habit of thinking of foreign relations and business ... which regard[s] the several nations of the civilized world as friendly and cooperating equals in aiding the progress of civilization.' By July of 1917 he was making a distinction between 'true internationalism and false internationalism.' The false creed would 'exalt the supernational brotherhood of man, and ... lay stress upon a world-wide community without national ties or national ambitions.' In opposition to this he offered true internationalism which 'would strengthen and develop nationalistic and patriotic sentiments and aims, in order that ... they may be used without impairment or weakening as elements in a larger human undertaking of which each nation should be an independent and integral part.'[51] Butler's true internationalism would seem an accurate description of the world at that moment in 1917. Each belligerent was busy developing nationalistic sentiments and aims, and they were indeed being used in a larger human undertaking – that undertaking was war.

Villard, who had fought every move for military preparedness, had challenged purveyors of German atrocity stories to produce evidence, had addressed peace meetings despite hostile crowds, and had hailed Wilson's 'Peace without Victory' speech as the greatest of his career, simply refused to accept the verdict of war. He wrote to Joseph Tumulty, Wilson's secretary, 'Believe me, I am ready for any concentration camp, or prison, but I am *not* at war and no one can *put me into war* – not the President of the United States with all his power; my loyalty to American traditions and ideals renders that impossible.'[52]

During the war Villard defended the right of free speech and worked with the Fellowship of Reconciliation in their efforts to protect the rights of conscientious objectors. The harassment to which he and his family were subjected left lasting scars.[53]

Back in the days before the war what had been the basis for Villard and

Butler's belief that peace was possible? Perhaps they believed, even more deeply than their colleagues, that it was not so much possible, as *necessary*.

Villard was the bearer of a torch passed from his maternal grandfather, to his mother, and thence to him. Several experiences served to reinforce this pacifist tradition. He had seen his professors at Harvard recoil from the anglophobia during the Venezuelan boundary dispute of 1895. His mentors Carl Schurz and E.L. Godkin had denounced the war against Spain. Villard had been indignant at the betrayal of American traditions in the brutal war against the Filipinos. He had seen first hand the military system of Germany and had been repelled by it. His convictions about war and militarism were bred in the bone. He and his fellow reformers knew that once the war spirit was unchained, the cause of reform itself would be crippled, if not destroyed.

In the years before the war Butler had believed in a rational world run by rational men. If the masses could not be trusted, the elite could. It was not an unreasonable assumption given the material progress of Europe and the fact that the continent had escaped a general war for nearly a century. More specifically, if he feared the sensation-seeking press, if he was troubled by the passions demagogues could arouse, he could still believe in the rulers of the great powers. He, Butler, could speak directly to them; they had listened to him. What he had to say made good sense. Though they might take great pride in their armies and navies, though they might be rivals for trade and colonies, still their best interests called for keeping the peace. After all, who would be the beneficiaries of a general war? Butler knew.

In the summer of 1908 Butler had met with a number of European leaders after the fashion of a practitioner of private diplomacy. Before returning home he journeyed to Switzerland for a few days of relaxation. There he met an intense man whose relaxation was enforced – brought about by his exile, a fugitive from the czar's police. V.I. Lenin and Butler held a number of conversations. There, high on the rooftop of Europe, the educator and the revolutionary must have discussed the future of the continent. What they said is not recorded; but these two dynamic men must have made a profound impression upon one another. The meeting served to reinforce Butler's long-standing antipathy to socialism.[54] As he emerged a leader in the international peace movement during the years that followed, Butler could well warn the heads of European states that their best interests cried out against a general war. Once such floodgates were opened, if they could not be quickly closed, he knew who waited in the wings.

In November 1917 his worst fears were confirmed when Lenin took power. Despite the German onslaught, civil war, and the foreign intervention that nearly brought it down, the Soviet state survived, though gravely weakened.

On 7 December 1920 the trustees of the Carnegie Endowment for International Peace gathered for their annual meeting. The war had ended, but an exhausted Europe was in a state of political disarray. Yet its problems seemed small compared with what Butler called the most fateful crisis for Western civilization since the spread of Mohammedanism. He warned the trustees: 'What is called Bolshevism is not a political theory. It is not even an economic doctrine. It is a faith. It is a form of fanatical belief which you and I cannot discuss because those who hold it reject every assumption upon which we proceed in our intellectual intercourse.'[55]

In attempting to alert his fellow trustees about what he called 'this new fanaticism,' Butler was giving voice to the modern secular expression of the American millennial idea, complete with Antichrist and a vision of the Apocalypse. Once again, as in the prophecies of old, the virtuous were called upon to redeem the world from the Satanic power.[56]

Whatever else might be said of these two proud and stubborn men, who represented different ends of the pacifist spectrum, both Butler and Villard, in their own ways, were prophetic in their fears of what the Great War would do to *their* world, once it was unleashed.

Notes

1 The author wishes to thank Robert Accinelli, Department of History, University of Toronto, for his helpful comments and suggestions.

2 Michael Howard, 'Reflections on the First World War,' in *Studies in War and Peace* (New York, 1972), 99–109.

3 Michael A. Lutzker, 'Present at the Outbreak: American Witnesses to World War I,' *Peace and Change* 7/1–2 (Winter 1981), 66. The witness was Oscar Straus.

4 Two able studies of the early twentieth-century peace movement are C. Roland Marchand, *The American Peace Movement and Social Reform* (Princeton, 1972), and David S. Patterson, *Toward a Warless World* (Bloomington, 1976).

5 Nicholas Murray Butler, *Across the Busy Years* (New York, 1939). There is as yet no full biography of Butler that assesses his peace activity. Lindsay Rogers, long-time professor of Political Science at Columbia, was at work on one for many years but never completed it.

6 Ibid., vol. 1, ch. 5.

7 *Dictionary of American Biography, Supplement IV*, 133–8.

8 The best study is Michael Wreszin, *Oswald Garrison Villard: Pacifist at War* (Bloomington, 1965). Villard's memoir is quite useful, *Fighting Years* (New York, 1939), as is an article by Stephen Thernstrom, 'Oswald Garrison Villard and the Politics of Pacifism,' *Harvard Library Bulletin* 14 (Winter 1960), 126–52.

9 *Fighting Years*, ch. 4.

10 Ibid., ch. 5.

11 Butler to Henry Cabot Lodge, Butler Correspondence, Butler mss, Columbia University, Special Collections, letter dated 22 Dec. 1989 (copy).

12 Ibid., Butler to William McKinley (copy), 14 Sept. 1898.

13 Wreszin, *Villard*, 33.

14 Michael A. Lutzker, 'The Patrician Peace Advocates. The Lake Mohonk Conferences on International Arbitration, 1895–1916,' unpublished paper presented to the New York State Historical Association conference, 1975.

15 Butler, *Busy Years*, vol. 2, 88; Butler to Hayne Davis (copy), 22 Oct., 9 Nov. 1906; Butler to Theodore Roosevelt (copy), 11 Dec. 1906, Butler mss. The executive committee consisted of Butler (chairman), Lyman Abbott, Richard Bartholdt, Richard Watson Gilder, Seth Low, James Speyer, and Andrew D. White. Butler to Theodore Roosevelt (copy), 21 Jan. 1907, Butler mss.

16 Butler to Roosevelt, 21 Jan. 1907, Butler mss.

17 For the nineteenth-century peace groups see Peter Brock, *Pacifism in the United States from the Colonial Era to the First World War* (Princeton, 1968).

18 *Fifteenth Mohonk Conference Report* (1909), 12–15. Britain did not include the United States fleet in her calculations.

19 Ibid., 18. The same speech of Butler's appears in abridged form in the *Advocate of Peace* 71 (July 1909), 157–61; and in full in *The International Mind* (New York, 1919), 21–44.

20 Ibid.

21 *Tribune* (New York), 15–16 Dec. 1910.

22 *Evening Post* (New York), 15–16 Dec. 1910.

23 Wreszin, *Villard*, 46.

24 Michael A. Lutzker, 'The Formation of the Carnegie Endowment for International Peace: A Study of the Establishment-Centered Peace Movement, 1910–14,' in *Building the Organizational Society*, ed. Jerry Israel (New York, 1972), 143–62.

25 Weardale to Butler, 11 Jan. 1911, Butler mss.

26 *Evening Post*, 15 Dec. 1910. See also Villard to Francis J. Garrison (copy) 14 Dec. 1910, folder 1461, Villard mss, Harvard University.

27 Carnegie Endowment for International Peace (hereafter CEIP) Archives, Columbia University, Document no. 4428, 9 March 1911.

28 Butler, 'The Carnegie Endowment for International Peace,' *Independent* 76 (27 Nov. 1913), 397–8.

29 Personal and confidential correspondence, Butler to John Bassett Moore, 10 Feb. 1914; Moore to Butler, 12 Feb. 1914; Butler to Moore, 13 Feb. 1914; Moore to Butler, 17 Feb. 1914; Moore Correspondence, Moore Papers, Box 25, Library of Congress.

30 This subject is examined in detail in Michael A. Lutzker, 'Can the Peace Movement Prevent War? The U.S.–Mexican Crisis of April, 1914,' in *Doves and Diplomats*, ed. Solomon Wank (Westport, 1978), 127–53.

31 Ibid.

32 Ibid., 140.

33 Ibid., 131.

34 *Fifteenth Mohonk Report* (1909), 18.

35 Butler to Weardale (copy), 12 Jan. 1915, Butler mss; Henri La Fontaine to J.B. Scott, 29 Sept. 1914; Butler to La Fontaine (copy), 22 Oct. 1914, III, CEIP Archives, 1914 Document no. 2299–2301.

36 Villard, *Fighting Years*, 248–9.

37 Butler, *A World in Ferment* (New York, 1917), 103–14. The speech was actually delivered 27 Nov. 1915.

38 New York *Times*, 19 Nov., 6 and 10 Dec. 1915, 2 Jan. 1916; Wreszin, *Villard*, 46.

39 Villard, Speech File, n.d. (ca. Jan. 1917), Villard mss.

40 Ibid.

41 Ibid.

42 Ibid.

43 Butler to Weardale (copy), 12 Jan. 1915, Butler mss.

44 'Cosmos,' *The Basis of a Durable Peace* (New York, 1917).

45 Hall Caine to Cosmos, 25 Nov. 1916, ibid., 125ff.

46 Wreszin, *Villard*, 50–5.

47 Villard, *Fighting Years*, 302–5.

48 Wreszin, *Villard*, 56–63.

49 Elihu Root to George Creel (draft), 27 Dec. 1917, Root Papers, Library of Congress.

50 J. McKeen Cattell, 'What the Trustees of Columbia University Have Done' (confidential statement for members of the American Association of University Professors, 1918), pamphlet in no. 422, Villard mss. The quote is from

William Leuchtenburg, *The Perils of Prosperity, 1914–1932* (Chicago, 1958), 45.

51 Compare Butler's *The International Mind*, esp. 102–5, with his *World in Ferment*.

52 Quoted in Villard, *Fighting Years*, 324–5.

53 Wreszin, *Villard*, 78–9.

54 Butler, *Busy Years*, vol. 2, 106–7. For more on Butler's concern about socialism, see Butler to Root (copy), 19 June 1908; Root to Butler, 30 July 1908; Butler to Root (copy), 17 Aug. 1908; Butler to Root (copy), 5 Oct. 1908, all in Butler mss. See also Butler to John Morley (copy), 29 Oct. 1906, ibid.

55 'Problems Confronting the Carnegie Endowment for International Peace,' 7 Dec. 1920, CEIP Document no. 48885, 10-11, CEIP Archives.

56 Earnest Tuveson, *Redeemer Nation: The Idea of America's Millennial Role* (Chicago, 1968), see esp. Preface and 214.

19

Pacifism and Revolution:
Bertrand Russell and Russia, 1914–1920

RICHARD A. REMPEL

Shortly after the March 1917 revolution Bertrand Russell invited his young mistress Constance Malleson to 'come to Russia with me after the war is over? We could get to know all the leading revolutionaries.' She could 'catch the fire from ... Lenin, and bear the torch here in years to come.'[1] Three years later, following a personal interview with Lenin, Russell remarked that the Bolshevik leader had 'as little love of liberty as the Christians who suffered under Diocletian and retaliated [on heretics] when they acquired power.'[2] These two comments encapsulate Russell's Russian odyssey and express the disillusionment of many pacifists and other dissenters. As with Russell, they had believed that the fall of tsardom would not only end the war; it would also usher in an era of peace and radical social reconstruction. The perception that the March revolution was a 'bloodless revolution' was shared by many Russians and by European sympathizers alike. They interpreted it as being distinctively different from previous revolutions, notably those of France in 1789 and England in the 1640s.

The thesis of this essay is that Russell did not merely assert that the March upheaval was a pacifist revolution; he integrated the revolution into a pacifist ideology that he had been developing during the Great War. In essays throughout 1915 Russell advanced his ideas on collective passive resistance as the best way to prevent conflicts in the future. Since such popular restraint would be difficult to inculcate, he predicted that such a transformation could only occur in the future after an intensive period of popular education. He refined these ideas in his *Principles of Social Reconstruction* (1916).

When men became conscientious objectors (COs) in 1916 rather than submit to the National Service Acts of January and May, Russell revised his prognostications from an uncertain future to the present for the creation of a politically effective body of people prepared to practise and proselytize for collective non-resistance. Throughout the spring and summer of 1916 Russell believed that such a large number of COs would come forward as to oblige the government to abandon conscription and enter into peace negotiations. Such a force of COs failed to materialize; nevertheless, Russell continued to see the COs as the moral vanguard of British society who would, by example and teaching, convert many Britons to peace advocacy. By the end of 1916 this conversion had not taken place. Indeed, the war raged with increasing ferocity. Then the sudden coming of revolution in Russia in March 1917 provided pacifists and other peace advocates in Britain and Europe with what they believed to be a dramatic example of a pacifist revolution. Encouraged, Russell wrote and campaigned actively, arguing that Russia had not only provided the road to immediate peace, but had also presented the British with the opportunity to transform their society from capitalism to guild socialism.

Russell acknowledged that the fall of tsardom had come with a degree of violence, but he believed that the force had been marginal or accidental and not the essence of the new movement. He was prepared to accept some violence if the goals of peace and a just society resulted. By early 1918, however, Russell thought that the opportunity presented to the Russians by the March revolution had been lost. Not only that, as his prescient warnings of 1920 in *The Practice and Theory of Bolshevism* were to demonstrate, he came to believe that Lenin had irrevocably perverted the aims of the revolution.

After 1920 Russell's lifelong hostility to communism blurred the extent to which he had reflected at length about the prospects for peace attendant upon the March revolution. Even Russell's most penetrating analysts, with the notable exceptions of Harrison, Kennedy, and Vellacott, have not related Russell's ideology of pacifism and socialism to the events in Russia. Most have accepted his major biographer's judgment that 'Russell, and men like him, saw the fall of the Tsar as a panacea for almost any political trouble.'[3]

To establish the effects of the Russian revolution on Russell's thought, three themes will be developed: (1) an account of the evolution of Russell's pacifist ideas up to the March revolution; (2) a reappraisal of Russell's efforts to link the events in Russia to the political role he had already helped establish for the No-Conscription Fellowship (NCF) in three specific campaigns before 1917; and (3) an examination of the impact of the March revolution on his pacifist thought and action in his fourth and last NCF crusade.

Theme 1: Russell's Pacifism and Dissent, 1901–1917

In all his essays on war and peace, Russell consistently claimed that he was not pacifist in all circumstances. This position is defined most clearly in his major essay on pacifism, 'The Ethics of War.'[4] In this essay he classified four types of wars, arguing that 'in the past' some types had been legitimate. But the present war and 'the objects for which men fought in the past, whether just or unjust, are no longer to be achieved by wars amongst civilized nations.'[5] His pacifism arose from a conviction that the destructiveness of war almost always outweighed any potential benefits, rather than from a belief that in and of itself war was immoral. Russell reasoned as a consequentialist or, in other words, as a 'utilitarian pacifist.' To employ Ceadel's typology, Russell was a 'pacificist,' not an absolute pacifist who condemned all wars.[6] Such abstract reasoning advanced in 'The Ethics of War,' however, omitted the quasi-religious or mystical dimensions of his pacifist impulse.

This quasi-religious aspect emerged suddenly in his 'conversion' experience of 1901 when, in the presence of Mrs Alfred Whitehead undergoing an apparent angina attack, Russell recalled that 'the loneliness of the human soul is unendurable; nothing can penetrate it except the highest intensity of the sort of love that religious teachers have preached ... a sort of mystic illumination possessed me ... Having been an imperialist, I became during those five minutes a ... Pacifist ... causing my attitude during the first war.'[7] Russell's 1901 pacifist impulse persisted with varying intensity throughout the Edwardian years, finding expression in *The Free Man's Worship* (1903). While in prison in 1918, he wrote to the NCF: 'Is it not odd that people can in "the same breath praise the free man's worship" and find fault with my views on the war? The free man's worship is merely the expression of the pacifist outlook when it was new to me ... Those who have known it cannot *believe* in wars any longer.'[8] Before 1914, however, Russell was too absorbed in philosophy and mathematics to devote his efforts to pacifist theorizing, much less to peace causes, although his 1904 campaign against tariff reform was primarily inspired by his conviction that free trade fostered international peace. Still, he was influenced by Norman Angell's thesis in *The Great Illusion* (1910) that capitalism had so intertwined the economies of modern states that war would be disastrous for the victors as well as the vanquished.

Prior to the war, Russell also regarded politics as secondary, even though by family upbringing he exemplified Cobdenite radicalism. As opposed to love of one's country, Russell loathed nationalism, which he termed the 'herd instinct.' On domestic issues before 1914 Russell battled against traditional forms of privilege, whether the male monopoly of the franchise or the power of the House of Lords. He did not share the New Liberals' belief in the beneficence of the state. Only during 1916 and 1917 did Russell shed aspects of his mid-Victorian radicalism in favour of guild socialism, an ideology in the tradition of the most decentralized form of socialism, which simultaneously with its socialism reaffirmed liberal beliefs in the rights of the individual.

In foreign policy Russell shared many of the shibboleths of dissent, especially Russophobia. Russian primitivism was symbolized by tsarist tyranny, peasant illiteracy, and what he regarded as the irrationalism of the Russian Church. Well before 1914, Russell had perceived in Sir Edward Grey's diplomacy a determination to 'extend the tyranny of the Tsar.'[9] In contrast, he was favourably disposed to Germany, despite its Bismarckian legacies of 'blood and iron,' and he despised both the kaiser and the Junker military caste. As well, he respected the German Social Democratic party, the greatest socialist organization in the world, beside which the Russian equivalent was weak and scattered. Despite its Marxist ideological basis, Russell sympathized with the 'peaceful' German revisionist wing led by Bernstein. Above all, Russell appreciated German culture, particularly since his two extended visits to Berlin in 1895. He had great respect for the intellectual achievements of German logicians and mathematicians, especially Georg Cantor and Gottlob Frege.

Comfortably ensconced in the privileged intellectual worlds of Cambridge and London, however, Russell was not particulary well informed on either foreign or domestic issues. It came to him as a shock, therefore, that a Liberal government could take the country into a war against Germany, although such a conflict had been widely anticipated. Led by Grey, an aristocrat practising secret diplomacy, Britain, as Russell saw the situation, had aligned herself 'in company with the Cossacks ... against a nation [Germany], which ... has contributed as much as any nation in the world to the permanent possessions of the human race.'[10] He believed that Germany, directed by Prussianism, was more at fault, but the unbridled nationalism of the other belligerents rendered them almost equally culpable.

When war broke out Russell claimed that he felt as if he 'had heard the voice of God,' calling upon him to 'protest,' for all that 'love of England' was 'nearly the strongest emotion' he possessed. Russell feared that if he failed to work for 'peace and internationalism' he would sink into 'doing nothing for the rest of my days.' But for some months he did not know how to mobilize his anti-war attitudes.[11] Although a participant in the early meetings that led to the establishment of the Union of Democratic Control, Russell soon became impatient. As he told Lady Ottoline on 8 June 1915, 'The UDC will be all right *after* the war, but at the moment they are tumbling over each other in their eagerness to disclaim any lack of patriotism or of determination that victory must be ours.'[12] Dissenting ineffectiveness was partly the result of the Asquith government's skill in presenting the conflict as a crusade against Prussian brutality. It also resulted from the disagreements among dissenters about how to oppose the war.

Early in 1915, Russell appealed to America over the heads both of his own government and the British people, the majority of whom he judged as imprisoned by official propaganda. He urged the United States to ban all armaments and other war supplies to both the belligerent coalitions. Although Russell's campaign to convince Americans to remain impartial was ineffectual, especially given the deep cultural and economic links between Britain and America, his articles in the *Atlantic Monthly* encouraged him to formulate a theory of pacifism which foreshadowed his 1917 linkage of peace with revolution. Russell's essay of August 1915, 'War and Non-Resistance,' as Brock has argued, 'provided the most eloquent exposition of the efficacy of nonviolence in the contemporary world.' It also represented 'an extension of pacifist thinking from a perhaps excessive concern for problems of moral conscience into the realm of international relations.'[13] Passive resistance, Russell was persuaded, could be initiated first in Britain 'if education and moral teaching were directed toward that end instead of to war-like prowess.'[14] He knew such a transformation would be difficult. Nonetheless, 'if England were to disband its army and navy after a generation of instruction in the principles of passive resistance' Germany would have no possible 'cloak' to disguise its aggression, since not even self-defence could offer a pretext.[15]

Throughout his 1915 writings, however, Russell believed that the imaginative effort required for world peace would be too great for ordinary people. Peace was more likely to come by the establishment of a world government prepared to coerce obedience until 'the great majority of men' recognized that force was useless and came to grasp the value of passive resistance.[16] These arguments were developed in his *Principles of Social Reconstruction* (1916), a book Russell regarded as the 'least unsatisfactory' expression of his 'own personal religion.'[17] Russell addressed what the pre-war peace movement had failed to explore searchingly, namely, 'the relationship between war and the economic order ... [and] the hidden seeds of war in the exploitation of labor or in imperialist expansion overseas.'[18] Wars occurred, he argued, because pernicious institutions and ideas led to possessive, destructive impulses. Change such institutions as marriage, education, and property so that creative impulses rather than alienating power relationships were instituted, men would cease to be warlike. The best political organization for the flowering of creative impulses would be guild socialism.[19]

Theme 2: Russell and the No-Conscription Fellowship

Russell's next campaign for peace came through his association with the No-Conscription Fellowship. Established in November 1914 by the Independent Labour party socialists Fenner Brockway and Clifford Allen, the NCF was founded to fight conscription, if and when the government resorted to such a policy. The two men were soon joined by a number of Quakers, other religious pacifists, socialists opposed specifically to 'capitalist' wars, and the suffragist, Catherine Marshall. The basis of the NCF was explicitly pacifist, for its members accepted the principle of refusing from 'conscientious motives to bear arms, because they consider human life to be sacred.'[20]

While Russell had been moved to speak for the NCF early in 1915, he felt no compelling need to do so until conscription became first a threat and then law. Parliament's decision late in January 1916 to pass the first Military Service Act meant that 'conscription became the harsh midwife of twentieth-century pacifism.'[21] Late in March 1916 Russell entered the NCF, initially only for a month; but he was to remain until the end of 1917. The NCF leaders gained an 'associate' member who not only had a reputation as a philosopher; they gained a writer of formidable polemical power, an advocate at the centre of Britain's intellectual aristocracy, and an activist from one of the country's most famous political families. On a practical level, Russell could, with the organizer Marshall, provide leadership of the NCF as those members eligible for conscription were sent to jail. For Russell, the NCF provided a forum that fulfilled his need to lead a crusade defending civil liberties. More significantly, Russell came to perceive the NCF as the organization whereby it might be possible to end the war by creating an 'army' of COs. After the NCF convention of 8 and 9 April, Russell wrote exuberantly to Lady Ottoline: 'I really believe they [the COs] will defeat the Government and wreck Conscription, when it is found they won't yield ... I can't describe to you how happy I am having these men to work with and for – it is *real* happiness all day long.'[22]

Nevertheless, since he was not an absolute pacifist, Russell's affiliation was soon to cause strain between him and many in the NCF. Russell wanted the NCF to advance well beyond its initial mandate of opposing conscription and assisting COs. In other words, he often involved NCF members in political campaigns, thereby directing them reluctantly, and at times rebelliously, into 'collaborative pacifism.'[23] Indeed, analysis reveals that Russell was instrumental in leading the NCF into four successive campaigns to assist COs and, more importantly for him, to attempt to secure a negotiated peace. However impatient Russell became with internal NCF opposition, he persevered with the organization, especially since the COs manifested examples of passive resistance that he had earlier believed possible only after extended popular education. He never relinquished his belief that they personified the moral vanguard of humanity. What Russell admired in conscientious objectors was their integrity and willingness to suffer for their convictions. While he respected liberty of conscience, he distrusted conscience as '*a cognitive faculty,*' which he divided into 'merely the combination which results from evolution and education.' Russell especially distrusted conscience when employed as an agency for the *enforcement* of moral judgments.'[24]

From April through July 1916, both by his writings and by a speaking crusade, Russell worked to create such an 'army' of COs that the government would be forced to repeal conscription and enter into peace negotiations. Second, when this army failed to materialize, he tried another policy. In the autumn of 1916, he tried to mobilize dissenting groups to persuade his countrymen that government invasions of civil liberties necessitated a new administration disposed to peace to replace the Asquith coalition. Third, when by November 1916 this strategy had not succeeded, he made a direct appeal to President Wilson on 23 December 1916 to impose mediation upon the belligerents; by virtue of Russell's eminence as a philosopher, he and the NCF earned wide publicity, although his letter had no impact upon the president. All three campaigns failed. Russell was completely unrealistic in his belief that so many men would opt for CO status that the government's existence would be threatened. He was also mistaken in believing that many would take an absolutist stand, for only 1,300 of the nearly 16,500 COs could face the absolutists' ordeals. The rest took some form of alternate service. He recognized his miscalculation by the summer of 1916.

In these campaigns, however, Russell confronted the military and civil authorities and Trinity College's 'establishment.' His punishments were harsh. During 1916 he was prosecuted for writing against conscription, forbidden to leave Britain to lecture in America, denied admission to all 'prohibited areas,' dismissed from his college lectureship at Cambridge, and in 1918 sent to prison. His greatest notoriety arose from his speaking foray into South Wales in July 1916, probably the largest centre in Britain for industrial militancy and workers' self-education. Russell was the first major dissenter to undertake such an ambitious anti-war enterprise. He was severely restricted thereafter precisely because the government feared his influence over discontented workers at home and on public opinion in America in what was avowedly a 'stop-the-war campaign.'[25]

However earnest President Wilson's peace diplomacy of December 1916 to January 1917, Russell could not have had a significant impact when no belligerent power was serious about peace negotiations. Only after the war did Russell acknowledge as much: 'At intervals, the German Government made peace offers which were, as the Allies said, illusory, but which all pacifists (myself included) took more seriously than they deserved.'[26] Moreover, by late 1916 his confrontations with his government meant that he was *persona non grata* with Wilson and his circle. By aligning himself with the NCF, the extremist end of the dissenting spectrum, Russell had effectively, if by miscalculation, placed himself on the political sidelines in America and in his own country. Nevertheless, during the diplomatic activity of January 1917 Russell assumed the acting chairmanship of the NCF. For the only time in his life, until the Vietnam War, he participated in exacting day-to-day political activity.

Theme 3: The Russian Revolutions of 1917

Pacifist disappointment over the collapse of Wilson's initiatives was soon overshadowed by excitement over revolution in Russia. The pacifists were convinced that 'within a week Russia had been transformed into the most free country in Europe.'[27] Their enthusiasm presents an eerie analogy to the 'progressive' responses to developments in the Soviet empire seventy years later. In that respect, Russell at first glance appeared just as gullible as millions in the West during the autumn of

1989 who asserted that politically backward, authoritarian regimes such as the Soviet Union and Rumania were peacefully embracing democracy virtually overnight. Western liberals were convinced that Gorbachev's *glasnost* and *perestroika* meant not merely the end of the Cold War, but that the policies also demonstrated a whole-hearted Russian commitment to social democratic ideals.

While a chorus of voices eulogized the March 1917 Russian revolution as pacifist in character, the explanations for its occurrence were diverse and often merely hortatory. Thus, Michael Ignatieff recounts how his uncles in Petrograd in the spring of 1917 listened to the slogans of revolutionaries near the Duma Palace calling upon Russians to 'secure the achievements of the Great Bloodless Revolution.'[28] Many interpretations in Britain were scarcely more penetrating. For George Lansbury and other ethical socialists with the *Herald*, 'The Russian Revolution – this is the vital point – is a *proletarian* revolution, and therefore a *pacifist* revolution.'[29] Russell at least had an explanation, however far-fetched in actuality, which went beyond mere slogans in accounting for the conversion of hitherto ignorant and docile Russian masses to political maturity. His explication, written on 2 April 1917 to Lady Ottoline, resonates with echoes of the intellectual and political elitism that characterized Russell's entire life:

It seems clear that the Army is on the side of the extremists, & that therefore they can't be suppressed. The "Committee of Soldiers & Workmen" seems to be the supreme power. Also, the Army internally is being democratized, with Committees of officers & men in equal numbers to look after the discipline. It seems that during the war the Revolutionaries have carried out a secret propaganda which has completely altered the views of peasant soldiers, & made them agree with the industrial workers.[30]

As we shall see, Russell's fuller interpretation, as developed in July 1917, reflected not merely his speculations of April. He had come to perceive in the revolution a real-life illustration of the validity of his 1915–16 arguments for non-violent resistance.

Russell and other dissenters believed that the new Russian Charter of Freedoms issued on 16 March would compel the British to learn lessons in civil liberties from Petrograd. By mid-March Russell and Marshall were leading a Committee for Anglo-Russian Co-operation. Indeed, on 17 March they had drafted a British Charter of Freedom based on the model proclaimed by the Russian provisional government. In trying to win over dissident labour to the pacifist cause, Russell and Marshall believed that a civil liberties campaign inspired by the Russian ideals could be linked to British workers' ideals. Such NCF high-mindedness seemed justified when on 31 March Russell, in association with anti-war labour leaders, notably George Lansbury, Philip Snowden, and Ramsay MacDonald, helped to organize the Albert Hall meeting. It was staged in support of the Russian revolutionaries' advocacy of the restoration of full civil liberties and a general amnesty for religious and political offences. This gathering demonstrated the degree to which pacifist and disgruntled labour now looked to Russia and not to America as the only hope for peace. It also reflected the standing Russell had gained with so many workers that a labour leader singled him out for a warmly applauded tribute.[31] Everyone at the Albert Hall, he told Lady Ottoline, wanted 'a real absolute change in everything ... the sort of thing the Russians have done ... A meeting of this kind would have been impossible a month ago.'[32]

On 10 April 1917 pacifists and many labour people were further encouraged by the Russian provisional government's startlingly new war aims – a declaration renouncing all claims to 'annexations and indemnities.' To Russell's satisfaction, this declaration evinced the Petrograd Soviet's victory over the 'Liberal Upper and Middle classes' of the provisional government. Since that government had attempted to keep Russia in the war and had asserted her right to imperialist ambitions, notably the acquisition of Constantinople, Russell had sided with the Petrograd Soviet from the beginning of the revolution. He took literally the claim of the coerced provisional administration that Russia's sole war aim was the maintenance of the country's integrity. Furthermore, the declaration that a constituent assembly was to be elected as soon as possible was more evidence to him that Russia was now in the forefront of civilization.[33]

The combination of the momentum from the Albert Hall meeting and the Russian proclamation of 'no annexations and no indemnities' led to the planning of the Leeds Convention for 3 June. This conference registered the highest hopes for revolution among anti-war workers and dissenters alike. The Independent Labour party and the Union of Democratic Control hoped that 'the Revolutionary people,' the Soviet, would prevail over the imperialist aims of the provisional government.[34] At Leeds the UDC, like the NCF, followed the lead of disaffected labour. For the ILP members in particular, the convention allowed them to attack what they saw as the misguided collaboration of many elements of the labour movement with the militaristic capitalism of the Lloyd George coalition. What Russell and other Leeds' enthusiasts overlooked, however, was the absence of labour leaders such as Arthur Henderson and members of many powerful unions. They still supported the war, despite, for example, anger at the government's attempts to conscript more skilled workers.

In such a heady atmosphere, the delegates, following the lead of the Petrograd Soviet, planned to establish Workers' and Soldiers' Councils in Britain. Here Russell again was acclaimed. As he told Lady Ottoline, 'To my great surprise, they gave me about the greatest ovation that was given to anybody. I got up to speak, and they shouted for me to go to the platform, and when I got there they cheered endlessly.'[35]

The momentum from Leeds seemed auspicious. As Russell told the philosopher Herbert Wildon Carr, he and some *Herald* journalists drew up plans for a 'People's Party,' whose guild socialist proposals were 'possible of immediate realisation'[36]: 'I am glad you welcome the revolutionary spirit. I have quite ceased to find the situation depressing since the Russian Revolution. There seems every hope of a real international spirit throughout Europe, combined with a far more humane economic system ... I wonder if you saw the enclosed in last week's *Herald*? It was drawn up by a small group of whom I am one, and probably represents the policy which will be adopted by the people who started operations at Leeds. We are distributing a million copies this week.'[37]

The government certainly took the Leeds Convention seriously, and had considered banning it. On 5 June 1917 the War Cabinet hurriedly decided to establish the National War Aims Committee, with virtually unlimited funds, to counter pacifist propaganda.[38] The coalition also incited riots against the councils.[39] The widespread May strikes coupled with the Leeds Convention not only seemed to presage severe economic dislocation; the two developments were perceived in official quarters as the possible prelude to revolution.

Simultaneously with his efforts to forge an alliance with labour, Russell attempted to persuade the NCF to seize the opportunity to join the loose peace-by-negotiation coalition emerging in Britain. As part of this mandate, Russell and the other members of the NCF National Committee had urged their members to support actively 'peace-by-negotiation' candidates at the forthcoming late March and early April by-elections. This decision brought down upon Russell the wrath of a number of NCF branches whose members believed that their mission was exclusively to oppose conscription. Russell's rebuttal was in keeping with his broader vision of a peace testimony: 'It is impossible for the NCF ... to retain mental health, or to keep free from self-righteousness, unless their thoughts are fixed upon what they owe to the community, rather than upon the rectitude of their own conduct.'[40]

Attacks continued and, after a particularly harsh onslaught, Russell on 18 May wrote out a letter of resignation, stating,

So long as the war lasts, any work that hastens the coming of peace is more important than anything else, particularly if peace comes in the spirit advocated by the Russian Revolutionaries ... I do not myself believe that there is any chance of a revolution in this country, but there is reason to suppose that the Government thinks otherwise, and that fear of revolution will be a powerful motive in leading them to desire an early end to the war. For this reason, anything that increases their fear of revolution is likely to do good ... I am a conscientious objector to the present war, and to almost any imaginable war between civilized states. But I have always held, and publicly stated, that the use of force in revolutions is not necessarily to be condemned. Until lately, this was a merely academic reservation, without relevance to the actual situation. Now, however, it has become a pressing practical consideration. A certain amount of bloodshed occurred during the Russian Revolution, probably unnecessarily. If it was unnecessary, I can of course condemn it; but if the revolution could not be accomplished without it, I cannot condemn it.[41]

In the event, Russell did not send the letter, deciding to remain with the NCF. From the vantage of the NCF, Russell must have thought he could accomplish more by retaining his official position within the 'peace coalition.' The value he placed on his connection with labour was demonstrated on 10 July when he joined the Independent Labour party, thereby severing forever his official links with the Liberal party his grandfather had twice led as prime minister.[42] The letter also demonstrates Russell's view in May that, however assertive the Shop Stewards' Movement and however weary many workers were of war, there seemed little or no chance of revolution in Britain. Yet this belief was modified, for throughout the summer and autumn of 1917 he seemed to see revolution as a distinct possibility. At least Russell alleged publicly that organized labour 'could achieve any change, however sweeping, by methods no more violent than those of ordinary industrial disputes.' By July, in summary, he was calling upon the pacifists to form an alliance with the Shop Stewards' Movement.[43]

By examining Russell's actions and thoughts from mid-to-late July

1917 his maturing pacifist thought and practice can be traced. Russell wanted to take an active part in the implementation of workers' and soldiers' councils. This role did not come automatically, for the arrangements were primarily the responsibility of the Provisional Committee of Labour. The pacifist organizations were, however, invited to participate. To this end, Russell was closely involved in the discussions among the NCF, the Friends' Service Committee (FSC), and the Fellowship of Reconciliation (FOR) about the advisability of sending delegates to the London 'Council,' scheduled for 28 July. The FSC and the FOR, two exclusively religious pacifist bodies, declined any official commitment. Russell and Marshall had to persuade some reluctant members of the national committee to participate in the London Council meeting. And both of them 'lobbied' their labour colleagues to get Russell 'elected to the Council of Workers' for the London meeting.[44] The gathering was eventually held at the Brotherhood Church, a well-known sanctuary for pacifist meetings.

The Joint Advisory Committee of the three major pacifist organizations decided to have Russell, two FSC members, and one FOR member contribute to a special *Tribunal* supplement 'on the theme of peaceful revolution.'[45] By July 1917 Russell argued that 'There is no need of violence in order to bring the reign of violence to an end. The instruments of violence are the armies and navies and police forces of the world, which are employed, in a very great measure, in order to keep the poor and the weak in subjection to the rich and the strong.' From these statements, Russell advanced his first and only extended argument for revolution, a revolution compatible with his ideals as developed in 1915 and 1916 and not merely an expedient designed to appeal to his pacifist audience:

It was by refusing obedience that the troops in Petrograd made the Revolution possible in Russia. Whatever acts of violence may have occurred in the course of the Revolution, it was not they that brought about the Revolution, but their exact opposite, the rebellion against violence when the troops were ordered to fire upon the people and did not do so ...

The word 'revolution' is associated, in the minds of many, with ideas of violence and bloodshed. But it is not violence and bloodshed that make the essence of revolution, or that insure its success. The success of revolution depends always upon the power of new ideas over men's minds ... The Russians have shown the way. Owing largely to them, our hopes can no longer be destroyed by the united armies of reactionary Europe, as they were at the time of the French

Revolution; and they have acquired a new depth and solidity by their application in the economic sphere.[46]

Russell's perception of what had occurred in Russia was that a spontaneous mass uprising had successfully brought together a coalition of soldiers laying down their arms, intellectuals articulating their concepts of freedom, and enlightened scientific managers, workers, and students taking over the institutions. This type of revolution always had his support, although he was to be disillusioned when these uprisings were debased from within or perverted by intervention from without. Russell supported this type of revolution when it occurred in Prague in 1968 and no doubt would have upheld the uprising in Tiananmen Square and in Berlin as well as in Central Europe in 1989.

By the summer of 1917 Russell had clarified the economic dimension of his thoughts on revolution. As Harrison has shown, by the time of the Leeds Convention in June 1917, Russell had 'largely shifted the emphasis from psychological to socio-economic considerations in accounting for war.'[47] The relationship between Russell's insistence on a collective as opposed to a merely individual pacifism was that fellowship, the essence of the NCF, had carried over into an identification with oppressed groups, whether workers or women. This shift towards comradeship is what delegates cheered him for at Leeds. It is in this context that Russell's article 'Pacifism and Economic Revolution,' published on 5 July 1917, must be read in conjunction with 'Pacifism and Revolution,' published on 19 July 1917. In the former, Russell claimed that 'the same principle of the brotherhood of man which has inspired our stand against war is bound to lead ... into a desire for a 'more just economic system ... It is impossible to doubt that the abolition of the capitalist would be a tremendous step towards the abolition of war ... [hence] pacifists ought to support the new movement with all their strength.'[48] Since the Russian revolution was based on the 'ideas of Socialism,' ideas shared by 'powerful factions in most civilized countries,' it had a much broader international base of intellectual and wage-earning support than had the French revolution. Because of its capitalist ethos, the French experiment soon had degenerated into a greedy, expansionist tyranny. Thus, fundamental economic change, which Russell believed to be occurring in Russia, became an essential ingredient of a 'people's peace.'

In Russell's mind the passing of tsardom and the coming of Russian democracy also offered a significant opportunity for revolutionaries peacefully to disarm militaristic societies, particularly Germany. Russell argued that the Russian example made the likelihood of democratic revolution in Germany probable. After all, the Junker hegemony only prevailed in Germany because those Prussian militarists could claim that they were the sole protectors of Teutonic civilization against the Slavic hordes.[49] With the revolution, Russell believed that the Russians were now leaders of humanity and not 'hordes.' These enlightened Russians, like Russell himself, were, he believed, encouraged in their hopes for peaceful revolution by the Reichstag resolution of 19 July 1917, sponsored by the Social Democratic party. The resolution endorsed the Russian call for a peace without annexations and indemnities.[50]

Russell's ideas of peaceful change represent his most developed thinking about pacifism and revolution. It is not surprising, therefore, that Russell declared at the concluding convention of the NCF in 1919 that during the war only two events had given him cause for hope – the Russian revolution (of March 1917) and the stand of the NCF.[51] His optimism faded, however, throughout the autumn and winter of 1917 and during 1918. As late as September 1917 Russell still believed that Germany had been willing to make peace by conceding every Allied demand in the West. By way of compensation, she would receive acquisitions from Russia, which would be 'willing to accept even very disadvantageous terms.' Russell understood, however, that the British government 'rejected' the idea. Thereafter, the 'opportunity which existed in September has been allowed to pass.'[52] As well, by the autumn of 1917 he had become increasingly impatient with Kerensky's determination to prosecute the war, for all that Russell blamed the Allies for forcing him 'into his ill-starred offensive.'[53] Nevertheless, Kerensky's war policy made Russell sympathetic to the Bolshevik coup of November 1917. Lenin was against continuing hostilities. Hence, Russell cast increasing responsibility for continued war upon America, writing on 27 December 1917 that had the United States 'remained neutral, there can be little doubt that peace would have come during the summer, as a gift of the Russian democracy.'[54]

Russell had become so disillusioned with Western governments who prolonged war, despite constitutionally possessing parliamentary majorities, that he even applauded Lenin's 'sacking' in March 1918 of the freely elected Constituent Assembly that contained a large anti-Bolshevik majority. Lenin was for peace; many other party leaders in the assembly were not. The latter, therefore, did not know their own and the world's best interests.[55] As late as 1919 Russell's hostility to elected governments that pursued war persisted. Arguing for direct action by industrial workers and other minorities whose interests such governments ignored, Russell alleged that, without economic democracy, the era when 'parliamentary government inspired enthusiasm' was now 'past.'[56] Such an illiberal view of majority rule did not persist, although it was to reappear during Russell's campaign for nuclear disarmament and Committee of 100 days during 1958 through 1961.

Russell was also disillusioned by events on the home front. When he and others in the London district Workers' and Soldiers Council meeting spoke at the Brotherhood Church on 28 July they were attacked by angry women and drunken soldiers. Philip Snowden described the incident as 'the worst riot seen in London for years.'[57] On 7 October Russell had to cancel a second speech at the same place, for he could not even begin to talk. At the national level, most revolutionary labour elements proved to be generally unsympathetic to pacifism; sectional wage claims mainly preoccupied the Shop Stewards' Movements.[58] And the majority of workers remained committed both to the war effort and to constitutional politics.

Russell was encouraged by the Bolsheviks' boldness in seizing power early in November, even if he feared that under their leadership Russia might be obliged to revert to a 'military dictatorship.' Russell's support of the Bolsheviks did not indicate that he had moderated his earlier antipathy to revolutionary Marxism as expressed as early as 1896 in his first book, *German Social Democracy*. It was enough for him that Lenin wanted Russia out of the war, while Allied capitalism continued the conflict. But Russell's support for Lenin lacked that optimistic belief of July 1917 that Russia had shown the way for spontaneous pacifist revolutions throughout the warring states. He still believed in December 1917 that peace would come from below, but it would 'be forced upon the reluctant rulers.'[59] By 10 January 1918 Russell was emphatic about the massive degree of violence that would result unless peace negotiations between Germany and Russia were extended to encompass a general settlement: 'The kind of revolution ... will be far too serious and terrible to be a source of good. It would be a revolution ... in which all that is best in Western civilisation is bound to perish.'[60]

Tired and depressed by early 1918, Russell 'gave up the Acting Chairmanship of the NCF.'[61] Following his resignation, ironically, the government pursued him with renewed vigour. Russell had written an article for the *Tribunal* on 3 January 1918. He was charged with making statements likely to prejudice Britain's relations with the United States.[62] He was tried, convicted, and sent to jail for six months on 1 May. While Russell and his friends attempted to have the charge dropped or at least modified, Germany imposed the punitive treaty of Brest-Litovsk upon Russia in March 1918 and in the same month launched the Ludendorff offensive. These events made Russell even more disconsolate. As he wrote to Carr on 30 March 1918, he had withdrawn 'from pacifist agitation ... solely due to the realization that I was achieving nothing.'[63] His contention that Britain and America were mainly responsible for continuing the war had been undermined by what was Germany's final thrust of the Great War for world power. From prison Russell wrote to Allen that 'since Brest Litovsk our duty to preach had ceased, because our chance of success has ceased.'[64] Russell's dismay reflected the concerns of other pacifists about Brest-Litovsk. A separate peace 'would be disastrous for Russia and Europe alike. Not only would it be a triumph for German militarism' but it 'would preclude the agreement of all the combatants that was necessary to secure a just and lasting peace.'[65]

It was to be the March revolution that Russell always looked back upon as the lost opportunity. While writing just before going to jail in May 1918, he reflected, 'If the Russian Revolution had been accompanied by a revolution in Germany, the dramatic suddenness of the change might have shaken Europe, for a moment, out of its habits of thought: the idea of fraternity might have ... entered the world of practical politics; and no idea is so practical as the idea of the brotherhood of man ... [but] the Millennium is not for our time. The great moment has passed.'[66] The 'moment' for peaceful revolution had been the summer of 1917 and not the Bolshevik revolution, for by November 1917 popular frustrations were so high, Russell believed, that revolution throughout Europe would have meant conflagration. Then his 1920 trip to Russia as part of a Labour party delegation brought disillusionment with the Bolshevik experiment. Upon direct contact in 1920 he perceived Bolshevism as being a secular religion 'with elaborate dogmas and inspired scriptures.' Since he was convinced that almost 'all progress ... is attributable to science ... [and] almost all the major ills are attributable to religion,' Russell believed that Russia had no constructive ideology to offer the West. Moreover, as Lenin's policy of authoritarian industrialization could be compared to the 'westernization' of Peter the Great, backward Russia had no practical lessons for the West.[67]

As well, Russell's personal encounter with Bolshevism turned him against revolutions, at least temporarily: 'I think it imperative that the Russian failure should be admitted and analyzed. For this reason ... I cannot enter into the conspiracy of concealment which many Western Socialists consider necessary.'[68] As Russell wrote to Gilbert Murray after his Soviet visit, 'I have returned more than ever a pacifist, as much against revolutionary wars as against others.'[69] Not only had Bolshevism failed to embody Russell's vision of a pacifist and socialist revolution; he attributed to naive Westerners' 'admiration' for the Soviet experiment the reason why genuinely free and peaceful movements such as guild socialism 'died down in the years following the end of the first world war.'[70]

What conclusion can one suggest from Russell's experience of the March revolution and its aftermath to 1920? After 1917, and especially after his 1920 Russian trip, Russell was reinforced in his belief that more politically mature societies had little to learn from politically undeveloped cultures.[71] Second, Russell was convinced after the disillusioning experience of the March revolution that sudden, dramatic changes were seldom likely to bring about constructive consequences. During the interwar period he often advocated socialism, but only 'without a devastating revolutionary war' and only so long as force would be employed solely to defeat 'small bands of malcontents.'[72] In the mid-1930s he also reaffirmed his advocacy of passive non-resistance; but this could only occur in politically advanced countries, particularly Britain. When confronted by Hitler's barbarism, Russell in 1939 supported Allied war policy. Finally, popular peace advocacy appeared so futile in the face of what he perceived as Stalin's imperialistic aspirations that Russell by 1945 had come to believe that the preservation of Western cultural values could only be ensured by a 'Hobbesian vision of peace.' How else but by referring to his disillusionment with the Soviet Union can one explain his advocacy from 1945 to 1949 of an American-dominated world order threatening Russia with nuclear war unless Stalin surrendered all Soviet atomic resources?[73]

Notes

1 6 May 1917, Constance Malleson Papers, Rec. Acq. 596, letter no. 200139, Russell Archives I, hereafter RAI, McMaster University.

2 *Bolshevism: Practice and Theory* (New York, 1920), 41.

3 Ronald Clark, *The Life of Bertrand Russell* (London, 1975), 318, and Alan Ryan, *Bertrand Russell: A Political Life* (New York, 1988), 82. Royden Harrison, 'Bertrand Russell, from Liberalism to Socialism?' *Russell* 6/1 (Summer 1986), 16–17, Jo Vellacott, *Bertrand Russell and the Pacifists in the First World War* (New York, 1980), ch. 11, and Thomas Kennedy, *The Hound of Conscience: A History*

of the No-Conscription Fellowship (Fayetteville, 1981), 226–39, provide the best accounts of Russell's pacifist thought during 1917.

4 'The Ethics of War,' *International Journal of Ethics* 25 (Jan. 1915), 63–73, reprinted as Paper 14 in *The Collected Papers of Bertrand Russell* (hereafter *CP*), 13 *Prophecy and Dissent*, ed. R.A. Rempel, with B. Frohmann, M. Lippincott, and Margaret Moran (London, 1988).

5 Ibid., 72.

6 Martin Ceadel, *Pacifism in Britain, 1914–1945* (Oxford, 1980), 1–8.

7 *The Autobiography of Bertrand Russell*, vol. 1, *1872–1914* (London, 1967), 146; hereafter *Autobiography*.

8 Russell to the NCF via Gladys Rinder, 30 July 1918, RAI, Rec. Acq. 5896, T.S. carbon 200299G, reprinted in *CP* 13 (1988), xxxi, and in *Autobiography*, vol. 2, *1914–1944* (London, 1968), 88.

9 'Principles and Practice in Foreign Policy,' written by Jan. 1915 and published as Paper 36a in *CP* 13 (1988), 207.

10 See 'Will This War End?' *Labour Leader* 11 (10 Sept. 1914), 2, reprinted as Paper 3 in *CP* 13 (1988), 14.

11 To Lady Ottoline Morrell, 14 Dec. 1914, no. 1168, courtesy of the Harry Ransom Humanities Research Center, University of Texas at Austin.

12 See letter no. 1240.

13 See Peter Brock's *Twentieth Century Pacifism* (New York, 1970), 38–9. Russell's essay is reprinted as Paper 28 in *CP* 13 (1988), 158–68.

14 'War and Non-Resistance,' *Atlantic Monthly* 116 (Aug. 1915), 166.

15 See 'The Philosophy of Pacifism' published in *Towards Ultimate Harmony*, Proceedings of the League of Peace and Freedom, 8 and 9 July 1915, reprinted as Paper 27, *CP* 13 (1988), 153.

16 'War and Non-Resistance,' 168.

17 Russell's 'Reply to Criticism,' in P.A. Schlipp (ed.), *The Philosophy of Bertrand Russell*, vol. 5, *The Library of Living Philosophers* (Chicago, 1944), 726.

18 Brock, *Pacifism*, 10.

19 *Principles of Social Reconstruction* (London, 1916), chs. 2–4.

20 John Rae, *Conscience and Politics* (London, 1970), 91.

21 Brock, *Pacifism*, 14.

22 10 April 1916, no. 1364.

23 Ceadel, *Pacifism in Britain*, 25, 51–2.

24 See Harrison, *Russell*, 15, who quotes from Russell's 'Greek Exercises,' 9–10, published as Paper 1 in *CP* 1, *Cambridge Essays*, ed. K. Blackwell et al. (London, 1983).

25 To Lady Ottoline, 1 May 1916, no. 1383, quoted in Vellacott's *Russell and the Pacifists*, 78.

26 'Some Psychological Difficulties of Pacifism in Wartime,' in Julian Bell (ed.), *We Did Not Fight* (London, 1935), 332.

27 Keith Robbins, *The Abolition of War* (Cardiff, 1976), 118.

28 *The Russian Album* (London, 1987), 117–18.

29 *Herald*, 14 April 1917, 9.

30 To Lady Ottoline, no. 1482.

31 *Herald*, 7 April 1917, 13.

32 1 April 1717, no. 1459.

33 See Russell's unpublished ms, 'The Russian Revolution,' written between 11 April and 3 May 1917, RA 220.011670.

34 See *The UDC* 2 (10 April 1917), 64.

35 5 June 1917, no. 1460.

36 See *Herald*, 23 June 1917, 8–9.

37 27 June 1917, printed in Michael Thompson, 'Some Letters of Bertrand Russell to Herbert Wildon Carr,' *Coranto* 10 (1975), 7–19.

38 Great Britain, Public Record Office, War Cabinet Minutes, WC154/22 Cab. 3/3, marked 'Secret.'

39 James Hinton, *The First Shop Stewards' Movement* (London, 1973), 240.

40 'Should the NCF Abstain from All Political Action?,' *Tribunal*, 26 April 1917, 2.

41 Unpublished letter to 'The Members of the National Committee,' 18 May 1917, marked 'Private and Confidential,' RAI 535 NCF folder.

42 Russell to Constance Malleson, 10 July 1917, Rec. Acq. 596, letter no. 200160.

43 See Russell's arguments in the *Tribunal*, 5 July 1917, 2.

44 See Russell's letter to NCF Branch Secretaries, 12 July 1917, RAI 535, and Russell to Lady Ottoline, 15 July 1917, no. 1463.

45 See Kennedy, *The Hound of Conscience*, 238.

46 'Pacifism and Revolution,' *Tribunal* (19 July 1917), supp., 2–3.

47 Harrison, 'Liberalism,' 16–17.

48 'Pacifism and Revolution,' *Tribunal*, 5 July 1917, 2.

49 'Russia Leads the Way,' *Tribunal*, 22 March 1917, 2.

50 'The Kaiser's Reply to the Pope,' *Tribunal*, 27 Sept. 1917, 2.

51 See *The No-Conscription Fellowship: A Souvenir of Its Work* (London, 1919), 21.

52 'The International Outlook,' *Pioneer*, no. 347 (10 Nov. 1917), 2.

53 'Freedom or Victory?,' *Pioneer*, no. 352 (15 Dec. 1917), 3.

54 'International Opinion during 1917,' *Tribunal*, 27 Dec. 1917, 1.

55 Cited without identifying the date in Alan Wood, *Bertrand Russell: The Passionate Sceptic* (London, 1957), 126.

56 'Democracy and Direct Action,' *ILP Pamphlet* (London, 1919), no. 14, n.s. (May 1919), 1–8.

57 Quoted in Stephen White, 'Soviets in Britain: The Leeds Convention of 1917,' *International Review of Social History* 19 (1974), 189.
58 See Hinton, *Shop Stewards*, 241.
59 'International Opinion during 1917,' *Tribunal*, 27 Dec. 1917, 2.
60 'The German Peace Offer,' *Tribunal*, 3 Jan. 1918, 1.
61 Letter to Lady Ottoline, 12 Jan. 1918, no. 1445.
62 Public Record Office, Great Britain, Home Office Records 314, 670, 9 Feb. 1918, and *Daily Express*, 11 Feb. 1918, 7.
63 30 March 1918, RAI 710.
64 See Russell's unpublished ms, 'Despair in Regard to the World,' ca. 20–4 June 1918, sent to Clifford Allen, RAI Rec. Acq. 596.
65 Beryl Haslam, 'From Suffrage to Internationalism,' PhD dissertation, McMaster University (1990), 226–7.
66 *Roads to Freedom* (London, 1918), 106.
67 *The Practice and Theory of Bolshevism*, 6, 117–20, 175.
68 *Roads to Freedom*, 108.
69 2 Aug. 1920, photocopy RA Rec. Acq. 71.
70 *Roads to Freedom*, Preface to the 3rd ed., 1948, 5.
71 Ryan, *Russell*, 170.
72 See 'The Case for Socialism,' in *In Praise of Idleness* (London, 1935), 124–5.
73 Mark Lippincott, 'Russell's Leviathan,' *Russell* 10 (Summer 1990), 6–29.

20

'Transnationalism' in the Early Women's International League for Peace and Freedom[1]

JO VELLACOTT

My focus in this essay is the response of a certain group of women, the founders of the Women's International League for Peace and Freedom (WILPF), to the end of the First World War and to the immediate post-war settlement, as it emerged from Versailles in the spring of 1919. My aim is to show not only the passion and dedication of the women involved but also something of the hard work, solid study, ability, and, above all, the originality that characterized their efforts. I believe that the approach they took is significant, in terms both of international relations and of feminist theory.

Feminist history has generally been written nationally rather than internationally, and, perhaps in part for this reason, the women of the WILPF have often been ignored, given only brief mention, or at best have been dealt with in separate monographs as something apart from mainstream feminism, let alone from malestream history.[2] Yet, even if we look only at British women, who will be at the centre of my argument, some of the most active, intelligent, and politically aware of feminists saw a most important future work of feminism as lying in the area of international relations and conflict resolution, and they dedicated themselves to this field of endeavour from the outset of the First World War.

The story of the Hague conference of 1915, which led to the founding of the International Committee of Women for a Permanent Peace (ICWPP), later to become the WILPF, has been told elsewhere.[3] Here we need to recall only certain salient features. The conference, conceived in February 1915 and taking place in April of the same year (a feat few of us would care to emulate even in peacetime and with all our technological aids), brought together over a thousand women from nations on both sides of the conflict and from neutral countries, including the United States. The women who came were predominately pre-war suffragists, most (though not all) of them from the non-militant bodies. Although they had not, in the main, been able to bring their national organizations into united support of the enterprise, it was as suffragists that they came together, and they had an impressive following among the rank-and-file of their organizations.[4] The pre-war suffrage movement had provided them with a great deal of international experience, and through it many of them had met each other personally, for instance, at conferences of the International Alliance of Suffragists (IAS). Many of the women, it is true, were from families accustomed to travel, but nevertheless the international suffrage movement must be credited with building a sisterhood across national boundaries and with helping to make freedom from xenophobia the norm within the women's movement.[5]

The conveners of the Hague conference established as a ground rule that there should be no recriminations, no laying of blame on one nation or another for the outbreak of war. Observed with remarkable commitment and discipline, this proviso not only served the obvious purpose of preventing the conference from breaking up into factional controversy, but also underlined that the women did not need to take on board the cargo of men's mistakes, nor of the patriotic fear and pride underlying those mistakes.

The discussions focused on two main themes. One, which led to deputations to the heads of state and the foreign ministers of belligerent as well as non-belligerent countries, was the attempt to find a process by which negotiations could be begun which might bring the war to an end. The second was the exploration of how to set up a new order after the war, an order within which international disputes might be settled by peaceful means. Underlying both, and firmly articulated, was the demand for women to have the vote in all nations and to have a voice in international affairs.

After the conference was over the activities of the ICWPP feminists continued. Although international communications were inevitably much restricted while the war lasted, the resources of the IAS, in which ICWPP influence was strong, were given over to trying to maintain links between feminists in various countries. Mary Sheepshanks, who edited *Jus Suffragii* (the IAS journal) throughout the war from IAS headquarters in London, struggled to keep channels open through neutral countries, and she strove consistently to publish 'as much news as possible from the two opposed sides as would present the human face of the 'enemy' to all women readers whatever their nationality.'[6] Aletta Jacobs, with the help of Rosa Manus, meanwhile kept the newly created ICWPP international office open in Amsterdam, despite extreme difficulties caused by wartime restrictions. Before the end of 1915 twelve national committees had been formed, and by 1919 the number was up to sixteen.

While the war continued, the British section of the ICWPP, already taking the name of 'Women's International League' (WIL), recruited many of those who were disaffected with the war-supportive stance of the major suffrage bodies and built a strong organization, active in international relief, in assistance to stranded 'enemy aliens,' in encouraging discussion of the peace that must end the war, and in doing whatever could be done to prevent the escalation of hatred of the enemy. Helena Swanwick was president of WIL and active in the Union of Democratic Control (UDC), which was dedicated to having the people have more knowledge of and say in foreign policy. Catherine Marshall, who had been one of the group who had gone to Amsterdam in February 1915 to plan the Hague meeting, and one of those prevented at the last minute from travelling there in April, remained an active member of WIL's executive, but gave most of her energies throughout 1916 and 1917 to the No-Conscription Fellowship (NCF).[7] By the end of 1917 Marshall was burned out and too ill to continue or indeed to resume work of any kind until early 1919. Other WIL officers with impressive international knowledge and experience were Irene Cooper Willis (international secretary), Kathleen Courtney (second vice-chair), Emmeline Pethick-Lawrence (treasurer), and Mary Sheepshanks (member of the executive).

At the 1915 Hague meeting the ICWPP had decided to gather again when and wherever the peace conference should convene at the end of the war. What they had envisaged at that time, however, was statesmen from both sides of the conflict meeting to hammer out terms of a negotiated settlement. When the peace conference convened in Paris on 18 January 1919 it was, of course, a meeting of statesmen and experts from the allied countries only. That the treaty was in the event worked out only by the politicians of the victorious powers had significant consequences for the women of WILPF, and provides us with a unique opportunity to understand the ground on which they stood, and to define what was new in their feminism and in their internationalism.

Because of the nature of the Paris conference, WIL stood aside while Millicent Fawcett, Ray Strachey, and Rosamund Smith of the National

Union of Women's Suffrage Societies (NUWSS) went to Paris in response to a call from French and United States suffragists 'who felt that the Peace Congress in Paris was developing on lines which gave very scant consideration to the special needs and responsibilities of women.'[8] Members of the ICWPP would undoubtedly have had no trouble with this statement, as far as it went. But their absence from Paris was a highly significant matter of principle and of ICWPP policy. Citizens of the defeated countries could not travel to Paris, so that the suffragists who could be there were from the victorious allied countries only, just as were the statesmen gathered to work out the peace terms. Although the decision was not reached without some regrets, in the end no national section of the ICWPP would send representatives where not all could go.[9]

An understanding of the work of those suffragists who did go to Paris helps to define the difference between them and the WIL group that will be our major focus. The Inter-Allied Suffragists held an informal gathering in Paris from 10 to 16 February 1919 and continued to maintain an even more informal presence throughout the following weeks. Their progress was reported almost weekly in the *Common Cause* (the organ of the NUWSS) and was watched with attention by the leaders of WIL, who were suffragists now more or less estranged from the NUWSS by differences over attitudes to the war. However, the issues addressed were of common interest to all feminist groups.

Indeed, the impressive common ground held among many forward-looking women's organizations was usefully mapped by a gathering convened by WIL at the Fabian Hall in London on 28 February 1919, under the title of 'Conference of Women's Societies to Draw Up a Minimum Feminist Programme.' Although she was not present, Catherine Marshall evidently had a hand in planning this meeting,[10] which was called during the most optimistic days, when there was thought to be a real 'possibility of a Commission of Women meeting in Paris' where 'the resolutions passed by such a body as this may assume great importance.'[11] At the time no one knew what might emerge from the peace conference, and the width of issues addressed by the women, going far beyond any actual peace terms, was based in part on the view that the peace conference might 'make certain Declarations of opinion, not binding on any National, but recommendatory.' (A precedent was seen in the declaration against slavery made at the Congress of Vienna in 1815.[12])

Forty people (thirty-nine women and one man, Oliver Strachey) came to the conference, from thirteen women's organizations.[13] An encouraging degree of unity emerged, and a catalogue of good feminist resolutions was passed. It was hoped that the congress of powers would put its weight behind equal suffrage, equal status in national and international bodies, equality of opportunity in training and employment, equal pay for equal work, woman's right to her own nationality independent of that of her husband, an equal share for both sexes in the rights and responsibilities of the guardianship of children, and the 'Endowment of Motherhood' (mothers' allowances). Other resolutions dealt with safeguards for consumers' rights, a minimum wage, the 'traffic in women', the 'Abolition of State Regulation of Vice,' international marriage laws, and the 'universal abandonment of conscription' (Catherine Marshall's hand can be detected here). As might be expected, the peace conference was also urged to appoint the hoped-for women's commission, 'composed of women representing organised bodies of women in their respective countries, to whom questions bearing on the life and employment of women should be referred,' and to recognize the eligibility of women on all bodies established by the League of Nations.[14]

Almost without exception, these were precisely the issues carried by the Inter-Allied Suffragists to Paris and less successfully to the ears of the men gathered there. Their first concern was to get some representation for women in the peacemaking process itself, specifically to look after the interests of women. Much of the spadework of the peace conference was done by commissions, meeting separately to hammer out proposals on different issues (such as minorities, mandates, reparations, and borders), and the women's first hope was to have a special women's commission set up to make recommendations, the members to be selected by national governments from names proposed by women's organizations.[15] The suffragists took the idea to Woodrow Wilson, who heard them out, and greatly encouraged them by supporting the concept of a special commission to tackle women's issues, suggesting, however, that one should be formed from among the peace plenipotentiaries present (all of whom were male), to which a second part should be added consisting of women named by the Inter-Allied Suffragists. The women understood Wilson to be committing himself to bringing this revised proposal forward. Yet no more was heard of the scheme, and as the weeks went by the suffragists desperately and repeatedly scaled down their goals. If there was to be no women's commission, they pressed at least to be allowed to appoint women representatives to the various existing commissions, and failing that to have some women, no matter whom, included by co-optation or appointment.

At the last, the suffragists would have been grateful to be granted brief official hearings by all the commissions, as they were by the one on international labour legislation, but they had to settle for what interviews they could get with this or that individual or occasionally with a sympathetic group from among the statesmen present. Although those who received the IAS representatives included some leading men, this procedure could hardly be deemed representation, and it was clearly granted as a favour rather than won as a right.

Despite their frustrating experience, the women's lobby at the Paris Peace Conference could claim to have contributed to two important developments. The first was the strong recommendation of the Commission on International Labour Legislation in favour of equal pay for work of equal value, enforced by government inspection, the inspectorate to include women.[16] This commission, in fact, had been the first to give a hearing to the suffragists, and it was surely supportive even before meeting them. The commission, chaired by Samuel Gompers and under pressure from a large international labour and socialist conference which met at Berne in February 1919,[17] was already the most progressive of the commissions – indeed, too radical for success, one may say in hindsight, since little came of their recommendation and the issue of equal pay for work of equal value is far from won in the 1990s. The phrasing also goes beyond what had been claimed in the 'Minimum Feminist Programme,' where the resolution had asked only 'that women should receive the same pay as the men for the same job.'[18]

The second triumph, rightly hailed as 'A Great Victory,' came when the Covenant of the League of Nations, first revealed to the public on 15 February, was amended in late March to include a clause declaring that 'all positions under or in connection with the League, including the Secretariat, shall be open equally to men and women.'[19] The concession was important even if – once more – it was to prove of small effect. The feminists were right in seeing a two-way relationship between this achievement and national suffrage: it came about largely because of successful suffrage struggles in Britain and other countries, and it would and did help support the suffragists' case in countries were women had not yet gained the vote. What it did not do, ironically if not surprisingly, was ensure women an effective or equal voice in the League of Nations.

The unwillingness of the ICWPP to convene a meeting in Paris did not mean that they sat idly by while the Inter-Allied Suffragists were there. Nationally and internationally the organization was extremely active, and no branch more so than the British WIL. Not only had WIL performed a most useful service to the women's movement in general (and made their own voices heard) by sponsoring the conference on the 'Minimum Feminist Programme,' but the leaders were taking an interest in aspects of the peacemaking that went beyond the conventional definition of 'women's issues,' important and far-reaching as the 'minimum' proposals had been. For the WIL leaders, however, the term 'minimum' had mean just that, and they were prepare to carry feminist intervention forward into a far wider field.[20]

When the draft Covenant of the League of Nations[21] appeared in the *Times* on 15 February 1919, Catherine Marshall was among those who studied it with great attention – and either she or some other WIL officer rushed out to pick up enough copies of the *Times* that the full text could be clipped for all the members of the executive, to whom it was duly sent with a covering letter and six typed and mimeographed pages of draft commentary and criticisms signed by Helena Swanwick. The text was amended in Catherine Marshall's handwriting and described as 'to be sent to British Delegation at Versailles and to Colonel House.'

Swanwick's commentary begins diplomatically by rejoicing 'that in this draft a number of principles have been broadly laid down.' The ten principles listed are referenced to articles in the covenant, and range from 'the abandonment of the absolute sovereign rights of States and the recognition that the world is one (Preamble and Article 11)' through 'the establishment of machinery for Arbitration and Conciliation (Articles 12, 13, 14, 15)' to 'the abolition of Secret Treaties (Article 23)' and 'provision for the revision of treaties which have become inapplicable.' Others refer to arms reduction (Articles 8 and 9) and freedom of transit. Catherine Marshall added a significant eleventh principle: 'The recognition (Article 22) that the league has important functions to perform in the furthering of constructive international cooperation.'[22]

Having enumerated the praiseworthy principles to be found in the covenant, the commentary continues: 'The universal recognition and practice of these principles would be the longest step the world has ever made towards international cooperation, but the Protocol [*sic*] in its present form makes such universal recognition and practice impossible.'[23]

Criticism, however, far outweighed praise. Much attention was paid to membership of the league, focusing on the discriminatory provisions, where eligibility for membership in the present and in the foreseeable future was weighted heavily in favour of the victorious Allies, with the Central powers initially excluded altogether. The flaw was seen as fundamental:

The first requirement for a League of Nations which is to establish and administer Courts of Arbitration and Conciliation is that it should be trusted by all the world to be administered impartially for the benefit of all the world. This will not be unless membership of the League is, from its inception, open without distinction to all self-governing States which express (a) their desire to become members, and (b) their willingness to perform the duties of members ... The omission of the Central Powers can be interpreted only as a sign of exaggerated and groundless panic or of a determination to use the League, not as an instrument for the co-operation of the world, but for the continued oppression of our late enemies.

The document describes the crippling economic effects that might follow from exclusion from the league, and Catherine Marshall added, 'This must lead to the most strenuous efforts on the part of Germany to make alliances outside the league.'

The constitution of the league is criticized for its failure to give significant function to the 'Body of Delegates,' for whom the writers hoped 'A more inspiring name may be found' and which indeed became the assembly. '[This] is the only body which is in the least likely to be democratically appointed and we are sorry that it should have no organic relation with the Executive Council and (with [one] exception ...) no function except to talk.' As for the executive council, the main criticism is for the action of the allied and associated powers in nominating five of their own number to be a permanent majority. In light of the important role laid down for the council, 'It is absolutely essential that the Executive Council should from the beginning bear the highest character for impartiality.'

The document raises questions on other parts of the draft, advocating, for example, that the mandate system should be applied not only to those colonies formerly under the defeated power but to all regions 'inhabited by peoples not yet able to stand by themselves' (that is, the colonies of the victors) 'with a view to granting them self-determination at the earliest possible moment.' As for the reduction of armaments, it seemed 'obvious' to the critics 'that no reduction of armaments imposed by a majority of the allied and associated powers upon their late enemies will be regarded by the latter as an act of impartial justice and it is, in fact, in the highest degree improbable that it would be such an act.'

On the subject of the Permanent Labour Bureau (Article 20), WIL's view was, 'The success of this branch of work will depend entirely upon whether the workers, including women workers, are given their due representation and upon whether those countries which have established socialism are freely admitted to carry their full weight in council.'

Regret was expressed at the omission of any mention of 'the principle of self-determination of peoples,' 'the freedom of the seas,' the universal abolition of conscription, or 'the duty of Mandatory Powers to assist in the gradual emancipation from sex slavery of women within the countries which they administer by mandate.' The document concludes with a 'summary of Recommendations.' Helena Swanwick shortly put out a full analysis on these lines in a pamphlet, published by WIL.

WIL's comments are striking for the extent and accuracy with which they identified those flaws that would contribute to the breakdown of peace in the following twenty years. At the same time they reveal how great was the gap between the internationalist women's hopes and expectations of the nature of the league and those of the statesmen who drafted its covenant. Catherine Marshall and Helena Swanwick were certainly among the many who would have liked to see the League of Nations set up as more than any mere treaty alliance; what they envisaged was a real step towards international government, with the renunciation of at least some small particles of national sovereignty in the interests of common welfare and peace, and the opening in time of the way to much more major abrogations of national sovereignty in the areas of conflict resolution and control of armaments and military forces. They also surely hoped for a new spirit in international affairs and believed it possible to develop structures that would provide both education in the new spirit and scope for learning its practice.

Of almost as much interest as the substance of WIL's criticisms is simply that they made them, and made them with confidence in their right and indeed obligation to be heard on the topic. These women were speaking out on all subjects and in all spheres, even the most traditionally male-dominated ones. Their idea of what it ought to mean for women's voice to be heard in international deliberations differed significantly from that of the IAS women who had gone to Paris to beg for a chance to have a say on recognized 'women's issues.'

The story of the ICWPP congress of May 1919 shows that the British critique of the Covenant of the League of Nations was no aberration, but indicative of a new kind of feminist initiative. A flurry of reorganization had begun by letter and cable between national sections and ICWPP headquarters as soon as it was made manifest that no truly international gathering could be held in Paris to coincide with the Paris Peace Conference. As an alternative Aletta Jacobs hoped for a return to The Hague, others proposed Berne, and when the United States delegates sailed, they were uncertain just where it was that they were to go on their arrival in Europe. An abundance of telegrams and no small feat of cooperation were needed finally to set the venue for Zurich, the date for 12 to 17 May 1919.[24]

By May the worst of wartime restrictions on travel were lifting. The 1915 decision to meet at the same time and in the same place as the statesmen's peace conference turned out to have been an inspired decision, even though circumstances prevented it from being carried out to the letter. There were many moving scenes and messages of sisterhood in Zurich. In Mary Sheepshanks's words: 'Women from the warring as well as the neutral nations joined hands in grief and horror at the misery and devastation, the loss of millions of lives, the mutilation and ruined health of millions more and the wretched plight of the hundreds of thousands of refugees now scattered over the face of the earth, homeless and deprived of everything that makes life worth living.'[25]

Shared grief was important. However, the women were in Zurich not to bewail the past as much as to try their utmost to make the future on a different pattern. Fortunately, the draft Covenant of the League of Nations had been published, as we have seen, far enough in advance for sections to have considered their responses, and the terms of the proposed peace treaty itself became available, by a remarkable coincidence, the very day that the delegates gathered. In a way that could hardly have been accomplished by any kind of correspondence or committee the congress hammered out a united and unifying response to these documents.

The resolutions passed at the congress in The Hague in 1915 were remarkably similar in tone and content to the points enumerated almost two years later by Woodrow Wilson, who had indeed studied them.[26] When Germany had been forced to seek an armistice, Prince Max von Baden, as Reichskanzler in the new, more democratic government formed at the beginning of October 1918, had addressed his suit to the president of the United States, stating his acceptance of Wilson's Fourteen Points and subsequent public statements 'as a basis for the peace negotiations.' After some tense discussion the allied powers had accepted this, with only one or two important reservations.[27] Accordingly, the Fourteen Points and The Hague resolutions alike provided the standard against which the peace terms were tried at Zurich – and were found wanting.

In words close to those of earlier feminist internationalists, Elise Boulding has said that 'the greatest strength of all for women is the strength of their commitment to a different future, and a lack of attachment to the existing international system.'[28] Unlike the statesmen at Versailles, the women at Zurich had no overt political constituency that they had to placate, and they foresaw only too accurately the negative effects of the harsh, dictated peace that replaced the hoped-for negotiated peace. Nor were they engaged in the standard diplomatic dishonesty and manoeuvring by which one's own nation is always flawless, the other always culpable. There was remarkable unity across national boundaries. The report reads, 'On the resolution on the Peace Terms there was little difference of opinion and criticism was unrelenting ... [and] the gloom of the settlement in the act of being announced from Paris hung like a shadow over the whole Congress.'[29] A strong resolution was forwarded to the peace conference in Paris:

This International Congress of Women expresses its deep regret that the terms of peace proposed at Versailles should so seriously violate the principles upon which alone a just and lasting peace can be secured, and which the democracies of the world had come to accept.

By guaranteeing the fruits of the secret treaties to the conquerors, the terms of peace tacitly sanction secret diplomacy, deny the principles of self-determination, recognize the right of the victors to the spoils of war, and create all over Europe discords and animosities, which can only lead to future wars.

By the demand for the disarmament of one set of belligerents only, the principle of justice is violated, and the rule of force is continued.

By the financial and economic proposals a hundred million people of this generation in the heart of Europe are condemned to poverty, disease, and despair, which must result in the spread of hatred and anarchy within each nation.

With a deep sense of responsibility, this Congress strongly urges the Allied and Associated Governments to accept such amendments of the Terms as shall bring the Peace into harmony with those principles first enumerated by President Wilson upon the faithful carrying out of which the honour of the Allied peoples depend.[30]

When discussion of the League of Nations Covenant began, some of the delegates from the United States and some from Britain initially spoke of it as so bad as to be irredeemable: 'while welcoming the fact that the idea of a League of Nations was so generally accepted, [they] declared that in its present form it was a league of conquerors against the conquered, that it maintained the old discredited system of the Balance of Power, excluded some nations from membership, and would not save the world from future wars. They therefore regarded it as useless as an instrument of peace.'[31]

Ultimately, the decision was made at Zurich to give support to the principle of the league and to work to improve the instrument. Leadership in constructive criticism came from the British section, Helena Swanwick being particularly interested and well prepared as a result of the preliminary work she had done in initiating discussion within the British section. The recommendations that were finally forwarded to Paris were closely in line with those she had made in her WIL pamphlet.

Another major topic of discussion and condemnation was the blockade, perhaps better called the breakdown in supply, from the effects of which some of the women present were visibly suffering. Historians have drawn attention to the complexity of the real situation behind what some call the blockade 'myth.' This complexity was already known to the women at Zurich. They knew that far worse conditions prevailed in Austria than in Germany herself; they knew how bad things were in parts of victorious France; they knew that the blockade was only one of the factors causing famine and distress. They may perhaps not have known of the difficulty of gaining the cooperation of the German government in the use of its ships for the importation of food supplies.[32] But in recognizing the role of general economic dislocation in inducing starvation and near-starvation that were no myth, these women foresaw the continuance of dislocation in the harsh economic terms of the peace, and they feared the political as well as the physical consequences that might follow. The British WIL had staged a demonstration against the blockade in Trafalgar Square on 6 April, followed by a plea carried by a deputation to the government. Now, they met face to face with women from some of the most seriously affected areas. Women from neutral and victorious countries mingled with women who had personally experienced the effects of the famine and were to return to it.[33] Their reality was very different from the reality of the allied statesmen, who, comfortable in Paris, met only with each other, as insulated from any direct contact with the starvation and disease ravaging Central and Eastern Europe as they were from the anger and despair burning in Germany.

As it happened, at that time many children from the disaster area of Vienna were being brought to Switzerland for emergency care, by an initiative of the Swiss Railwaymen, and a trainload of eight hundred was met at the station by the congress delegates, providing them with a first-hand experience denied to the Paris statesman:

They were told that 1,500 had been rejected as medically unfit to bear a twenty-four hours' journey. The children left behind had been slowly done to death by starvation and illness. Those that had arrived had been selected as being robust enough and sufficiently free from illness to make it safe for them to associate with children in another country. As they poured out of the train, they might have been a party of East-end children going off their summer holidays, yet these were in many cases the children of professional men and officials, and were years older than they looked, thin, undersized, and too often poorly clad. One of the delegates took a child in her arms, thinking it was an infant. She was told that it was six years old.[34]

A resolution presented to the Paris Peace Conference described the situation 'as a disgrace to civilization,' and went on to urge positive steps towards relief, and that it be given the highest priority:

This International Congress of Women ... urges the Governments of all the Powers assembled at the Peace Conference immediately to develop the inter-allied organizations formed for the purposes of war into an international organization for purposes of peace, so that the resources of the world – food, raw materials, finance, transport – shall be made available for the relief of the people of all countries from famine and pestilence.
   To this end it urges that immediate action be taken –
(1) To raise the blockade, and
(2) If there is insufficiency of food or transport;
      (a) To prohibit the use of transport from one country to another for the conveyance of luxuries until the necessaries of life are supplied to all peoples.
      (b) To ration the people of every country so that the starving may be fed.
   The Congress believes that only immediate international action on these lines can save humanity, and bring about the permanent reconciliation and union of the peoples.[35]

Before and after the congress some of the delegates travelled to the afflicted regions to see conditions firsthand. Dr Ethel Williams, for example, was in Vienna at the end of May and beginning of June (after the worst of the famine there was over), and she examined the condition of children, the attempts to provide care, and records of the disease and death rates during the previous year.[36] Jane Addams noted the emaciated children in Lille, as she passed through France on her way to Zurich, and later when she travelled for several weeks in Germany, seeing starving children everywhere. Her vision, shared by many other women, was that the machinery of the newly created League of Nations could have been put to no better purpose than to alleviate this misery. Addams later wrote, 'Could it [the League of Nations] have considered this multitude of starving children as its concrete problem, feeding them might have been the quickest way to restore the divided European nation to human and kindly relationship.'[37] Departing from the sanitized academic discourse, I have to ask, Can any one doubt that even today we might have a better world, and probably a more peaceful one, had this simple recipe been followed?

Note that this goes far beyond taking up starving children as a stereotypical 'women's issue.' Certainly, the women were deeply moved by what they saw, but they refused to take comfort in mere palliative measures. Such horrors were for them indicators of the need for the radical political change towards which their efforts were directed. Here I do not want to go into a detailed explanation of what this means in terms of feminist theory, where the role of feminist pacifism and internationalism has generally been neglected or misunderstood. In brief, the core is that the founders of WILPF held that the contribution of women's ways of thinking were needed at every level, not just to gain better conditions for their sex, but to promote change in the whole governance of the world. Certainly, they often used the rhetoric of motherhood, but they showed themselves neither passive nor sentimental. They simply saw women as being qualified by nature or experience to bring something new to public life, and they brought a fresh perspective to the most jealously guarded bastions of male dominance – economics, war-making (now politely called 'defence'), and international affairs. I see the assumptions they were making as more radical than separatist feminism, more radical than equity feminism (although implicit was a demand for absolute equality of opportunity), more radical than socialist feminism (though many of them were, in fact, socialists), because they were claiming the right neither to stay outside the system and do their own thing, nor to be admitted to it on the men's terms, accepting the established rules of thinking and behaviour.[38]

Moving out of the realm of pure feminist theory, here I shall move into an area lying somewhere between feminist theory and pacifist/ internationalist theory, to focus my conclusions on what was different in the international work of these women from the common approach to such work.

The claim of the women of the ICWPP to bring something different to international affairs had solid experience to back it by 1919. As we have seen, their two conferences, the one at The Hague in 1915 and the one in Zurich in 1919, had both been full of images scarcely available to men at the time. The participants had created an ambience hard to envisage in a men's conference, let alone in any meeting taking place at that time and including participants from both sides of the conflict. Nevertheless, at the most obvious level, the central topics under discussion at the peace conference of the allied statesmen in Paris in 1919 and at the women's conferences at The Hague in 1915 and in Zurich in 1919 were the same.

Of course, one cannot infer that the difference in approach was simply the result of the special nature of women. In fact, their legal disabilities as women were an important factor: the gatherings were in large part able to be held exactly *because* the women were excluded from full political citizenship and from equal participation in the peacemaking process. The concept of 'transnationalism' is useful in defining what the women created from the difference.[39]

In common usage, the word 'transnational' means little more than 'extending beyond national boundaries,'[40] as in the phrase 'transnational railroad.' But even in this technical definition there is an element which helps towards the concept I am reaching for. Where 'international' means 'between nations,' and reinforces the idea of nationhood, 'transnational' represents a disregard or crossing of the barriers between nations. Similarly, 'international negotiation,' for example, suggests a balancing of national interests between high-level representatives of both sides, charged with getting the best possible for their own country at the least cost in concessions to the other side, while 'transnational' can appropriately be used for negotiation based on common interests among people on either side of the artificial line on the map. The term can, of course, be applied to any cross-border organization – for example, the pre-war International Council of Women, the IAS, the Socialist International, or, more recently, the multiplicity of non-governmental organizations or NGOs (some of which may also meet my definition).[41] I shall use the term here only for something going beyond a sectarian interest.

By this criterion, I cannot use 'transnational' to describe the pre-war international women's suffrage movement.[42] But the movement had enough of the elements of cross-border understanding that it is no coincidence that it provided the seeds from which WILPF grew. Because the women kept alive throughout the war their sense of each other's humanity, as well as their personal love and respect for each other, and kept in touch with one another as far as possible, the seeds grew, rather than perishing in the climate of the conflict that set the nations against one another, or at best turned them into military allies, not friends. The trust of this group of feminists that they could transcend boundaries and hold a meeting at The Hague in 1915 among women from both sides of the conflict, as well as with those from neutral countries, was a huge step forward. The success with which the conference was carried off, despite gloomy predictions from those of a narrower vision, reaffirmed that they were moving towards a truly fresh approach. Their ability, against odds, to avoid recriminations for the outbreak of war, shows them conscious of the need to detach themselves from the existing international system. Significant indicators, too, may be found in the nature of the wartime work of ICWPP sections within their own countries, trying to replace hatred of the 'enemy' with a recognition of shared humanity, educating themselves and, as far as possible, the public towards a new postwar world order, struggling against the overwhelming tide of patriotic fervour.

The 1919 Zurich conference saw further developments. The rejection of a meeting with women from only the victorious allied countries was a rejection of international divisions and national interests, as well as a courageous violation of the sanitary cordon that could shield the victors from any glimpse of the suffering of the vanquished.[43] Indeed, faced with immense postwar pain, the WILPF women developed a significant process; already in 1919 it began to be 'a tradition ... that, if a wrong has been done, it should be the section belonging to the country which *does* the wrong that should appeal for right.'[44] Under the leadership of Jane Addams, the league adopted the practice of arriving at decisions consensually, 'not by imposing the will of the majority, but by a genuine collective activity.' As Emily Balch put it, 'We try both to create agreement and to bring clear expression to all the agreement there is latent among us. We must all the time be trying as much to agree with others as trying to get others to agree with us.' She added, 'This is as new in debate as peaceful settlement of disputes is new in international politics.'[45] The criticisms of the text of the covenant and treaty, detailed above, may seem naive if read in the context of traditional international discourse. They are part of a logical and consistent whole, however, if the premise is recognized: the women gathered at Zurich stood outside the international structure, and they were free to look at what their own experience led them to believe would lead to lasting peace, rather than at what would be politically advantageous in their own countries. They hoped to see a League of Nations that would be both more representative and more empowered to take a positive constructive role, standing outside or beyond narrow national interests. Professor Abrams's term 'fundamental peacemaking' well fits their vision.[46]

The insistence that wartime wrongs would be better forgotten, that to put relief and healing at the centre of postwar international organization would make a better basis for a lasting peace than punishment would are part of the same holistic approach. Significantly, the women of WILPF were to resist as far as possible attempts to sideline them into bandaid operations directed, in effect, to healing the injuries brought about by what they saw as the failures of the existing (male-dominated) system. Their attitude to suffering associated with the blockade is an example. Although they were willing to publicize the damage, and to respond with a certain amount of direct aid, they were more concerned to focus attention on finding solutions to the economic dislocation and to attack the underlying faults in international relations that made such a thing possible.

Transnationalism, in the sense in which I have used it, is clearly something that must be practised as well as preached. It is not a structure (like the League of Nations), nor a system (like diplomacy), nor a treaty, nor a set of rules. I hope, at some future date, to examine how far the feminists of WILPF managed to maintain their commitment to what was both a vision and a practical way of life. I want to look at the extent of their influence on international affairs and discuss its limitations. This last, I think, should not be done in simplistic and dualistic terms of success or failure in their own time. After all, who runs may read. If there is something to be learned from the actions of these women, it may still be learned, and so perhaps the effect of the work of the early Women's International League for Peace and Freedom is not yet finished.[47]

Notes

1 I appreciate the support which I have received, at various times, while engaged on the research on which this essay is based, from the following: the Social Sciences and Humanities Research Council of Canada; the Friends' Study Centre at Woodbrooke, U.K.; Lucy Cavendish College, Cambridge, and the Calouste Gulbenkian Foundation; the Simone de Beauvoir Institute (Con-

cordia University), where I am an honorary fellow; and the Canadian Institute for International Peace and Security, from which I held a Barton Award when writing this essay. I am also indebted to the following collections for use of material: Cumbria Record Office, Catherine Marshall Papers; Western History Collection, University of Colorado, Boulder, WILPF International Papers; City of London Polytechnic, Fawcett Collection; British Library of Political and Economic Science, WIL Papers; Swarthmore College Peace Collection. The theme of this essay and some of the material used will also appear in my second book on the life of Catherine E. Marshall, 1880–1961.

2 For a comparable view that 'radical feminist philosophy has always been more internationalist and more working class than the historians who have studied it,' see Jane Marcus, 'Transatlantic Sisterhood: Labor and Suffrage Links in the Letters of Elizabeth Robins and Emmeline Pankhurst,' *Signs* 3 (Spring 1978), 744–55; for some thoughts on the relationship between feminist and malestream history, see Jo Vellacott, 'Double Tunnel Vision,' *Le Bulletin/Newsletter* 10/1, Simone de Beauvoir Institute, Concordia University (1990), 26–30. I have explored the theory of feminist pacifism in more depth in 'A Place for Pacifism and Transnationalism in Feminist Theory: The Early Work of the Women's International League for Peace ad Freedom,' *Women's History Review* 2/1 (1993). For other recent work on international feminism, see Sandra Stanley Holton, '"To Educate Women into Rebellion": Elizabeth Cady Stanton and the Creation of a Transatlantic Network of Radical Suffragists,' *American Historical Review* (AHR) 99/4 (Oct. 1994); and Leila J. Rupp, 'Constructing Internationalism: The Case of Transnational Women's Organizations, 1888–1945,' *AHR* 99/5 (Dec. 1994).

3 Gertrude Bussey and Margaret Tims, *The Women's International League for Peace and Freedom* (London, 1965), Ch. 1; Jane Addams, *Peace and Bread in Time of War* (New York, 1945); Jane Addams, E. Balch, and A. Hamilton, *Women at The Hague* (New York, 1915); Mercedes Randall, *Improper Bostonian: Emily Greene Balch* (New York, 1964), ch. 6; Anne Wiltsher, *Most Dangerous Women: Feminist Peace Campaigners of the Great War* (London, 1985), ch. 5; Johanna Alberti, *Beyond Suffrage: Feminists in War and Peace, 1914–1918* (London, 1989); Catherine Foster, *Women for All Seasons* (Athens and London, 1989), 7–17; Jo Vellacott Newberry, 'Anti-War Suffragists,' *History* 62/206 (Oct. 1977), 411–25.

4 There were, for instance, at least 180 British women willing to pay the cost and take the risk of crossing the North Sea to attend The Hague conference, although they were prevented from doing so by actions of the British government. Sybil Oldfield, of Sussex University, is engaged on a valuable project to recover what can be found of the histories of all these women, some of whom

were well known, some obscure. She is finding that, in addition to suffragists, many were Quakers and/or socialists. I appreciate her making this information available to me, and also her helpful comments on this essay.

5 See also Sybil Oldfield, *Spinsters of this Parish* (London, 1985), 176–8; for
Catherine Marshall's formative years in the National Union of Women's Suf-
frage Societies, see Jo Vellacott, *From Liberal to Labour with Women's Suffrage:
The Story of Catherine Marshall* (Montreal and Kingston, 1993).

6 Oldfield, *Spinsters*, 186.

7 For the NCF, see Thomas C. Kennedy, *The Hound of Conscience: A History of
the No-Conscription Fellowship, 1914–1919* (Fayetteville, 1981); Jo Vellacott,
Bertrand Russell and the Pacifists in the First War (Brighton, 1980).

8 Fawcett, M.G. *What I Remember* (Westport, Conn., 1976) 253–6. Margery Cor-
bett Ashby, in the Preface to D.M. Northcroft's *Women at Work in the League of
Nations* (Keighley, 1927) says that the Allied women gathered at the invitation at the ICW and the IWSA.

9 Extensive telegrams and correspondence, WILPF International papers, Western History Collection, University of Colorado, Boulder (hereafter Col/
WILPF).

10 The copy of the preliminary agenda in Col/WILPF has an addition in Marshall's handwriting.

11 Preamble to preliminary agenda and to final agenda, both in Col/WILPF. See
also 'Proceedings' and Swanwick's 'Chairman's Remarks,' Col/WILPF.

12 Agenda, item A, Col/WILPF.

13 The participating organizations were: Actresses' Franchise League, Association for Moral and Social Hygiene, Association of Women Clerks and Secretaries, Catholic Women's Suffrage Society, Fabian Women's Group, Friends'
League for Women's Suffrage, Independent Women's Social and Political
Union, National Union of Women's [Suffrage] Societies, Voter's Council,
Women's Deliberative Council, Women's Freedom League, Women's Industrial Council, Women's International League.

14 Proceedings, Resolutions 6 and 7.

15 *Common Cause* (hereafter *CC*), 21 Feb. 1919, report by Ray Strachey.

16 *CC*, 4 April 1919.

17 Paul Kellogg and Arthur Gleason, *British Labor and the War: Reconstructors for
a New World* (New York, 1919; reprint ed. with Introduction by Jo Vellacott
Newberry, New York and London, 1972), 285.

18 WIL Feminist Programme Conference, 28 Feb. 1919, Resolutions as passed,
Col/WILPF.

19 *CC*, 4 April 1919; Ferdinand Czernin, *Versailles 1919* (New York, 1964), [145];
Covenant, clause 7; Northcroft, Preface.

20 See also Vellacott, 'A Place for Pacifism,' 30–1.
21 Czernin, [140–63, unpaginated], contains a useful chart placing three successive versions of the covenant side by side. The one under discussion here is Czernin's second, his first being the Anglo-American draft, little more than a working outline.
22 H.M. Swanwick, 'Draft of criticism ...,' 4 March 1919, Col/WILPF. The Article 22 to which Marshall referred dealt with an agreement to place under league control already existing international bureaux, presumably referring to such things as the regulation of international mail services.
23 Marshall has substituted 'draft' for 'protocol' throughout, Swanwick rather curiously having been under the impression that the two words meant the same.
24 Various material, Col/WILPF.
25 Mary Sheepshanks, unpublished autobiography, seen by courtesy of Sybil Oldfield, 61; for a vivid description of the Zurich congress, see Randall, *Improper Bostonian*, ch. 12.
26 Mercedes Randall, Introduction to Garland reprint of Jane Addams, E. Balch, A. Hamilton, *Women at The Hague* (New York, 1972), 11.
27 Czernin, 5–43.
28 E. Boulding, *Women in the Twentieth-Century World* (New York, 1977), 181. The theme recurs throughout the women's international movement: see, e.g., Rosika Schwimmer, quoted in Bussey and Tims, 80; Virginia Woolf, *Three Guineas* (London, 1938); Maude Royden (*London Mail*, 22 April 1920, quoted in Sybil Oldfield, *Women against the Iron Fist* (Oxford, 1989), 57–8; see also Jane Mackay and Pat Thane 'The Englishwoman,' in Robert Colls and Philip Dodd (eds.), *Englishness: Politics and Culture, 1880–1920* (London, 1986), 220–1.
29 *Towards Peace and Freedom* (Zurich, 1919), 6.
30 Ibid., 18.
31 Ibid., 7.
32 Erich Eyck, *A History of the Weimar Republic* (Cambridge, Mass: 1962–3) vol. 1, 88–9; Sally Marks, *The Illusion of Peace: International Relations in Europe, 1918–1933* (London, 1976), 7.
33 Addams, *Peace and Bread*, 158–9; H.M. Swanwick, *I Have Been Young*, (London, 1935) 313–19; Wiltsher, *Most Dangerous Women*, 208–10; Randall, *Improper Bostonian*, 265–6.
34 *Towards Peace and Freedom*, 12; see also Addams, *Peace and Bread*, 169–70.
35 *Towards Peace and Freedom*, 18.
36 Ibid., 10–11.
37 Addams, *Peace and Bread*, 172.

38 The category of 'social feminist,' as elaborated in a recent work by Naomi Black, is illuminating and most nearly fits the early WILPF women, though Professor Black does not carry its definition quite far enough to include all that I see as significant about the approach of this group of women. *Social Feminism* (Ithaca and London, 1989). There is a great deal of recent work on gender and war, (e.g., Margaret R. Higonnet (ed.), *Behind the Lines: Gender and the Two World Wars* (New Haven and London, 1987); see also Vellacott, 'A Place for Pacifism.'

39 For an interesting and closely related use of the word and discussion of its application, see Charles Chatfield, *For Peace and Justice: Pacifism in America, 1914–1941* (Boston, 1973), 36–7.

40 *Concise OED.*

41 See, e.g., Boulding, *Women in the Twentieth-Century World*, esp. ch. 8.

42 In a useful article, which is however acknowledged to be no more than intro-ductory, Rebecca Sherrick examines the concept of 'universal sisterhood' as illustrated in the women's international movement before, during, and immediately following the First World War. 'Toward Universal Sisterhood,' in Elizabeth Sarah (ed.) *Reassessments of 'First Wave' Feminism* (Oxford, 1983, 655–61. Rupp's recent impressive article (note 4 above) provides thought-provoking data on the difficulty experienced in attempting to move beyond the Western-centred conditioning of the women making up the international organizations, but treats WILPF as only one of the series comprising the ICW, the IAS, and WILPF. I still hold that a new term is needed to describe the nature and aspirations of the early WILPF, in particular, of its international section. There is a qualitative and functional difference between the genius of the international suffrage movement, truly a sisterhood of women struggling together for their rights against the male-dominated system which prevailed in every country, and the transnational humanistic feminism of the WILPF, still consisting of women working with women, but directed towards a vision for all humanity, and refusing to be limited to 'women's issues.'

43 As I first wrote this (March 1991, with the Gulf War just declared to be over), I learned that holders of United States passports were forbidden by their own government to enter Iraq, on penalty of a $10,000 fine and five years impris-onment, a startling example of the literal enforcement of such a sanitary cordon.

44 For examples of the application of this principle, see *Towards Peace and Free-dom*, 7. It is, of course, not unusual for people in peace movements to tackle what they see as the errors of their own leaders, at least in countries with some pretensions to democracy. Before the dissolution of the Iron Curtain, the writer remembers observing the curious phenomenon, at a women's

peace conference, of all the participants from the West beating their breasts and blaming their own leaders for the tensions of the Cold War; in that instance, however, the representatives of the nations on the other side of the Iron Curtain – whose attendance had had to be officially sanctioned by their governments – cordially concurred with all criticisms of the West, but (under the eye of their monitoring compatriots) became incensed when the slightest hint was made that their nations, too, might bear a share of the blame.

45 Randall, *Improper Bostonian*, 273.

46 Irwin Abrams, 'The Quaker Peace Testimony,' in this volume.

47 See Adam Curle, *Tools for Transformation* (London, 1990), where he points out that we can never know what measure of effect our actions and attitudes have, but that every small act of peace adds to the foundation of peace in the world rather than contributing to the hostility; see, for example, 90. I explore this further as it relates to WILPF in a paper, 'How Do We Measure Success?,' given at the 18th International Congress of Historical Sciences, Montreal, August 1995.

21

A Question of Respectability and Tactics: Vera Brittain and Food Relief for Occupied Europe, 1941–1944[1]

Y. ALEKSANDRA BENNETT

The twentieth century has blurred the distinction once drawn – at least in theory – between the soldier and the civilian. During the Second World War allied bombs rained down upon cities, and the peoples of occupied Europe suffered starvation because of the occupation practices of the Nazis and the allied blockade. These policies have raised troubling questions about the nature and methods of modern warfare.[2] Of area bombing, much has been written.[3] By contrast, the allied blockade has been comparatively neglected, though in some ways it demonstrated even more completely the totality of modern war.[4] It effects were universal and pervasive. Those of the population it did not kill were often left in damaged health and with a lowered resistance to disease.[5]

In September 1939 Britain blockaded Germany as the only practical method of taking the war to the enemy, but in June 1940 the blockade was extended to include all of occupied Europe.[6] This placed the civilian populations of occupied allied countries at far greater risk than those of the enemy. In the official history of the economic blockade, W.N. Medlicott admits, 'The Ministry [of Economic Warfare] did its best to avoid a discussion of its ultimate dilemma. Could the blockade really harm the enemy, except at the cost of widespread starvation?'[7]

At the time only a few determined voices spoke out against blockade. In the vanguard of the protest was Vera Brittain, the English writer and pacifist. For her, the exercise of humanity and morality in wartime was essential to the preservation of 'the whole foundation of law on which Society rests.'[8] Some of Brittain's concerns were shared by others in the pacifist community, the churches, and even in Parliament and in the government bureaucracy. The voices of dissent were, however, deeply divided.

Indeed, by 1941 Vera Brittain was fighting a stiff rearguard action against those who might have been thought her natural allies. She was attacked by fellow pacifists on philosophical grounds and – most difficult of all – by non-pacifist Christians who also worked for famine relief. Common goals were overshadowed by quarrels over political efficacy and methods of moral suasion, over perceptions of respectability as a means of access to government decision makers, and – fundamentally – over whether pacifism itself would discredit the movement for food relief by tarring its 'respectable' advocates with defeatism and fifth columnism. For Vera Brittain, the long and bitter struggle would propel her from the position of 'respectable' insider, who moved comfortably in upper-middle-class liberal and left-wing intellectual circles, to 'unrespectable' outcast: 'I am afraid I have come to the conclusion, though I have long resisted it, that to work effectively on behalf of oppressed humanity you have got to give up all hope of remaining respectable. Like Christ himself you have to put yourself among felons and just endure as best you can the calumnious and malicious assertions that are made about you.'[9]

On 15 November 1939, within weeks of the outbreak of war, Brittain launched her protest against the blockade with an article in the *Daily Herald* headlined, 'Should We Blockade Germany? It's war on babies says Vera Brittain.'[10] Her revulsion at the 'social misery and individual suffering' caused was heightened by first-hand experience. A trip to Germany in 1924[11] had exposed her to lasting evidence of the 1914–18 allied blockade: 'Long after States have ceased to quarrel the consequences of their disputes are visible in the impaired development, the depleted vitality, sometimes even the living death, of their weakest and most vulnerable citizens.'[12]

After this initial statement Brittain's public criticism of the blockade was suspended for the next two years. During this time, she worked within the Peace Pledge Union (PPU), Britain's premier non-sectarian pacifist organization, and directed her energies towards support for its Stop-the-War Campaign, which advocated a negotiated peace settlement with Germany.[13] Although preoccupied with this platform, the PPU did publish three pamphlets on the blockade. A fourth, which called for controlled food relief in Poland, had to be withdrawn when Hitler's invasion of France and the Low Countries precluded any positive public response.[14]

In March 1941 the issue of food relief was taken up again, and appeals began to appear in the PPU's weekly *Peace News*.[15] By the fall, as food supplies on the continent dwindled, the campaign against the blockade acquired a priority status for the PPU and for Vera Brittain.[16] In a speech at the Aeolian Hall on 24 January 1942, she revealed the shocking fact that in Greece the expected average number of deaths from starvation was two hundred a day.[17] Brittain blamed the food shortage in occupied territories on both the German invaders and the British blockade. She chided her compatriots for their schizophrenia, for showing themselves to be a nation capable of being 'moved to righteous wrath by the crimes of others, while remaining singularly insensitive to the victims of ... [their] own policy.'[18]

To Vera Brittain it was essential that her audience understand that the integrity of the values for which the British were fighting could not be preserved by adopting methods akin to those of the Nazis.

The real opposite of a Nazi, is not another belligerent who uses the Nazi's own weapons in the hope of subduing him; it is a pacifist who refused to touch those weapons at all.

I am not a defeatist. I want to see our victory in this war, but victory for me *does not mean acquiring the power* to push another people into outer darkness of desperation, which gave birth to the ugly militarism in Germany and Japan, that is now our Nemesis. It means the triumph of those *spiritual qualities* to which many individuals in this country are sadly indifferent as those whom we call our enemies – truth, justice, brotherhood and compassion.[19]

From 1942 until 1944, when food supplies began to flow freely into liberated Europe, Brittain appealed 'to the conscience of Great Britain.'[20] Her diary and collection of newspaper clippings bear eloquent witness to a punishing round of addresses and meetings in support of food relief. These activities intensified after she came to head the PPU's Food Relief Campaign Committee in March 1943.[21] Pursuing all avenues, Vera Brittain also published several pamphlets and articles that reached a wide audience.

A pamphlet, *One of These Little Ones*, appeared in February 1943. By 12 July it had sold 32,862 copies.[22] In it she maintained that Britain, while not responsible for food shortages in Europe, had contributed to worsening conditions through an unbending application of the blockade – only minor concessions having been made to Greece because of acute circumstances in that country.[23] She argued that this limited relief should be followed by further minimal supplies that, even if commandeered by the Axis powers, would do little to damage the allied war effort: loss through seizure was far outweighed by the psychological benefit to the occupied populations of the knowledge of aid extended in the name of common humanity.[24] The same themes appeared in Brittain's *Letter to Peace Lovers*, a personal, fortnightly newsletter, which reached over two thousand regular subscribers.[25] Between January 1942 and December 1944 it devoted thirteen issues, in whole or in part, to famine relief.[26]

Much of the moral and intellectual rationale for Brittain's work was summed up in her article, 'Should We Humanise War?'[27] The innocent elements of the population needed to be distinguished – the aged and the infirm, the children, and the mothers of the unborn – in order to preserve humanitarian and Christian values in the face of Nazism. The retention of some semblance of morality and the recognition of international law would preserve a basis of appeal – however narrow – for all civilian victims of war.[28]

Other pacifists, however, believed that to mitigate war's worst effects, as Vera Brittain was attempting to do, would humanize war, rendering it more tolerable and prolonged. Some pacifists felt that to focus on starvation ignored other atrocities and was inconsistent with a true pacifist position. Still others recognized the humanitarianism of those involved in food relief, but felt that their efforts might deflect the limited energies of the PPU away from the campaign for negotiated peace.[29]

These philosophical differences within the PPU blighted the food relief effort from its inception, although a majority of the PPU's executive committee had agreed to the campaign, which had been 'strongly taken up by local PPU groups.'[30] Symptomatic of this internal discord was the behaviour of John Middleton Murry, editor of the PPU's *Peace News*. Vera Brittain and Roy Walker – the secretary of the PPU's food relief campaign – felt that Murry was deliberately obstructionist in his editorial policy by denying essential publicity to the effort.[31] For his part, Murry considered it 'to be an unwise use of the small forces of pacifism to concentrate them on a campaign which has no hope of success.'[32]

In fact, the public conscience was being pricked, in large part because of Vera Brittain. The success of the Aeolian Hall meeting in January 1942 was followed by an extraordinary response to the PPU's 'harrowing' news bulletin *Famine*, to which she had also contributed.[33] By 3 March 1942 sales had reached 50,000 copies.[34]

The problem, as Brittain fully appreciated, was one of effectiveness. In general, pacifists were condemned to leprous isolation in wartime, while the PPU in particular was seen as an 'unrespectable' body – a group with a propensity to embarrass the establishment and, specifically, in the matter of food relief, to do so by a sustained program of agitation and protest.[35]

Vera Brittain's response was not the defeatism of Murry. As she explained, 'One cannot switch off a deep religious faith like a tap just because the reason for its expression is inconvenient to the wielders of power, or put one's ideas into cold storeage [sic] expecting to find them still vital and unimpaired when it is again safe to express them.'[36] Given the climate of opinion, however, Brittain recognized that PPU members who wished to help the hungry would have to adopt a more neutral political stance.[37] Without denying their pacifism, they would have to show that their opposition to government policy was loyal. It appears that Brittain's strategy was adopted in February 1942. After much discussion, the PPU leadership decided to establish a national committee to coordinate the publicity, discussion, and advocacy of food relief.[38] This committee was to be composed of `notables' and would not be expressly pacifist. By the same token, it was decided that the PPU would cooperate with any group working for famine relief, even if it otherwise supported the war.[39]

Some thirty-six `notables' were contacted, including George Bell, the Anglican Bishop of Chichester, who expressed doubt about the viability of such a mixed national committee. Subsequently, it became clear that Bell was really concerned about the adverse effect of PPU involvement.[40] Accordingly, he pirated and recast the PPU's idea, to form an exclusive committee of notables – the Famine Relief Committee (FRC).

Since the main purpose of the FRC, as Bell conceived it, would be to obtain authoritative information about the food situation on the continent, and to advocate relief measures through cordial contact with government parties, no member of the PPU was asked to join.[41] As Edith Pye, a well-known Quaker chosen by Bell to be secretary of the newly formed group, explained, 'Those responsible for action on any scale should not be known as pacifists.'[42] Ironically, a member of the Society of Friends was arguing that pacifists involvement would antagonize the government.[43]

The PPU's exclusion was therefore pointed, intentional, and tactical. Bell reported to the Archbishop of Canterbury that his group had 'decided against the proposal made by Stuart Morris [of the PPU] and others that we should try and agitate, and in favour of a small committee, the purpose of which would be to keep in friendly touch with the

Government and see what could be done through representation from time to time.'[44]

Not only did Bell's committee, including its Quaker members, opt for a quietist approach, it also contacted the mixed food relief committees, of pacifist and non-pacifist members, that the PPU had been organizing since the fall of 1941. The circular announcing the new group, stated that 'it is not considered that public agitation is necessary or advisable.'[45] This stance ran directly counter to the PPU's strategy of bringing pressure to bear on the government. By May 1942 the issue of food relief had thus been taken up by two groups of supporters, the respectable and the unrespectable, 'the PPU being that unrespectable portion.'[46]

In July 1942, in keeping with its strategy of making discreet representations to the government, Bell's committee approached Lord Selborne, the minister of economic warfare. He received the delegation cordially, no doubt because, in official eyes, it commanded 'a certain volume of support from responsible persons and ... [had] been careful to keep itself apparently free from pacifist associations.'[47]

Respectability, however, did not translate into effective political pressure. Nothing of substance came of the meeting. In October 1942 Bell appealed to the Archbishop of Canterbury, William Temple, requesting that he join with the Cardinal Archbishop of Westminster, Arthur Hinsley, in taking 'the scheme [of relief for children and nursing and expectant mothers in Greece and Belgium] to the Prime Minister, or at least to send it to him so that he would be obliged to look at it.'[48] Temple and Hinsley agreed, and in late October Temple wrote to Winston Churchill. A meeting with the foreign secretary, Anthony Eden, took place on 5 November 1942.[49]

Once more, the FRC did not appear to make any headway. Rather, it was Eden who used the occasion to obtain assurances that the FRC's detailed proposal for relief in Greece and Belgium would not be published, lest it expose him to immense pressure from the governments of other occupied countries.[50]

The FRC appeared satisfied for the moment to maintain a watching brief. But as hunger mounted in Greece, Vera Brittain was unwilling to accept such a timid approach. On 8 October 1942 she responded by publicizing the plight of the Greeks in her *Letter to Peace Lovers*. Hunger experienced during the winter of 1941–2 had 'been partly checked by the shiploads of various food-stuffs' the British government had let pass through the blockade, she wrote, but 'babies ... cannot live on bread alone,' and supplies of milk and other suitable foods were not being given navicerts by the Ministry of Economic Warfare. Brittain urged her readers to undertake a vigorous letter-writing campaign to reverse this policy.[51]

Minutes and notes in the Ministry of Economic Warfare's files record the public response to her appeal. One report noted, `We are receiving letters from widely separated parts of the country which, however, betray very clearly a common origin. They all take the same line of demanding the issue of navicerts (an expression which I suspect most of the authors have just learned for the first time) and their authority for accusing us of withholding navicerts is a representative of the Greek Red Cross ... Several of them also contained references to one of Miss Brittain's latest outbursts ... Eight of these effusions came by second post today and they are no doubt, only the first taste of the wrath to come.'[52] This prognosis was correct, for two days later the number of letters received had mounted to sixty. Undoubtedly, the common inspiration behind the flood of pro-relief letters to the ministry was Vera Brittain's spearheading of what officials came to regard as a new relief campaign in the country.[53]

The renewed interest stirred by Brittain explains Anthony Eden's anxiety to win the support of the two archbishops, Temple and Hinsley. Were the efforts of the 'respectables' and the 'unrespectables' to have been joined, a groundswell of protest might have emerged powerful enough to challenge government policy.

Yet the prospects for a common front were slight. The divisions separating the famine relief forces emerged clearly in the circumstances surrounding the publication and reception of Brittain's pamphlet, *One of These Little Ones* in February 1943. Her difficulties showed how realistic were her concerns that the 'unrespectability' of her pacifist connections would impair the effectiveness of her work.

In a symbolic gesture of her willingness to cooperate with the FRC, Brittain sent a draft copy of her pamphlet to the committee. Bishop Bell pronounced it 'not quite in accord with the majority of the Famine Relief Committee i.e. friendly pressure on the Government, and an unwillingness to despair of success resulting from friendly pressure.'[54] Accordingly, the FRC would distribute the pamphlet to all its groups and help in its sale, but the officers of the FRC 'felt that its tone was a little too anti-Government for the Famine Relief Committee to put its name to it.'[55]

Brittain made no changes, but she wrote to the Peace Pledge Union requesting them not to circulate the pamphlet because it might 'be less effective with MPs.'[56] Whether these fears were justified is a matter for speculation, but there was no ambiguity in the response of the *Evening*

News. A reporter informed Brittain that he had written about her pamphlet, but his story had been stopped by the editor on the grounds that Brittain was a member of the PPU and 'notorious.'[57] She was given to understand that the policy of the paper was to attack the PPU and anyone belonging to it.[58]

Making the best of adversity, Brittain came to see the 'pacifist Food Campaign ... as a kind of spearhead to make way for the more discreet Famine Relief Committee to follow.'[59] In her view, 'Somebody has to take the official kicks, and that is the PPU's function.'[60] Magnanimously, she divided the substantial royalties from *One of These Little Ones* between the two campaigns.[61]

Notwithstanding this gesture, and similar signs of a willingness to act in concert on the part of the PPU, relations between the two groups did not improve. In July 1944 Vera Brittain berated the FRC for its continuing, un-cooperative attitude.[62] Undaunted, however, the PPU's Food Relief Campaign kept up its efforts for food relief, encouraging local committees, lobbying members of Parliament, engineering questions in the Commons and in the Lords through sympathetic members, and holding public meetings throughout the country. It did not allow the pressure on the government to ease even though, as Temple was to remark to Bell, in February 1944, 'I am afraid the Government's reply is horribly easy at present. They will just say – We have every reason to hope that before long these countries will be liberated and it will be possible to make available for them the stocks that have been prepared.'[63] The FRC did not relax its own brand of pressure either, and, like the PPU's Food Relief Campaign, worked through its own local committees and through both houses of Parliament. George Bell became increasingly outspoken on the famine issue – a measure of his frustration with the lack of success achieved by the FRC's methods – but, to the end of the struggle for food relief, he did not renounce the FRC's quietist tactics and its claim to respectability.[64]

It is difficult to assess, in quantitative terms, the impact of the two campaigns. That they did maintain a constant pressure upon the government is clear, but it is also clear that there were only limited and very controlled concessions to food relief. The result, in personal terms, of the determination of Bell and Brittain to adhere in principle to their respective tactics – albeit with some deviation in practice on both sides – was richly paradoxical. Bell's increasing outspokenness on famine relief (and area bombing) may well have rendered him unrespectable enough to be eliminated as a candidate for the see of Canterbury. Brittain's outspokenness, however, made her sufficiently prominent to appear with Winston Churchill on a German list 'of British people (approximately 3,000) to be shot [or] imprisoned by the Gestapo when the Nazis landed in England.' As she was to observe, 'With this came an ironic sort of respectability ...' It placed me once and for all, above further possibility of suspicion, yet left me with the experience of knowing that being a "suspect," & humiliated, had meant; of losing prestige and gaining kinship with the outcasts.'[65]

'Outcast' though she may have become, Vera Brittain nevertheless succeeded in making a signal contribution to keeping the nineteenth-century tradition of moral protest alive in wartime Britain by reminding the nation of the threat posed by total war to the very fabric of Western civilization. In the official history of the economic blockade the efforts of Vera Brittain and the PPU's food relief campaign are dismissed as little more than an irritant or nuisance. As Medlicott comments, 'In the United Kingdom the relief campaign was never a challenge to the Government.'[66] Yet this is to deny the moral significance of the issues raised by Brittain (and her pacifist and non-pacifist allies) and the place of such protest in the history of English dissent.[67] As Vera Brittain sought to remind those who would listen, the questions she asked were perennial questions, which a civilized society ceases to ask at its peril if there is to be any respect for the 'sacredness of individual life.'[68]

Notes

1 I would like to thank the Social Sciences and Humanities Research Council of Canada for funds in 1989–91 to complete some of the research for this project. I also thank my colleagues, Robert Goheen and Mark Phillips. I owe an inexpressible debt to my colleague Frances Montgomery. Finally, to Peter Brock my appreciation for the example of his dedicated scholarship.

2 See Geoffrey Best, *Humanity in Warfare: The Modern History of the International Law of Armed Conflicts* (London, 1983), 216–85.

3 A recent example is Stephen A. Garrett, *Ethics and Airpower in World War II: The British Bombing of German Cities* (New York, 1993).

4 An excellent article on the 1939–45 blockade and food relief is Joan Beaumont, 'Starving for Democracy: Britain's Blockade of and Relief for Occupied Europe, 1939–1945,' *War & Society* 8/2 (Oct. 1990), 57–82. Also Peter Hoffman, 'Roncalli in the Second World War: Peace Initiatives, the Greek Famine, and the Persecution of the Jews,' *Journal of Ecclesiastical History* 40 (1989), 77–99.

5 See C. Paul Vincent, *The Politics of Hunger: The Allied Blockade of Germany, 1915–1919* (Athens, 1985).
6 Detailed account of the 1939–45 economic blockade in W.N. Medlicott, *The Economic Blockade* (London, 1952–59).
7 Medlicott, *Economic Blockade*, vol. 2, 277.
8 Vera Brittain, 'Should We Humanise War?,' *Christian Pacifist* (July 1944), in the Vera Brittain Collection (hereafter VBC), William Ready Division of Archives and Research Collections, McMaster University, Hamilton, Ontario, G596.
9 The idea of 'respectability' is frequently used by Brittain. VBC/Correspondence-Replies (hereafter VBC/C/Rep) Brittain to M.L. Moll, 8 Dec. 1941. Also Alan Bishop and Y. Aleksandra Bennett (eds.), *Wartime Chronicle: Vera Brittain's Diary 1939–45* (London, 1989), 223.
10 Vera Brittain, 'Should We Blockade Germany? It's war on babies says Vera Brittain,' *Daily Herald*, 15 Nov. 1939, VBC/G535.
11 Vera Brittain, *Testament of Youth: An Autobiographical Study of the Years 1900 1925* (London, 1978), 632–42. *Testament of Youth* was originally published by Victor Gollancz in 1933.
12 VBC/G535.
13 In the fall of 1939 alone Vera Brittain spoke at innumerable meetings across the country in favour of an armistice and a negotiated, early peace. See *Oxford Mail*, 1 Nov. 1939; *Glasgow Herald*, 13 Nov. 1939; *Birmingham Evening Post*, 24 Nov. 1939. On the Peace Pledge Union, see Peter Brock, *Twentieth Century Pacifism* (Toronto, 1970); Martin Ceadel, *Pacifism in Britain, 1914–1945: The Defining of a Faith* (Oxford: 1980); Richard A. Rempel, 'The Dilemma of British Pacifists during World War II,' *Journal of Modern History* 50 (1978), D1213–29.
14 See VBC/Famine Relief Committee Files (hereafter FRCF).
15 For example, *Peace News*, 7 March 1941.
16 Peace Pledge Union, Executive Committee Minutes (hereafter PPU/ECM), 2 Dec. 1941, Peace Pledge Union Offices, Dick Sheppard House, 6 Endsleigh Street, London, England.
17 Vera Brittain, 'Food Relief in Europe,' 24 Jan. 1942, VBC/F76. Brittain was speaking at the Aeolian Hall in London. VBC, Holograph Daily Diary 1 Jan. 1942–31 Dec. 1942 (hereafter D25), 24 Jan. 1942.
18 VBC/F76. Also Procopis Papastratis, *British Policy towards Greece during the Second World War, 1941–1944* (Cambridge, 1984).
19 VBC/F76.
20 Ibid.
21 See VBC/E24, a scrapbook of cuttings on Brittain's lectures and public addresses over the period Jan. 1941–Dec. 1946.

22 Vera Brittain, *One of These Little Ones* (London, 1943), VBC/G588. VBC/Correspondence-Received (hereafter VBC/C/Rec), Andrew Dakers to Vera Brittain, 12 July 1943; Bishop and Bennett, *Wartime Chronicle*, 208–13; VBC/FRCF, Roy Walker to Martin Parr, 7 Jan. 1944.
23 Brittain, *One of These*, 2–3, 7–9.
24 Ibid., 6–17, 19.
25 Winifred and Alan Eden-Green (eds.), *Testament of a Peace Lover: Letters from Vera Brittain* (London, 1988), Introduction.
26 Vera Brittain, *Letter to Peace Lovers* (hereafter *LPL*) no. 73, 1 Jan. 1942; no. 86, 2 July 1942; no. 93, 8 Oct. 1942; no. 102, 11 Feb. 1943; no. 108, 6 May 1943; no. 114, 29 July 1943; no. 116, 26 Aug. 1943; no. 120, 21 Oct. 1943; no. 126, 13 Jan. 1944; no. 136, 1 June 1944; no. 148, 16 Nov. 1944; no. 149, 30 Nov. 1944; no. 151, 28 Dec. 1944. For government reaction to Brittain's newsletter, see PRO CAB 75/7 HPC (40) 103, Memorandum on Anti-War Publications, 4 May 1940.
27 VBC/G596.
28 Ibid. On international law and war, see Best, *Humanity in Warfare*. Also, G.I.A.D. Draper, 'Humanitarianism in the Modern Law of Armed Conflicts,' *International Relations* 8/4 (Nov. 1985), 380–96.
29 Sybil Morrison, *I. Renounce War: The Story of the Peace Pledge Union* (London, 1962), 58–9. Also interview with Sybil Morrison, London, England, 6 July 1979, and VBC/G596.
30 PPU/ECM, 2 Dec. 1941; Morrison, *I Renounce War*, 58.
31 Interview with Roy Walker, Ipswich, England, 8 Jan. 1980.
32 *Peace News*, 19 June 1942. Also PPU/ECM, 20 Jan. 1942; VBC/D25, 20 Jan. 1942. VBC/C/Rep Brittain to Alex Wood, 20 June 1942; Brittain to Andrew Dakers, 9 Nov. 1942.
33 Medlicott, *Economic Blockade*, vol. 2, 278. Vera Brittain, 'Wanted: Simple Human Pity,' in *Famine*, published for the PPU Information Service from 6 Endsleigh Street, London, 24 Jan. 1942, 4. It was priced at one penny. See VBC/FRCF.
34 PPU/ECM, 17 Feb. 1942; PPU/ECM, 3 March 1942; Medlicott, *Economic Blockade*, vol. 2, 278.
35 PPU/ECM, 3 Feb. 1942; VBC/D25, 3 Feb. 1942; PPU/ECM, 17 Feb. 1942. Peace Pledge Union, National Council Meeting Minutes (hereafter PPU/NCM), 13–14 Dec. 1941.
36 VBC/C/Rep Brittain to Harold Latham, 16 Nov. 1942.
37 VBC/C/Rep Brittain to Wood, 18 Sept. 1941. Also Brittain to Stuart Morris, 26 Sept. 1941; PPU/ECM, 7 Oct. 1941.
38 PPU/ECM, 3 Feb. 1942; PPU/ECM, 17 Feb. 1942. Starvation in Greece was

acute. See FO 371/33175 Greece 1942; FO 371/33176 Greece 1942; Medlicott, *Economic Blockade*, vol. 2, 254–67; FO 837/1231, W.P. (42) 80 'Greece: The Blockade,' Memorandum by the Minister of Economic Warfare for the War Cabinet, 14 Feb. 1942. See also FO 837/1222, Memo by W.A. Camps, 11 Aug. 1941.

39 PPU/ECM, 3 Feb. 1942. Also PPU/NCM, 23 Sept. 1941.

40 PPU/ECM, 3 March 1942. See Kenneth Slack, *George Bell*, (London, 1971).

41 PPU/ECM, 19 May 1942. The administrative work was done in the office of the Friends Service Committee.

42 George Bell Papers (hereafter GBP), Lambeth Palace Library, London, England, vol. 58, Edith Pye to Bell, 26 Apr. 1942.

43 Walker interview, 8 Jan. 1980. Some of the notables contacted by Bell were also opposed to Quaker involvement. See GBP vol. 58, Barbara Ward to George Bell, 13 April 1942; Douglas Woodruff to Bell, 19 July 1942.

44 William Temple Papers (hereafter WTP), Lambeth Palace Library, London, England, vol. 50, Bell to Temple 1 May 1942; GBP, vol. 58, Bell to Arthur Hinsley, Cardinal Archbishop of Westminster, 30 April 1942.

45 PPU/ECM, 14 June 1942; VBC/C/Rep Brittain to Emile Cammaerts, 21 May 1942.

46 Walker interview, Jan. 1980.

47 FO 837/1214, Note on Blockade Policy Respecting Relief, Ministry of Economic Warfare, Jan. 1943, W3225/4/49. For Bell on meeting, see GBP, vol. 58, 'Report of Meeting between the Minister of Economic Warfare and the Famine Relief Committee at the Ministry of Economic Warfare, 17 July 1942.'

48 WTP, vol. 50, Bell to Temple, 7 Oct. 1942.

49 WTP, vol. 50, Temple to Churchill, 25 Oct. 1942. Brittain recorded in her diary, 'The *respectable* Food Relief Committee ... is shortly to take a deputn. to Churchill ...' VBC/D25, 3 Nov. 1942.

50 WTP, vol. 50, 'Confidential. Memorandum by the Archbishop of Canterbury of his and Cardinal Hinsley's interview with Mr Eden on Thursday, November 5th, at the Foreign Office.' Eden commented, 'My visitors expressed satisfaction at what was being done ... [They] are ... [not] associating themselves with attacks on His Majesty's Government ... I have some hope that as a result of this interview they will use their influence to dissuade the Committee from interfering in what is essentially a government matter.' FO 837/1214, Eden to Halifax, 16 Nov. 1942, telegram no. 7108.

51 VBC/LPL no. 93, 8 Oct. 1942. On navicerts see Beaumont, 'Starving for Democracy' 78, 1.

52 FO 837/1224, Minute by R. Morrison (MEW) for Mr Camps and Mr Foot (MEW), 13 Oct. 1942.

53 FO 837/1224, Note for Minister by R. Morrison, 15 Oct. 1942.

54 GBP, vol. 59, part 1, Bell to Pye, 2 Feb. 1943.

55 VBC/FRCF, Pye to Brittain, 9 Feb. 1943. Also VBC/FRCF, Pye to Brittain, 27 Jan. 1943. In her diary Brittain wrote, 'Andrew Dakers rang up this morning to say that the Bp. of Chichester sent my pamphlet on to the Archbp. of Canterbury, who doesn't want it publicly associated with his address to the members of both Houses of Parlt. on Feb. 17th because of its mild & vague criticism of Govt.! So Dakers, to his disgust with the Church, cannot mention the Archbp.'s address in his advts. to booksellers ... I said that both the Archbp. & I had the same object, & if his type of approach failed, it would never do for him to think this was due to my pamphlet.' Bishop and Bennett, *Wartime Chronicle*, 212.

56 VBC/C/Rep Brittain to Howard Whitten, 9 Feb. 1943.

57 VBC/D26 Holograph daily diary, 1 Jan. 1943–10 Oct. 1943, 16 March 1943.

58 VBC/C/Rep Brittain to Dakers, 16 March 1943.

59 VBC/C/Rep Brittain to Cammaerts, 21 May 1943.

60 VBC/C/Rep Brittain to W. Seymour, 12 Feb. 1942.

61 VBC/FRCF, Walker to Parr, 7 Jan. 1944.

62 VBC/C/Rep Brittain to Pye, 29 July 1944.

63 WTP, vol. 50, Temple to Bell, 8 Feb. 1944.

64 VBC/C/Rep Brittain to Bell, 18 Dec. 1944; Brittain to Selborne, 18 Dec. 1944; GBP, vol 59, part 2, Walker to Bell, 18 Dec. 1944. Also, Medlicott *Economic Blockade*, vol. 2, 616–17. The PPU's Food Relief Campaign finished its work in March 1945, PPU/NCM, 17–18 March 1945. A farewell concert was held on 20 July 1945 at Guildhall School of Music, with Peter Piers and Benjamin Britten. Speakers were Vera Brittain and Michael Tippett.

65 Vera Brittain, *Testament of Experience: An Autobiographical Story of the Years 1925–1950* (London, 1957), 398.

66 Medlicott, *Economic Blockade*, vol. 2, 277–9.

67 See K.O. Morgan, 'The army of the peacemakers,' *Times Literary Supplement* (8 Aug. 1980), 887.

68 VBC/LPL, no. 151, 28 Dec. 1944.

22

Ambivalence in the Post–Second World War French Peace Movement, 1946–1952

NORMAN INGRAM

The title of an article by Karl Holl in the German weekly *Die Zeit* describes French pacifism of the interwar period as 'permanently discredited.'[1] This is certainly the commonly held view in France where for the man on the street pacifism has become associated with defeatism, collaborationism, and the Vichy experience. As one French commentator has written, 'In denying the virtue of war, rendered sacrosanct by tradition, pacifism shakes established ideas. It is lumped together with defeatism, with cowardice, with treason. Pacifism has, therefore, often taken on a pejorative connotation. It is perversion. It is to peace what formalism is to form, simplism to simplicity, sentimentality to sentiment.'[2] And he goes on to say that 'pacifism played its role in the birth of the Vichy regime.'[3]

Since the war, the French peace movement has been divided into two mutually antagonistic parts. On the one hand, there is the numerically large communist-dominated and -inspired Mouvement de la paix; while, on the other hand, there is a small and struggling genuinely pacifist movement represented today by the Union Pacifiste de France. This essay examines the attempts of French pacifism to regroup after the experience of the Second World War and considers the extent to which the legacy of Vichy and the interwar period can be held responsible for the weak and divided nature of the French peace movement in the immediate postwar era.

Dissent from Political Society

The first point to be made is that the experience of the Second World War does not appear to have changed the anti-political, dissenting outlook of the representatives of what I have called in the interwar period *pacifisme nouveau style*, or new-style pacifism. Fernand Gouttenoire de Toury, a former infantry captain, a graduate of the prestigious Saint-Cyr military academy, and a veteran who had lost a leg in the Great War, wrote in May 1946, for example, 'In a few weeks our unhappy France will be called upon to pronounce itself on the politics of the country. At other times we should have rushed to the ballot boxes, as we did in the interwar years, when, as exemplary militants, we showed our confidence in the great movements which proclaimed their pacifism or antimilitarism: the Socialist party, the League for the Rights of Man, and this Communist party whose antimilitarism constituted [our] Gospel, and which today is at the forefront of the fight to militarise the country.'[4]

There was not a single electoral candidate, of any of the parties, in whom de Toury thought a pacifist could place his confidence. Not one of the political parties had had the courage to condemn the political direction followed since the war. There were anti-Pétainistes in great number, but de Toury underlined their opportunism, given that many of them had been pro-Pétain during the war. With regard to de Gaulle, de Toury wrote that his policies were just as nefarious as those that preceded them. His principal grievances against the general were threefold. First, that de Gaulle had claimed that 'those Frenchmen who were partisans of the Armistice in June 1940 are evil Frenchmen and traitors,' while everyone knew, according to de Toury, that in 1940 there was only a handful of resisters, and they were either abroad or in the colonies. The truth of the matter was that all of France, generalissimo included, realized that resistance to the Germans was useless. Following this line of reasoning, the entire Gaullist regime was based on a lie.[5]

The second complaint was that de Gaulle had regilded the escutcheon of the communists, 'these communists whom we reproach not for being communists, but for placing themselves deliberately in the service of a foreign government.'[6] Finally, de Toury condemned the Gaullist government for having made a mockery of justice during the *épuration*.

Thus, for de Toury, both Gaullist and Pétainist regimes ought to be censured: 'Just as the Pétain régime should be condemned – not for having signed the Armistice – but rather for having spoken of "collaboration" and having thrown its lot in with Germany, at a time when the strictest neutrality was required between the Nazi victor and our allies, in like manner de Gaulle deserves to be condemned for having sown throughout the country ferments of hatred which have yet to be extinguished.'7

A year later de Toury proclaimed the necessity of a Franco-German rapprochement. As far as the Nazi war crimes were concerned, he wrote that they in no way justified the cruel treatment of which Germany was the victim, because the German people could not be held responsible for the crimes of their former Nazi masters. Even if it could be proven that German people were guilty of heinous crimes, it did not make sense to turn Germany into a 'foyer of virulent infection' which would only create future problems.8

Pacifisme ancien style: Down and Almost Out

The movement of which de Toury was a member has left few written traces of its activity. But what of the old-style pacifism of the Association de la Paix par le Droit? The APD is the quintessential example of the liberal, internationalist, juridically oriented form of French pacifism that exemplified the old-style pacifism from which the new, virulently dissenting variety evolved in the interwar period. The APD was formed in 1887, originally as a discussion group of lycéens in Nîmes; it gradually expanded across France until by the outbreak of the Great War it was probably the most important and influential of the pre-war peace societies – certainly in terms of the high intellectual level of its review *La Paix par le Droit*.

The APD had gone underground in May 1940 at the time of the German invasion of France. In October 1947, after almost eight years of silence, it reactivated its journal and resumed its role in French pacifism. As Théodore Ruyssen, the association's president, wrote at the time, the APD had ceased publication of the review in June 1940 because it was felt strongly by the association's leaders that to continue publication would be nothing short of treason.

In reality we did not even attempt it [he wrote], because if we had succeeded, success would have been more unbearable than failure. In effect, within the hypocritical confines of 'collaboration' it would undoubtedly have been easy to improvise some formula of 'conciliation,' or of international 'rapprochement' which might have obtained the approbation of the defeatists of Vichy and maybe even the dishonouring approval of the occupying Power ... We did not dream for an instant of attempting such an inglorious adventure. La Paix par le Droit has always taken pride in being free of all occult influences, be they financial, political, confessional, or otherwise. Less than ever, during the cruel period of national humiliation, did we feel disposed to renounce what had been our freedom of expression in order to give the illusory appearance of life.[9]

The APD held its first postwar meeting in Paris in November 1945 and mandated the Comité directeur to do everything in its power to breath new life into the association's old body. But it quickly became apparent that old-style pacifism was experiencing a crisis of age even more profound than that traversed ten years previously at the time of the fiftieth anniversary congress. Ruyssen wrote that the APD suffered first of all from the general economic chaos buffeting modern society, which meant that the middle class, 'from which the APD had always recruited its most loyal adherents, had seen itself become impoverished, ruined, proletarianized by the unequal rise of resources.'[10] But the November 1945 meeting had also brought into relief another pressing problem: the obvious aging of the association's ranks. This, too, was a theme that had first seen the light of day ten years previously.[11]

Charles Rousseau, another long-time member of the APD and a professor of law at the University of Paris, tackled directly the question of whether a pacifist attitude 'in the traditional sense of the word' was relevant in 1947 and whether it had any chance of success. With regard to the first question, Rousseau wrote that there was hardly any doubt: 'The world of 1947 is far from knowing peace through the application of law which still remains the ideal of the readers of this review.'[12] As to the second question, Rousseau wrote that it was difficult to know whether pacifist action would have any effect in 1947. There were a number of reasons for this. First there was the dullness of public opinion, which was partially explicable by the mediocrity of the French press, which was in turn the result of the low level to which internal French politics had sunk since 1945.[13] But, in an interesting departure for the usually rather conservative APD, Rousseau went further and argued that 'in order to be useful, pacifist action will have to abandon the conformism which before 1939 rendered it largely a supporter of the then existing international institutions, that is to say above all of the League of Nations. It is today intellectually, morally, and juridically impossible for a constructive pacifist propaganda to defend the Charter of the United Nations in its present form. One of the first objectives of any pacifist campaign will have to be the abolition of the absurd and nefarious right of veto.' Rousseau was not at all certain that French public opinion was up to the fight. It had been broken by four years of occupation, by the lies of Vichy, deceived by the succession of governments since the Liberation, demoralized by the incoherence of an omnipotent bureaucracy, and abandoned by a press that was careless of its duty to provide objective information. He concluded that his statements could well appear disillusioned, but given the state of the world, Rousseau wrote that it would be highly inappropriate to abandon oneself to the idea of reconstructing reality to suit one's dreams. No, French pacifism would have to show courage and realism. 'Only on this condition will it be given the opportunity to answer the hopes of those who do not resign themselves to live in a world barely less acceptable than that of yesterday.'[14]

The final statutory annual general meeting of the APD took place at the Reid Hall in Paris on 8 February 1948 and was, all things considered, a rather tired affair. Ruyssen, Jules Prudhommeaux (the association's secretary-general), and Mme Marie-Louise Puech (vice-president) all either announced their immediate resignation or gave notice of their intention to resign. It was hoped that new, young hands would be found to take up the work of the APD, but the association was able to struggle on only until the end of 1948, after which it disappeared without a trace.

The Legacy of Vichy

The Second World War undoubtedly had a momentous impact on the peace movement in France, particularly on that section of pacifism that called itself 'integral' or absolute. In a speech delivered on 3 January 1947 to the central London Peace Pledge Union, Gérard Vidal noted that from the outset of the war, French pacifist newspapers such as *Le Barrage* and *La Patrie humaine* had ceased to be published. Instead, according to Vidal, 'from the beginning of the war, the press had given credence to the idea that pacifists were part of a fifth column, and public opinion immediately believed it.'[15] During the Nazi occupation of France the German authorities were quite indulgent towards the pacifists, according to Vidal. This was likely the origin of the commonly held idea that pacifists could be equated with collaborators. 'Certainly there were collaborators,' he wrote, 'but these were above all within the parties which supported pre-war patriotism (the Action Française, PSF, PPF, and so on) ... All of this shows that pacifism is not well-regarded in France, and this is above all the fault of our new super-patriots, the Communists.'[16]

Despite Vidal's comments, it would seem possible to suggest that there *was* a connection between some representatives of interwar *pacifisme nouveau style* and the collaborationism of the Vichy years. René

Gerin, Félicien Challaye, and Léon Emery, to name but three examples, were all tried for collaboration after the war. Gerin died in 1957 still protesting his innocence.[17] The first number of Marcel Déat's newspaper *Germinal* (published in Paris from April to August 1944) contains articles by a constellation of former contributors to *Le Barrage* (the organ of the Ligue internationale des combattants de la paix) and *La Patrie humaine*.[18]

In this case of Challaye, it seems clear that the man's visceral hatred of war had clouded his moral judgment by the time Vichy was a political fact. In a preface dated December 1941 to a book by Raoul-Albert Bodinier of the Ligue scolaire internationale de la paix, Challaye called for 'grateful recognition' to Pétain who had 'saved the country in imposing the armistice' and who had had 'the courage to go to Montoire.' Furthermore, he wrote that the politicians and journalists responsible for 'pushing' France into war, ought to be sentenced to prison terms or have their civic rights removed 'for at least ten years.' In a terrible misapprehension of the nature of Nazism, Challaye proclaimed the 'duty to COLLABORATE with Germany, to hasten the return of our dear prisoners, to save our people, first from extreme misery, but also from political annihilation, and finally, to hasten the advent of a reconciled Europe and world.'[19]

The accusations of collaborationism did not sit well with French pacifists. In another postwar speech to a meeting of the War Resisters' International (WRI) held in Cambridge, England, Gérard Vidal defended both Gerin and Challaye, saying that 'this is the point we have reached in France, where we are accused of being "collaborators," despite the fact that the patriotic-communist furore is diminishing little by little.'[20]

Perhaps because of this ambiguous position *vis-à-vis* Vichy, not much seems to have happened in the five years immediately following the end of the war. Or, rather, not much seems to have happened in the camp of the former integral pacifism of the interwar years, not much seems to have happened in the independent, non-Soviet peace movement in France. In his 1946 speech to the WRI Vidal had explained that in France 'we can hardly hope, for the moment at least, to win the masses to our ideas, especially since the communists have become patriotic fanatics – and we have many communists.'[21] Instead, Vidal said that French pacifism would have to content itself in the short term with the maintenance of the small groups that did exist. The important presence of the French Communist party in the French war and peace debate was thus undoubtedly a deforming influence for pacifists, like Vidal, who insisted on the non-political nature of their pacifism.[22]

In 1949 the French Communist party (PCF), in conjunction with communist parties elsewhere, organized a massive peace congress and rally in Paris. It seems clear that the PCF was trying to lay claim to a pre-eminent place in French pacifism. It was with this as a backdrop that Emile Bauchet, the former secretary-general of the Ligue internationale des combattants de la paix, emerged from self-imposed silence at the end of 1950 and began publication of *La Voie de la paix*, creating at the same time the Comité national de résistance à la guerre et à l'oppression (otherwise known as the CNRGO), and shortly thereafter the Comité d'action pour un référendum.[23]

La Voie de la paix attacked the communist notion of pacifism in its February 1951 number, writing that 'contrary to so many imposters, we, here, want to *serve* peace and not merely to *use* it.' The writer (almost certainly Bauchet) attacked those who used the pacifist platform only to gain electoral support: 'Others are pacifists in fits and stars: pacifists to the bitter end until 1935 [year of the Laval-Stalin Pact], then *bellicistes* to the bitter end until 1939. Once again pacifists from 1939 to 1941, and then war-mongers from 1941 to 1945, they still dare to proclaim themselves pacifists today, while waiting for another opportunity to perform a new pirouette.'[24] Later that same year, Bauchet defined the pacifism of *La Voie de la paix* in terms not a little reminiscent of the LICP in the thirties: 'our position [he wrote] is that the fight for the freedom and security of the peoples, for liberty and resistance to oppression must be envisaged as much on the individual as on the national level, and by any and all means – non-violence, or violence if non-violence is impotent – everything except a war of nation against nation.'[25] There are strong echoes here of Victor Méric's editorials in *La Patrie humaine* in the early thirties, and especially of Félicien Challaye's definition of pacifism in his essay *Pour la Paix désarmée, même en face de Hitler*, published in 1933.[26]

Challaye himself returned to this theme in an article published in November 1951 in which he analysed the notion that war could provide protection. He defined his pacifism as far from strictly non-violent and wrote that, while happy to cooperate with Tolstoyans, he did not share their moral conception of the fight against war. 'We fully accept that the individual should defend himself, should defend his life and his freedom, should defend his own, by force.'[27] But he argued that it was an 'old sophism,' nurtured by governments and by the pedagogues in their pay, to confuse legitimate individual or familial defence with the so-called national defence. Legitimate individual defence had as its goal the 'saving of several precious existences,' while the national defence had as its inevitable result the 'destruction of innumerable precious existences.' It was this 'radical and essential difference' that was at the base of Challaye's pacifism. Moreover, he noted (again in a reprise of a theme from the early thirties) the means of destruction had made war untenable, unthinkable. War had changed from an essentially two-dimensional exercise into a three-dimensional one with the advent of air power, and thus 'no front, no matter how courageously defended, can be held against an onslaught of airborne troops, no front can prevent enemy airplanes from dropping incendiary or atomic bombs on our homes.'[28] According to Bauchet, the conclusion that had to be drawn from such a line of reasoning was that 'all peoples are victims of this abominable war propaganda,' and so, together with Alain and La Fontaine, pacifists would say, 'Power, that is the enemy' and 'Our enemy is our master.'[29]

In March 1951 Challaye described the different pacifist currents of the day. First of all there were the so-called Combattants de la paix, or the Partisans de la paix, who had stolen the old name of the pre-war LICP. But Challaye could not believe in the sincerity of what he called these 'communists or crypto-communists,' nor in the sincerity of their Soviet *inspirateurs*. Having said that, Challaye wrote that he was thankful in a certain way to the militants of the Partisans de la paix because they, too, condemned the Atlantic alliance. But here the community of interest ended. He admitted that both groups condemned the production and use of atomic weapons, but he noted acerbically that the communists did so only because the Soviet Union did not yet possess a great number of such weapons. *La Voie de la paix* condemned *all* weapons, including atomic weapons, something which 'the so-called Partisans de la paix' never did.[30]

Like *La Voie de la paix*, the Partisans de la paix were opposed to the rearmament of Germany, but for reasons that were the precise opposite. Challaye wrote that the communists appealed to the basest hatred for the German people, representing it as the perpetual aggressor and 'forgetting that in 1870 and in 1939 it was France which had declared war on Germany, and that in 1914 the war emerged from an intrigue woven by the *revanchard* Poincaré and the tsarist leaders.'[31] The CNRGO was opposed to German rearmament because it would make Germany the target for a future war. The German people, according to Challaye, wanted none of it. The great lie of the Partisans de la paix was to present the Soviet Union as a rampart of peace – and it was in this affirmation, according to Challaye, that their hypocrisy was most manifest. 'We denounce this lie,' he wrote: 'It is no pacifist state that by military force and against all international law, has chased or is chasing a good ten million Germans from the territories inhabited by their ancestors. It is no pacifist state which by the force of its arms has subjected to its imperialism, and colonised, a part of Europe. It is no pacifist state which does not cease to utilise the presence or the threat of its red army to serve the ends of its own policies. The peace of the murderers of the red army is not our peace.'[32]

In terms of pacifist methods, little seemed to have changed in the immediate postwar era. There was a recognition that whatever pacifist action was undertaken, it needed to be at a global level. The peoples needed to signify to their governments that they wanted nothing whatsoever to do with a future war. The way to achieve this was through a referendum on a global scale, which Bauchet wrote did not preclude that it be at the national level first. *La Voie de la paix* was composed of integral pacifists who approved of any sincere action against war. There were numerous approaches to a practical pacifism, but none that promised to be able to galvanize public and pacifist opinion. 'From conscientious objection to the social revolution, there are numerous means envisaged by one or by the other, all of which have a certain value which we will not dispute, but which cannot at present be practically efficacious.'[33] Bauchet proposed instead a concerted effort by all pacifist groups around the idea of a referendum rejecting war in all cases. 'This means of giving a voice to the peoples is both legal and democratic; it is based on the notion of popular sovereignty.'[34] And so, from the CNRGO was also born the Comité national pour un référendum.

In fact, the call for a mandatory referendum was only one part of the CNRGO's program. The other two planks were a call for some form of world government (*mondialisme*), and disarmament, if need be unilaterally.

The attack on the communist view of peace was an integral part of the CNRGO's pacifism. In June 1951, for example, *La Voie de la paix* attacked the communist approach to peace and pacifism in the recent French election campaign: 'Only the Communists declared themselves fiercely in favour of peace, but their pacifism is merely circumstantial and occasional. It is neither honest, nor sincere. During the elections, the French communists demonstrated – as during the Resistance – that they were nothing but Russian *francs-tireurs* speculating either on war or on peace according to the needs of the Russian cause. One cannot have confidence in such a pacifism which hoaxes the credulous masses. Their patriotism of yesterday is to be denounced as firmly as their pacifism of today. For us, pacifism is internationalist and could never be a means of manipulating public opinion to the advantage of a state.'[35]

In more general terms, Robert Jospin (father of Lionel Jospin, sometime secretary-general of the French Socialist party) wrote in September 1951 about the choices facing France and French pacifists. Two options were possible: to take a position, or to remain neutral. To come out for one camp or the other in the East-West debate was to accept the possibility of war, perhaps even to increase its likelihood. Neutrality was the other option, and it brought with it two possibilities as well. Neutrality could be either armed or disarmed. The idea of an armed neutrality for Europe presupposed that there existed a unified Europe with a common will, but as Jospin wrote, 'One has only to refer to the work of the Strasburg Assembly, or to measure the traditional resistance of England, to realise that there is no such thing as Europe. At least for the moment.'[36] The other flaw in the argument for an armed neutrality was the mistaken belief that France or Europe would be able to defend itself in the event of an attack by either the Soviet Union or the United States. Economically and militarily Europe would never be strong enough.

Instead, Jospin made the case for disarmed neutrality and unilateral disarmament. If, despite all of France's efforts to remain outside the fray, she were invaded and occupied by a foreign power, at least according to Jospin she would have saved the tremendous cost of a defence program that could have no hope of success anyway. And in his view, disarmed neutrality would put France in a better position morally *vis-à-vis* the conqueror. He asked whether this plan had any chance of success and had to admit frankly that he doubted that it did. The reason was the presence of the communists in France; comparing the French situation to that of Britain, he wrote,

This neutrality might be respected if we were talking about a country like England where the Communist party has neither the manpower, nor sufficient leadership. Let us not forget that we are in France ... the temptation would be very great to try the 'great experiment,' the experiment that only the presence of American troops aborted at the Liberation ...

The Communists will try again – they cannot *not* take this chance offered by History – aided by the Red Army ... We shall therefore first of all be occupied by the Russians, and then bombed by the American liberators ... France must take up again its role of mediator. She must become the hyphen (*trait d'union*) between East and West. Her geographic position, as much as her past, have defined her mission.[37]

And he concluded that France needed twenty years of peace.

Europe as a whole was caught in a dangerous vice between East and West, between the two big power blocs that faced one another across the northern hemisphere. Jospin believed that in throwing its lot in with the Americans, 'Europe has signed its death warrant. It will become the scene of the great battle. The dispute will be resolved on our doorsteps. At our expense.'[38] Jospin saw the annihilation of Europe as the inevitable first stage in this coming conflict of superpowers: 'the neutralisation of Europe by annihilation will constitute the first phase of the conflict.' So, the choice for Europe was between this neutralization and what he called 'neutralism': 'May Europe become a rigorously independent entity (something it no longer is), may it manifest its united and formal desire for peace, may it address a manifesto to the world announcing that its lands will serve as ossuary to neither side, and all might yet be saved. This must be the policy which we defend. In denying support to both America and Russia, and in saving itself, Europe runs the magnificent risk of saving the Peace of the world.[39]

The 1951 congress of the CNRGO was notable for its lack of success.[40] In 1952 things were apparently much different. *La Voie de la paix* reported that there were some five hundred people from eighteen different nations either present or represented when the two-day conference opened 1 November.[41] The final charter was a recitation of every issue dear to the hearts of French pacifists: everything from the outlawry of war, to a mandatory referendum to be held before any declaration of war, to demands for total, universal and, if need be, unilateral disarmament, denunciation of the notion of collective security as long as nations retained the right to maintain armies, a demand for the free movement of merchandise, ideas, and people, a clause contesting the legitimacy of the United Nations, a demand for an end to colonialism, and for a rational policy regarding natality (a subject of great importance in the French mind).[42]

Korea

The Korean War provided the first real test of the pacifist convictions of *La Voie de la paix* and of the CNRGO. Challaye drew a direct lesson for France from the events in Korea. He had been particularly incensed in reading a line from a United Press report reproduced in *Le Monde* of 10 January 1951. Without the slightest intention of irony, the American correspondent had written that 'Korea has become a sort of symbol for what the world organisation [the United Nations] can do for a friendly country.'[43] Challaye concluded,

The present situation in Korea is the greatest masterpiece of what is so appropriately called collective security. Let us appreciate from this example what the 'World Organisation' can provide us in terms of security as individuals grouped in a collectivity.

We in France are, just like Korea, a friendly country of this 'World Organisation,' and especially of the United States which dominates and manipulates it at will. If we arm and over-arm ourselves in order to remain members in good standing of the U.N., then the Americans have had the good grace to promise us the same help as that given to that other friendly nation, Korea. Their airmen have already shown us in the last war what they are capable of – at Rouen, Caen, Saint Lo. Now they are ready to do even more. What a magnificent scorched earth will stretch from Cherbourg to Marseille!

Forgive us if we prefer integral disarmament and political neutrality to the Korean solution of U.N. intervention.[44]

This ostrich-like approach to world politics was not new in Challaye; he and the other representatives of *pacifisme nouveau style* had been preaching the politics of denial since the early thirties. They hoped that simply by refusing to get involved in the international crises of the day, these problems would somehow pass France by. And if, against all odds, France were attacked and occupied, Challaye wrote that a foreign occupation would be less damaging than participation in a war; 'the occupying power, whoever he might be, would treat an innocent victim less badly than a vanquished adversary.'[45] Having said all that, Challaye had to admit that in the present state of the world, he would much prefer to see a loved one in Boston or London, rather than Moscow or Prague, but conversely he would prefer Moscow or Prague infinitely more than the 'smoking ruins' of Seoul.

Conclusion

It is instructive to note the extent to which some of the old pre–Second World War theses of what I have called *pacifisme ancien style* were wedded in the postwar period to the ideas of the new-style, dissenting pacifism. *La Voie de la paix* proclaimed the trilogy of 'Referendum–World Government-Disamament' as its goal in 1951.[46] In an article in which Bauchet mentioned that *La Voie de la paix* was written and led by women and men who had been the prime movers behind the LICP from 1930–9, he also described the group's goals in terms not a little reminiscent of the APD's interwar program: 'We want the union of all the peoples, disarmed and in a world confederation, we want a code of real justice which will resolve pacifically conflicts between states, if need be with the help of an international police force recognised by all.'[47] Admittedly, Bauchet's insistence on unilateral disarmament put him at odds with the former pacifism of the APD, but he came close in his emphasis on world government, the codification of international law, and the creation of an international police force, to some of the theses of the interwar APD. Having said that, there can be no doubt as to the continuing dissenting stance of Bauchet and his ilk; Bauchet was careful to underline that he condemned the defunct League of Nations as well as its successor, the United Nations, as organs of the victorious states that made a mockery of the real justice to which the peoples of the earth aspired.

It would seem possible to suggest in conclusion that the post – Second World War French peace movement has been substantially weakened by a number of factors. First must undoubtedly be the effects of the German occupation during the war, an occupation which presented French pacifism with some very difficult choices, not all of which were resolved in an honourable fashion. Second, there is the thorny question of the continued presence of the French Communist party in the war and peace debate. And finally, there is the ongoing balkanization of the French peace movement into antagonistic parts, each representing a slightly different constituency.

Notes

1 Karl Holl, 'Pazifismus in Frankreich, 1919–1939: Dauerhaft diskreditiert. Die Irrtümer der französischen Friedensbewegung – damals,' *Die Zeit*, 8 Feb. 1991, 38. See also my book, *The Politics of Dissent: Pacifism in France, 1919–1939* (Oxford: 1991). I have discussed aspects of the pacifist experience in the Second World War in 'Pacifism and the Liberation' in Roderick Kedward and Nancy Wood (eds.), *The Liberation of France: Image and Event* (Oxford, 1995).

2 Jean Defrasne, *Le Pacifisme*, Collection 'Que sais-je?' (Paris, 1983), 3.

3 Ibid., 111.

4 Fernand Gouttenoire de Toury, 'Un Pacifiste devant les urnes,' *Les Cahiers du Pacifisme* 1 (May 1946), 1. This was the official publication of the Ligue d'action pacifiste et social, Section française de l'Internationale des Résistants à la guerre.

5 Ibid.

6 Ibid.

7 Ibid.

8 Fernand Gouttenoire de Toury, 'Nécessité du rapprochement franco-alle-mand,' *Les Cahiers du pacifisme*, 12 (March 198), 1. Nos. 3–11 of the collection I consulted in the Bibliothèque de documentation internationale contempo-raine at Nanterre seem to be missing.

9 Théodore Ruyssen, 'La Paix par le Droit rentre en scène,' *La Paix par le Droit* (hereinafter cited as *PD*) 51/1 (Oct. 1947), 1–2.

10 Ibid., 2. On the 1938 Fiftieth Anniversary Congress, see 'Le Cinquantenaire de l'Association: A nos amis,' *PD* 47/8–9 (Aug.-Sept. 1937), 297–8; and Théodore Ruyssen, 'Presant appel aux membres de l'Association et aux lect-eurs de la Revue,' *PD* 47/11–12 (Nov.–Dec. 1937), 385–6; and Jules Prudhom-meaux and J. Lahargue, 'L'Assemblée générale et le Congrès du cinquantenaire, Nîmes, 19–21 avril 1938,' *PD* 48/6–8 (May-June-July 1938), 209–99.

11 Ibid.

12 Charles Rousseau, 'L'après-guerre ou la pré-guerre?,' *PD* 51/1 (Oct. 1947), 14.

13 Ibid., 16.

14 Ibid., 17.

15 Gérard Vidal, 'France and Pacifism,' 1 (text of a speech delivered mainly in French to the central London PPU on 3 Jan. 1947), in archives of the War Resisters' International, International Institute for Social History, Amsterdam (hereafter cited as WRI Archives). These papers were consulted when they were still stored in the Chelsea garage of the late Myrtle Solomon, Chairper-son of the War Resisters' International.

16 Ibid., 2.

17 See René Gerin, *Un procès de la libération ... La justice enferrée* (Paris, 1954). There are a number of letters from Michel Alexandre in Bibliothèque de documentation internationale contemporaine (BDIC) Dossiers Alexandre/ FΔRés. 348 attesting to the character and probity of both Emery and Chal-laye.

18 *Germinal*, 1 (28 April 1944) contains articles by Marcelle Capy and Félicien Challaye, both former presidents of the LICP, as well as articles by Claude Jamet (a former member of the LICP's Comité directeur), Maurice Rostand, Gérard de Lacaze-Duthiers, Pierre Hamp, etc.

19 See Félicien Challaye, Préface in Raoul-Albert Bodinier, *Vérités d'Avant-Paix* (Paris, n.d. [1942]), 18–19. The emphasis is Challaye's.

20 'Discours de Gérard Vidal (France) à la Conférence Préparatoire WRI Cam-bridge, 30 décembre 1946,' 4, in WRI Archives.

21 Ibid., 3.
22 Ibid. Vidal had said in his speech, for example, that 'les pacifistes, en général, ne s'intéressent pas à la politique et je crois que c'est bien ainsi.'
23 The first number of *La Voie de la paix* was called *La Voie nouvelle*, but this title had to be dropped because another regional newspaper in France was already using it.
24 'Sans ambiguité!,' *La Voie de la paix* 2 (Feb. 1951), 1.
25 Émile Bauchet, 'Vers un Front mondial des toutes les forces libres de la paix,' *La Voie de la paix* 7 (Sept. 1951), 1.
26 Félicien Challaye, *Pour la paix désarmée, même en face de Hitler* (Le Vésinet, n.d. [1933]). See also Ingram, *Politics of Dissent*, 182, and also 69–78 for a discussion of the antecedents of Challaye's essay.
27 Félicien Challaye, 'La Protection par la guerre,' *La Voie de la paix* 9 (Nov. 1951), 1.
28 Ibid.
29 E. Bauchet, 'Vers un front mondial.'
30 Félicien Challaye, 'Courants pacifistes,' *La Voie de la paix* 3 (March 1951), 1–2.
31 Ibid.
32 Ibid.
33 Emile Bauchet, 'Peut-on empêcher une 3ème guerre mondiale?,' *La Voie de la paix* 3 (March 1951), 1.
34 Ibid.
35 La Voie de la paix, 'Après les élections,' *La Voie de la paix* 6 (June 1951), 1.
36. Robert Jospin, 'Faisons le point,' *La Voie de la paix* 7 (Sept. 1951), 3.
37 Ibid. Cf. Régis Messac's comments about how France must become the *trait d'union* between Nazi Germany and the Anglo-Saxon nations in 1939 in Régis Messac, 'Pour un esprit civique européen,' *Le Barrage* 147 (20 April 1939), 1. See also Ingram, *Politics of Dissent*, ch. 9 ('Munich and all that').
38 Robert Jospin, 'Neutralisation ou neutralisme?,' *La Voie de la paix* 2 (Feb. 1951), 1. See also the instructive articles by Jean-Baptiste Duroselle, 'Les précédents historiques: pacifisme des années 30 et neutralisme des années 50,' in Pierre Lelouche (ed.), *Pacifisme et dissuasion* (Paris, 1983), 241–52; and Maurice Vaïsse, 'Le Passé insupportable: les pacifismes, 1984, 1938, 1914,' in *Vingtième Siècle* 3 (July 1984), 27–39.
39 Ibid.
40 Emile Bauchet, 'Premiers pas,' *La Voie de la paix* 9 (Nov. 1951), 1–2.
41 La Voie de la paix, 'Magnifique succès du Rassemblement Universel de la Toussaint,' *La Voie de la paix* 18 (Nov. 1952), 1. According to this report there were some 250 people *actually* present at the congress.

42 'Charte finale,' *La Voie de la paix* 18 (Nov. 1952), 1. For a more detailed discussion of the points raised by the charter, see 2–3 of this number of *La Voie de la paix*.

43 Cited in Félicien Challaye, 'Corée et désarmement général,' *La Voie de la paix* 2 (Feb. 1951), 1–2.

44 Ibid.

45 Ibid.

46 *La Voie de la paix* 4 (April 1951), 1.

47 Emile Bauchet, 'Qui sommes-nous? Que voulons-nous?,' *La Voie de la paix* 4 (April 1951), 1.

23

The Dilemma of Canadian Pacifists during the Early Cold War Years

THOMAS P. SOCKNAT

Following the Second World War, Canadian pacifists faced in inescapable dilemma. On the one hand, their optimistic hope for the postwar world was shattered by the threat of atomic weapons and, most particularly, by fear of a Third World War between the United States and the Soviet Union. Under such circumstances the moral relevance of pacifism was seriously questioned. On the other hand, as they attempted to face reality and to help avert atomic warfare, their support for efforts to ease East-West tensions and to promote disarmament made them extremely vulnerable to Cold War red-baiting, with a resulting loss of credibility.[1] By the early 1950s, therefore, the peace movement was in disarray and pacifists were in retreat, having been forced to defend their beliefs, their sincerity, and their loyalty. They generally remained disorganized until late in the decade, when they refocused their attention and that of the Canadian public on the single issue of nuclear disarmament.

The 1945 peace movement in Canada bore little resemblance to its pre-war predecessor. The peace campaign that gained momentum through the interwar years had mushroomed by the mid-1930s into a broad alliance of groups and individuals scattered across the country but united in the cause of disarmament. The peace movement was further strengthened by the fact that a new political party, the Cooperative Commonwealth Federation (CCF) was headed by Canada's leading pacifist, J.S. Woodsworth, and endorsed a neutralist foreign policy. As it successfully staged public demonstrations, conferences, rallies, and torchlight parades, the peace movement continued to widen its base of support.[2] It was at this time, for instance, that pacifists first began to cooperate with Canadian communists organized through the Canadian

League against War and Fascism (later the League for Peace and Democracy), a communist front organization.

By the late thirties, however, the fortunes of the peace movement began to change. The Spanish Civil War, in particular, took a heavy toll, since it triggered a crisis of conscience that caused many peace activists to abandon their commitment to non-violence for the fight against fascism. Such defections, which continued into the Second World War, had devastating consequences for the peace movement.

After a heated debate at the beginning of the war in September 1939 the CCF reversed its traditional neutralist policy. So did the Canadian branch of the Women's International League for Peace and Freedom (WILPF). Although it still condemned Canada and Britain for not properly supporting the League of Nations and for helping to arm Germany 'right up to the eleventh hour,' the WILPF executive explained that it could not be indifferent to the war's outcome, since the democratic rights of common people appeared to hang in the balance.[3] Laura Jamieson, a WILPF activist in Vancouver, urged Canadian women to continue working for a peaceful, just world by cooperating in international relief schemes and by defending the rights of free speech and assembly at home.[4]

Despite the continued work of such groups as the WILPF, for all practical purposes the wartime peace movement was reduced to a small core of Christian pacifists organized through the Fellowship of Reconciliation (FOR). Carlyle King, the outgoing FOR chairman from Saskatoon, urged fellow pacifists to become islands of sanity 'in the midst of surrounding chaos.' Although there was little they could do 'in a public way' with the War Measures Act in force, he suggested they could still promote human understanding and goodwill by minimizing atrocity stories and checking the harsh treatment of aliens in their communities.[5]

The most dramatic anti-war protest came in October 1939 with the publication of a pacifist manifesto signed by over seventy-five United Church ministers.[6] Some of the ministers, such as Lavell Smith and James Finlay, helped make the FOR a dynamic peace group in Canada and launched the first Canadian pacifist magazine, *Reconciliation*. Although pacifist activities were limited by official wartime constraints, pacifists did manage to organize support for international relief projects, offer assistance to refugees, and spearhead the defence of civil liberties and the individual conscience.

This type of civil libertarian and humanitarian work, a comfortable and socially acceptable alternative for pacifists during wartime, continued to monopolize their attention well into the postwar years. Although they recognized the threat posed by the atomic bombing of Hiroshima and Nagasaki, Canadian pacifists were slow and almost reluctant to face and atomic issue. Rather, they agreed with FOR spokesman Lavell Smith that the first duty of pacifists was to respond to pressing postwar social problems.[7]

Canadian Quakers immediately launched a massive drive for refugee relief with the full support of the pacifist community.[8] The Canadian Friends Service Committee purchased the supplies, such as cod liver oil, powdered milk, medical articles, blankets, and clothing, and shipped them directly to the needy areas of the Far East and Central Europe. There the American Friends Service Committee organized relief teams that included Canadian volunteers.[9] For instance, Barbara Walker served in Germany and Paul Zavitz worked in Poland along with a future Canadian, Peter Brock. In Canada the Friends Relief Fund raised over fifty thousand dollars and became part of a postwar network of relief agencies such as the Canadian Save the Children Fund and the Canadian Church Relief Abroad.[10]

The FOR also tried to heighten public awareness of social problems at home. James Finlay, the postwar FOR chairman, headed the campaign organized through the Canadian Cooperative Committee on Japanese Canadians to assist Japanese Canadians relocated during the war and to prevent their proposed deportation.[11] Special issues of the FOR journal, *Reconciliation*, were devoted to the Japanese Canadian question as well as to such issues as racial discrimination and industrial disputes. A race relations institute was held in Toronto in May 1947, and the FOR also sponsored concerts by Bayard Rustin, the black American singer and fieldwork secretary of the American FOR, and Rosa Page Welch, the black American mezzo-soprano.[12] It also sponsored addresses by a number of internationally known pacifists including A.J. Muste, H.H. Farmer, Vera Brittain, A.D. Belden, E. Stanley Jones, and James M. Swomley.

Despite such an impressive roster of speakers, by 1947 the FOR and the entire Canadian peace movement was in trouble. The movement was plagued by a lack of financial resources, a dwindling membership, and general public apathy. The previous summer, Scott Nearing, the American anti-war radical, had recognized the crisis and blamed it on the failure of Canadian pacifists and anti-war socialists to attract young converts. Few of those who came to meetings were under forty, and most were over sixty. 'They are the stalwarts who learned to hold the torch on high before World War I,' he wrote, but since then they had gained few adherents, while death and disaffection had decimated their ranks. 'It is a rebel remnant, still rebellious, but thinning out with the years.'[13] The future of pacifism in Canada looked bleak. As a last resort, James Finlay, FOR chairman, appealed to the American chapter for financial help, but it was not forthcoming.[14] John Nevin Sayre replied that Canada was considered a 'financially-arid country' for pacifist fund-raising.[15]

One of the first casualties of the financial crisis was the FOR publication, *Reconciliation*. It was already appearing less and less frequently, but by October 1947 the national journal was forced to suspend its publication permanently.[16] In its place Canadian subscribers would receive the American journal, *Fellowship*, and perhaps come under increased American influence.

Obviously, the appeal of the FOR was in decline, a fact that was even noticeable in its last major campaign, the familiar struggle against cadet training in schools. During the interwar years the movement against the cadet corps had actually succeeded in abolishing the programs in various school systems throughout the country. Although cadet training was again compulsory during the war, by 1947 it was either placed on a voluntary basis or eliminated from school programs altogether in most provinces. The glaring exception was Ontario, where cadet training remained compulsory with the full support of Ontario Premier George Drew.[17] The FOR launched an all-out campaign to disband the Ontario cadet corps, labelling it 'Mr Drew's army.' The FOR revealed that the Drew government required all boys in the province's high schools to devote the majority of their physical and health education periods to military drill. When the government defended the cadet system as valuable training in 'good citizenship,' the pacifist critic Abe Watson replied that 'it was not possible to train boys in democratic citizenship, by compelling them to submit to the authority of a military system.'[18] Instead of recruiting an army of boys, Drew was challenged to support alternative measures that would help achieve lasting peace in the world, such as the improvement of race relations, decent labour legislation, and improved social services.

In an angry reaction, Premier Drew charged that the Fellowship of Reconciliation was a 'crypto false front communist organization.' Pacifists expected as much from Drew, but they were surprised and disappointed when they were criticized by their former liberal ally, B.K. Sandwell, the editor of *Saturday Night*. In an editorial entitled, 'Pacifism

Again' Sandwell accused the FOR of being inconsistent in supporting Canada's role in the United Nations, which involved the supplying of military forces, on the one hand, while advocating the under-mining of Canadian preparedness on the other.[19] While he agreed that a good argument could be made for the exemption of students from compulsory cadet training for reasons of conscience, Sandwell did not share the logical conclusion of the pacifist line of thinking – the complete disarmament of Canada. Considering the inconsistency in the FOR's position he also wondered if pacifists really desired that end, implying that perhaps they wanted 'to be defended while doing nothing for defence.'

It was a stinging accusation that pacifists found difficult to refute because it exposed the ambiguity of their arguments. It also exposed pacifist vulnerability, for the responses of Sandwell and especially of Drew were indicative of the Cold War, anti-communist mentality taking root in Canadian society. FOR pacifists recognized the dangers of a possible war between the democratic West and the communist East but they failed to confront its political ramifications. It was not that the FOR was politically naive but, as one of the last major vestiges of a liberal Christian pacifism founded upon faith in a divine force working on its behalf, FOR pacifists believed that in time religious pacifism would lead to a peaceful and just social order. By 1948, however, their organization was in decline, their journal had folded, and their dynamic general secretary, Abe Watson, had resigned to take up a new position with the American FOR. They could no longer ignore the fact that the threat of atomic warfare, heightened by East-West tensions, had undermined the social hopes of liberal pacifism.

One side of the pacifist dilemma was clearly exposed as early as 1946 in a *Reconciliation* article by J.J. Brown, the director of the Canadian Association of Physicists.[20] Before Hiroshima, he argued, pacifists might not have expected to see much change in the common attitude towards war in their lifetime, but they still believed their efforts would ultimately reach fruition. After 1945, however, liberal pacifism and its efforts to mould public opinion and build model communities were irrelevant, since the world had run out of time. Brown concluded that pacifism and its corollary, pacifist social action, were in need of an urgent and 'thorough overhauling.' Carlyle King, the first national chairman of the FOR in Canada, agreed that the pacifism of the FOR was simply outmoded by the realities of the atomic age, but no Canadian pacifist took on the task of rethinking or redefining religious pacifism. Instead, pacifists were conveniently diverted by the campaign to halt the atomic arms race and to promote understanding and friendship between Canada and the Soviet Union.

Other than the escalation of Cold War tensions in 1948, the stimulus for revitalizing and redirecting the energies of Canadian pacifists was an appeal made by Harry Ward, professor emeritus of Christian Ethics at Union Theological Seminary in New York City.[21] On his way home from his Ontario summer cottage in October of that year, Ward stopped in Toronto to address an FOR gathering that included James Finlay, I.G. Perkins of Donlands United Church, his former student Lavell Smith, and his old friend A.A. MacLeod, business editor of the radical Christian journal *The World Tomorrow* in the 1920s and communist head of the Canadian League for Peace and Democracy before the war. Ward told his audience that there was a dangerous war psychosis in the West and, after reviewing the origins of the Cold War, he warned that United States President Truman was determined, especially after the recent Berlin blockade, to mobilize the Western world to destroy the Soviet Union, if need be with atomic weapons.[22] Ward therefore urged his fellow pacifists to do something to prevent this folly.

The Toronto group was stirred to action by Ward's address and immediately established a provisional committee to launch a new national movement and to find a politically seasoned, dynamic speaker as its head. The committee's choice of James G. Endicott to organize a wider peace movement was not without risk, since he was already *persona non grata* in the United Church and in government circles because of his outspoken support for the Chinese communists while a United Church missionary in China. As a result of the controversy, Endicott had resigned from his missionary post and from the ministry. Could such a man generate public support for pacifism? Those pacifists desperately seeking a realistic response to the current world crisis genuinely hoped he could.

Although definitely not a pacifist, Endicott agreed to take on the task, and under his guidance a new politicized peace movement grew rapidly. A Vancouver Assembly for Peace was founded by Norman Mackenzie, president of the University of British Columbia, Harry H. Stevens, leader of the Reconstruction party during the 1930s, and Watson Thompson, an educator and promoter of cooperatives.[23] A similar peace council in Edmonton was founded and headed by George Hunter, a professor of biochemistry at the University of Alberta. As Endicott tried to form more local peace committees, leaders of Canada's Communist party, including Tim Buck and Leslie Morris, urged him to organize a broad coalition of all peace forces in the country.[24] Endicott was sympathetic to the idea, especially after attending the 1949 international gathering in Paris of the World Partisans of Peace (later called the World Peace Council), the Soviet-sponsored popular front for peace during the Cold War.[25]

Endicott returned to Canada just in time for a national conference of peace groups, as three hundred delegates from across the country gathered in Toronto's Bathurst Street United Church in May 1949. The historic conference launched a new national organization, the Canadian Peace Congress, with Endicott as chairman and Toronto CCFer Eva Sanderson as vice-chairman. Although it was not exactly clear at the time, the Canadian Peace Congress was also destined to be the Canadian branch of the World Peace Council. In his keynote address, however, Endicott emphasized the openness of the movement and his respect for the individual conscience. There was room for all, he claimed, who shared 'the simple conviction that disagreements between nations which threatened world peace should be settled through the United Nations.'[26] He assured Canadians that the purpose of the peace congress was neither to defend nor to attack the foreign policy of the Soviet Union. 'If you are not planning war, he explained, 'you have no need to fear a peace movement! If you are planning and working for peace, there will be no need for military alliances and vast schemes of re-armament.'

There followed a remarkable explosion of public support for the peace movement. Through the year there were hundreds of meetings in towns and cities across Canada, including four packed meetings in Toronto's Massey Hall and a hugh rally of twelve thousand people at Maple Leaf Gardens.[27] By May 1950 the second national conference of the Canadian Peace Congress attracted over 1700 delegates.

Obviously, much of the credit for the amazing success of the Canadian Peace Congress belonged to Endicott himself, who was a skilful organizer and a forceful, charismatic speaker. Public interest in peace was also heightened by the visits to Canada in 1948 and 1950 by Dr Hewlett Johnson, the so-called Red Dean of Canterbury. An outspoken and controversial churchman, Johnson drew large crowds in Canada. Five thousand turned out in Winnipeg, while another 'five thousand were turned away from an overflow meeting of almost three thousand in Toronto's Massey Hall.'[28] Although Johnson was criticized and denounced in the press as a communist dupe, people greeted him warmly; 'crowds rubber-necked and besieged him for pictures and autographs.' He was a true celebrity, and at the close of his 1950 tour ten thousand people packed Maple Leaf Gardens to give him a standing ovation.[29]

Johnson, Endicott, and the peace movement in general gave expression to the fears of ordinary Canadians about the atom bomb and the possibility of war with the Soviet Union. It was also comforting to be told that common people had the power to prevent another war simply by saying no. As a result, a wide range of people were attracted to the movement. As the American consul in Montreal confirmed, Endicott's peace congress enjoyed 'a considerable amount of support from people in different walks of life.'[30]

During its first few years, the Canadian Peace Congress concentrated on mobilizing public opinion against atomic weapons and for increased understanding between the Soviet Union and the West. Both goals generally received widespread support from the pacifist community. The FOR, for instance, urged its members to help improve Canadian-Soviet relations and to help stop the atomic arms race.[31] Although the FOR itself refused to affiliate with the Canadian Peace Congress, individual FOR members lent their support to the Endicott campaign.[32] Within a year, the peace congress collected an astonishing 200,000 signatures on its 'ban-the-bomb' petition. The following year, as the colourful ban-the-bomb campaign continued with demonstrations, family peace picnics, rallies, and door-to-door canvassing, 300,000 Canadians signed the Stockholm Appeal, a simple statement demanding that atomic weapons be outlawed and that the first government to use them be condemned as war criminals.[33] Although the Stockholm Appeal was sponsored by the Soviets, many, probably most, of the Canadians who signed it did so because of their legitimate desire for peace, only later to discover they were in danger of being branded communists.[34]

As the politicized peace movement gained momentum, its critics became more vocal. Pacifism itself came to be labelled dangerous, subversive, and communist-inspired. The press in general dismissed peace activists as 'fellow travellers' or 'dupes' of the communists.[35] Many prominent Canadians, even M.J. Coldwell, leader of the CCF, claimed the ban-the-bomb petition was an instrument of Soviet policy and warned Canadians to stay clear of the peace movement. Although journalists Gerald Waring discovered that only nineteen of one hundred Canadian Peace Congress national council members were indeed communists, that was enough in the minds of many to brand the whole peace movement as a communist front.[36] Given Endicott's ties to the World Peace Council and his visit to Moscow in 1950, it was impossible to refute completely the communist connection. Still, some non-communist Canadians, including religious pacifists, saw no reason why they should not cooperate with communists in the cause of peace. For instance, over one hundred ministers representing several denominations signed the Stockholm Appeal in Canada. One of those, E. Crossley Hunter, pastor of Trinity United Church in Toronto, later explained: 'The Stockholm Appeal I carefully read and willingly signed. I see no reason why any Christian should not sign it.'[37]

Nevertheless, reinforced by McCarthyism in the United States, the anti-communist crusade in Canada began to take its toll in the peace movement. As early as 1949 Professor George Hunter, a Fellow of the Royal Society of Canada, was fired from his teaching post at the University of Alberta after making political comments critical of NATO in his classes. It was no accident, claimed his defenders, that he was also the founder of the Edmonton chapter of the Canadian-Soviet Friendship Association and the head of the local peace council.[38] Hunter's dismissal was a grim warning to activists of what was to come as they increasingly 'saw friends go to jail, or lose their jobs or place in the community because of red smears.'[39]

Amid the allegations of communist subversion and stern reprisals, Canadian pacifists seriously questioned Endicott's motives and the direction of the peace movement. Religious pacifists, in particular, criticized Endicott's inconsistency in working for peace while at the same time supporting revolutions of national liberation as in China. It was all too similar to the pacifist dilemma of the 1930s, when the pursuit of social justice came into conflict with the pacifist commitment to non-violence. The comparison was all the more vivid because much of the grass-roots support for the Canadian Peace Congress came from former members of the defunct, communist-inspired League for Peace and Democracy.

The disenchantment of the pacifist community became acute during the Korean War when Endicott politicized the peace movement even more with his attacks on United States foreign policy, both in public addresses and in his personal publication, the *Canadian Far Eastern Newsletter*.[40] As the war dragged on the Canadian Peace Congress and its chairman were continually accused of repeating the communist line. External Affairs Minister Lester Pearson denounced the congress as an 'agent of a foreign aggressive imperialism,' and the RCMP and secret police agents were used to further discredit the peace movement.[41] Meanwhile, Justice Minister Stuart Garson introduced changes into the Criminal Code of Canada making it a treasonable offence for a person to say or do anything that could be considered helpful to enemy forces.[42]

The public storm that had been building for some time finally erupted in the spring of 1952 following Endicott's visit to China. After touring the Chinese-Korean border, he made the startling charge that the Americans were using bacteriological warfare. Moreover, he claimed that the preparations for germ warfare were conducted in Canada at Suffield, Alberta. Consequently, cries of treason and sedition reverberated from Parliament, press, and pulpit.[43] Despite the emotional reaction, Endicott did make some important revelations, especially regarding the experiments at Suffield. By this time, however, most liberal and religious pacifists had already distanced themselves from the peace congress. Once Endicott accepted the Stalin Peace Prize in Moscow later that year he and the Canadian Peace Congress were almost totally discredited in the eyes of most Canadians. The peace coalition was shattered, and pacifists retreated to safer ground while the Canadian Peace Congress was reduced to a leftist fringe group.

Following their brief brush with Cold War politics, Canadian pacifists returned to their more familiar humanitarian work. They remained relatively silent and disorganized until the late 1950s, when again they joined together in the campaign for nuclear disarmament. By that time they were better prepared to conduct a politicized campaign, partly because of their experiences during the early Cold War years. They had learned, for instance, that pacifism, by its very nature as a form of dissent, was as much a political as a moral or religious belief. They also learned that in the nuclear age pacifism could attract a large number of supporters merely because of the 'survivalist' instinct in most people. Endicott had taught them how to draw a crowd, but it was up to pacifists to mobilize that support into political pressure in order to achieve their own goals. In short, pacifists were politicized by their experience. By the end of the decade, James Finlay, the postwar chairman of the Fellowship of Reconciliation in Canada, totally dismissed the argument for nuclear deterrence and endorsed Canada's withdrawal from NATO and NORAD as long as those military alliances relied on nuclear power.[44] A decade earlier he might have feared being branded a communist for making the same statement. On the one hand, therefore, the experience of the early Cold War years, as disappointing as it was, helped prepare Canadian pacifists for a more activist political role. On the other hand, it is also probable that the communist-backed Canadian Peace Congress and Endicott's various political antics not only discredited pacifism but actually thwarted the development of a respected, viable campaign for nuclear disarmament in Canada during the crucial years of the early 1950s.

Notes

1 Canadian peace promoters consistently denied the charge that the movement required its members to support Soviet policy. See James G. Endicott, *Canadian Far Eastern Newsletter*, no. 331 (July 1982).
2 Thomas P. Socknat, *Witness against War: Pacifism in Canada, 1900–1945* (Toronto, 1987), chs. 4 and 5.
3 Saskatchewan Archives Board, Saskatoon (SABS), Violet McNaughton Papers, Al.E95 (5), Statement of the WILPF Executive, Sept. 1939.
4 Ibid., Laura Jamieson, 'Women and the Present War,' n.d.
5 SABS, Carlyle King Papers, vol. 27 153, King to Mrs Corner, 21 Sept. 1939.
6 Socknat, *Witness against War*, ch. 7.
7 J. Lavell Smith, 'Whither the FOR?,' *Reconciliation* (Dec. 1945), 14.
8 Fred Haslam, *A Record of Experience with Canadian Friends and the Canadian Ecumenical Movement* (Toronto, 1970), 66.
9 'Minutes of the Canada and Genessee Yearly Meetings,' 1948, 20–1; Canadian Quaker Archives (CQA), Canadian Friends Service Committee Papers, War Victims Relief File, 'Canadian Friends and War Victims,' newspaper clipping.
10 *Reconciliation* (Sept. 1949), 2.
11 United Church Archives (UCA), FOR Papers, box 1, file 4, The Co-operative Committee on Japanese Canadians, Bulletin 17, no. 7, 14 Sept. 19456; Edith Fowke, *They Made Democracy Work: The Story of the Co-operative Committee on Japanese Canadians* (Toronto, n.d.), 11.
12 UCA, FOR Papers, box 1, file 1, Report of the General Secretary, June 1947.
13 Scott Nearing, *World Events* (Sept. 1946), 6.
14 UCA, FOR Papers, box 1, file 5, James Finlay to John Nevin Sayre, 19 July 1947.
15 Ibid., Sayre to Finlay, 28 July 1947.
16 Ibid., box 1, file 1, Minutes of FOR National Council Meeting, 3 October 1947.
17 Ibid., 'Memo on Cadet Training.'
18 A.G. Watson, 'Mr. Drew's Army Must be Disbanded,' *Reconciliation* (Feb.–March, 1947), 10.
19 B.K. Sandwell, 'Pacifism Again,' *Saturday Night* (3 May 1947), 5.
20 J.J. Brown, 'Pacifism after Hiroshima,' *Reconciliation* (July 1946), 1.

21 Socknat, *Witness against War*, 291; Stephen Endicott, *James G. Endicott, Rebel out of China* (Toronto, 1980), 262.

22 Ibid., *Toronto Daily Star*, 14 Oct. 1948.

23 Socknat, *Witness against War*, 290.

24 Endicott, *Rebel out of China*, 272.

25 Norman Penner, *Canadian Communism: The Stalin Years and Beyond* (Toronto, 1988), 22.

26 Endicott, *Rebel out of China*, 264–5.

27 Ibid.

28 Ibid., 268.

29 '10,000 Cheer Red Dean,' *Toronto Star*, 8 May 1950.

30 As quoted in Endicott, *Rebel out of China*, 265.

31 Canadian Fellowship of Reconciliation, *The Atom Bomb Demands that War be Abolished*, n.d.

32 Charles Huestis, letter, *Saturday Night* (21 June 1947).

33 Endicott, *Rebel out of China*, 267; James G. Endicott, *The Best of Jim Endicott* (Toronto, 1982), 55.

34 The same situation appears to have existed in the United States. Lawrence S. Wittner, *Rebels against War: The American Peace Movement, 1933 1983* (Philadelphia, 1984), 204–5.

35 Blair Fraser, 'How Dr Endicott Fronts for the Reds,' *Maclean's* (15 July 1952), 51.

36 Gerald Waring, 'The Canadian Peace Congress,' Montreal *Star*, 16–18 Aug. 1950, also cited in Endicott, *Rebel out of China*, 264.

37 As quoted in Endicott, *Rebel out of China*, 288.

38 L. Freeman, 'Dr. Hunter's Dismissal,' *Canadian Forum* (Oct. 1949), 1; 'Around Campus,' *New Trail*, University of Alberta Alumni magazine (Jan. 1944), 28.

39 Barbara Roberts, 'Women's Peace Activism in Canada,' in Linda Kealey and Joan Sangster (eds.), *Beyond the Vote* (Toronto, 1989), 293.

40 Endicott, *Rebel out of China*, 274.

41 Ibid., 286–7.

42 Canada, House of Commons Debates, 25 June 1951.

43 Ibid., 12 May 1952; *Toronto Star*, 14 May 1952.

44 James M. Finlay, 'Christian Responsibility in the Atomic Age,' *United Church Observer*, (1 Feb. 1960), 8–9.

Bibliography

BOOKS AND ARTICLES ON PEACE HISTORY BY PETER BROCK

The work of Peter Brock in synthesizing the history of pacifism has been made possible by the expansion of peace history – that embraces much more than the history of pacifism – since 1945. There were notable pioneer peace historians active in the interwar years – Merle E. Curti and W. Freeman Galpin, for instance, in the peace movement in antebellum America, or A.C.F. Beales in England. The Quaker peace testimony found an able historian in Margaret E. Hirst, a classical scholar by training. In the case of the Church of the Brethren one of its ministers, Rufus D. Bowman, wrote a competent account of his denomination's attitude to peace and war. Two learned accounts of the history of internationalism appeared during this period from the pens of the Norwegian Christian L. Lange and the Dutchman Jacob ter Meulen. Ter Meulen's compatriot Bart de Ligt published thought-provoking volumes on the history of what he called 'creative peace,' highlighting direct action against war. But the breakthrough came only after the Second World War, as may be seen from the bibliographical data in Peter Brock's books as well as in the notes of his essays listed below.

1957
The Political and Social Doctrines of the Unity of the Czech Brethren in the Fifteenth and Early Sixteenth Centuries. The Hague: Mouton, 302 pp.

1964
'The Spiritual Pilgrimage of Thomas Watson: From British Soldier to American Friend,' *Quaker History* 53 (2) 81–6.
Ed., 'Colonel Washington and the Quaker Conscientious Objectors,' *Quaker History* 53(1), 12–26.

1965
'The Peace Testimony in a "Garden Enclosed,"' *Quaker History* 54 (62) 67–80.

1967
'A Pacificist in Wartime: Wojciech Bogumil Jastrzębowski,' *Polish Review* 12 (2), 68–77.

1968
Pacifism in the United States: From the Colonial Era to the First World War. Princeton, NJ: Princeton University Press, 1005 pp.
Radical Pacifists in Antebellum America. Princeton: Princeton University Press, 298 pp. (Excerpted from *Pacifism in the United States.*)

1970
Pioneers of the Peaceable Kingdom. Princeton: Princeton University Press, 382 pp. (Excerpted from *Pacifism in the United States.*)
Twentieth-Century Pacifism. New York: Van Nostrand Reinhold, 274 pp.

1972
Pacifism in Europe to 1914. Princeton: Princeton University Press, 556 pp.

1974
'When Seventh-day Adventists First Faced War: The Problem of the Civil War,' *Adventist Heritage: A Magazine of Adventist History* 1 (1), 23–7. (Excerpted from *Pacifism in the United States.*)

1975
'The Hutterites and War, 1530–1800,' in Bela K. Kiraly (ed.), *Tolerance and Movements of Religious Dissent in Easter Europe.* Boulder, Col.: East European Quarterly, 43–51.

1978
Ed., 'A Polish Anabaptist against War: The Question of Conscientious Objection in Marcin Gzechowic's *Christian Dialogues* of 1575,' *Mennonite Quarterly Review* 52(4), 279–93.

1980
'The Nonresistance of the Hungarian Nazarenes to 1914,' *Mennonite Quarterly Review* 54 (1), 53–63.
'Tolstoyism and the Hungarian Peasant,' *Slavonic and East European Review* 58 (3), 345–69.

1981
The Roots of War Resistance: Pacifism from the Early Church to Tolstoy. Nyack, NY: The Fellowship of Reconciliation, 81 pp.
'Gandhi's Nonviolence and His War Service,' *Peace and Change* 7 (1–2), 71–83 (Also in *Gandhi Marg*, n.s., 2(11), 601–16.)

1983

The Mahatma and Mother India: Essays on Gandhi's Non-violence and Nationalism.
Ahmedabad: Navajivan Publishing House, 223 pp.
Ed., 'Some Materials on Nazarene Conscientious Objectors in Nineteenth-
Century Hungary,' *Mennonite Quarterly Review* 57(1), 64–72.

1984

'The Peace Testimony of the Early Plymouth Brethren,' *Church History* 53(1),
30–45.

1988

*The Military Question in the Early Church: A Selected Bibliography of a Century's
Scholarship, 1888–1987.* Toronto: privately printed, 15 pp.

1990

The Quaker Peace Testimony 1660 to 1914. York (England): Sessions Book Trust,
387 pp.

1991

*Freedom from Violence: Sectarian Nonresistance from the Middle Ages to the Great
War.* Toronto: University of Toronto Press, 385 pp.
Freedom from War: Nonsectarian Pacifism, 1814–1914. Toronto: University of
Toronto Press, 436 pp.
'Marcin Czechowic in Defense of Nonresistance, 1575,' *Conrad Grebel Review* 9(3),
251–7.
Studies in Peace History. York: William Sessions, 103 pp. Ed., 'Gregorius Paulus
against the Sword: A Polish Anabaptist on Nonresistance,' *Mennonite
Quarterly Review* 65(4), 427–36.

1992

A Brief History of Pacifism from Jesus to Tolstoy. Toronto: Distributed by Syracuse
University Press, 80 pp. (Second edition of *Roots of War Resistance*.)
'Conscientious Objectors in the Polish Brethren Church, 1565–1605,' *Slavonic and
East European Review* 70(4), 670–87.
'Faustus Socinus as a Pacifist,' *The Polish Review* 38(4), 441–6. Ed., *Records of Con-
science: Three Autobiographical Narratives by Conscientious Objectors,   1665–
1865.* York: William Sessions, 66 pp.
Ed., 'Martin Czechowic on the *Via Crucis*, Self-Defense, and Government (1575),'
Mennonite Quarterly Review 67(4), 451–68.

1994

'The Birth of the Antibomb Campaign,' *Reviews in American History* 22(2):
316–21.

'Conscientious Objectors in Nazi Germany,'*Reconciliation Quarterly*, Summer issue, 21–6.

'Dilemmas of a Socinian Pacifist in Seventeenth-Century Poland,' *Church History* 63(2), 190–200.

'Why Did St Maximilian Refuse to Serve in the Roman Army?' *Journal of Ecclesiastical History* 65(2), 195–209.

Index

Aarek, Wilhelm, 209
Aberli, Heini, 113
Abrams, Irwin, 378
Action Française, 401
Acts of Thekla, 75; as document of women's resistance, 83–5
Addams, Jane, 209, 316, 375, 377
Adler, Clemens, 117
Ahiṁsā, 227, 234, 237, 246–7, 278; see also Buddhism, Gandhi, M.K., and Hinduism
Alara, King (Tamil), 249
All-India Muslim League, 284–5
All-India National Congress, 284–5
Allen, Clifford, 346
Allen, Devere, 60
Allen, J. Hope, 272
Altamira, Rafael, 60
alternative service, 194
Amana Society, 129
American Association for International Conciliation, 321, 326
American Bankers Association, 335
American Civil War, 131, 185, 314, 324
American Friends Service Commit-

tee (AFSC), 77, 138, 207–11, 217, 220n27, 221n28, 415
American peace movement, 8, 299, 320–37
American peace organizations, 320–1
American Peace Society, 321
American Revolution, 129–30, 159
American School Peace League, 321
American Society for International Law, 321, 325
American Society for the Judicial Settlement of International Disputes, 321
American Union against Militarism, 334
Ames, William, 39
Amish, enter Canada, 131
Anabaptism, 112–18, 120n13, 125–7
Anabaptists, 5, 8–9, 75–6, 177; Polish, 426–7
Angell, Norman: authorship of The Great Illusion, 343
Anglo-American rapprochement, 321
Anti-Imperialist League, 324
Apology. See Barclay, Robert